TEE
IN
JAPAN
A Realistic Vision

TEE IN JAPAN
A Realistic Vision

**The Feasibility of
Theological Education by
Extension for churches
in Japan.**

W. Frederic Sprunger

William Carey Library

P.O. BOX 128-C • PASADENA, CALIFORNIA 91104

Library of Congress Cataloging in Publication Data

Sprunger, W. Frederic, 1940–
    Theological Education by Extension in Japan.

    Originally presented as the author's thesis
(M. Th.)--Fuller Theological Seminary.
    Bibliography: p.
    Includes index.
    1. Theology--Study and teaching--Japan.
2. Seminary extension--Japan. 3. Mennonites--
Japan. I. Title.
BV4140.J3S67   1981   230'.973   81-7739
ISBN 0-87808-434-7   AACR2

Published by the William Carey Library
P.O. Box 128-C
Pasadena, California 91104
Telephone (213) 798-0819

In accord with some of the most recent thinking of the academic press, the William Carey Library is pleased to present
this scholarly book which has been prepared from an author-
edited camera ready copy.

PRINTED IN THE UNITED STATES OF AMERICA

Dedicated to

ELLEN

and to each of our dear brothers and sisters

who have labored or are laboring

for Christ in Japan

Contents

Figures

Foreword

There has been an annual flow of TEE books. All have been about the same with a repeat of the basic Winter concepts with some local applications. I have been asked about the relationship of TEE and Church Growth very often. Does TEE effect church growth? Here is an honest look at these real problems.

It is just now that some of these real questions can be answered. TEE has been around nearly twenty years although many of us have been involved for just over ten years. It has been impossible, or at least difficult, to statistically demonstrate TEE's value. To many of us who were concerned about the church and involved in training its ministry TEE seemed to solve many of our problems on the one hand and to reach the right people with valid theological training on the other. As we observed TEE in practice we THOUGHT it was doing the right things and participant feedback was support-ive. It is just now that we can hold up examples and see some demonstrable evidence; Sprunger has done this in the first church growth type in-depth study of the possibilities of TEE in a particular setting. While Japan is not typical of the vast areas of Africa, Latin America, or Asia where TEE is being widely used, it does serve as a critical test area of observation.

Bless Sprunger and his book -- may it have followers.

May 2, 1980   Frederic Holland, Adjunct Professor
                               Theological Education by Extension,
                               Fuller Theological Seminary

Preface

My interest in Japan and the Japanese Church began during a
short term of service in that country (1964-1967). While
there, I had a chance to participate in as well as observe
what was happening in some of the Mennonite churches. The
churches were typically small, averaging perhaps 10 or 20
active members. They appeared to be made up of very dedicated believers. But what hit me most perhaps were some of
the struggles these young churches and Christians were going
through. It seemed to be assumed, for example, that in
order to be a church, you needed to have both a church building and a paid pastor. The churches being relatively small
in size, needless to say it was hard for them to support a
full-time person, let alone put up a special meeting place.
Yet many were trying to do this, though it was a constant
battle for them, and for the pastors and their families
financially.

Along with this hardship was a shortage of leaders.
Those who felt led to become pastors as a rule left the
rural areas to go to Bible schools located in the big cities.
Many of them had support problems while in school. Some of
them did not return. Those who did often found it difficult
to fit back in, or to make ends meet. There was also no
provision made for the continuing education of these leaders.

But while there was at least the possibility of getting
training in Bible and related subjects for those who could
go away, for those who could not leave their homes and
families and jobs it seemed there was practically no way

for them to get some training except what was offered on a
local level, which in most cases was quite limited. Yet
these people who could not get further training were in many
instances the real leaders of the church! It was out of a
concern for reaching them with more advanced training that I
began to think about this subject. How could they be
trained? Surely there must be a way, not only to train them,
but also many of those who would otherwise go off to school
somewhere and be lost to our churches. The interest that
had been sparked by seeing a need led me to begin collecting
material relevant to the topic over a period of several
years.

Besides the problem of leaders and training mentioned
above, there was also that of slow growth or no growth by
the churches, and a seeming lack of goals on a local as well
as conference level in spite of there being many opportunities. Somehow I felt all of these problems might be
connected. Along the way, I was also exposed to the concept
of Theological Education by Extension (TEE), and the unique
possibilities it holds for training leaders. It seemed to
me it just might be possible to adapt some of the principles
found in TEE to the Japanese situation, and by so doing
begin to solve some of the main problems we faced. And it
is with whether that can be done or not that this study
wrestles.

The basic research for this project was carried out in
1974-1975, during our furlough year. It has taken a few
years since then, working at it as time has allowed, to com-
pile the data, analyze and interpret it, and put it all
together. But while the basic research (such as questionnaires and interviews) was done some time ago, wherever
possible the study has been brought up to the present time.
And while there are some disadvantages in working at a project over a number of years, there are also some advantages.
One of these being that it has a chance to mature. This
paper at least is much different than originally conceived
because of the time it has had to "simmer." The disadvan-
tage is that some of the material may become a bit dated,
but in this case that is only a small part of the whole,
and I do not feel it takes anything away from the major
findings. The basic data then is from 1974, unless noted
otherwise. It might be helpful to take another survey of
some key questions about 1984 or so for the sake of comparison with the earlier situation.

In addition to the interviews and questionnaires (mostly
in Japanese), archival research has also been engaged in.

Extensive use has been made of records found in the Mission
and Church files. Such minutes, reports, and correspondence
clearly document the problems we as one group have faced.
Many articles and books were also read as background material and are occasionally referred to. Personal experiences
have been shared too where it was felt it would be appropriate to do so. An attempt has been made to integrate
these various sources in a balanced way. I have also tried
to be accurate, objective, and fair in interpretation of the
data, although I realize that 100 percent objectivity is
never possible. Where the reader may feel I have been
inaccurate or unfair, correction and dialogue is welcome and
would be much appreciated.

There has been some minor editing of minutes and other
non-copyrighted material for spelling, capitalization, and
punctuation, although insofar as it seemed reasonable,
things were left as is. For the most part, use was made of
the English translation of Japanese minutes. Where an
English translation was not available, the page number in
the reference is followed by a "J" (for example, 1969:1J)
to indicate that fact. Translation in such cases was by the
author, and he takes full responsibility for any "mistrans-
lations."

Monetary references are usually given in both dollar and
yen amounts. The dollar equivalent for yen is calculated
according to the approximate average exchange rate for the
year. Up to 1970 that was about 360 yen per dollar. For
1971 it is figured at 310; 1972, @ 300; 1973, @ 280; 1974,
@ 290; 1975, @ 300. Effort has been made to keep the text
understandable, but the Glossary may be consulted for an
explanation of the meaning of foreign words, and the list of
Abbreviations for any which may be unfamiliar.

The study deals mainly with the history and problems as
well as the possibilities of the Japan Mennonite Christian
Church Conference (*Nihon Menonaito Kirisuto Kyōkai Kaigi*). And
while as pointed out earlier, one of my chief concerns was
with the need for a leadership training program, it soon
became evident that any kind of training program is based on
one's concept of the church and its ministry, or should be,
and that those concepts needed to be dealt with before one
could try to propose any kind of a training program. Thus
the study is made within the larger framework of those
issues. And though it deals primarily with a rural church
as a case in point, the lessons learned can apply to urban
churches as well.

It strikes me as more than mere coincidence that among several studies done on the Church in Japan in recent years, one has had to do with the church (*Laity Mobilized* by Neil Braun), another with the ministry (*Whose Ministry?* by K. Lavern Snider), and this one with training. It may be somewhat unfortunate that all three were made by expatriates. But the issues dealt with are basic -- church, ministry, and training -- and in light of that each of these works ought to be evaluated for whatever they may be worth. Hopefully they along with many other such studies can at least act as a catalyst in stimulating further discussion and action in the areas under consideration. The Bibliography should be consulted for some of the other relevant literature on the topic.

While the focus of the study is on the Mennonites, and on some of the Mennonite churches in Japan in particular, the applicability is much broader than that. To be sure, the information brought together here does reveal a lot about the Mennonites, who they are and what they have done (and have not done) in their mission endeavor in one part of the world. The objective has not been to expose some of the many weaknesses which may be found in Mennonite circles, but undoubtedly there are many "spots and wrinkles" there, and in the process of reporting, for better or worse, some of them do come through. It is hoped some good, positive images will come through as well.

But the point is, I submit, that we can learn from each other, our failures as much as our successes. Perhaps there are lessons others can learn here too, not only from the way things have been done, but perhaps even more so from the way things have *not* been done or should have been done. So whether you are "Mennonite" or from some other denomination, whether it is Japan or elsewhere where you labor, it is desired the application will be visible to each one. Although Appendix K deals more specifically with issues related to Mennonite churches, and is really a chapter in itself, it may be of interest to those from other traditions also.

It is readily admitted that much of what is said here is not new, such as the need for various kinds of leaders (part-time and full-time, paid and unpaid), or trying to develop an extension program on different levels (for laymen and leaders) and possibly combining it with residence study too, or making use of pastors and missionaries as well as faculty from a recognized school as itinerant teachers.

These and many other suggestions come out in the material in the files, and have all been proposed before. But I have tried to undertake a new synthesis of these and other options, and as others catch the vision trust they can take it even further. If this research can be of benefit to the churches of Japan in even a small way in helping them become more what they have the potential to be, personally, I will be very humbled and happy. Hopefully this edition can be followed by a future update, and chapter on how the vision has become reality, and is actually being done. To see that happen would be most rewarding, and make all the effort seem even more worthwhile.

The work in hand was actually begun as a thesis for the M.Th. in Missions program at Fuller Theological Seminary, but has turned into more of a dissertation, so it is not quite clear where it belongs on that score. But a 30-page summary of it has been made and translated into Japanese for the churches there, and is available upon request (free) from the Japan Anabaptist Center, 1-17 Honan, 2 Chome, Suginami Ku, Tokyo 168, JAPAN.

May 1980   W.F.S.

Acknowledgments

How can a person express one's thanks? Words often seem so inadequate, yet it is all we have. And in reflecting on the many who have had a part in this study, I would first of all like to offer my heartfelt thanks to each of the laymen and pastors as well as missionaries who filled out some rather lengthy questionnaires, and for the data provided. Also to the General Conference Mennonite Mission in Japan and the Japan Mennonite Christian Church Conference for free access to their historical records. Without such cooperation the research done would not have been possible.

A word of thanks is due Fumio Kuroki, who graciously translated the questionnaires into Japanese. And to Mr. and Mrs. Philip Tsuchiya, Mr. and Mrs. Masaharu Asayama, and others who helped decipher and interpret many of the answers for me.

I would also like to express my gratitude to those who so kindly granted interviews for the case studies -- Hugh Sprunger in Taiwan, and Morris Jacobsen, Dale Oxley, and Takio Tanase from various schools in Japan.

Then I would like to offer a word of appreciation to Ralph Winter and Fred Holland, both from the School of World Mission, Fuller Theological Seminary, for the comments and suggestions they made to improve the content, most of which were incorporated in revision. And to the latter too for being so gracious as to write a fitting word of commendation in the Foreward.

Also, a word of thanks to my missionary colleagues who looked the study over, raised questions here or there and provided missing information. A special thank you to Henry Kliewer, who took time to read the project critically, and for the many helpful remarks he had to offer.

Appreciation is also extended to the following individuals and publishers for permission to quote rather extensively from their material:

Abingdon Press, *The Interpreter's Dictionary of the Bible*, III, copyright © 1962.

William B. Eerdmans, *The New Bible Dictionary*, James D. Douglas, ed., copyright © 1962.

Faith and Life Press, *The Christian Mission of the General Conference Mennonite Church*, S. F. Pannabecker, ed., copyright © 1961.

Friendship Press, *How Churches Grow* by Donald A. McGavran, copyright © 1966.

Herald Press, *The Complete Writings of Menno Simons*, John C. Wenger, ed., copyright © 1956.

John H. Leith, ed., *Creeds of the Churches*, Doubleday, copyright © 1963.

Macmillan, *The Origins of Sectarian Protestantism* by Franklin H. Littell, copyright © 1964.

Mennonite Library and Archives (North Newton, Kan.), *The Witness of the Martyrs' Mirror for Our Day* by Cornelius Krahn, copyright © 1967.

Paul Peachey, excerpts from "Seminary and Bible School Study" (Richards and Peachey), 1959; "*Mukyōkai-shugi*: A Modern Japanese Attempt to Complete the Reformation," *Mennonite Quarterly Review*, January 1961.

University of California Press, *Japanese Society* by Chie Nakane, copyright © 1972.

William Carey Library, *An Extension Seminary Primer* by Ralph R. Covell and C. Peter Wagner, copyright © 1971; *Theological Education by Extension*, Ralph D. Winter, ed., copyright © 1969; *The World Directory of Theological Education by Extension* by Wayne C. Weld, copyright © 1973.

Takashi Yamada, *Experiments in Church Growth: Japan*, Paul W. Boschman, ed., Japan Church Growth Research Association, copyright © 1968.

Tetsunao Yamamori, "The Sōka Gakkai: A Religious Phoenix," *Practical Anthropology*, July-August 1972.

Permission was also sought from Forum House for quotations from *The Base Church* by Charles M. Olsen, copyright © 1973, but letters were returned as undeliverable or unforwardable, so use of this material is hereby gratefully acknowledged without having been able to secure formal permission.

A note of thanks too to the William Carey Library for their assistance in getting the study into print. And to the Commission on Overseas Mission of the General Conference Mennonite Church for willingness to contribute something toward publication of the work.

Before I forget, I also want to express in a special way my indebtedness to Ellen, who obligingly made a lot of rough places plainer, and without whose patient typing and constant encouragement this project would never have seen completion.

And finally, thanks be to God for His help in seeing the study through. From the hundreds of times I have sat down at the typewriter and asked His help to the time my train ended up going the wrong way in Hokkaido and I almost missed the boat, I have experienced His guiding and strengthening and presence in a very real way. For any good that may come out of the finished product, to Him be the glory!

Abbreviations

AMBS	Associated Mennonite Biblical Seminaries
BIC	Brethren in Christ
CES	China Evangelical Seminary
EHBS	Eastern Hokkaido Bible School
FOMCIT	Fellowship of Mennonite Churches in Taiwan
GCMC	General Conference Mennonite Church
GCMM	General Conference Mennonite Mission
HBS	Hitoyoshi Bible School
ICWE	International Congress on World Evangelization
JCC	Japan Christian College (now TCC)
JMCCC	Japan Mennonite Christian Church Conference
JBPM	Japan Bible Protestant Missions
JMC	Japan Mennonite Church (Hokkaido)
MC	Mennonite Church
MCC	Mennonite Central Committee

OM   Old Mennonite (now MC, Mennonite Church)

OMS   Oriental Missionary Society (now OMS
            International)

PI   Programmed Instruction

PIM   Programmed Instruction Material

TCC   Tokyo Christian College (formerly JCC)

TEAM   The Evangelical Alliance Mission

TEE   Theological Education by Extension

TEF   Theological Education Fund

UCCJ   United Church of Christ in Japan (*Kyōdan*)

1

Introduction to the Japan Mennonite Christian Church Conference

Many people have visions, but too often those visions are simply not realistic. Other people are so realistic, they tend to seldom if ever have visions. Our world is full of both realists and visionaries. And we need both. We need people who are visionary. We also need people who are realistic. But does it have to be a choice of being one or the other? Is it not possible to combine the two, to have what we might call a "realistic vision"? A vision that is both realistic and visionary?

Take the subject of this book, for example, the possibilities of TEE (Theological Education by Extension) in Japan. A realist, on the basis of his experience, might say quite frankly, "I don't think it could ever be done." A visionary, on the other hand, might say rather glibly, "I don't see any reason why it couldn't be done." But is it not possible to bring these two views together and say, "I think TEE could be done in Japan under certain conditions." I believe it is. I believe that it is possible to be both visionary and realistic. In short, to have a realistic vision. I also hold that TEE has real possibilities for Japan (and elsewhere), providing that certain conditions are met. But before we get into that, perhaps it would be in order to back up a little and trace something of the history of the Mennonites and the Mennonite Church for those who may be unfamiliar with them.

WHO ARE THE MENNONITES ANYWAY?

The Mennonites are, first of all, Christians. They are
in fact one of the oldest Protestant denominations, their
roots going back to the Reformation of the sixteenth century. The Mennonites get their name from Menno Simons
(c.1496-1561). Menno Simons is not as well known as some of
the other reformers, but was one of the leaders of the
Anabaptist movement in the Netherlands. He would probably
"turn over in his grave" if he knew there was still a group
of Christians named after him, for it was not his intention
to found a Mennonite Church any more than it was Luther's
intention to start a Lutheran Church. But just as Luther's
followers came to be called "Lutherans," so Menno's followers came to be called *Menists* or *Mennonists*, and later on
"Mennonites." And though we might sometimes wish there was
not such a proliferation of denominations, looking back on
the history of the Christian Church, it is probably inevitable things worked out that way. Within the Mennonite
tradition itself there are various groups, but all together
Mennonite Christians today are said to number about 600,000
worldwide (GCMC 1977:86).

As has already been mentioned, the Mennonites originated
in the Anabaptist movement which began in the city of
Zurich, Switzerland, in 1525. There was a small group of
Christians there, followers of Zwingli, who could not agree
with him at certain points. One of these was whether there
should be a union of church and state, or whether they ought
to be separate. Zwingli was in favor of a state church, but
this little group of believers was not. They felt that the
church should consist of believers only, and it was over
this issue that they finally parted company with him. Two
of the men in this small group were George Blaurock and
Conrad Grebel. Like everyone else in their day, they had
been baptized in the state church as infants, but they
rejected that baptism as being invalid, since they had not
had faith at the time. They were convinced that the New
Testament taught believers' baptism. So they refused to
have their own children baptized.

On January 17, 1525, the Zurich council held a public
debate between "the advocates and the opponents of infant
baptism." According to the council, "Grebel and his com-
panions were defeated by Zwingli." The council therefore
declared that "all parents who had neglected to have their
children baptized were to do so within a week, on pain of
banishment." As a result of this, on January 21, 1525,

Blaurock, Grebel and others met secretly. Blaurock asked Grebel to baptize him, which he did, and he in turn baptized the others present. They "re-baptized" one another. Thus it was that the first Anabaptist congregation, the first Protestant free church, was born. This small group of believers simply thought of themselves as brethren, as brothers and sisters in Christ, and became known as the "Swiss Brethren." But it was not long until they were nick-named "Anabaptists," literally meaning "rebaptizers," by Zwingli and others who opposed them. Fearing for the unity of their city-state, the Zurich council met again in March 1526, and declared that anyone found guilty of rebaptizing would be drowned. Within less than a year, in January 1527, Felix Manz became the first Anabaptist martyr (at the hands of the Protestants) by drowning (Hershberger 1957:58-65).

On the surface it would appear as if baptism was the main issue separating the Anabaptists and their opponents, but actually it was much deeper than that. While baptism was symbolic of their differences, it was not the most basic issue. As Cornelius Krahn and Melvin Gingerich state in a little pamphlet introducing the Mennonites,

> The Anabaptist Mennonites originated in Zurich, Switzerland, in 1525, where they parted company with Ulrich Zwingli over the issue of a free church versus a state church. The Anabaptists rejected infant baptism and baptized only those who freely chose to become members of a voluntary church of believers. The order was "repent, believe, and be baptized" (1967:5).

The Anabaptists did not have their children baptized. They practiced believers' baptism instead. They believed that membership in the church should be voluntary. But baptism was not the basic issue at stake. The real issue at stake was the whole concept of the church. The Anabaptists held a concept of the believers' church. But if the church is to be made up of believers only, one of the implications of this is that only believers should be baptized. If only believers are to be baptized, then membership must be volun-tary. If membership is to be voluntary, then the church and the state must be separate rather than united. And it was over this issue of a free church versus a state church that the Anabaptists differed with the other reformers.

Further confirmation of this is found in the earliest Anabaptist confession, "The Schleitheim Confession" of 1527

(Leith 1963:282-292). Interestingly, there are no articles in the Confession on God, man, Christ, and so forth. Why? Because those were not the issue. They were agreed on those things. They were agreed on such things as the authority of the Scripture (*sola scriptura*) and justification by faith (*sola fide*). There was little or no disagreement on fundamental Christian doctrine, but the implications drawn from these doctrines were different.

Perhaps a little diagram would be useful in showing the relationship between the Anabaptists and the other reformation movements. The diagram (Figure 1.1) is oversimplified, to be sure, ignoring some previous divisions within Christendom, such as the East-West schism in 1054. But if we take 1517, the year Martin Luther nailed his Ninety-five Theses to the Wittenberg Church door, as the beginning of the Reformation, from that point on there were both Catholics and Protestants. The Protestants themselves, however, soon became divided into several factions. There were the followers of Luther, Calvin, Zwingli, and so on. The Lutheran and Reformed groups formed some of the main strands of the Reformation.

Figure 1.1

MAJOR REFORM MOVEMENTS

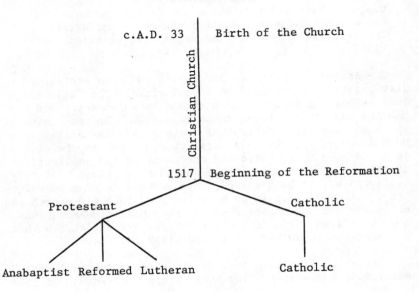

The Anabaptists are sometimes referred to as the left
wing or the "radical wing" of the Reformation, and we have
seen that they were actually a split off Zwingli and his
group. This was not really what they wanted to happen, but
to the Anabaptists, the whole nature of the church, the concept of a free church over against a state church was the
crucial issue at stake. It was one on which they felt they
could not compromise. They believed that Luther and the
other reformers were achieving only a "halfway reformation."
They were leaving the problem of the church itself untouched.
But the Anabaptists rejected the concept of *corpus chris-
tianum*, where church and state are united to form one body.

> Instead of a reformation they wanted *restitution* --
> to restore the church as described in the Bible. The
> church had fallen by becoming a state church under
> Constantine in the fourth century and could be
> restored only by returning to a point before the fall.
> It was with the fall, they believed, that infant bap-
> tism, militarism, clericalism, and all the un-Christ-
> like characteristics had come into the church (Dyck
> 1967:314).

The Anabaptists believed the church had fallen with Constantine, and that it could not be restored to its original
nature without a truly radical reformation, requiring the
separation of church and state. Therefore, they sought to
complete the reformation which had been initiated by others.

We have just reviewed briefly some of the basic differences between the Anabaptists and the other movements
which were a part of the Reformation. But so far we have
been using the word *Anabaptist* without distinguishing
between different Anabaptist groups. Actually, there were
about three main streams within the Anabaptist movement itself. First there were what we might call the peaceful
Anabaptists. They believed that being a Christian meant
following Christ in life. They took the teachings of the
Sermon on the Mount very seriously. They believed that
Christ had taught the way of peace and therefore refused to
take up the sword, to hold a civil office, or even to use an
oath. Another group are what we might call the mystical
Anabaptists. As the name suggests, they were of a rather
mystical frame of mind, and tended to rely more on the
direct guidance of the Spirit rather than the Scripture as
their teacher. They stressed the work of the Holy Spirit in
the individual believer but played down the importance of
the fellowship of believers.

A third group are what we might call the radical Anabaptists, "radical" used here in the sense of violent. There were the Munsterites, for example, who expected Christ's immediate return, and wanted to establish the new Jerusalem at the city of Munster. The movement had started out peaceably in the beginning, but with a change in leadership turned to violence. Regrettably, an attempt was made to usher in the Kingdom of God by force, resulting in tragedy when the city fell to the authorities in 1535. It was a tragic incident, giving a bad name to all Anabaptists. But as Anabaptist scholar Walter Klaassen has said, "There should be no attempt to conceal from public view these skeletons in the Mennonite family closet, much less to deny that they were there" (1973:2).

Unfortunately, to many people even today, the radical Anabaptists are thought to be representative of the whole movement. The fact is, studies have shown that they were not. Both the mystical and the radical Anabaptists composed only a small minority of all Anabaptists. The majority were of the peaceful type, and along with the other reformers condemned the extremes of the minority. And yet, because of their beliefs, even the peaceful Anabaptists were persecuted. They were persecuted by churches, both Catholic and Protestant, as well as by the state. The result was that the movement spread from Switzerland where it began to South Germany, Austria, and the Netherlands.

In the Netherlands, there was a group of peaceful Anabaptists who invited a man by the name of Menno Simons to be their leader. Menno Simons had been born in Witmarsium, Friesland, about 1496. He trained for the priesthood and later served as a Catholic priest in his hometown. But he began to have doubts about the actual presence of Christ's flesh and blood in the bread and wine offered in the Mass, as he had been taught. From a study of the New Testament, which he claimed he had never read before, he came to the conclusion that he had been deceived. The Church was wrong in its teaching on the matter.

The Anabaptists did not arrive in the Netherlands until about 1530, and when he first heard of them, the idea of a "second baptism" sounded strange to him. But again, from an examination of the Scriptures, he discovered that there was no report concerning infant baptism. He also consulted various writers on the subject, but eventually came to the conclusion that he had been deceived about this also. The Anabaptists were right in their teaching on the matter. He

was also influenced no doubt by the testimony of the many
martyrs who so willingly died for their faith. It is
thought, too, that a certain Peter Simons, who was killed in
one of the battles connected with Munster, may have been his
brother. Undoubtedly there were many factors that led up to
it, but Menno describes his conversion in his own words as
follows:

Meanwhile it happened, when I had resided there [in
Witmarsium] about a year, that several launched adult
baptism. ...

Next in order the sect of Munster made its appearance, by whom many pious hearts in our quarter were
deceived. My soul was much troubled, for I perceived
that though they were zealous they erred in doctrine. ...

...I saw that these zealous children, although in
error, willingly gave their lives and their estates
for their doctrine and faith. And I was one of those
who had disclosed to some of them the abominations of
the papal system. But I myself continued in my com-
fortable life and acknowledged abominations simply in
order that I might enjoy physical comfort and escape
the cross of Christ. ...

My heart trembled within me. I prayed to God with
sighs and tears that He would give to me, a sorrowing
sinner, the gift of His grace, create within me a
clean heart, and graciously through the merits of the
crimson blood of Christ forgive my unclean walk and
frivolous easy life and bestow upon me wisdom, Spirit,
courage, and a manly spirit so that I might preach
His exalted and adorable name and holy Word in purity,
and make known His truth to His glory.

I began in the name of the Lord to preach publicly
from the pulpit the word of true repentance, to point
the people to the narrow path, and in the power of the
Scripture openly to reprove all sin and wickedness,
all idolatry and false worship, and to present the
true worship; also the true baptism and the Lord's
Supper, according to the doctrine of Christ, to the
extent that I had at that time received from God the
grace.

I also faithfully warned everyone against the
abominations of Munster, condemning king, polygamy,

kingdom, sword etc. After about nine months or so,
the gracious Lord granted me His fatherly Spirit, help,
and hand. Then I, without constraint, of a sudden,
renounced all my worldly reputation, name and fame, my
unchristian abominations, my masses, infant baptism,
and my easy life, and I willingly submitted to distress
and poverty under the heavy cross of Christ. In my
weakness I feared God; I sought out the pious and
though they were few in number I found some who were
zealous and maintained the truth (Wenger 1956:669-671).

So it happened that Menno was converted, left the priesthood, and went into hiding. That was in 1536, and he was
about forty years old at the time. He goes on to relate,
however, that about a year later several Anabaptists
approached him and requested that he be their spiritual
leader. At first he was hesitant to comply, but seeing the
need of those who were like "sheep without a shepherd," he
finally consented to preach, teach and baptize. He was
ordained as an elder. He married and is said to have had at
least three children. But for the next 25 years, he,
together with his family, spent most of his time fleeing
from one place to another seeking refuge where he could,
preaching and teaching as he went. He spent about seven
years in the Netherlands, and then the last 18 years of his
life in Northern Germany, where he died and was buried in
1561. He not only taught, but did considerable writing
which has been published under the title, *The Complete
Writings of Menno Simons* (Wenger 1956).

Persecution continued after Menno's death as it had
before. As noted earlier, the first Anabaptist martyr was
put to death just two years after the movement began.
Several thousand others met a similar fate, some by drowning, others by being strangled, beheaded, or burned at the
stake. Only a few recanted. Most were willing to die a
martyrs death rather than give up their faith. They were
literally "baptized in blood." But extreme as the measures
were, it did not extinguish the movement as the authorities
had hoped it would. In fact, it had just the opposite
effect. It drew attention to the movement and caused it to
spread even more rapidly. As Tertullian reportedly once
said, "The blood of the martyrs is seed," the seed of the
Church. The church continued to grow because of the testimony of many witnesses. There is the dramatic account of
Dirk Willems case, for example:

In the year 1569 a pious, faithful brother and
follower of Jesus Christ, named Dirk Willems, was
apprehended at Asperen, in Holland, and had to endure
severe tyranny from the papists. But as he had founded
his faith not upon the drifing sand of human command-
ments, but upon the firm foundation stone, Christ Jesus,
he, notwithstanding all evil winds of human doctrine,
and heavy showers of tyrannical and severe persecution,
remained immovable and steadfast unto the end; ...

Concerning his apprehension, it is stated by trustworthy persons, that when he fled he was hotly pursued
by a thief-catcher, and as there had been some frost,
said Dirk Willems ran before over the ice, getting
across with considerable peril. The thief-catcher
following him broke through, when Dirk Willems, per-
ceiving that the former was in danger of his life,
quickly returned and aided him in getting out, and
thus saved his life. The thief-catcher wanted to let
him go, but the burgomaster, very sternly called to
him to consider his oath, and thus he was again seized
by the thief-catcher, and, at said place, after severe
imprisonment and great trials proceeding from the
deceitful papists, put to death at a lingering fire by
these blood thirsty, ravening wolves, enduring it with
great steadfastness, and confirming the genuine faith
of the truth with his death and blood, as an instructive example to all pious Christians of this time, and
to the everlasting disgrace of the tyrannous papists
(Krahn 1967:28).

There were many others like Willems who remained faithful
to their Lord to the end. It is a moving experience to read
how so many endured under such persistent persecution, such
terrible torture, even unto death. Numerous accounts of the
Anabaptist witness have been gathered together in a large
volume entitled *Martyrs Mirror* (Braght 1951), a most unusual
collection. The *Martyrs Mirror* was first published in the
Dutch language in 1660, and for many years is said to have
taken its place beside the Bible in Mennonite homes.

A greatly abbreviated edition called *The Witness of the
Martyrs' Mirror for Our Day*, from which the above selection
was taken, was also published a number of years ago (Krahn
1967). Not all Anabaptists were Mennonites, of course, but
all Mennonites were Anabaptists, or at least stood within
the Anabaptist tradition. No one knows exactly how many
lost their lives as a result of persecution, but one of the

last Anabaptist-Mennonite martyrs was put to death in
Switzerland in 1614 (Schowalter 1957:525), almost 90 years
after the movement began.   There are said to be many more
who continued to be put in prison, some of whom died because
of mistreatment during their imprisonment.

In spite of their great devotion and missionary zeal, and
a willingness to suffer for their faith, persecution began to
take its toll.   The Mennonites began to migrate to other
areas seeking religious freedom.   From the Netherlands they
spread into Prussia and Poland, and in the late 1700s and
early 1800s, into Russia.   They had been promised many things
in Russia -- freedom of religion, vocational freedom, freedom
from military service, free land, freedom from taxes and so
on. For a while things were better. But as they gradually lost
their freedom there also, they once again began to migrate,
this time from Russia, as well as other European countries, to
the United States and Canada.   Some also migrated to South
America.   Most of these migrations took place in the late
1800s and early 1900s, although some came as late as World War
II and after.   Not all Mennonites migrated, however, and while
it is reported that there are only 3,000 or so left in Switzerland today, there are said to be considerably more in such
countries as Germany (10,000), the Netherlands (26,000), and
Russia (55,000 est.)   (GCMC 1977:82).

The earliest Mennonite immigrants had come to America in
the late 1600s, the first permanent Mennonite settlement
being at Germantown, Pennsylvania, in 1683.   As they
migrated, they naturally brought their faith with them, and
the oldest Mennonite congregation in America is the Germantown Mennonite Church.   The largest concentration of
Mennonites in the world is said to still be in Lancaster
County, Pennsylvania, where many settled when they first
came.   Others moved further on into the states of Ohio,
Indiana, Illinois, Iowa or even as far west as Kansas, or
north into some of the provinces of Canada.   But just as
they had brought their faith along with them, so they also
brought their various cultures.   The Swiss Mennonites
brought their Swiss culture; the German Mennonites their
German culture; the Dutch Mennonites their Dutch culture;
the Russian Mennonites their Russian culture.   Many of them
formed communities composed largely of their own people, in
which they felt at home.

There still exist many predominantly Mennonite communities today.   Take my hometown, for example -- Kidron, Ohio.
Kidron is just a small farming community in rural Ohio, but

as you enter there is a sign which says, "Entering Kidron, an Energetic Swiss Community." Downtown is a Swiss cheese factory. Some of the businesses feature Swiss storefronts. You might even have the pleasure of hearing some Swiss cow bells if you go to the right place. Many of the older people still speak a Swiss dialect. There are many people with Swiss names. Sprunger, for instance, is a Swiss name. The ancestors on my father's side came from Switzerland in 1890 (Herr 1975:82). My wife's maiden name, Hostetler, is also of Swiss origin, her ancestors having gone down the Rhine and come to America in 1736 (Hostetler 1974:1). Except for my mother's side of the family, which was Presbyterian, you might say we are both ethnic Mennonites. Because Mennonites originated in the two countries of Switzerland and the Netherlands, and from there spread into other parts of Europe and to America, all ethnic Mennonites have either a Swiss-German or a Dutch-German background. There are, of course, many other-culture Mennonites today also.

As you might expect, the original settlers in the Kidron area being Mennonites from Switzerland, the only churches in town are Mennonite churches. There are three in fact. One of the churches, the Sonnenberg Mennonite Church, was founded first and is named after a community in Switzerland. My home church, the Salem Mennonite Church, and the third one, the Kidron Mennonite Church, are both splits off the first one. The three churches have a total membership of perhaps a thousand or more, although the population of the town is only about six hundred. The difference is due to the fact that many people who belong to these churches live in the wider area and not right in town. In fact, the first group of pioneers who came way back in 1819 lived a couple of miles from what is now the center of town. But in 1969, Kidron celebrated its sesquicentennial anniversary, and a survey taken for that occasion revealed that 76 percent of the 594 inhabitants are affiliated with various kinds of Mennonite churches; 22 percent are affiliated with churches of other denominations; only about 2 percent gave no church affiliation (Lehman 1969:338-339). The report goes on to mention that

Kidron forms something of a hub around which are clustered over 7,500 Mennonites of about a half-dozen varieties and nearly 60 congregations. Within the same area are nearly 5,000 Amish in about 50 congregations. ... The Amish settlement of this five-county area is the largest in the world (1969:340).

There are many other communities in other areas of the
States which, like Kidron, are made up primarily of Mennonites.

From what has already been said, you can see that there
are actually many different kinds of Mennonites. There are
the Amish, for example, with their beards and buggies and
plain clothes. The Amish are the result of a schism in
Switzerland led by Jacob Ammann (1693-1697). Then there are
the Hutterites, who practice a community of goods. The
Hutterites originated even earlier in Austria with Jacob
Hutter (d. 1536). But while these groups are Mennonite
related, at least in their origin, they are the only Mennonites many people have heard of. The result is that
Mennonites are often thought of in terms of their cultural
peculiarities rather than their religious convictions. They
are known for their superb cooking and superior farming
(although many of them are not farmers anymore), but perhaps
not much else.

The fact is that today, while there are exceptions, most
Mennonites and Mennonite churches do not differ greatly from
other Protestants. In terms of basic Christian beliefs such
as the deity of Christ, His atoning death and resurrection,
His coming again, the necessity of the new birth, discipleship and so on, there would be general agreement. Among the
different Mennonite groups this would also be true. Part of
the reason for the existence of various Mennonite groups is,
of course, slight doctrinal differences, each having freedom
to interpret the Bible in their own way. But cultural
difference and geographical distance have undoubtedly played
just as great or a greater part in the formation of the
different Mennonite groups. Many splits have unfortunately
taken place over little things such as using a catechism,
starting Sunday schools, having a church constitution, keeping minutes, wearing proper attire and the like. Even the
validity of holding prayer meetings was at one time an
issue. But basically, Mennonites are agreed among themselves and with other evangelical Christians.

If there is any teaching that might distinguish the
Mennonites from other denominations, it would probably be a
greater emphasis on "peace." The Mennonites, along with the
Church of the Brethren and the Society of Friends (Quakers),
are known as one of the "historic peace churches." And
while there may be points of difference among the various
Mennonite groups, they also cooperate in many ways, especially in relief, service, and reconcilation work done

through the Mennonite Central Committee (MCC), an inter-
Mennonite service organization. It is regrettable in many
ways that there are so many different Mennonite groups, or
for that matter, a Mennonite Church at all. The same could
be said, perhaps, of any and all other Christian denominations, although, as implied before, denominations are
probably an inevitable phenomena and we simply have to live
with them.

We have seen how one of them, the Mennonite Church, came
into being. As was pointed out, it got its name from Menno
Simons, one of the leaders of the Anabaptist movement in the
Netherlands at the time of the Reformation. It should be
remembered, however, that while Mennonite churches today
continue to stand within the Anabaptist-Mennonite tradition,
it was not Menno's intention to start a new denomination or
a new church. "Mennonite" was simply a label given to Menno
and his followers by their opponents, which has stuck to
this day. Mennonites, though, like many other Christians,
see themselves as Christians first, and Mennonites second.

The three largest Mennonite groups are the Mennonite
Church, the General Conference Mennonite Church, and the
Mennonite Brethren, respectively. Several other groups are
the Brethren in Christ Church; Church of God in Christ,
Mennonite (Holdeman); Hutterian Brethren; Old Order Amish
Church; and Old Order Mennonite Church (Horsch 1979:151).
My wife and I happen to belong to churches which are part of
the General Conference Mennonite Church. My wife's home
church, the Oak Grove Mennonite Church at Smithville, Ohio,
is also a member of the Mennonite Church (MC). That is,
like a number of other congregations in recent years, they
have opted to become members of more than one conference,
which suggests how much in common these groups really have.

Anyway, the General Conference Mennonite Church was first
organized at West Point, Iowa, in 1860. This union grew out
of a desire on the part of several congregations to do some
things together that it was difficult to do alone, namely,
missions and education. The Conference began with only two
congregations and 200 or so members. Today it has over 300
congregations and approximately 60,000 members in the United
States and Canada (GCMC 1977:69). This figure also includes
a few thousand members in South America, but does not
include the approximately 45,000 members in the younger
churches overseas (1977:80-84). The number of members in
these churches may soon surpass those at home.

The General Conference has no legislative power over the
member congregations. It is simply an advisory body, with
the final authority residing in the local churches. It does,
however, operate various institutions on behalf of the
churches such as camps, colleges, hospitals, homes for the
aged, mental health centers, a joint seminary (with the
Mennonite Church) and so on. It also has its own publishing
house and several bookstores and publishes a weekly conference paper, *The Mennonite*. The headquarters of the General
Conference Mennonite Church is in Newton, Kansas. The motto
of the General Conference is the same one Menno Simons took
for himself, which was, "No other foundation can any one lay
than that which is laid, which is Jesus Christ" (I Cor.
3:11). (Note: For the reader who would like to learn more
about Mennonites in general or the history of the General
Conference Mennonite Church in particular, the book, *An
Introduction to Mennonite History* (Dyck 1967), would be a
good place to begin.)

It has sometimes been remarked that the "cement" which
holds the General Conference Mennonites together is missions.
In addition to the institutions mentioned above, the Conference does have a Commission on Home Ministries (CHM) and
a Commission on Overseas Mission (COM). The Conference
approved its first volunteer missionary candidate, Samuel S.
Haury, in 1872, but it took several more years to find a
suitable field of service. Haury, together with his wife,
finally went out in 1880 and established the first American
Mennonite mission work among the Arapahoe Indians, in what
is now Oklahoma (Smith 1957:683). At the time, it was
called a "foreign" mission, but overseas work did not really
begin until 1900 when P. A. Penner and J. F. Kroeker and
their wives went to India as the first foreign missionaries
(1957:684). Today the CHM continues its ministry among the
American Indians, as well as in other parts of the States.
There are about 135 missionaries serving abroad under COM.
They are working in 14 different countries: Bolivia,
Botswana, Brazil, Columbia, Costa Rica, India, Japan,
Lesotho, Mexico, Paraguay, Taiwan, Upper Volta, Uruguay, and
Zaire (GCMC 1977:39-40). Hong Kong was also entered in 1980.
(For a survey of General Conference Mennonite mission work
overseas, the recent book *A People of Mission* by James C.
Juhnke is highly recommended.)

Our interest, here, of course, is in Japan where our
first workers were sent in 1951. Fortunately, we have a
good record of the opening of the work there. In a report
called *The Christian Mission of the General Conference*

Mennonite Church, we are given a summary of the main reasons
for considering Japan as a new mission field:

> At least four distinct reasons can be isolated for
> General Conference interest in Japan as a mission field
> in the immediate post-World War II period. In the
> first place, Japan represented an unparalleled challenge
> to Christian missions. The military defeat and the
> overthrow of the traditional emperor worship had left
> a void in the lives of the Japanese. This made them
> open and receptive, not only to Christianity, the pro-
> fessed national religion of their conqueror, but to
> anything new that had promise in it.
>
> In the second place, and closely allied with the
> first, was General MacArthur's request for one thousand
> missionaries for Japan as soon as possible. Third,
> immediately following the war, the Mennonite Central
> Committee began relief work in Japan as a member of
> the Licensed Agencies of Relief in Asia. As has
> usually been the case in the past when Christians
> minister to the physical needs of people, they become
> more keenly aware also of their spiritual needs, and
> thus relief work becomes the springboard for missionary
> effort.
>
> The fourth reason, however, became the immediate
> reason why the General Conference seriously considered
> opening a missionary work in Japan. This was prompted
> by the closing of our field in China. The decision to
> investigate the Japanese field and the appointment of
> W. C. Voth as field investigator took place at the
> annual meeting of the Board of Missions in Mountain
> Lake, Minnesota, in 1949. In the spring of 1950 Rev.
> Voth traveled through Japan. Finding conditions most
> favorable on Kyushu, the island farthest to the south,
> he recommended that work be established in Miyazaki
> Prefecture (county) on the eastern coast of this
> island. The board authorized him to make tentative
> arrangements for housing and sought for two couples
> to go to the field immediately. Here churches and
> Christians were least in number.
>
> At the triennial session of the General Conference
> in Freeman, South Dakota, in August, 1950, Rev. Voth
> gave his first-hand report on Japan, and an official
> decision was made to open a mission there. Leonore
> Friesen, who was attending the conference, volunteered

to go immediately and was accepted as the first missionary. She arrived in Osaka in January 1951 to begin the
study of the difficult Japanese language (Pannabecker
1961a:55).

In addition to the above reasons, Voth made clear elsewhere in a written report that it was his deep conviction
that "the paramount reason for our mission work in Japan is
THE CALL OF GOD" (Voth and Unruh 1951:16). In response to
this call other missionaries were sent out to join Miss
Friesen, and by the end of the first year, there were 10
missionaries on the field. We want to say a little more
about them and their work. But before we get into that,
perhaps we should take a little time to get acquainted with
Japan and describe the area to which they went.

WHERE IN THE WORLD IS KYUSHU?

As already pointed out in the quotation just given,
Kyushu (pronounced "cue-shoe") is the southernmost of the
four main islands of Japan. Actually it is more to the
southwest than to the south of the other islands. Okinawa
is still further to the south and west. From the map
(Figure 1.2) you can see where Kyushu is located in relation
to the rest of the Japanese islands. You will also see that
an area has been darkened in the lower right hand side of
Kyushu. That represents Miyazaki Prefecture, where the
General Conference Mennonites (GC) have primarily been working. There are other Mennonite groups working in Japan.
The Mennonite Brethren (MB), for example, in the Osaka area
on Honshu, and the Mennonite Church (MC) in Hokkaido. The
Brethren in Christ (BIC), a Mennonite-related group, are
working in Yamaguchi Prefecture in southern Honshu. Several
of these groups are also working in the Tokyo aı a, where
they are cooperating through the Greater Tokyo Evangelism
Cooperative Fellowship (*Keihin Dendō Kyōryokukai*, KDK, reorganized in 1979 as TAFMC, Tokyo Area Fellowship of Mennonite
Churches), composed of representatives from the various Mennonite churches. But as we are dealing here with the General
Conference work, we want to concentrate our attention on
Kyushu, more specifically on Miyazaki Prefecture.

Geographically, the island of Kyushu is less than 300
kilometers (185 mi.) from South Korea. Miyazaki Prefecture
itself is on the opposite side of the island, lying about
1,400 kilometers (870 mi.) southwest of Tokyo, the capital.
The prefecture is approximately 65 kilometers (40 mi.) wide
and 160 kilometers (100 mi.) long. It is primarily a rural
area, although there are some good-sized cities such as

Miyazaki City (pop. 250,000), the prefectural seat. Like
the rest of Japan, Miyazaki is quite mountainous. It is
famous for its stately palm trees, its striking coastal
areas, and its scenic national parks. Endowed with great
natural beauty, it has become a popular honeymoon resort.
It borders the Pacific Ocean, and tourist literature sometimes refers to it as the "Hawaii of Japan." One of our
friends visiting us commented that Miyazaki City was the
"Pasadena of Japan."

Figure 1.2

MAP OF JAPAN

Compared to northern Japan, the climate is rather mild,
almost semitropical at places. The fact is, however, it is
not warm year round like Hawaii or Southern California. The
latitude is more like the state of Georgia, and it can be
quite cold and clammy in winter, hot and humid in summer.
June is the rainy season, and an occasional typhoon comes
through, but generally the weather is quite pleasant. Deli-
cate cherry blossoms in spring, picturesque rice paddies in
summer, clear blue skies in fall, and frosted brown fields
in winter all add to the beauty. Miyazaki is sometimes
referred to as the "province of the sun," and the prefectural flag has three yellow stripes on a green background to
represent it as the land of sunshine and green.

Historically, it is one of the most significant areas in Japan. It is the "land of legend" as well as "province of the sun." Take the origin of the imperial line for instance. As former ambassador to Japan Edwin Reischauer recounts it, according to Japanese mythology,

> The Sun Goddess, one of the chief objects of worship
> by the ancient Yamato clan, was considered to be the
> progenitress of the imperial line, and her grandson
> was described as descending to Japan from heaven and
> the latter's grandson, in turn, as becoming the first
> emperor, ascending the throne in 660 B.C. (1964:30).

That descent is supposed to have taken place on Mt. Takachiho, one of Miyazaki Prefecture's most beautiful spots. Thus the prefecture is the home of Jimmu Tenno, supposedly the first emperor of Japan.

Because the emperor was believed to be a direct descendant of the Sun Goddess, it gave both him and his subjects a divine origin, and every autumn sacred dances are held to reenact some of these old legends. Most of these myths originated with the *Kojiki* and the *Nihon Shoki*, two of Japan's oldest existing books, dating from the early eighth century and a combination of both history and mythology (1964:29-30). But while these legends are not believed by most people anymore, the present emperor, Emperor Hirohito, is said to be the 124th in succession, and eras in Japan are still reckoned according to the reign of the emperor. So it is not only 1979 in Japan, when this is being revised, but also the 54th year of *Shōwa*, the name (meaning "bright peace") which the emperor chose for his particular era. Although the Imperial Family does not live in Miyazaki today, it supposedly had its beginnings there.

Besides the many places associated with the legends, there are also numerous old burial mounds and other historic sites to visit. It is said there are over 2,200 ancient burial mounds scattered throughout the prefecture (Miyazaki Prefectural Government 1966:8). Built on top of one of these huge burial mounds in Miyazaki City is the Peace Tower. It was originally constructed to commemorate the 2600th anniversary of the emperor, but later became a memorial to those who have died in war and a symbol of the desire for peace. There is much more one could say, but Miyazaki indeed has a rich cultural and historical heritage.

Economically, Miyazaki is primarily an agricultural area. As throughout Japan, however, farms are small and most of

the farming is done by the women while the men go to work in
the factories. There are lumbering, fishing, chemical and
many other industries too. Unemployment has traditionally
been low, although in recent years even that situation has
been changing. As far as food production is concerned,
though all of Japan would fit in a state the size of California and less than 20 percent of the land is arable, the
people are able to raise a large proportion of the rice and
other food they need. Some items such as meat, soybeans,
wheat and the like are largely imported. But what has hurt
most is that Japan is plagued with a scarcity of natural
resources such as oil, 99 percent of which must be imported.
With an industrially based economy, and rising oil prices,
that can make things extremely difficult.

Yet Japan has come a long way since the war years, and in
spite of some serious problems such as inflation, outwardly,
at least, the economy still appears to be booming. In the
city of Miyakonojo (pop. 120,000), for example, where we
lived, three large new department stores were built in the
early 1970s within a year's time (one eight stories, another
nine stories), whereas there had been only one large one
before. Even though inflation has driven many prices way
up, wages have been going up accordingly and people seem to
have money to spend. A high percentage of the people now
have cars and color TV, and many are buying or building
their own homes.

While Miyazaki is said to economically rank toward the
bottom of the scale in comparison with other prefectures,
the economy is certainly growing. New roads, schools, and
hospitals are being built. Prefectural harbors, airports,
and railways are being improved. When the Japanese National
Railways completes the "bullet train" lines down Miyazaki
way, that will also no doubt give a boost to the economy.
Back in 1964, it took about 24 hours to get to Tokyo by
train from down here. At present it takes only about 12,
and when the new lines are finished they say it will take
only about eight or nine hours. Or, you can fly there in
less than two, if you are in a hurry. So a lot is happening.
In many sectors of the economy such as shipbuilding, syn-
thetics, radio, television, movies, motorcycles, and auto-
mobile production, Japan has consistently been at or near
the top in recent years. Her GNP is one of the highest in
the world. Truly Japan's recovery is nothing short of an
"economic miracle" and materially, at least, people appear
to be well off, even down in Miyazaki.

Ecologically, the prefecture is still one of the cleaner areas. There is some air and water pollution from pulp, chemical, and other factories, but it is nothing like Osaka, Tokyo and other vast industrial areas with their photochemical and other smog problems. It surely must be a dubious honor to be one of the largest cities in the world with all the problems it creates. Yet Kyushu has had its share of problems too. One example of this is the mercury poisoning, the cause of the Minamata disease, which has crippled many so horribly. When one sees films about the victims of man's carelessness, it makes you realize how widespread the problem is. It even extends to the countryside. Compared to the rest of Japan, Miyazaki's problems may seem small. But many voices are calling for constant vigilance, lest people awake some day to find the trees no longer green, the sky no longer blue.

Educationally, as in the rest of the country, schools abound. Schools function on a five-and-a-half-day week. Since everyone must go through at least junior high (nine years of compulsory education), literacy is about 99 percent. Beyond that there are high schools -- commercial, industrial, agricultural, college prep and so on. To get into high school, you must pass a stiff exam, so preparation starts early, way down in kindergarten. To get the best possible job, you must graduate from the best schools all the way along. Thus competition is intense. One's classmates are one's competitors. But an attempt is made to ensure that everyone has an equal chance at a good education. I was reminded of this when we visited a small elementary school on a little island only about a kilometer or two off the coast of the prefecture. Most of the residents were fishermen and their families. The school had only 19 children in six grades. But for those 19 there were six teachers, a head teacher, a principal and even some office workers! Education is highly valued.

To get into the university of one's choice you must also pass a very difficult exam. University exams are referred to as "examination hell." So it is difficult to enter university, but once you get in, you are almost assured of graduating. And once you graduate and enter a company, you are virtually certain of lifetime employment. So there is a considerable amount of security in the system for those who make it. There are several junior colleges, but only two universities in Miyazaki, so most of the students must go to one of the larger cities to study, and many stay to work there after graduation.

Linguistically, there is a standard Japanese which is used in the schools, also on television and in the newspapers. The Tokyo dialect is considered to be the standard. But there are also numerous other dialects, carrying over from feudal days. Miyakonojo, our city, has one. Miyazaki City, an hour away, has another. Just several minutes away, in Kagoshima Prefecture, is still another. These dialects are not mutually understandable, even to the Japanese. Especially for an outsider, they are difficult to learn as they are unwritten languages. The Japanese, of course, borrowed many of the Chinese characters (*kanji*) and use them as part of their writing system. Japanese and Chinese are so different, however (for example, one is monosyllabic, the other polysyllabic), that the Japanese have an alphabet of 50 characters of their own they must use with the Chinese characters to write most words. They also have another alphabet of 50 characters which they use to write foreign or loan words or names. Thus learning written Japanese can be even more complicated than spoken Japanese, depending on one's ability.

Politically, Japan has five major parties: Liberal-Democratic, Democratic-Socialist, Socialist, Clean Government, and Communist. There are also some more recently formed parties such as the New Liberal Club. The Liberal-Democratic Party is now in power, with Mr. Ohira as Prime Minister. The Emperor has become just a figurehead of the nation, making occasional appearances in public, but not having any real political power himself. The postwar Constitution contains an "anti-war clause" which forbids Japan to have any forces that might be used in making war on another nation. But it has been interpreted in such a way as to allow them to have what they call a "Self-Defense Force." It is the equivalent of an army, navy, and air force all in one, but they do not call it such. These forces are not to be used for aggression. They are to be used only in case of an invasion. Japan also has a "Joint Defense Treaty" with the United States for mutual defense purposes.

Be that as it may, Japan is a democratic nation, and anyone twenty years or older can vote. While I do not have any statistics to go by, it is said that Miyazaki is basically a conservative area. It is also said that a majority of Christians lean toward the policies of the Socialist party, fearing that some of the other parties might lead Japan back toward militarism and nationalism. Recent attempts on the part of the current government to nationalize the Yasukuni

Shrine (Shinto) as a memorial to the war dead may be a confirmation of that fear. In addition to the federal government, there are naturally regional governments that take
care of local matters.

Racially, the population of Miyazaki is very homogeneous
as throughout Japan. Short stature, black hair, dark eyes
-- these are some of the more notable physical characteristics. There are no blue-eyed blondes, and foreigners can
be spotted a block away by the way they look, the way they
walk, the way they talk. There are no Ainu (a race physi-
cally somewhat different from the typical Japanese) in the
area as there are in Hokkaido, but there are a number of
people considered foreigners. When I was at the city
office one day to register ourselves, I casually asked them
how many foreigners there were in town. They said, "about
250." I could hardly believe my ears, for to our knowledge
we were the only American family in the city, and we had
seen only a few other Americans or other foreigners around.
But upon further inquiry, I found out they were mostly from
Korea. There were over 200 Koreans in our city! To us they
did not look any different from the Japanese. But they were
not Japanese citizens, and like us, had to carry an alien
registration card.

Sociologically, the people of Miyazaki make up a rural
society. The total population of Japan is over 115 million,
and increasing at the rate of about 1 percent per year.
Approximately 10 percent of the population lives in Tokyo.
By comparison, Miyazaki, with only slightly over a million
people, is indeed sparsely populated. A recent census
showed that from 1965 to 1970, the prefecture's population
declined by almost 30,000 people (1,080,692 to 1,051,105),
but at present is estimated to more or less be holding its
own (Bureau of Statistics 1974:14). Being a rural area, the
people are perhaps not as responsive to new ideas as in the
cities where they may have cut more of their ties with the
past. This may be especially true of the older generation,
and the *buraku* (close-knit communities) which appear to be
extremely resistant to change. On the other hand, rural
young people, as young people in urban areas, seem to be one
of the most responsive groups, but about 90 percent of them
leave their hometowns after graduation from high school so
it is hard to build a church out of them.

People are very mobile, moving frequently. There are the
rich and the poor, but about 90 percent of the population
are said to claim they belong to the huge middle class

somewhere in between. As indicated before, the per capita
income in the prefecture is said to be below the national
average, and yet people seem to have more and more time and
money for golf, eating out, travelling and other leisure
activities. The family is still the basic unit of society,
although it is undergoing many changes too. Families are
smaller than they used to be, with an average of only about
two children per family. Many marriages are now "love
marriages" instead of arranged, where you marry first and
then learn to love each other later. Divorce is quite
common. Juvenile delinquency and crime are on the increase.
Parents and grandparents do not live with their children as
much as they used to. Young families like to have their own
house or apartment, even if it is small. The elders usually
live nearby in a separate house or in an "old peoples" home.
But while on the surface things are changing rapidly, under-
neath they remain very much the same. To the tourist, Japan
may look quite western, whereas in fact it is still, and
probably always will be, very much eastern. An excellent
book on Japan is *Japan: Images and Realities* by Richard
Halloran (1969). His chapter titled "We Japanese" is "must"
reading for anyone interested in Japanese society, and the
Japanese way of looking at things.

Religiously, there have been two main religions in Japan:
Shintoism and Buddhism. Shintoism, a kind of nature worship
(literally, "the way of the gods"), is indigenous to Japan,
and was at one time the state religion. Buddhism, on the
other hand, came from China by way of Korea about A.D. 552
(Reischauer 1964:18), and gradually came to take its place
alongside Shintoism as one of the traditional religions.
To this day Shinto shrines and Buddhist temples dot the land
wherever you go. But a third force has also taken its place
beside the other two, and that is Christianity.

There have been three main comings of Christianity to
Japan. The first was with the arrival of the famous
Catholic missionary, Francis Xavier, at Kagoshima in 1549
(Boxer 1951:37). This was almost a thousand years after
Buddhism had come, but Xavier, and those who came after him,
had considerable success, so great in fact that by 1580
there was a total Christian community of 150,000 (1951:114).
It looked as if Japan might soon become a Christian nation,
and it might well have except for the fact that the government, fearing for the unity of the empire, began to perse-
cute the Christians. This persecution continued for about
50 years. It finally culminated in the Shimabara rebellion
of 1637-1638, by the Christians, in which about 37,000 of
them were subsequently slaughtered (Drummond 1971:105-108).

For about two centuries after this, Japan remained a
closed country. But with the arrival of Commodore Perry's
ships, Japan opened itself to the world again, which paved
the way for the second coming of Christianity. This second
coming took place in 1859, 310 years after the first one,
with the arrival of several Protestant missionaries. Samuel
R. Brown, Guido F. Verbeck, and James C. Hepburn were some
of the more famous of these, and like a number of the other
first Protestant missionaries who came, two of them had been
former missionaries to China (Iglehart 1959:31-32). The
third coming of Christianity then took place in the late
1940s, with the arrival of both many new Catholic and
Protestant workers, some of whom were also transferred from
China. In fact, it is interesting to note that Xavier himself having come from China to Japan, all three major
comings of Christianity to Japan have involved coming from
the West by way of China.

In addition to the three main religions, there are also
hundreds of new ones which sprang up after the war. Many of
them are sects of Buddhism, and some, like Sōka Gakkai, have
had amazing success, having won over 10 percent of the population in only a couple decades. Others were short-lived,
having died out already. Like Christianity, most of the
so-called "new religions" were seeking to fill the religious
vacuum that had been created when the Emperor denied his
divinity, January 1, 1946. But unlike Christianity, many of
them are syncretistic, often including selected parts of
Christianity as well (Thomsen 1963:29). This tendency has
been a characteristic of Japan. In 1972, for example, the
total population of Japan was estimated at 107 million
(Bureau of Statistics 1974:11). But in the same year, the
total adherents of the various religious bodies was over 178
million (1974:590)! The official explanation given is that
"Total adherents exceed the total population of Japan,
because some persons often belong to both Shintoism and
Buddhism" (1974:591).

In this connection, Catholic scholar Joseph Spae also
notes the saying that for the Japanese, religion is often
"Shintō at birth, Christianity at marriage, and Buddhism at
death" (1968:92). For the Christian, of course, this would
not necessarily be true. But for many others it could well
be, for they are taken to the Shinto shrine to be blessed as
children, they may be married in a Christian church even
though they are not Christian, and when they die they are
buried as Buddhists, Buddhism being largely a "funeral
religion." Thus many people claim more than one religion,

without feeling any contradiction, and it is sometimes difficult to know exactly how many Christians there really are.
According to the *Kirisutokyō Nenkan* [The Japan Christian
Yearbook], as of 1978 there were approximately 406,000
Catholics and 694,000 Protestants (*Kirisuto Shimbunsha* 1979:
443), which means that less than 1 percent of the population
are church members. But whenever a religious survey is
taken, there are usually about 3 percent who claim to be
Christian, so there may actually be more Christians than is
thought, or at least many secret admirers.

In any case, the progress of Christianity has been slow
in Japan. In fact, percentagewise, there are less Christians today than there were back in the early 1600s, over
350 years ago, when approximately 300,000 out of a total
estimated population of 20 million were believers (Boxer
1951:320-321). One of the reasons for this, of course, is
the persecution which we have already mentioned. Some
other reasons may be the late arrival of Christianity, its
exclusivism or its westernness, the competition of other
religions and so on. But one of the biggest problems today
is not persecution, as it was with the Anabaptists or the
early Christians of Japan (incidentally, at about the same
time), but simply indifference to the Gospel. There are
some indications, however, that the situation is changing,
among the younger generation in particular, and we certainly
hope it will improve. But up till now, with few exceptions,
the growth of the church has been painfully slow, especially
in the more rural parts of the country such as Miyazaki.

WHAT ARE THE GENERAL CONFERENCE
MENNONITES DOING THERE?

One of the main reasons for choosing the Miyazaki area
was that, as noted before, "churches and Christians were
least in number." This does not mean there were not any
churches. C. A. Clark, the first Protestant missionary to
work in the prefecture, had founded the first church in the
area in Miyakonojo in 1887 (Boschman 1968:40). William C.
Voth and Verney Unruh, who surveyed the situation in 1951,
found 17 churches and three missionaries working among a
population of 1,052,000 (1951:7-9). But churches were few
and far between. So the Mennonite missionaries, after a
year or two in language study, began working in Miyazaki in
1952. Their strategy was to start work in the larger cities,
and then later on try to work the area in between. As Japan
had good schools and hospitals, they did not start any educational or medical work. But they carried on various types

of work such as Bible classes and prayer meetings, English classes, street meetings, tent campaigns, radio evangelism, literature evangelism, hospital visitation, Sunday schools, Sunday worship and so on. They also began bookstore work, a camping program, a kindergarten, and a student center for university students.

Until the early 1970s, there were on the average 15 or 20 long-term missionaries serving in the area. This would include about eight couples and three or four single workers (both husband and wife are counted as missionaries). One missionary put most of her effort into the bookstore work; others have concentrated on kindergarten or student center work (which has since developed into a church). The missionaries have not all worked in Miyazaki all of the time. Some have served for several years or more doing pioneer work outside the prefecture. One couple has also been working in the Tokyo area as self-supporting missionaries for about 15 years. But by and large most of the workers have spent most of their time working in the Miyazaki area, mainly because it was an unchurched area.

There have also been a number of short-termers (a two- or three-year term), from 1958 on, assisting with the work. Today they are called "mission associates," but for many years they were called "pax-workers" or "peace-workers," "*pax*" being the Latin word for "peace." Most of them came to do alternative service, instead of going into the army or some other branch of regular military service. Their duties have been varied. Some have spent most of their time teaching conversational English in public schools. Others have taught in junior colleges or universities. A few have taught the children attending the Miyazaki Christian School in Miyakonojo, an elementary school operated by the Mennonites for their missionary children but including some non-Mennonite children as well. Still others have served as houseparents to the children, who stayed in the dorm four days a week, returning to their homes each week for a long weekend. The school has now closed, however, as most of the missionary children have grown up. Some of these workers have helped in other ways too, such as doing Mission office work. Many have also helped out at retreats and church camps or English seminars. But much of the work short-termers have done has been only indirectly related to the work of the churches.

It was hoped that through English teaching and helping teach and take care of the missionary children, short-

termers could release the long-termers for more direct evangelism and church planting, and that hope was no doubt to
some extent realized. Yet while it has been a good witness,
the short-term program in itself seems to have had little
real impact on the growth of the church. It has, nevertheless, produced some long-term workers. One of the short-
term single girls and two of the short-term couples have
felt God's call to stay on, and have returned for one or
more additional terms. There has been a total of over 50
workers serving in Kyushu at one time or another, divided
about equally between long-termers and short-termers. (See
Appendix A for a list of all those who have served.) At
present (1978), there are about 20 missionaries still in
Japan, but only one of them is a "mission associate." Of
the original 10 missionaries who went out the first year,
only one couple is still serving in Japan, and they have not
been here continuously.

As a result of the labor of the various workers, 10 new
churches ("church" being defined as a group of 15 or more
believers) have been established; three "evangelistic
centers" have also been opened (as of 1977). Of the ten
churches, seven have Japanese pastors, two are pastored by
missionaries, and one has invited a missionary to come in
the near future. As for the three centers, two are pastored
by two of the above mentioned pastors, one is pastored
jointly by another pastor and a missionary. Two of the
churches and one of the centers are not in Miyazaki Prefecture. One of these churches is located in Oita City (Oita
Prefecture) to the north, the other is located on Honshu, in
the city of Kobe (Hyogo Prefecture). This latter church was
started by the missionaries when they were in language
school. The one evangelistic center is located in northern
Kyushu in the city of Fukuoka (Fukuoka Prefecture).

There is a total of about six hundred baptized members
belonging to the churches, although resident active membership is only about half that figure. The churches range in
size from about 15 to 50 active members. Two of the evangelistic centers are sponsored by local churches -- the one in
Miyazaki (Otsukadai) by the Oyodo and Kirishima churches,
and the one in Miyakonojo (Takao) by the Namiki Church. The
newest center (Muromi) in Fukuoka is sponsored by the Church
Conference. For several years there was a center in Kagoshima
City also, but that work has since been terminated.

The map (Figure 1.3) will give you an idea where the
various churches and centers are located on Kyushu. One of

the groups, the Kirishima Christian Brotherhood (Kobayashi)
does not call itself a "church," but for the sake of simplification, it is listed along with the others as a church.
In addition to the churches, a camp, a kindergarten, and
three bookstores (one was closed in 1979, another in 1980)
have also been established. The church in Kobe, being
several hundred kilometers away (near Osaka), is not represented here, but is also very much a part of the work of the
Conference. The work being done in Tokyo is not included as
it is more of an inter-Mennonite-Brethren in Christ venture.

Figure 1.3

CONFERENCE WORK IN KYUSHU

+ church
* evangelistic center

WHY THE JAPAN MENNONITE CHURCH CONFERENCE?

As Christians were won and churches were formed, it was
felt that the churches needed each other in order to grow.
The goal was to plant "indigenous churches," that is,
churches that were "self-supporting, self-governing, and
self-propagating." But the churches were so small that in
order to strengthen them it was felt that a larger

brotherhood to which they could belong was necessary. This
followed the pattern of General Conference Mennonite
churches in the United States and Canada. Mennonite
churches have traditionally been congregational in polity.
At the same time, they have often formed conferences where
groups of congregations have joined together to do some
things they could not do by themselves. This has been
especially true in the area of missions and education. A
conference has no authority except that which the member
churches give it. Membership is voluntary. No congregation
is forced to join. But, as pointed out earlier in the study,
nowadays some churches are even taking out membership in
more than one conference.

In any case, when the missionaries first came to Japan
there was just the mission organization. The Mission had
its own constitution, and was known as the General Conference Mennonite Mission in Japan (GCMM). Then as churches
came into existence, the Mission and the churches worked
side by side, the churches forming a loose organization of
their own. For a while, the Mission and the churches each
had their own education and evangelism committees and so on,
but it was felt that such duplication was unnecessary, so
joint committees were formed. More and more the Mission
decreased and the churches increased, so that finally the
pastors and missionaries agreed that it would probably be
best to become one body and form a conference. So it was
that in 1964, the Japan Mennonite Christian Church Conference (JMCCC) was officially born with seven member churches.
(See Appendix B for the *Constitution of the Japan Mennonite
Christian Church Conference*.)

When the Church Conference was formed, it was assumed by
the pastors that the mission organization would cease to
exist. To them that was understood in the idea of becoming
"one." To some of the missionaries, though, the idea of
"oneness" was more or less to run on two parallel tracks,
like a train, rather than on one track, like a monorail. In
other words, while the missionaries were willing to cooperate in all matters pertaining to the work of the churches,
some of them felt there were certain areas which were
uniquely their own and that the Mission should continue to
exist in some form. Some were afraid total dissolution of
the mission body might hinder expansion in the future. Or
that some of the missionaries might not be able to come
back. Or that the Conference might be able to control all
the finances, including money for missionary housing and
salaries. This was threatening. It was felt that some of

these things would only create unnecessary tensions, and so for the time being the mission organization continued to exist.

Most of the business was already in the hands of the Church Conference, however, and now that the pastors at least had an equal voice, they began to speak up. They questioned many of the things the missionaries were doing. They decided to drop the radio work as too expensive and ineffective. The camp and bookstores and kindergarten were all questioned too. Also whether short-termers were needed or not. There was considerable criticism of what was called "missionary paternalism." They felt the organizational structure they had inherited from the missionaries was too heavy, so they decided to dismantle the Education, Evangelism, and Literature committees and start over from scratch. They reorganized, beginning with only an Executive Committee, later adding an Evangelism, Personnel, and other committees as the need arose. Many of these decisions did not have the full backing of the missionaries, but they were no longer in the driver's seat and so there was not too much they could do. It was in many ways a very difficult time.

In other ways, it was encouraging to see such developments. The national leaders were maturing. They were interested in doing things their way. After all, it was their country and their culture. And while Church-Mission relationships were in the fore for several years, a much healthier relationship seems to have developed between the two. The Church Conference now has its own constitution. It also has equal representation on the Religious Juridical Person (*Shūkyō Hōjin*), which controls all church-, Mission-, and Conference-owned property. The camp, kindergarten, and bookstores are now under the supervision of the Conference or conference-appointed committees. The Church Conference Executive Committee consists of one representative from each church (not necessarily the pastor), and there is one missionary on it to represent their group. The offices of chairman, secretary, and treasurer can theoretically be held by anyone, but at present are all occupied by nationals. The Conference has an annual meeting in February, and between conferences the Executive Committee transacts any necessary business.

The Mission continued to operate under its old constitution until 1972 when it finally realized how outdated it was, and so a one-page "Memo of Understanding" was drawn up instead. (See Appendix C for the "Statement of

Understanding.") This was presented to and accepted by the Church Conference in 1973 (JMCCC, Decision 4, Annual Conference 1973:1) and means that for all practical purposes, except for a few items peculiar to missionaries such as language study, children's education, missionary housing and so on, the "two" have finally become "one."

God has blessed and the work has progressed through three stages. It has gone from foreign mission, to Mission and Church working side by side, to national church. The "mission" still has an annual conference of its own in fall, but this is primarily for fellowship. For over a decade already, missionaries have been invited back by local churches rather than by the Mission, and placement is given final approval by the Conference. The Conference is an advisory body. It is in a sense a larger brotherhood. A larger expression of the Church. And together the Mission and the Conference are trying to do what needs to be done everywhere, "to make Christ known and to plant His Church."

WHAT MAJOR ISSUES DOES THE CONFERENCE FACE?

We have talked briefly so far about who the Mennonites are, and what one group of them, the General Conference Mennonites, are doing in Japan. We have also said a little about the formation of the Japan Mennonite Christian Church Conference. The next thing we want to do is discuss a few of the major issues facing the churches and the Christians that make up the Conference. Shortly before returning to the States, in May 1974, I distributed questionnaires to all the pastors and missionaries associated with the Conference. One of the questions asked was, "What do you feel is the greatest need of the Church Conference?" The following were some of the pastors' replies:

"Concrete vision and deep personal fellowship in the
   Lord."
"Having a broader perspective and turning our eyes
   toward reaching out."
"Greater planning and carrying out the things decided."
"If you mean all the churches participating in the
   Church Conference, then the most important thing is
   to endeavor to carry out faithfully our mission as
   God's people placed in the world, and I think that
   any and all methodologies that might be helpful to
   that end are worth a try, as long as they are com-
   patible with the essence of the Gospel."

"Joint research on our Confession of Faith and Church
   Constitution."
"I feel things are fine just as they are at present."

The following were some of the missionaries' replies:

"Lack of vision and lack of faith in the Lord to do
   the impossible ..."
"More faith in God -- that He leads specifically when
   we ask for direction."
"Goals."
"Spiritual unity and vision, especially among the
   leadership."
"A coordinated, systematic leadership training program."
"Money! From their own churches for their own
   programs."
"A sense of brotherhood and willingness to share."
"More heart to heart fellowship and sharing in depth.
   Less business and discussion of finances."
"Maybe more openness and love."
"A love that will cast out the fear of man."
"Humility."
"Perhaps a greater spirit of optimism, more expecta-
   tion that God is going to act. I feel we are
   caught in a rut of pessimism where we really don't
   expect much to happen any more. There is little
   aggressiveness or enthusiasm. A good 'charismatic
   encounter' I believe would help a lot."
"I am unable to suggest any concrete needs at present."

Those are a few of the needs that were felt at that time
on the part of both pastors and missionaries. Being
acquainted with the situation myself, I feel that they all
have a certain validity. There does not seem to be any one
thing which these various answers have in common, unless it
would be vision or faith or love or planning and carrying
out what we plan, each of which was mentioned a couple of
times. No one suggested any one specific thing. All spoke
in general terms. Interestingly enough, except for my own
suggestion, there was no one else who mentioned the need for
some kind of lay leadership training program, the subject of
this study. Be that as it may, if I might be so presumptuous as to suggest what I feel are the three biggest problems of our Church Conference today, it would be lack of
growth, lack of leaders, and lack of goals. I would like to
elaborate a little more on each one of them so you will know
why these three have been selected out of so many that could
be chosen.

First, the lack of growth. When one looks at the annual "Church Growth Surveys" from 1964, when the Church Conference was born, to the year 1974, it is evident that the churches have grown in various ways. For example, the number of churches has increased from seven to 10, without counting one of the seven (Nango) that closed down. (Actually, only seven of the ten churches meet the requirement of having 15 or more resident active members to be considered "churches." They should really be termed "evangelistic centers," according to the Conference Constitution. In the most recent "Church Growth Surveys" which have been taken, however, 10 churches are listed, although not all of them are full-fledged members of the Conference yet. So practically speaking, there are actually 10 groups which I believe can rightfully be termed "churches," depending on how you define "church." Therefore, throughout this study, it will be assumed that we are dealing with a total of 10 churches.) (See Appendix D for a complete list of all the churches and their pastors.)

Another area in which growth has taken place is in membership. The surveys reveal that resident active membership during these years has grown from 157 to 229. Total membership (baptized members) has increased from 316 to 556. There has been over a 50 percent increase in the number of Christian homes. The church offerings have well over tripled during these 10 years. These are all indications that in many ways the churches and the Church Conference have grown.

On the other hand, if you look a little more carefully, you will discover that, as pointed out, one of the original seven churches is no longer functioning. You will also see, as indicated in the graph (Figure 1.4), that there has been considerable fluctuation in the number of baptisms, from a low of 12 to a high of 55 per year. In 1973, for example, there were 33 baptisms, an average of 3.3 baptisms per church. What this graph does not show, however, is that over half of those 33 baptisms were from only two of the ten churches listed, from two of the newest groups. It also does not show that one of those two groups did not have any baptisms the year before. And another thing it does not reveal is that in one of the ten churches there were no baptisms at all from 1970-1974, and in some of the others there have been none for one or two years at a time. In 1974 also, well over half of the baptisms were from only two of the churches. Growth has been very spotty. These same trends hold true for the years 1975 and 1976 also. In 1977

too, 13 of the 20 baptisms were from but two of the churches,
five churches had only one or two, and three reported none.

Figure 1.4

ANNUAL BAPTISMS, 1965-1976

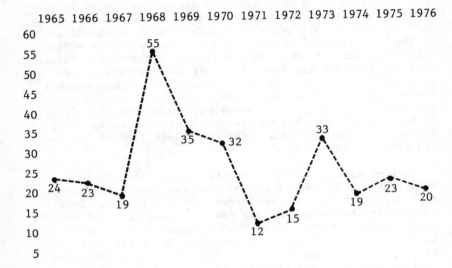

(Source: JMCCC "Church Growth Surveys," 1965-1976. Note:
From 1965 to 1968 the figures are based on an Oct.-Sept.
year. Thus the 1965 figure, for example, actually represents the number of baptisms from Oct. 1964-Sept. 1965 and
so on. The figure for 1968 (55) is an estimate rather than
an exact figure as it also includes some baptisms from Oct.-
Dec. 1968. The reason for that is that from 1969 on, the
figures are based on a Jan.-Dec. year rather than Oct.-Sept.
as previously.)

     There is also the fact that while resident active member-
ship is up about 70, or 45 percent over what it was 10 years
ago, percentagewise it has shown a notable decrease in
relationship to the total number of baptized believers.
That is, the total membership increased by 240, but only
about 43 percent is resident, whereas it was almost 50 percent before. Part of the reason for this is mobility,
especially from rural to urban areas, a phenomenon which

seems to be continuing and raises questions as to the growth potential of the churches in the future.

As far as seekers go, the statistics available to me were not complete, but it would appear that some churches seem to have considerably more than others. The total number of serious seekers in 1974 (56, or an average of seven for each of the eight churches who reported this item) is not especially large, and again, there is considerable fluctuation, anywhere from zero to 20. This may account in part for the small number of baptisms, at least in some of the churches. As former missionary to Japan, Paul Boschman, has observed, "The number of baptisms will always depend on the number of seekers available in each church" (1968:60).

In any case, I think it is quite apparent that while the churches have grown in some ways, in others they do not seem to have grown much at all. In fact, some of the churches have very serious problems. They simply are not growing, or growing only very slowly. Qualitatively there has hopefully been growth in all of the churches, which is, of course, to be desired. But quantitatively, growth has been very slow and uneven, and leaves much to be wished for. It is not only that not much is happening, but as one of the missionaries put it, "We are caught in a rut of pessimism where we really don't expect much to happen anymore." Or as one of the pastors said, "We need to have a broader perspective and turn our eyes toward reaching out." Lack of growth is certainly one of the main problems facing the Conference today.

Second, the lack of leaders. As we have mentioned before, only seven of the ten churches have national pastors; the other three are or will be pastored by missionaries. From these figures it is fairly simple to see that we are short of trained national leaders. The problem, however, is not only that we are short of leaders for the churches. It is much bigger than that. To state it briefly, one leader can do only so much. He can handle only so many meetings by himself, which means that the number of meetings that can be held is in direct proportion to the number of trained leaders that we have. Without more leaders we cannot start more meetings. Without starting more meetings, the number of seekers will not increase. If the number of seekers does not increase, neither will the number of baptisms. If the number of baptisms does not increase, the churches will not grow any faster than they are now. In other words, a lack of leaders can have a direct bearing on the growth or non-growth of the church.

As pointed out earlier, no one else listed this as one of
the biggest problems facing the Conference. It was mentioned indirectly, perhaps, by the missionary who said that
he felt "spiritual unity and vision, especially among the
leadership," was one of the greatest needs facing us. But I
suppose one of the main reasons it was not mentioned is
simply that the churches are not growing all that fast. As
long as churches do not grow, leadership is not felt to be
such a problem. We feel we can make do somehow with who we
have. On the other hand, if the churches were growing
rapidly, we would be faced with a leadership problem, and be
forced to do something about it. Since the churches have
not been growing much, we have done very little about the
leadership problem. But we need to see that this, in turn,
is part of the reason we are not growing. It is a vicious
circle, which perhaps can be summarized something like this:

When the church does not grow, there is little need
     for more leaders;
When there is little need for more leaders, few new
     leaders are produced;
When few new leaders are produced, few new groups can
     be started;
When few new groups can be started, the church does
     not grow.
When the church does not grow ...

So, you see, the lack of leaders, the second problem, and
the lack of growth, the first problem, are intimately
related. Without doing something, without producing more
trained leaders, our expansion will always be limited. For
many years we have been sending men away to be trained as
leaders. There have also been some attempts to train lay
leaders locally, but there has been no systematic attempt
at doing it together as a Conference. Yet I am convinced
that this matter of leadership training is one of the
crucial problems that confronts the Japan Mennonite Church
Conference today. Until it is solved, there is little hope
that the churches can or will grow.

Third, the lack of goals. This one is probably the
hardest of the three problems to get ahold of, because
goals are often difficult to define. Perhaps that is at the
heart of the problem. Our goals as a Conference have been
largely left undefined, with the result that there is no
specific goal to unify the churches. This does not mean
there has been a lack of good ideas. Many worthwhile proposals have been made from time to time. The problem may

rather be, as one pastor has put it, we need both "greater
planning and carrying out of the things decided." We have
been especially weak on the latter, as we will see in
Chapter 2. Goals have occasionally been decided on, but too
often left uncarried out. It is revealing, though, to see
what can happen when goals are both set and carried out.

Going back to the baptism chart on page 34 you will
notice that in one year, 1968, there were 55 baptisms,
almost three times higher than the year before, and higher
than any other year before or after. There are no doubt a
number of factors involved here, but one of the main ones
I believe is that in the year 1967, the churches set as a
goal for themselves having 60 baptisms in the year 1968.
Decision 1, made at the Annual Conference in 1967, read:
"That we as a Conference, strive for 60 baptisms during the
coming year" (JMCCC, October 1967:2). In order to help the
churches carry this out, it was decided to prepare a list of
all the potential baptismal candidates in the churches
(JMCCC, Executive Committee, January 1968:3), and the
churches prayed together and worked together to achieve that
goal. And look what happened! There were greater results
than ever before, over twice the average number of baptisms
for any of the other years.

For some reason, a similar goal was not set the following
year when the emphasis switched from the local church to
"wider-area evangelism," but it does illustrate what can
happen when we work toward a goal. The individual churches
usually set annual goals for themselves, but it seems to be
much harder at the conference level. Yet I feel, and one of
the other missionaries listed this too, that "goals" are one
of the greatest needs of our Conference. It is risky to set
goals, for we might not reach them. But without goals, we
lack for direction and something to give unity to the Conference. In all fairness, however, it should be pointed out
that the Conference did decide to begin a new work in the
city of Fukuoka, which was actually begun in 1976, and that
is at least a step in the right direction. Work in other
cities is also under consideration.

One of the pastors has well summed up this latter problem
when he said that what we need most is "deep personal fellowship in the Lord and concrete vision." How true! We need
intimate fellowship both with the Lord and with one another,
and also a specific vision. As the Bible says, "Where there
is no vision, the people perish" (Prov. 29:18a, KJV). And
if there is any one thing which can give us the vision we

need, I believe it lies in the area of a coordinated, systematic leadership training program.

Such programs have been proposed before, but they have
never been carried through. If they had, this paper would
likely not be being written. But just as pointed out in
connection with the second problem that leadership is related
to growth, so leadership is also related to goals. That is,
a leadership training program could give us something to
rally around. It could make our vision concrete. It could
be the thing that unites our churches, that really pulls them
together. It would do so, first of all, by hopefully providing the churches with the leaders they need. But in addition,
it should also make possible the expansion and the growth of
the church through providing the leaders necessary for that.
And it should also bring greater unity to the Conference by
giving us a goal around which we could rally. This is not
to suggest that a leadership training program would cure all
of our ills. But I am convinced that it is the greatest need
of the Church Conference today, and that it just might make
it possible for us to "kill three birds with one stone."

Growth. Goals. Leaders. These are the major problems
we need to deal with. How can the churches be helped to
grow? What goal might bring the churches greater unity?
How can adequate leadership be provided for the churches?
Those are the big questions. Now we need to begin searching
for some answers. But before doing that, we need to take a
look at how things have been done up till now, which is the
subject of the following chapter.

2

Leadership Training Patterns and Problems

What training patterns have been employed up till now? How effective have they been? What have been some of the problems encountered? These are a few of the questions we want to explore here. As is the case with many other missions and churches, we have not had a school of our own. We have had to depend on the schools of others. This has perhaps had its advantages as well as disadvantages. But what we want to do is take a good hard look at the patterns we have been following, and see if they are in fact the most effective way to train leaders for churches in rural Japan.

Being in a rural area, with no Bible schools near us, we will see how from the beginning we have been sending our leaders to the larger cities for training. We will also see how when that did not prove to be the best solution, plans were made for a school of our own. But whatever became of those plans? We want to try to find out. We also will see how various attempts have been made at training laymen locally, and the problems connected with that, which led several years later to a second proposal for a school of our own. But whatever happened to those plans? We want to try to find that out too. At the end of the chapter, we will try to pull together the various problems that remain.

EXPORTING OUR LEADERS TO THE CITY FOR TRAINING

Leaders can be trained in many ways. Five of our six pastors have been trained in the city. The other one, the first of the six, is an exception in being self-educated

rather than having had any formal Bible school or seminary
training. (As noted in the first chapter, there are now
actually seven pastors. When the pastors were surveyed in
1974, however, there were only six. Since that time, one of
them resigned as pastor in 1976, and two others came in 1977,
for a total of seven pastors. The data included here, therefore, and throughout this paper, are based on the questionnaires filled out by the six who were pastors in 1974.)

Of the five who were city-trained, four of them received
their training at Tokyo Christian College (TCC, formerly
JCC, Japan Christian College). But Tokyo is a great distance from Miyazaki Prefecture, where most of our churches
are. And Tokyo is a highly urbanized area, whereas we are
working in a rural situation. The differences between city
and country are many, as one might expect. This has naturally created problems in training a ministry that is
suited to the needs of rural churches. While it has been
over 20 years already since we first started sending men
away for training, correspondence between representatives of
the Mission and the school reveal some of the problems that
have existed. We want to take a close look at some of these
letters, but first, it might be well to give a little introduction to TCC as it was in the beginning. Later on, in
Chapter 4, we will give a little more attention to the
school as it is today.

Tokyo Christian College began as the Alliance Bible
Institute in 1950. A few years later, in the "Prospectus"
sent out about the new school, it was stated that

The Japan Christian College, an evangelical
Christian training school on the college level, will
open in Tokyo in April, 1955.

Specific objective of the Japan Christian College
is the discipling of key Christian youth to serve
the Lord Jesus Christ throughout Japan. To build a
firm spiritual foundation under these future evangelists, pastors, teachers, and Christian workers, the
college program will center on a thorough teaching
of the Word of God, application of Biblical principles
to the basic problems of Japanese life ... and careful
discipline in the spiritual life. ...

The Japan Christian College will offer work in
four divisions:

1. *Four-year college course* -- leading to the degree
   of bachelor of arts. At the outset this program
   will concentrate on two majors: Bible-Theology and
   Education. Other majors will be added from year to
   year. ... A carefully organized program of practical Christian work, under experienced leadership,
   will give laboratory training in evangelism, man-to-
   man follow-up, and Bible teaching, as well as
   relating the student to the intimate life of a
   church group of his own background.

2. *Three-year Bible school.* This division offers a
   concentrated program in Bible, Bible-related subjects, and a minimum of arts courses (music,
   psychology, etc.) to the student who wishes a
   shorter program of Bible only, the older student,
   and the student inadequately prepared for college.

3. *Kindergarten teachers' course.* A three-year
   "junior college" course leading to kindergarten
   teacher's certificate is planned to provide fruitful training for young women. ...

4. *Evening school.* In a downtown Tokyo location
   evening extension courses in Bible, Christian
   philosophy, and English will be featured. Chapel
   services and other spiritual advantages will
   accompany this program for adults, working young
   people, and students in other universities. ...

The Japan Christian College is a project of faith,
seeking to serve the church of the Lord Jesus in Japan
on an inter-denominational, inter-mission basis ...

Your prayers, your counsel, and your recommendation
of the college to God-called young men and women are
earnestly sought by the administration (TCC 1955:1-5).

So it was the school began. Our Mission responded to
their appeal for students by sending five young men to study
there. The "Prospectus" had optimistically stated that "A
maximum of 100 will be accepted the first year" (1955:3),
but the "Prospectus" of the following year recorded that
"the Japan Christian College last year enrolled 112 students" (TCC 1956:1). The optimism had been justified, and
the school got off to a good start.

From the beginning, however, the school anticipated that there would no doubt be certain problems along the way, as with any new venture. In a letter to the various missions, dated November 8, 1954, six months before the school even opened, College President Donald Hoke said that some of the problems they were already facing were securing an adequate faculty, the accreditation process, and the screening of new students. He also mentioned that there seemed to be a few "key questions" in the minds of missionaries. One of these was "the basic purpose of the school." Another concerned "the spiritual attitude and level of the college course." The final one, he said,

> ... concerns the possibility of students being weaned from their own churches or missions while in school and then failing to return. This is also basically a spiritual problem. We will make every possible effort to guard against this. ... I can only say we will do our best to see that no student leaves his own group, is spoiled by the city, or is tempted to change his loyalty. For we sincerely want to serve the whole evangelical church of Christ in Japan (1954:1-2).

The Mennonites, not having their own school, were indeed grateful for the opening of Japan Christian College. As Verney Unruh, then chairman of the Mission wrote to President Hoke in a letter of April 27, 1955,

> As you know our Mennonite Mission has 5 boys attending JCC. For us it was an answer to prayer that the school was founded for we were looking for a place where our future leaders could get a sound, evangelical training. There was some concern voiced in our group about fellows going to the city, lest they never come back to the work here (1955:1).

There was evidently a feeling of both gratitude and concern. And it soon became clear that this concern, earlier expressed by Hoke himself, was not unfounded, for Unruh goes on in his letter to say that

> ... less than a month has passed and what we feel is a temptation has already been put in front one of the boys. H-san [Note: Some of the names in this chapter have been abbreviated to protect confidentiality.] who is working at ... for his "arbeit"

[part-time work] has been asked to stay there and
work for them through the summer vacation.

We have made plans for the boys to come back and
work as a team for tent evangelistic campaigns during
the summer vacation so that he is already engaged.
However, it is the principle of the thing which we
are vitally concerned about. Of course H-san is very
capable, especially in English, and we are not surprised that ... has discovered this and would like to
use him. Working just during the summer may be only
a small thing but the longer these boys are away from
home the less they will want to come back. Nor is it
the kind of work. But we are depending on him as a
future leader. ...

We feel a word of caution is also in order regarding M-san. We understand that he is no longer staying at school but has gone to live with a missionary
family, to help them in language as part of his
"arbeit." It has been our experience down here that
it is unwise to take a young man like that in as one
of the family. M-san comes from an extremely poor
family. They live just from day to day and there
are times when their prayer for daily bread is not
answered. For him to live with a missionary, in the
midst of wealth, could spoil him as far as future
work with us is concerned.

It may be difficult for you who live in Tokyo to
see these problems like we do who live out in the
country. Among all young people there is the urge
to go to the city. At first we thought this was
only true of youth who do not know Christ. But we
know other missionaries who have sent their young
people away to school, only to lose them. With the
trend to the cities we believe Japan can never be
evangelized until rural Japan responds to the Gospel.
City folks will never evangelize the country so we
must evangelize the country and let them take the
Gospel to the city (1955:1-2).

Already we have seen two or three problems that existed
from the very first month we sent students away to school.
They could not support themselves adequately. Consequently,
they had to do part-time work. The result of that, in one
case at least, was that a student was tempted to not come
home for the summer, which the Mission had expected him to

do. In spite of such problems, however, the Mennonites continued to support the school, and in January 1956 were
elected to be a member of the College Board (Hoke 1956:1).
In May of the same year, Verney Unruh again wrote a letter,
this time to John Reid, Acting President. In his letter he
says that

> JCC is often in our prayers that it might truly be-
> come a school that will give leadership and produce
> leaders for the Church in Japan.
>
> We enjoyed having the boys back for the spring
> vacation. They matured a good bit since last summer
> which is, I feel, a fine testimony for the school.
>
> In connection with their return a few points have
> come up which I want to write about. First, this may
> be just the boys own ideas or wishful thinking on
> their part, but they spoke about some of the present
> students being sent to America for further training
> so they could come back to be teachers at JCC, and
> the intimation was that some of them (that is, our
> boys) are under consideration. As I say, I do not
> know whether it is fact, or just wishful thinking,
> but if you at the school have any plans like that,
> I'm sure our Mission would appreciate it if it were
> discussed with us as well. I believe you recall that
> JCC has pledged that it will do all it can to send
> students back to the churches or Missions from which
> they have come. We appreciate that, although we
> know there is a limit to what you can do. We are
> proud of the students we have there and are looking
> forward to the time when they can assume leadership
> of our churches here in Miyazaki Ken [Prefecture].
> In case there is any thought of using them at JCC
> in the future we would be happy if there can be
> mutual agreement on this.
>
> A second matter concerns either teaching or influ-
> ence which they have received at JCC. One thing they
> seem very much taken up with is the idea of election
> and predestination; in other words there seems to be
> a strong Calvinistic influence at the school. Now,
> I am not criticizing you for this. Mennonites have
> never quite fit into either the Arminian or Calvinist
> camp. You could probably classify us Calvinist
> Arminians or Arminian Calvinists. So we would simply
> shy away from an extreme either way. Above all we

put the Scriptures at the center with the teachings
and work of Christ as the key to both Old and New
Testaments. And of course, we recognize the Holy
Spirit as the Teacher of all truth. Now I hasten to
add that I am not trying to dictate school policy.
I am urging that as much as possible a moderate road
be followed; where there definitely are issues where
evangelicals are on both sides of the road, try to
present both sides and trust the Holy Spirit to lead
the students from there.

One more thing regarding a couple of the boys,
apparently H-san and Y-san, who it seems are in big
demand as interpreters for many missionaries in the
Tokyo area. This aspect came out when we were discussing aid for them. Their one complaint was that
they did not have time for both "arbeit" and studying
(1956:1).

Three more problems! Temptation to study abroad. Undesirable teaching or influence. Inadequate time for both
study and work. These are all stated very clearly in
Unruh's letter to the school. But in spite of these additional problems, the Mennonites continued to send their
students off to the city for training. Instead of getting
better, however, things went from bad to worse. Some students dropped out. Others did not return. This is docu-
mented in another of Unruh's letters to the school, this
one written March 9, 1959:

We also were somewhat surprised by H-san's interest
in Wheaton. I've had a chance to think it over for
several days and though I still am unenthused about
anyone going to the States for study I feel there are
exceptions and I believe H-san is one of them.

I believe that the whole experience was quite painful for H-san. We were very sorry that he dropped
out of JCC, especially right in the middle of a term,
but I also feel he did not make it on the spur of the
moment. Though some have judged him severely and
accused him of succumbing to the temptation of money
I don't think that is the case. When he was home
some weeks ago his testimony seemed as strong and
radiant as ever and he frankly admitted that he feels
his present work is only an interlude until he clearly
knows the Lord's leading. So I for one am inclined to
believe the Lord may be leading him in this and if
that is true then who are we to stand in the way? ...

Now about M-san. We also are somewhat disappointed
that he is not returning to Kyushu but he has expressed
his wish and desire to go on to school ever since last
fall, and we have not pushed him on it. We had no
agreement with the first bunch of boys that they were
expected to return for a couple of years of service
with us. There is an opening at Nichinan now ... and
I believe M-san would fit in quite well. I have
written him about it but again he replied that he felt
led to go on to school, ...

One other matter I've wanted to write about is
A-san. I don't know if you've been aware of it but
he has been considering quitting at the end of this
year. He always gave financial difficulties as the
reason. ...

But ... there seems to be something else bothering
him. Do you or any of the teachers have any idea
what it might be (1959a:1-2)?

With regard to A-san, who was considering dropping out,
it is interesting to read what Unruh had written in a
letter of recommendation for him less than a year before.
In a letter dated March 14, 1958, he said:

A-san became a Christian a little over 3 years ago
in January, 1955. He was baptized in April of the
same year and has been a faithful member of the ...
Christian Church.

For the past two years he has been working ... in
Nobeoka. Though there are none of [our] Mennonite
churches in Nobeoka he found an evangelical group
that had been started by the Soul Clinic and has been
attending there and helping them.

A-san has had a definite call from God for Christian service, although he is not quite clear yet just
which field it is -- a pastor, evangelist or other
type of service. But he feels it is time for him to
start school and go ahead as the Lord leads.

Though A-san may not be quite as talented as some
of the other boys who have gone from Kyushu, he has
a pleasing personality and a radiant testimony.
Brother Derksen joins me in recommending him as a
prospective student (1958:1).

Here was a boy who was thought to have a call to serve the
Lord. He had been a Christian for a few years. He had
worked in a company for a couple of years. He was recommended to the school and accepted. But less than a year
later he was thinking of quitting. One wonders why. Was it
financial problems as he suggested? Was it a loss of call
to serve the Lord? Did he become disenchanted with the
school for some reason or other? He, of course, is the only
one who could answer such questions.

But, it causes us to raise other questions. What if he
had really been called of the Lord? And what if he had
stayed at his company job? And what if an attempt had been
made to train him locally? Would it have made any difference? Would he possibly be working with us today? Why is
it that out of the first five men we sent away for training
only one eventually came back to work here? Is there any
way the pattern could have been improved? President Hoke
speaks to this matter in a September 22, 1959 letter to
Unruh:

... speaking frankly, I am very concerned that of the
four or five young men that came from your work to JCC
five years ago now, only one is back full-time at the
present time, S-san is back part-time, T-san is still
studying, H-san is working, and M-san studying. And
I know this is probably a disappointment to you. We
can naturally expect a certain shrinkage of those who
put their hand to the plow and turn back. And also
some who have other guidance. But I feel sure that
you are somewhat disappointed in this.

I also see one or two inherent weaknesses in our
setup here which can and should be remedied I believe
to obviate these situations. I believe there are
tremendous advantages and strengths in an inter-denominational school, as well as tremendous economies of
both men and money. On the other hand, there are
certain weaknesses. I am in correspondence with the
Yeotmal Seminary in India which has a school which has
a much closer degree of cooperation including large
financial investments of various mission groups, including yours. A letter from one of their prominent
men there has told me much of their setup, some points
of which it would be well for us to adopt.

But the thing that comes to me as a single most
important matter which would solve many of the problems

of keeping the students more closely related with their
own denomination and their own mission, of keeping
them under direct instruction with regard to their own
particular church and mission distinctives, and also
keeping them under the supervision in practical Christian service of one of their workers, would be the
appointment by each cooperating mission group of one
pastor or missionary to our faculty here. This person
would teach one or two courses in the college, have
seminars as a regular part of the curriculum in which
he would teach those of his denomination and mission
affiliation the distinctives of their own work, and
then work with them in active Christian work on weekends. This would mean that in Tokyo this missionary
could establish a strong work of his own church. Then
when members move in this direction, members could be
united with it. And it also will be a splendid base
in this, the world's largest community growing at the
rate of a quarter million a year.

So, I would like to put this before you for your
prayerful consideration. I believe that the appointment of such a Japanese worker or missionary would
meet all of the problems and needs, substantially, and
would still be able to share in all the blessings that
the combined effort provides (1959:1-2).

Responding to Hoke's letter on November 9, 1959, Unruh
said,

We do appreciate your concern about students not
returning to their member missions to work. However,
in our case, I certainly would not want to place blame
on anyone else before acknowledging our own short-
comings in our student aid program. When our first
students left for JCC we said that we would help them
but it was our mission policy not to hire anyone with
foreign funds and that they should therefore not look
to the mission for employment on graduation. Of
course we were hoping that the churches would be ready
to take them. Hindsight is always better than foresight and now I've wished many times that we would
have assured the boys that we would do everything
possible so that they could come back when finished.
But that is past history and I trust we've learned our
lesson. I might add, further, though, that we haven't
given up entirely on those who haven't returned and as
far as we are concerned the door is always open.

The suggestion you raised about having a set-up
something like Yeotmal in India appealed to all of
us. ...

The idea of faculty representation also appealed to
us and we went so far as to pass the following resolution: "Resolved that in response to Don Hoke's letter
the education committee begin consultation with Japan
Christian College regarding representation of our
mission on the faculty" (1959b:1).

Thus the Mennonites began to consider the possibility of
having one of their own men on the college faculty, hoping
that might help solve some of their problems. Several of
these problems have already been seen in part of the correspondence that took place between the Mission and the school.
But one of them that has not been mentioned was what to do
in the case of someone who was a little older but could not
meet the requirement of having had a high school education.
This comes out in another of Unruh's letters, this one from
February 17, 1960. His letter to the school reads as
follows:

I'm writing about another one of our boys who is
interested in studying at JCC but there is a question
of whether he will be accepted because of the high
school requirement.

K-san was converted about 3 years ago and since
then has shown steady spiritual growth. ...

In the fall of 1957 he felt led to the Child
Evangelism School in Ashiya where he spent one year. ...

We have strongly urged him to consider JCC but he
hesitates because he did [not] finish high school.
He is somewhat older (27 or 28 now I believe) and had
his high school under the old set-up before there was
[the] educational reform program. He finished what
would be the equivalent of present 2nd year high
school.

We would like to recommend him because he is more
mature and since he has had further training. If he
can pass all his other tests successfully would you
consider accepting him as a student? If you would
rather maintain a rigid standard I'll understand but
would appreciate giving this your consideration
(1960a:1).

With regard to this request, I was not able to find any
direct confirmation in the correspondence in the Mission
files as to whether K-san was actually accepted by JCC or
not. The files seem to be complete for the most part, but
with regard to certain matters there evidently are items
missing here and there. Be that as it may, after reading
this, one of the missionaries commented to me that he was
quite sure K-san had been accepted, and after doing some
further searching, I was able to find at least indirect
documentation of that fact. This was in an April letter
from Unruh to the school in which he thanks them for their
help to K-san, and speaks of his presence at JCC (1960b:1).
In any case, this was another problem the Mission faced --
what to do with more mature men who could not meet the
entrance requirements set up by the school. So on the one
hand the Mission had its share of problems. But on the
other hand, so did the school. This is evident in a letter
of May 24, 1961 from President Hoke to friends of the
school, in which he says that

> Until now Japan Christian College has operated as an
> inter-denominational school in the sense that it
> offered to train young people for the service of the
> Lord from any groups who are interested in sending
> young people. We have had our problems and also our
> blessings and our successes.
>
>   However I feel for the future stability of our
> work, the growth of the school, and the best interests
> of those who do send young people here, that a more
> active form of cooperation and commitment to the edu-
> cational program on the part of the denominations or
> mission boards is desirable. This may take several
> forms:
>
> 1) Simple endorsement of Japan Christian College as
>   the school for the training of young people from
>   your group.
> 2) The above endorsement, plus a financial commitment
>   yearly, plus membership on the Board of Trustees
>   or Board of Directors.
> 3) The above two commitments, plus the further guar-
>   antee of interest to the degree that money will also
>   be given for capital investment and growth and
>   membership will be guaranteed on the Board of
>   Directors.
> 4) Possible just continued interest in JCC, but recog-
>   nizing it as only one of several schools in Japan

to which some of your students may be recommended
(1961:1).

It was suggested that the various missions or groups concerned discuss these proposals, and share their questions or
opinions at the Japan Council of Evangelical Missions meeting to be held the following month. What came out of that
meeting is not indicated in any of the materials I have had
to work with, but apparently the talk of greater cooperation
between the College and churches and missions supporting it
continued, for a couple of years later in a letter dated
May 17, 1963, Robert Ramseyer, who was then the Mennonite
representative on the College Board, writes to Donald Hoke
that

> Peter Derksen reported last year that you were
> interested in a reorganization of the college at the
> board level with missions and churches being offi-
> cially related to it. With that in mind, we have
> been discussing this in the education committee of
> our church conference. This problem, of course, is
> directly related to the whole problem of training
> church workers and evangelists for our conference.
> The leaders of the church here are much concerned to
> develop a plan of training which will prepare young
> men for evangelistic and pastoral duties here in the
> rural areas of Kyushu. We feel that in many ways the
> situation here is a peculiar one and that in some way
> specialized training must be provided to prepare men
> to face this kind of a situation.
>
> The committee has asked me to share some of our
> thinking on this matter with you.
>
> 1) We feel that our first step should be the
> strengthening of the educational program of our
> churches here on the field. We feel that no one
> should be sent away to school for Bible or other
> specialized training until [he] has been firmly
> grounded in the basic teachings of the Faith.
> This should be done in the local church, accom-
> panied by a program of practical work in the
> local situation.
> 2) We feel that our students who have gone away to
> school and come back to Miyazaki have not been
> adequately trained in pastoral work and evange-
> lism. Someone suggested that persons who are
> capable of teaching this sort of thing are very
> rare in Japan.

3) The feeling was expressed that the conservative
   schools in Japan have tended to neglect the practical and social applications of the gospel. Students
   come away from these schools without a real understanding of their own society and the culture in
   which they live and work. They are not able to
   apply the gospel to the real world in which they
   find themselves when they graduate.

We feel that we want our students to have a good
sound education in the Christian faith as it has been
revealed in the Scriptures. This, of course, is basic
for any Christian worker. However, we feel that this
is not enough. We also want our students to understand modern Japan and the people who live here, the
background and thought patterns of the people to whom
they will be bringing the gospel. Our pastors and
church leaders feel that it is a big mistake to assume
that because a man is a Japanese he understands Japan,
especially rural Japan. I understand that the United
Church has one or more rural evangelistic training
centers, and our people are very much interested in
this kind of training. Whether or not it is possible
to provide this kind of training in a Tokyo center is,
of course, a separate question which none of us here
can answer. However, we wanted to share our needs
with you in the hope that JCC might move in the direction of being the kind of school which would meet
these needs. At our spring conference in April, it
was decided to defer any decision on our future relationship to JCC until the education committee has
studied our total training program more fully and is
prepared to make a recommendation. ...

   ... I would like to emphasize that we are not
being critical of JCC, nor are we trying to tell JCC
what kind of a school it should be. Rather we wanted
to share with you the thoughts which have come to our
committee as we considered the kind of training which
we feel is necessary for training workers for our
situation here. Some in our church feel that the only
real answer is to have our own school here. Others
feel that this will not be a realistic answer for many
years to come. We want to continue to seek the Lord's
will in this matter and do what is fitting in his
sight (1963a:1-3).

Here we have a good summary of how the Mennonites felt
after seven or eight years of experimenting with exporting

their men to the city for training. It had not proved to be
as satisfactory as they had hoped it would be. In short,
they felt it was not meeting the needs of the churches. As
noted in the correspondence, President Hoke had suggested
that a partial answer to some of the problems might be to
have a Mennonite on the faculty. For a while the Mennonites
considered this, hoping to appoint someone to the faculty
who could also possibly serve as their representative in the
work of the Mennonite Central Committee's Peace Section in
Japan (GCMM, Annual Conference, October 1959:6). As it
turned out, however, they appointed someone to serve as
their representative in the peace work, but never appointed
anyone to serve on the faculty (GCMM, Business Session, June
1960:1)! But although they did not officially appoint anyone to be their representative on the faculty, consultations
must have continued, at least privately, for in the
Mission's Annual Conference minutes of October 1963, it is
noted that

> A letter from Donald Hoke (Japan Christian College)
> was read requesting Robert Ramseyer as lecturer at
> the College once or twice a year. This apparently
> in connection with getting recognition with the
> Department of Education. The Mission would encourage
> Bob to make use of this opportunity (GCMM, 1963:2).

Then in a letter of October 25, 1963, Ramseyer accepted
President Hoke's invitation to lecture. He said:

> With regard to your request that I be listed as a
> lecturer at the school and give lectures once or
> twice a year, I have taken up the matter with our
> mission, and I would be very happy to serve in this
> way. Our mission is glad to have me do this. Per-
> haps you could send me details when you have them
> more clearly in mind (1963b:1).

Hoke replied in a letter of October 29, 1963, saying,
"We're delighted that you'll be willing to lecture with us.
I'll let you know later as to just what time will be best"
(1963a:1). It looked like the Mennonites would at last be
represented on the faculty, at least part time if not full
time, but the fact is that neither Ramseyer nor any of the
other Mennonites ever taught at the school. As to just what
happened, a personal letter in November 1974 from Ramseyer
suggests that at the time he was invited to lecture, the
college was working on getting accredited with the Ministry
of Education (as the Mission minutes noted also), and that

his invitation may have been more for accreditation purposes
(wanting his M.A. credentials), rather than ever really
intended to actually be carried out. At any rate, he says
that after his acceptance he never heard anything more about
this again (1974:1).

In a letter of July 1975 to the author, Hoke confirms
that Ramseyer had been invited to lecture at the college,
and that this was never followed up on. As to why not, he
said he feels there may have been inadequate follow-up on
both sides. But as to whether he concurred with Ramseyer's
interpretation of what happened, that the invitation may
have been given primarily for accreditation purposes, he has
this to say:

> Actually at that time we were interested in having him
> lecture not solely for accreditation or even most
> importantly for that, but because of special insights
> that he would be able to give, particularly from the
> viewpoint of Mennonite theological emphases (1975a:1).

After so many years, memories are naturally hazy, and it is
difficult to trace just what did happen and why things
turned out the way they did. But whatever the reason why
this was never followed through on, the above information
brings us about as far as we want to go for now.

One may wonder why it was seen fit to use so many lengthy
quotations in this first section. It has been done simply
because I feel the material itself reveals so vividly the
situation as it was. It does not speak in generalities. It
is specific. It focuses on the problems as they were. It
is sufficient, I believe, to demonstrate the problem.

As we have seen the problems were many: financial
support while in school; maintaining a healthy balance between study and work; occasional exposure to undesirable
teaching influences; inadequate integration of the academic
and the practical; dropping out before graduation; employment after graduation; temptation to study abroad; failure
to return; inability to readapt to their own culture; un-
certainty of call in some cases; what to do with older
students who did not perhaps qualify for formal schooling
and so on. It is quite obvious from this that at least in
a number of cases, sending young men off to the city was not
in their best interest, nor in ours. But undoubtedly the
greatest disappointment was when students did not come back,
and to find out that even those who did were not really

trained for a rural ministry. It was primarily for that
reason that the Mennonites began considering opening their
own school. But that is another story.

WHATEVER HAPPENED TO OUR OWN SCHOOL IN 1963?

"Resolved that the combined Education Committee continue to make plans for a Bible School and come with
definite plans for aims, curriculum, faculty, site,
etc., to be presented at the spring conference."

"Resolved that we aim to put this program into operation in 1963."

The above two resolutions were made at the annual Mission
conference in October of 1961. Part of the reason for them
was certainly some of the negative experiences or problems
that have already been related in the previous section. But
actually, these resolutions had their origin back in the
early 1950s before we ever started sending our students off
to school somewhere.

What we want to do now is trace the process whereby the
resolutions were formed. To do this we want to simply look
at some of the minutes and reports that were in the Mission
files, and let them speak for themselves. Most of these are
minutes of executive, committee, or other meetings, or
annual conferences and reports, especially by the Education
Committee. There were a few dates and pages missing here
and there, but for the most part the material seemed remark-
ably complete. So we will just let the record speak for
itself, first of all, to see how the Mission came to feel
they should start a Bible school of their own, and then,
what happened to their resolutions. (Note: Unless otherwise indicated the following references from 1953-1964 all
pertain to the General Conference Mennonite Mission.)

1951 If there is to be an indigenous church there must be
native leadership. The Japanese do not lack education
but they do lack Bible training. We must, therefore,
plan for Bible classes for leadership training from
the beginning (Voth and Unruh 1951:17).

1953 The problem of giving our Christians Bible School
training was brought before the group.

Resolved that we elect a committee of three this
session to study the needs for and possibilities of

a Bible School and when the mission is ready, to
launch into that direction (Resolution 16, Annual
Conference, September 1953:6).

1954   Resolved that as a guiding principle for our mission
for the next five years we do not hire regular
national workers for such work as pastors, evangelists,
Bible women, and Bible teachers for a period of more
than six months (Resolution 5, Spring Conference,
April 1954:2).

Resolved that the mission create a fund for the purpose of assisting young people to formally prepare
themselves for the ministry and other Christian service ... (Resolution 9, Annual Conference, September
1954:4).

Moved and seconded that the chairman send a formal
letter to H-san offering to pay his tuition at the
Japan Christian College, should he consider attending
school (Executive Committee, September 23, 1954:1).

1955   Qualifications for accepting students [who apply for
mission aid]:

1. Must be a baptized believer.
2. Must be regular in weekly church attendance at
    least one entire year after conversion.
3. Must show spiritual stability and growth and evi-
    dence of a separated Christian life.
4. Must show leadership qualities.
5. Must be recommended by the local church and by one
    G.C. missionary.
6. Must have consent of parents until of age (20).
7. Students must apply through the local church for
    mission aid.
8. Aid will be limited to one new student from each
    station, including Kobe, per year. If stations do
    not fill their quota the committee in charge can
    serve as a clearing house to fill in from another
    station.
9. Students receiving mission aid are expected to
    return services to our churches.
10. The school to be attended must be mission approved.
11. Mission aid is as follows:
    (Each student will be considered according to need)
    a. Tuition
    b. 1000 yen per school month ...

Our present students are:

1. H-san, a student in the Tokyo Theological Seminary since April 1955
2. Y-san of Kobe at J.C.C. since April 1955
3. H-san of Miyazaki at J.C.C. since April 1955
4. S-san of Miyakonojo at J.C.C. since April 1955
5. M-san of Miyakonojo at J.C.C. since April 1955
6. T-san of Miyakonojo at J.C.C. since April 1955
(Education Committee Report, Annual Conference, September 1955:2).

The students now receiving mission funds have encouraged us to start our own school. Problems of faculty, students, etc. were discussed. Short-term Bible schools or station Bible conferences were suggested as a possible solution for the present (Annual Conference, 1955:13).

1956 Short reports were heard from those who had had a short winter Bible school course at their stations. Rev. Thiessen [secretary of the Mission Board] suggested that we continue with, say a 6 week course and working up to a 3 month course, and perhaps eventually getting to a 3 year course whereby we could train our workers here instead of sending them all the way to Tokyo (Spring Conference, May 1956:6).

Some of the "firsts" of this year:

3. Student pastors took over for several months during the summer at four different places.
4. One full-time pastor was called (Annual Conference, October 1956:1).

In the field of evangelism there were two firsts this year, namely the Family Camp and the Bible Conferences. Both of these were very worthwhile and proved to be a real blessing to our churches (Evangelism Committee Report, Annual Conference, 1956:1).

Evangelism Chart 1955-56

Bible Conf.	Date	Bldg.	Tent	Days	Aver. att.
Tomitaka(a)	Feb.	x		5	23
Kobayashi(b)	Mar. 17-20	x		4	22?
Kyomachi(c)	Mar. 12-16	x		5	13
Miyazaki(d)	Feb. 22-26	x		5	24

Remarks: (a)February is too cold a time
           (b)Was very worthwhile for Christians
           (c)Found that few people came to all meet-
              ings
           (d)60 different people came to meetings
              (1956:2).

That our mission sponsor a 3-week spring vacation
Bible School in Miyazaki in 1957 (Recommendation 4,
1956:1).

1957   The Evangelism Committee has been working on the
         curriculum for the "Spring Vacation Bible School." ...
         The tentative curriculum includes the following sub-
         jects:

Bible -- Old and New Testament
Personal Work
Child Evangelism
Devotional -- Private devotions
                   How to give testimonies
Chorus
Art

The evenings would be more or less taken up with
special lectures including Christian Ethics and Personal Work Labs (Business Session, January 28,
1957:1).

The [Spring Bible School] curriculum and working out
of further details regarding tuition etc. was turned
over to the Education Committee. It was felt that
there should be at least five students in order to
operate the school for the first time (1957:3).

Moved and seconded that we begin sending out a
correspondence [course] from our own office. ...

Recommended that under the Student Aid Program each
student may receive up to 3,500 yen [$10] per month
("in view of the fact that some of the students seem
to be having financial difficulties") (Business
Session, April 16, 1957:2).

Our Mission conducted its first short-term Bible
School this year in Miyazaki from March 25th to April
7th. Seven people served as teachers, including one
missionary, one outside teacher, and several of our

own young people who have been and are studying in different schools.

The enrollment was as follows:

        Miyazaki   - 10
        Kobayashi   - 4
        Miyakonojo - 3
        Nichinan   - 3
            Total   - 20 (14 for 2 weeks, 6 for 1 week).

In addition to the daily study program, the students assisted in special evangelistic meetings which were held in Kiyotaki during week-ends. The total expenses of the school were a little more than 80,000 yen [$222].

In general, judging from the testimony of those who attended, we believe it was a very worthwhile and rich experience for them. ...

One of the needs in our student aid program seems to be to maintain more personal contact between the missionaries and the students receiving aid. This might help to give them a greater sense of responsibility toward the Mission, their home churches, and the work of evangelism in Miyazaki Prefecture (Education Committee Report, Annual Conference, October 1957:1).

Recommend that we have another two-week Bible School in the spring of 1958 (Recommendation 1, 1957:2).

The question was raised [by the Mennonite group in Hokkaido] whether we did not feel the necessity of a Bible School in Kyushu.

Resolved that the Education Committee study the possibilities in cooperative education for Japanese in the future and come with a definite proposal at the next annual conference (Resolution 3, Annual Conference, 1957:3).

Resolved that we inform our churches when students will be graduating and urge our churches to utilize their services, at the same time we inform the following, H-san, M-san, S-san, T-san, Y-san, T-san, and H-san that if none of our churches call them they have no further obligation to us but remind them again of our mutual obligation to our Lord (Resolution 74, 1957:13).

From the beginning of sponsoring a radio broadcast, all our contacts were enrolled in the Pacific Broadcasting Associations correspondence school in Tokyo. This spring we received permission to use the Emmaus Bible School correspondence lessons and send them out from our own office. Since May we have done this, with a total of 174 enrolled as of Oct. 25. Of these enrolled students of the Word, 22 have finished the course, 11 are studying the second course and 4 are ready for the third. The Emmaus Bible School courses that are offered are "What the Bible Teaches" (12 lessons), "Lessons for Christian Living" (12 lessons) and "The Servant of God" (12 lessons on the Gospel of Mark). Following these we would like to use our own courses, on which work has been begun, but nothing is ready for presentation yet (Radio Report, Annual Conference, 1957:1).

Spring Bible School (during school spring vacation) Aims:

1. Provide short period of intensive Bible study which should create an appetite for personal Bible study.
2. Give systematic instruction in the doctrines of the Bible.
3. Provide an atmosphere of warm Christian fellowship.
4. Encourage and instruct in Sunday School work, personal work, and other types of witnessing.
5. Create an appreciation and understanding for Church History and Missions.
6. Create appetite and desire for a closer walk with God (Education Committee, December 2, 1957:1).

1958 Send congratulatory telegrams as from the mission to T-san and H-san at the time of graduation (Education Committee, January 4, 1958:1).

Resolved that if students do not comply with this request [to help the Mission, if requested, in its spring and summer evangelistic programs] they will not receive support during that time (Resolution 18, Spring Conference, April 1958:3).

Several things have been suggested [for discussion at a meeting of the chairmen of the Mennonite missions]: a joint seminary, a joint dormitory with someone appointed to give supplementary lectures, a joint effort to place a Mennonite teacher at the seminary now being started by Hatori and others (Peter A. Willms to Chairmen of Mennonite Missions, April 5, 1958:1).

Since there are no plans for establishing a united Mennonite Bible School or Seminary and since Mennonite students are in a number of different schools it was felt that it would be of value to donate several key Mennonite books and periodicals to several schools. These books would then also be available to other students to study Anabaptist and Mennonite history (Chairmen of Mennonite Missions Meeting, July 2, 1958:2).

Spring Bible School: There was considerable talk that it was of greater importance to have a one-week school at all of our stations. The purpose then would be to encourage and build up *all* believers. However, the purpose of the two-week school (longer school) is for *special* instruction and could be a bit more concentrated being longer and all day. It was agreed there is a place for both (JMCCC, Church Council, October 18, 1958:1). [Note: From 1958 until the Conference was born in 1964, representatives of the different churches and the Mission occasionally met together, and these meetings were referred to as Church Council (*Kyōgiinkai*) meetings.]

A brief review of students who have received support in the past and their present place of work:

1. Miss K of Nichinan graduated from J.C.E.F. [Japan Child Evangelism Fellowship] Bible School in March, 1957, and is now serving as teacher in our kindergarten.
2. Miss K of Miyakonojo graduated from J.C.E.F. Bible School in July, 1957, and is also serving as teacher in our kindergarten.
3. Mr. H. of Miyazaki attended J.C.C. and is now employed at ... in Tokyo.
4. Mr. T of Miyakonojo graduated from J.C.C. (Bible School course) in March, 1958, and has been doing evangelistic work with a TEAM [The Evangelical Alliance Mission] missionary in Nagano Prefecture.

5. Mr. H, formerly of Kobe, graduated from Tokyo
    Theological Seminary in March, 1958, and is now
    serving as pastor of our Miyazaki church.

Students who are now receiving aid:

Japan Christian College
1. Mr. Y - will graduate in March, 1959.
2. Mr. M - will graduate in March, 1959.
3. Mr. I - will leave school in March, 1959, for a
    year of practical training.
4. Mr. A
Japan Bible Seminary
5. Mr. T - will graduate in March, 1959.
J.E.B. [Japan Evangelistic Band] *Bible School*, Kobe
6. Mr. M
In Practical Training
7. Mr. S left school in March, 1958, for a year of
    practical training. He is serving the Miyakonojo
    church and will return to JCC in April, 1959.
8. Mr. K graduated from J.C.E.F. Bible School in July,
    1958, and is now serving the Hyuga church. He is
    planning to continue his studies in April, 1959.

The following young people from our churches are not
receiving financial support, but are studying in
different Christian schools:

1. Mr. N of Miyazaki, at Japan Bible Seminary.
2. Miss U of Miyazaki, at J.C.C.
3. Miss F of Nango, at J.C.C.
4. Miss O of Kobayashi, at Ikoma Bible School.
5. Miss M of Takazaki, at Osaka Christian College
(Education Committee Report, Annual Conference,
October 1958:1-2).

The [Spring Bible] school was conducted from March
24th to April 5th with a total enrollment of 30 students. However, only a few of these attended throughout the two weeks (1958:3).

I believe that the basis of J.C.C. is sound and that
we are in complete agreement with its aims. One of
the main needs is more devoted, full-time Japanese
faculty members. It might be of interest to some that
Mr. Niwa, who graduated from the Mennonite Brethren
Bible College in Winnepeg this spring, is now teaching
at J.C.C. One of the main questions before J.C.C. is

whether it should remain a Bible college or try to expand and become a liberal arts college (1958:4).

Resolved that we continue to give our whole-hearted support to Japan Bible Seminary and recommend it to our Christian students for seminary training.

Resolved that we continue our whole-hearted support of Japan Christian College and recommend it for Bible college and pre-seminary training.

Resolved that in view of the need we feel for our own Mennonite Bible School, we present this need to our pastors, churches, and students and urge them, together with us, to make this a special matter of prayer.

Resolved that we again have a two-week Spring Bible School in 1959.

Resolved that we change point I. 2 of our Student Aid Program, making it read as follows: "Must be regular in church attendance for at least *two years* after conversion" (Resolutions 1-5, Annual Conference, 1958:1).

Japan Christian College is considering sending graduates under a scholarship plan to the States for further training at Fuller Seminary. If one of our students were chosen and had the opportunity of going what would be our position?

Resolved that we inform Japan Christian College that we as a mission are not enthused about any of our students going to America for further study. However if a student is chosen we recommend that he have at least two years practical experience after college graduation before going (Resolution 57, 1958:7).

The correspondence course enrollment has increased considerably this past year with the largest number of enrollment coming through village evangelism rather than radio contacts. At present the total enrollment is 604 (Radio Report, Annual Conference, 1958:1).

1959 Resolved that the property committee look for land for a future Bible School and Training Center to be purchased with special funds up to 200,000 yen ($550) to be made available by a gift, a decision to be made by

the property and executive committees by April 15
(Resolution 17, Spring Conference, March 1959:3).

1. Selecting of students for the ministry and the
   giving of scholarships. It was felt that applicant should work with missionary or pastor prior
   to going to school. ...
3. There is a definite need for assisting the pastors
   in their own further training such as the purchasing of books (500 yen [$1.40] per month was
   suggested), a travelling stipend for attending
   spiritual life conferences etc. (Missionary-
   Workers Conference, September 18-19, 1959:2).

Mr. Y graduated from Japan Christian College and is
now employed by the Mission as a literature worker.
Mr. M. graduated from JCC and is continuing his
studies at Aoyama University in Tokyo.
Mr. T graduated from Japan Bible Seminary and is
employed full time by the Japan Sunday School
Union (Education Committee Report, Annual Conference, October 1959:1).

The [Spring Bible] school was again conducted at the
Oyodo Church in Miyazaki from April 2-9. 5 women
attended full time and 3 men and 12 women attended
part time for a grand total of 20 as compared to 30
over a two-week period in 1958. ...

Courses included Bible (Philemon), Doctrine (Inspiration and Authority of the Bible) Mr. Homma, Evangelism
(street, hospital and visitation) Pastor Yoshima, and
early Mennonite History by V. Unruh. P. Voran had
charge of the early morning prayer meetings.
Expenses for the Bible school this year were 23,231
yen [$65] (1959:2).

The [Spring Bible] school has been appreciated but the
attendance has been small. The suggestion was made to
bring the school to the churches. The mission Education Committee and the churches Education Committee
should draw up a curriculum, select teachers who would
go around to the churches and run a three-night Bible
school with three periods each night (JMCCC, Church
Council, September 19, 1959:1).

Resolved that we seek to assist churches in the continuing education of pastors and student pastors.

Resolved that to implement resolution 3 we plan with the churches a full three days (between Sundays) of intensive Bible study and fellowship twice a year, this to be based on a carefully planned curriculum.

Resolved that we plan to have a Spring Bible School in 1960.

Resolved that together with the Japanese Education Committee we plan for a three-night evening Bible School at each church in 1960 (Resolutions 3-6, Annual Conference, 1959:1-2).

1960 The mission has passed a motion that we again have a Spring Bible School as in previous years. The tentative dates were set for April 3-9. We decided to pay travel and the "orei" [honorarium] for one outside teacher.

Later in the day we met with the Japanese Church Education Committee and they were not interested in the Spring Bible School but felt it should be dropped and time and effort put forth to make the local Bible schools worthy and effective (Education Committee, January 23, 1960:1).

Mission representative on the Japan Christian College faculty. Suggested that we write to the other Mennonite missions in Japan (esp. the O.M.s [Old Mennonite, now Mennonite Church (MC)] in Hokkaido) to see if they are interested in making a cooperative venture (Education Committee, February 11, 1960:1).

There was discussion on beginning our own local Bible School. It was felt that we are not ready to begin a Bible School for training Christian workers. We see the need of training the laity but cannot see the possibility of having a formal school in the immediate future. Therefore we encourage lay groups to get together.

Therefore we recommend fellowship conferences for lay groups in our church groups: teachers, office workers, nurses, farmers, women, etc. In these fellowship and study conferences we want to guard against pastor or missionary domination. We want it to be a lay movement (Education Committee, October 1, 1960:1).

The second annual [Christian workers'] retreat was
again held at Isegehama, Hyuga, March 28-29. 20
Japanese and 11 missionaries registered. ... This is
the only time of the year that all missionaries and
Christian workers have an opportunity to be together
for fellowship, inspiration and sharing.

Following the recommendation of last year's conference
this committee, together with the Japanese committee,
planned the first pastors' seminar. This was held at
Matsubashi, March 29 to April 1. 8 pastors and students attended as well as several of the men missionaries. ...

This first seminar was well received and gave us
direction in planning for the continued training of
the pastors. ...

We had planned to have another spring Bible school but
the Japanese committee discouraged this. Instead,
evening Bible schools and conferences were held at
Hyuga, Miyazaki, Miyakonojo and Kobayashi. Reports
from these were not too encouraging. Perhaps the
results were in direct proportion to the enthusiasm of
the pastors. Somehow we must do more to help them
catch the need and vision of strengthening the laity.
Along this line, but in a different direction the
committee has a recommendation to present.

At the last pastors' meeting enthusiasm was expressed
for starting a Bible school in Miyazaki Ken. The
committee, however, feels that the time is not yet
ripe. The churches are still too young to contribute
financially, teachers would be a problem and prospect
for students at present is rather slim. The committee
favors continued support of JCC and exploring areas in
which we can have a stronger voice in shaping school
policy (Education Committee Report, Annual Conference,
October 1960:1).

Resolved that we sponsor a fellowship and study conference for Christian teachers in public schools in
our churches in the spring of 1961.

Resolved that we sponsor a fellowship and study conference for office workers in our churches, perhaps
in the fall of 1961.

Resolved that we utilize the services of Dr. Howard
Charles [New Testament professor, AMBS] for the time
he is available to us in the fall of 1961 --
   a) for our lay people -- how to use the Bible.
   b) for pastors and missionaries -- book study and
      Bible interpretation.

There was some discussion of the possibility of having
Jake Enz [Old Testament professor, AMBS] come out to
[the] Japan field for a year in the interests of
teaching Old Testament to help in the training of the
laity as well as pastors.

Resolved that we aid the pastors in purchasing books
and periodicals to the extent of 5,000 yen [$14] per
pastor per year.
(By pastors we mean those who are full-time pastors
serving in our organized churches. The list of books
to be drawn up by the Education Committee together
with the pastors) (Resolutions 1,2,3,5, Annual Conference, 1960:1-2).

In the correspondence course Bible studies we have an
enrollment of 1055 but of these the addresses of 115
have become unknown. Patients leave the hospitals and
leave no forwarding address, or else people move and
do not inform us of change of address. ...

The following is a breakdown of those enrolled in the
courses. The courses are sent out in the order here
given.

		Present enrollment	Finished no.
1.	Servant of God (Gospel of Mark)	575	122
2.	What the Bible Teaches	308	118
3.	Christian Living	57	47
4.	Gospel of Luke	14	4
5.	Sermon on the Mount	5	1

The larger portion of those enrolled in the study
courses have not come through radio listeners. In
fact, during the last three months we have had exactly
five people enrolled in the course because they
listened to the program (Radio Report, Annual Conference, 1960:1-2).

1961   [Note: From 1961 on, the Church Education Committee
         and the Mission Education Committee sometimes met to-
         gether. Such meetings will from here on be referred
         to as Joint Education Committee meetings. Those not
         designated as "joint" will refer to Mission meetings
         only.]

         We agreed our own local Bible School is needed, on a
         full-time training basis, to partly train our future
         workers.

         A possibility would be that we have some kind of
         agreement with J.C.C. whereby they attend here for two
         years and perhaps finish at J.C.C. Shall aim at be-
         ginning in the spring of 1962.

         Teaching staff:
              Definitely one full-time missionary teacher
              Part-time teachers: missionary and Japanese

         Location: (possibilities)
              Rural area: perhaps together with camp site
              Urban area: Miyazaki City (Education Committee,
              April 18, 1961:1-2).

         Need: We have failed to give adequate leadership
              training in our local churches.

         Aims: a. Need to train people in the Word of God
                  (1) So that they will have a solid founda-
                      tion for victorious Christian life.
                  (2) So that they will be more adequate to
                      lead others to Christ and help them grow
                      spiritually.
                  (3) To prepare them for a place of responsi-
                      bility in the local church such as elders,
                      deacons, S.S. teachers, youth workers,
                      women's workers, etc.
               b. To give those who have had a special call a
                  basic training.
               c. To create an appetite and desire for a closer
                  walk with God (Education Committee, June 12,
                  1961:1).

         Our Own Bible School:
         A.   It was agreed that a Bible School is necessary.
         B.   It was agreed that the purpose is not only to
              train those who plan to go into full-time work but

those who have an interest in studying the Bible
and will become lay leaders in the churches.
C.   Agreed that the students should be high school
graduates. Exception should be made for older
students -- entrance would depend upon ability.
Only born again believers will be considered.

Discussion followed on: housing, teaching staff,
curriculum, student support while in school.

Tentative date is still the spring of 1962 (Joint
Education Committee, June 27, 1961:2).

It may seem a bit strange that 6 months previously
[Annual Conference, 1960] we could not see the possibilities of having our own school and then suddenly we
agreed it was necessary. My personal interpretation
of this is the experiences we have had with our students who have gone to Tokyo. This spring one of the
students at JCC decided to accept a call from another
church and said he would not be coming back to our
work. Another 2nd year student questioned whether he
would come back. At least four others who have received aid from the mission have found work elsewhere.
So when we heard how these two felt it seemed as
though it was time to seriously start working on getting our own training program set up. ...

So as things are shaping up we are thinking of the
needs of three different areas -- training for full-
time Christian service, training for present laymen,
and training for future laymen. It is beginning to
look as though the resolution of 8 years ago may be
finally carried out in the not too distant future
(Verney Unruh, Education Committee chairman, to Board
of Missions, June 29, 1961:3-5).

Yamada san, having just returned from Hagi, gave an
enthusiastic report about their lay leadership training program. The Japanese committee seemed to be
enthusiastic about a similar program here -- perhaps
dividing our areas into four units and have one
teacher going from one unit to the next, weekly, thus
making the training program available to more laymen
(Joint Education Committee, September 23, 1961:1).

Last year at conference it was decided that we begin
sponsoring fellowship meetings for Christians who have

the same occupation so that they share and discuss
ways in which they can be a more positive witness
where they are. The first of these was the fellowship
for Christians who are public school teachers.

11 were present and entered freely in discussing
problems and temptations such as social drinking,
discipline, teaching morals, school responsibilities
on Sunday, responsibilities at funerals and the relation of a Christian to Japanese culture. ...

In 1960 seminars to encourage and help the pastors
study and grow were initiated. This program was continued this year but in March was expanded to make it
an All-Mennonite church leaders seminar in Tokyo.
Those attending included the 5 pastors from Kyushu, 2
from Hokkaido, 2 lay leaders from Hagi, and several
lay leaders and students in the Tokyo area. Daytime
discussions centered around the Bible and Anabaptist
studies. In the evening Dr. Charles lectured on the
Bible.

Enthusiasm was expressed that this become an annual
meeting. However, because of distance, time and
expense are factors which must be considered seriously
(Education Committee Report, Annual Conference,
October 1961:1).

JCC is in the process of moving the entire campus to
the outskirts of Tokyo. Along with this move the
entire aims and purpose of the school are being re-
studied. There seems to be a need for both a strong
liberal arts college and a strong Bible college for
training pastors and evangelists. Personally I have
been encouraging ... making JCC a Yeotmal type of
school where we would have a greater voice and also
greater responsibility in the financial aspect. However, future relations with JCC should be determined
in the light of our own Bible school plans (1961:2).

There was considerable discussion particularly concerning the Bible School. Some of the questions
brought up were:

Is this to be a Mission project? a Church project?
Would it not rather be both? Should this project be
geared to the laity or to higher training like the
training of pastors and other church workers? ...

What is the solution for the need of more training for church workers? Would keeping them in a local Bible School not give them a more constant vision of the work which needs to be done right here in their own churches? and consequently [not] losing them to other groups when they leave for the schools in the larger centers? Could the Bible School prove to become a unifying factor between Mission and Church (Annual Conference, 1961:3-4)?

RESOLVED THAT THE COMBINED EDUCATION COMMITTEE CON-TINUE TO MAKE PLANS FOR A BIBLE SCHOOL AND COME WITH DEFINITE PLANS FOR AIMS, CURRICULUM, FACULTY, SITE ETC., TO BE PRESENTED AT THE SPRING CONFERENCE. [Caps added]

By Bible School we mean an institution which will provide a program for full-time instruction and study and also an extension program providing opportunity for systematic study in the local churches.

RESOLVED THAT WE AIM TO PUT THIS PROGRAM INTO OPERA-TION IN 1963 (Resolutions 8,9, 1961:4). [Caps added]

Resolved that we continue the seminars for the pastors.

Resolved that we have another Christian Workers' Retreat (Resolutions 13,15, 1961:4).

The following papers were presented on the conference floor. Copies of the same were distributed at the time.

Leadership in the New Testament Church and Summary of Conclusions by Dr. S. F. Pannabecker
Bishops, Elders, Teachers, Deacons in the New Testament by George Janzen
Review of Dr. Waltner's "The Church in the Bible" by Verney Unruh
Applying the Principles of Church Leadership to our Local Church in Japan by Bernard Thiessen
Leadership in our Churches by Paul Boschman
The Place of the Bible School in Training for Christian Service by Peter Derksen (Devotional, Annual Conference, 1961:4).

Miss Kushima has made two trips each to Nobeoka and
Miyakonojo to visit correspondence enrollees. She has
also visited those from Miyazaki City, but found many
not at home or it was inconvenient on their part to
visit.

At the request of the evangelism committee she tried
to arrange a meeting for these enrollees in different
localities but without success. The plan was to
gather them for an evening of fellowship and then
begin a regular meeting in those areas.

At present 755 are on the mailing list of the *Yoki
Otozure* [Good News] paper. These have at sometime or
other all started the Bible study course, but not all
have continued. This year 36 new ones have enrolled
in the *Mark* course, 15 in *What the Bible Teaches*, and
13 in *Christian Living* (Radio Report, Annual Conference, 1961:1).

The *Bible School* has been proposed off and on and considerable opinion has crystallized in the direction of
starting one. The Education Committee presented a
favorable report and conference acted favorably on it.
Though not unanimous the vote was by large majority.
What concerned me more was that the Japanese brethren
were unenthusiastic or negative. The plan is to combine training in one institution for lay workers and
for moderately trained full-time workers. The reasons
are logical: students go away and find jobs elsewhere
and do not return; distances are too far for any but a
few; schools that are both "safe" and academically
creditable are few; Anabaptist-Mennonite background is
unknown in the schools and young Christians trained
away. Personally I feel it will be difficult to combine the two purposes -- training lay workers and
training full-time workers -- in one institution. The
whole program and plan needs to be worked out in
greater detail than has been done yet (S. F. Pannabecker, conference speaker, to Board of Missions,
October 12, 1961b:2).

The objectives of the [Bible] school were discussed
briefly. Reference was made to the objectives stated
in the paper presented at the annual conference: "The
Place of the Bible School in the Training for Christian Service." The objectives could probably be
divided into 3 areas:

1) Devotional; 2) Academic; 3) Service: a) Laymen
                                            b) Pastors,
                                                etc.

A comparative curriculum will be drawn up from the catalogues of various Bible schools and seminaries in Japan and abroad and this is to be studied by the committee members before the next meeting.

The suggestion was made that a pastor and missionary visit all of the churches in order to discuss this matter with them. No action on this taken (Joint Education Committee, December 12, 1961:1).

1962 The general attitude was that we were not ready to begin a Bible School. The problems of getting a student body and a suitable faculty seemed to be the two main barriers, and these appeared insurmountable to some at the present time. More favorable attitudes were expressed in regard to local lay training, and first gradually building up church enthusiasm for a larger effort. ...

The O.M.s have invited our cooperation on an equal basis in a continued program of the Dr. Charles type. ... Not much enthusiasm was expressed. Cost too high. Too few really benefiting. Too difficult for laymen to digest and apply practically. Willingness was expressed to continue cooperating in the same way we did in the Dr. Charles program.

Until now pastors have been bound in their choice of book purchases with the 5,000 yen donation to the prepared Book List. This year they will not be limited, but will be asked to report purchases at the end of the year and share with one another the ones they found more profitable (Joint Education Committee, February 23, 1962:1).

In reading the minutes I got the feeling that the committee is not at all sure we need a Bible School. It seems to me mission action has already settled that. Over 2/3 of the mission has said in effect, "We need an adequate leadership training program and we are asking the committee to make plans for getting it into operation." Further, $1000 was put into the budget to begin this and I believe the budget was accepted unanimously. Also, while the pastors did not

have opportunity to vote they did have the privilege
of floor discussion and in talking to them since conference I know that the majority support conference
action. So I feel that the committee need not feel
hesitant in going ahead with plans. ...

I fully agree that we should have as much church support as possible and for that reason I have suggested
that two members of the committee (a missionary and a
Japanese) visit all of the churches to present the
challenge to them (Verney Unruh to Education Committee,
March 10, 1962:1-2).

Thanks for your letter to the education committee. I
can well understand your feelings and there may be
others in the mission who share them. If the education committee were a mission committee then I would
agree with you a hundred percent.

As it is, we are in a little bit of a peculiar situation on this committee. Half of the committee is
responsible to the mission and half is responsible to
the "kyogiinkai" [church council]. The mission has
made a decision on a Bible school, the "kyogiinkai"
has not even discussed it.

At the committee meeting in question, all of the
missionaries were quite ready to go ahead and try to
make the plans called for in the mission resolution.
... However the other three members of the committee
did not feel bound, since they had no responsible part
in making the decision and Y-san especially felt that
the basic question needed to be reopened.

This situation pointed up to me again the urgent need
that we have for some kind of organization... If our
committee were responsible to some one body which had
made a decision to open a Bible school then all of the
members of the committee would have felt a responsibility and I rather think that their whole attitude
would have been different. If our Bible school is to
be a success, then somehow or other we need to change
the attitude of the pastors from their present attitude which is lukewarm at best to active support.
Somehow they must feel that this is their school and
the church's school and that they are involved in it.

Perhaps the best thing to do would be to wait and represent the basic question to a joint conference in

the fall. After being discussed and passed there I
think it would not only have the support of pastors
and church, but also of the missionaries who have not
yet become reconciled to the idea. At least I think
that the reluctance on the part of some of the missionaries was on the basis that the church was not yet
prepared and ready for this step (Robert Ramseyer,
Joint Education Committee member, to Verney Unruh,
March 13, 1962:1).

On the assumption that the decision of the Mission at
Annual Conference regarding the Bible school will
stand, the Committee proceeded to make further plans,
recognizing that if it is desired, discussion on this
decision may be re-opened at the Spring Conference.

RECOMMENDATIONS RE BIBLE SCHOOL:

1. *Aims & Objectives*:
   a) To help young people develop Christian char-
      acter and attain spiritual growth through a
      study of the Scriptures, through devotional
      exercises, and through practical Christian
      activities.
   b) To help young people towards a greater zeal in
      seeking the lost for Christ.
   c) To emphasize the importance of a fully conse-
      crated life, revealing itself in a willingness
      to do God's will in whatever field of service
      to which He may call.
   d) To offer Christian young people a comprehensive
      understanding of the Bible and related subjects
      through a totally Bible-centered curriculum.
   e) To provide general basic Biblical instruction
      leading to further theological studies.
   f) To prepare laymen as well as full-time Chris-
      tian workers to serve with competence in
      different areas of Christian activity and
      service and any worthy vocation.

2. *Curriculum*: that in general the J.C.C. curriculum
   be adopted for the time being. Thus our school
   would be fully accredited by J.C.C. and a graduate
   of our school could enter J.C.C. as a third-year
   student. This would still allow room for a certain amount of variation. There would be a
   separate course for laymen.
      Relationships with other schools could also be
   established, e.g. the "Osaka Biblical Seminary"

(Mennonite Brethren, Baptist General Conference,
North American Baptists) now has a 5-year program:
2 years Bible school and 3 years seminary (with
junior college in between). Our graduates could
thus, after completing junior college (J.C.C. is
planning to begin with a junior college program in
1964) enter the seminary department of Osaka
Biblical Seminary. For entrance into Japan Bible
Seminary (Tokyo) our graduates would have to complete J.C.C.'s four-year course.

During the Spring Seminar we plan to meet with
the J.C.C. students and ex-students to discern
their views on the above recommendation.

3. *Faculty*: no agreement, no recommendation. There
   was considerable discussion as to whether the
   principal of the school should (or could) be:
   a) A missionary.
   b) A Japanese person from our own group.
   c) A Japanese person with some experience invited
      in from outside of our group to take over the
      leadership of the school.

4. *Site*: also no recommendation. It was felt that
   site would have considerable bearing on faculty,
   especially if the principal was a missionary.

5. *Extension Course*: no recommendation. The members
   of the Joint Education Committee are requested to
   attempt to discern the following in their local
   churches.
   a) Local interest for an extension training
      program in the churches.
   b) Desired subject matter: Bible? Other?
   c) Desired teacher: Pastor? Missionary? An
                       outside person?
   Education Committee members are asked to be ready
   to report their findings by the time the
   "Kyogiinkai" meets, April 21. If there is no real
   apparent interest in the local churches, plans
   will be made to send a representative to tour the
   churches in an effort to create interest.

6. *Finances*: no recommendation, but the following is
   presented to the Mission for discussion at the
   Spring Conference:
   a) Plant: to be financed by the Mission.

b) Faculty salaries: (national) Would the
   churches be willing and able to undertake this?
c) Tuition: free.
d) Room & Board: to be paid by students ("arbeit,"
   scholarships, etc.) (Joint Education Committee,
   March 12, 1962:1-2).

Due to the cut in the budget the following adjustments
were made: Resolved to cut out the $1,000 allotted
for the Bible School.

Resolved that the aims and objectives of the Bible
School be as follows: [same as *Aims & Objectives*,
page 75].

Moved and seconded that Recommendation 2 of Education
Committee reading: "Recommended that in general the
Japan Christian College curriculum be adopted for the
time being. There would be a separate course for
laymen" be tabled and that Resolution 9 of Fall Conference 1961 reading, "Resolved that we aim to put
this program (Bible School) into operation in 1963" be
reconsidered.

In the discussion it was generally felt that a Bible
School in Miyazaki Ken is desirable in the future but
that the churches at present are not ready.

The following substitute motion was passed:
*Resolved that we aim to begin this Bible School when
the churches feel the need and are anxious to have it.*
[Italics mine]

Resolved that the Education Committee begin a promo-
tion campaign in the churches to create interest and
enlist support for the Bible School.

Resolved that our mission cooperatively investigate
seminaries in Japan together with the OMs and BCs
[BIC] (Resolutions 3,11,12,13,15, Spring Conference,
1962:2-4).

Representatives from various churches reported briefly
on the results of their local investigations as to
types of programs desired, who would be the instructor,
how often to meet, etc. No action was taken at this
meeting. However, a few general observations may be
made as to the results of the investigation.

1. The majority favored a strictly local-church program led by the local pastor and missionary.
2. Courses in Bible survey and personal evangelism
   seemed to take prior interest.
3. No agreement as to how often to meet. Some would
   like to begin with two meetings per month, others
   with a weekly meeting -- none more than that.

Again, no particular action was taken. This was simply a discussion of ways and means to promote interest
in the Bible school. It was emphasized that the above
local church training course might be the primary
means to gain this goal. Two important factors to
keep in mind as we work towards a Bible school were
suggested: a teacher and the development of a library.
Suggestion was made that perhaps a major requirement
in thinking of qualifications of teachers ought to be
that he have as much a local background as possible
plus several years of pastoral experience. Perhaps
even one of the present pastors, should he feel such a
calling, might be considered as future teacher of the
Bible school (Joint Education Committee, April 21,
1962:1).

Till now there have been two organizations -- the
Mission conference and the "Kyogiinkai." There has
been some difficulty in operations e.g. the Bible
School. There is need for cooperative action (JMCCC,
Joint Executive Committee, May 14, 1962:1).

[Note: From 1962 on, the Mission and the Church held
a joint conference annually. Such conferences will
from here on be referred to as a Joint Conference.
Those not designated as "joint" will refer to the
Mission conferences only.]

During the past years believers from our churches
have attended the following schools for biblical
training:
1) Japan Christian College
2) Tokyo Theological Seminary (Tokyo Shingakujuku)
3) Japan Bible Seminary (Nihon Seisho Shingakusha)
4) Kansai Bible School
5) Kyoritsu Bible School for Women
6) Ikoma Bible School
7) Child Evangelism Fellowship Bible School
8) Seinan Gakuin
9) Osaka Christian College

10) Bible Institute, Karuizawa (Education Committee Report, Joint Conference, October 1962:2).

Resolved that we have one pastors' seminar in the fall of 1963.

Resolved that we have a Christian Workers' Fellowship in the spring of 1963.

Resolved that the revised Student Aid Program be approved by this conference. ... Aid will be as follows:

3) Upon request of the church(es) the student is expected to help in the spring and summer evangelistic programs.
4) Upon graduation a student is expected to serve one year in practical training working together with a pastor or missionary.
5) Application for support must be renewed each year (JMCCC, Resolutions 6-8, Joint Conference, 1962: 3-4).

Yamada sensei reported briefly on the present local training program undertaken at Kobayashi. It has been operating since June of this year. Twice a month with five students attending. The aim is to make disciples and create a closer fellowship in the church.

Nango is using the weekly bulletin as a means of Bible teaching.

Miyakonojo has a Young People's Bible class.

Miyazaki has an annual Sunday School Teachers' study meeting.

The concern was expressed that if too many meetings are scheduled we will ultimately lose out on the essential ones like Sunday worship and prayer meeting.

A centralized training program would make for a greater oneness in our future church conference. Several expressed a desire for such a program (1962:4).

... after the business was all finished Yamada sensei who was bringing the closing message gave opportunity for testimonies.

Some of the statements brought out in the testimonies
were something like this:

The feeling of brotherhood and oneness had struck
him forcefully and he was so happy for it.

It was a real revelation. Up to this time he had
thought that our denomination had been rather dis-
organized but his eyes had been opened.

Even the most lowly were given a voice and it was
respected.

This conference had showed him that there were
others bearing the same burdens and concerns. He no
longer felt that he was in this alone.

It was a revelation to know where the money comes
from.

It was a real answer to prayer (1962:1-2).

Up to this point there has been a gap between missionaries and pastors. This gap is again apparent between
pastors and churches. Perhaps it is a question
whether the churches at this time are "ready" for joining the two organizations in as far as the pastors are.
We feel it is simply a matter of time and teaching and
that further steps in joining the two organizations
will be possible (Annual Conference, October 1962:8).

1963   The whole matter of training of those who have been
       called to be pastors and evangelists and who have
       dedicated themselves for this task was discussed. In
       general, the following viewpoints were expressed.

   A. Problems with the present theological education
       offered in Japan:
       a. There is no clear distinction between Bible
          schools and theological seminaries (with refer-
          ence to curriculum and entrance requirements).
       b. There is no real training in the churches be-
          fore students are educated in seminaries.
       c. As a result, those who enter seminary often do
          not know even the very rudiments of the Chris-
          tian faith.
       d. There is a definite lack in practical training
          in pastoral work and evangelism. There are few
          persons capable of teaching this.

   B. Unless the individual churches understand the
       importance of theological training for pastors and
       evangelists and are willing to strengthen the
       basic training within the church, and raise the

level of such training, we cannot expect an improvement in seminaries or in theological education.

C. There seems to be a tendency for the so-called evangelical schools to neglect the practical and social applications of the gospel while preserving what is probably an orthodox faith. On the other hand, schools which are said to be comparatively liberal seem to show an opposite tendency.

D. It is necessary to provide training for evangelism in Miyazaki Prefecture, or at least for this general area of Japan.

E. We need our own agency for providing this training.

F. However, in the present situation it would be difficult for us to open our own school and provide the necessary training for evangelism in this area of Japan in the immediate future. ...

G. In the present situation we might consider the following:
  a. First, strengthen the laity in our churches, and then with this as a base, build on this the educational organs for training those who are going into the ministry.
  b. After students have received an education at an evangelical school, they spend one or two years at a place like the rural evangelism training center.

After the above discussion, the following viewpoints were expressed with reference to support for JCC.
1. What are the reasons for the Mennonite support for JCC?
2. This support comes from the fact that JCC is evangelical and undenominational.
3. Is JCC really evangelical in the light of the Anabaptist understanding of the gospel?
4. Education received at JCC is not adequate for evangelism in this part of Japan.
5. Would it not be safest to continue our support of JCC for the present (Joint Education Committee, February 19, 1963:1-2)?

Resolved that we reserve our final judgment on our future attitude toward JCC, waiting to see how the

situation develops. In the meantime the Education
Committee will continue to study the training of
church workers (JMCCC, Resolution 1, Joint Spring
Conference, April 1963:1).

Leadership Training
Resolved that using the Catechism and the Articles of
Faith we fill out the content of the baptismal preparation class using it effectively to strengthen general
believers' training.

Resolved that the education committee provide opportunities and materials to help believers understand
the historical background of the Mennonites and grasp
the fullness of their own faith.

Resolved that we use materials like the Bible Outline
Course which was sent out by the person in charge of
the correspondence courses and evaluate the response.

Resolved that definite educational training for non-
professional leadership (elders, deacons, deaconnesses)
be provided and that the education committee prepare a
standard for guidance.

Resolved that in view of the present situation of the
Sunday School in order to work out a basic reform, the
education committee appoint a study commission to prepare a plan for revision of the Sunday School.

Resolved that hereafter those called to become professional church workers, before leaving for theological training, spend a definite period of time (about
one year) in practical training and study under the
direction of a pastor or missionary. This period to
be considered a time for observation of this person.

Resolved that in order to guide and help the study of
ministerial candidates, a research problem be given
them.

Resolved that in order to aid the study and training
of all professional church workers, study assignments
be given them and time provided at the seminar for
reports and discussion (JMCCC, Resolutions 8-15, Joint
Conference, October 1963:1).

Resolved that Step I of the Church Polity Study of the
Executive Committee be accepted: It reads:

a) The present joint organization (Kyushu Mennonite churches and Japan Mennonite Mission) become one Church Conference in 1964.

b) Representation as at present (two delegates per church plus missionaries).

c) All committee members to be elected at fall conference 1964 with the provision that there be equal national believer and missionary representation.

Resolved that Step II reading as follows be tabled till fall conference 1964:

a) Representation - 4 delegates per member church.

b) At fall conference 1965 all committee members be elected irrespective of national-missionary status.

Resolved that the organization of Resolution 28 shall consist of Executive Committee; Education Committee; Evangelism Committee; and Literature Committee (Resolutions 28-30, 1963:3).

1964 After over two years of careful thought, planning, and study, at our last combined meeting of the boards of directors and trustees we drew up a plan for cooperation of member missions and denominations in the work of Japan Christian College.

... in brief the plan provides for full cooperation in the government and the guidance of Japan Christian College by mission and denominational church groups in Japan. There are two levels of such cooperation:

1. By previous and longstanding agreement with the T.E.A.M. board of directors, a mission or church may have a member elected to the property-holding board of directors on condition that they endorse the school as their official training school and that they make a capital investment in the college itself.

2. In the event that the capital investment cannot be made, the mission may nevertheless participate in the governing "administrative committee" of the school and have membership on the board of trustees according to the following conditions:

   a. That the mission endorse Japan Christian College as its official training school (college level) for Christian workers.

   b. That the mission nominate to the board of trustees and to the school administrative

committee official representatives to serve in
the guidance and policy making of the college,
according to the plan outlined in the by-laws.
...

Kindly study this carefully. I sincerely hope that
the nine years of cooperation and fellowship that JCC
has enjoyed with the General Conference Mennonite
Mission shall be continued in a more formal way. And
I sincerely hope that you will take the step of making
this official endorsement and then that you'll nominate to our board of trustees and our administrative
committee your representative or representatives
(Donald Hoke to General Conference Mennonite Mission,
January 23, 1964:1).

In reflecting on the evangelism and church planting of
the past 12 years it was recognized that there have
been mistakes made and that the goal of what we were
trying to do has often been vague. We have been
strong on evangelism but have had no program for training church leadership or no specific guides for a new
church just starting. We need to study especially the
pattern and structure of the local church. What kind
of church are we trying to establish? Who are the
leaders? How are they chosen? How do we train for
leadership (JMCCC, Joint Executive Committee, April 10,
1964:2)?

Pete Voran, chairman of the education committee,
explained that the recommendation to be presented to
the Church conference next week means that if passed
we will officially approve JCC as our training school
on a high school graduate level. This, however, does
not mean that it will bind us to send all prospective
Christian workers to JCC for training (Annual Conference, October 1964:11).

Agreed that the name of this Church Conference shall
be Kyushu Mennonite Christian Church (JMCCC, Resolution 1, Joint Conference, October 1964:1).

Agreed that the Kyushu Mennonite Christian Church
become a member of the standing [administrative]
committee of Japan Christian College.

Agreed that the chairman of the education committee
for 1965 be the representative on the standing
committee for 2 years.

Agreed that funds for the student-aid program be budgeted (Resolutions 17-19, 1964:3-4).

Budget (Education)

committee operation	40,000	[$111]
pastor's seminars	20,000	[$ 56]
worker's retreat	25,000	[$ 69]
pastor's libraries	30,000	[$ 83]
contribution to schools	90,000	[$250]
local leadership training	70,000	[$194]
student support	100,000	[$278]
(1964:4).		

This brings us to the end of the minutes, reports, and letters bearing on the question raised in this section. That is, Whatever happened to our own Bible school in 1963? We have simply sought to let the materials tell their own story. But to summarize briefly, we have seen that there was talk of making plans for leadership training back as early as 1951, the very first year the G.C. Mennonite missionaries arrived in Japan. By 1953, it was definitely felt there was need of a Bible school. In 1954, a fund was created to assist those training for the ministry. From 1955 on, a number of students were sent away for training, primarily to Japan Christian College.

In 1956, several four- and five-day Bible conferences were held in various places. The first short-term spring Bible school was held in 1957. Another was held in 1958. The third one was held in 1959, and in the same year was the first Christian workers' retreat. In 1960, there was no spring Bible school but several of the churches held three-day local Bible schools instead, and that was also the year of the first pastors' seminar. In 1961, the Mission made a decision to start their own Bible school which was to open in 1963. The next year, 1962, aims and objectives of the school, curriculum, faculty and so on were discussed, but it was decided to wait to begin until the churches were ready. In 1963 it was felt that rather than starting our own school we should try to first of all strengthen the laity on the local level. In 1964, the Church Conference was formed and became a member of the administrative committee of Japan Christian College.

As we went through the minutes I am sure you noticed that there is a certain amount of overlap with the first part of this chapter, which is unavoidable as both sections cover approximately the same period of time. A number of the same

problems are evident -- student support while in school, the
failure of many students to return, the difficulty of providing continuing education for the pastors and the like.
, These are the sort of problems that lay behind the missionaries' decision to begin their own school. But they do not
explain what ultimately happened to that resolution. No
doubt there were numerous factors involved.

One may have been a lack of someone to see it through.
For example, one missionary remarked to me that he had been
asked to help out in this area, but did not accept because
he felt it was "not his calling." Personnel and other such
things may have been a problem. But if there was any one
reason why the proposal failed, it seems to me from a reading of the minutes and a reading between the lines that the
failure lay in the area of Mission-Church relationships. By
this I mean relationships between missionaries and pastors;
relationships between the churches and the Mission. And on
top of that, relationships among the missionaries themselves,
for the decision to start their own school was not unanimous.
There were 14 who voted in favor of it, four against it, and
two who abstained (GCMM, Annual Conference, 1961:4).

But, forgetting about that for a moment, we have seen how
from the outset the idea to open a Bible school was a
missionary idea. When it resulted in a decision to actually
begin such a school, again the decision was a missionary
decision. The Church had no part in making it. And since
they had had no part in the original decision, they felt no
responsibility to carry it out. While they may not have
come right out and said they were not in favor of such a
school, personally I believe that was actually the case.
The fact that the Japanese were not behind the proposal
comes out clearly in S. F. Pannabecker's letter to the
Mission Board, which we have looked at before. Commenting
on the 1961 Mission conference and the Bible school proposal,
you will remember he expressed concern that "the Japanese
brethren were unenthusiastic or negative" (1961b:2). It
seems that the missionaries finally came to realize this too,
for at their spring meeting of 1962 they decided to wait to
begin the Bible school until "the churches feel the need and
are anxious to have it" (GCMM, Spring Conference, 1962:3).

Behind all this, however, would seem to be the problem of
Church-Mission relationships as suggested above. Pannabecker's letter also brings this out when it says,

Church and Mission Relations are still in the beginning
stage. Churches are small in members and in some cases

hardly enough to organize formally. Yet there are
committees of some kind in most of the places where
work is carried on and a fairly full organization in
the older places. ...

I believe we can expect the Japanese to assume responsibilities for church operation earlier and faster
than in most of the other fields. The first decade
which we have just celebrated was the decade of the
missionary. Another decade may be given to joint participation but I feel that should be about the limit.
In other words this decade should be devoted to getting
Japanese pastors into every church and making them feel
responsible and also to preparing and setting up an
organization in which missionaries can participate as
necessary but which can be made predominantly Japanese
by the end of this decade (1961b:3).

That all moved in this direction is very clear in the
minutes of the next few years. Things, indeed, went much
faster than Pannabecker had anticipated. The Kyushu (now
Japan) Mennonite Christian Church Conference was officially
organized only three years later, in 1964.

Besides Church-Mission relationships, there were other
concerns also that diverted attention from a Bible school.
The bookstore work was one. The kindergarten (Nichinan) was
another. The opening of the Miyazaki Christian School for
missionary children was still another. Incidentally, my
wife and I first went to Japan as houseparents for the
missionary children studying at that school in the fall of
1964. At the time, there was little if anything being said
about starting a Bible school. It was not until 1974, in
fact, when I spent some time going through the Mission files,
that I learned of the extensive plans which had been made
for a Bible school. I could hardly believe some of the dis-
coveries I made! I had not known anything about those plans
before, and we arrived just a year after the Bible school
was to have opened. But at that time, they were not talking
about it anymore. Almost everything had to do with Church-
Mission relationships. That was the big issue of the day.
And I believe that is above all the thing which caused the
Bible school to move from the foreground into the background.
The preoccupation with Mission-Church relationships over-
shadowed everything else.

What would have happened if the Bible school had opened?
Or if the Mission had earlier employed a Bible teacher?

That, of course, could lead to all sorts of conjectures.
But if the churches and pastors were not behind it, it is
difficult to see how anything could have really succeeded.
In any case, a school which had been conceived over a period
of about 10 years died before it was ever born. The Church
seemed to be thinking in other directions. But it still
needed leaders. They needed to be trained. We want to take
a look next at some of the efforts that were made to train
leaders at home.

EXPERIMENTING WITH LAY TRAINING IN THE COUNTRY

When the plan to send men away to the cities for training
did not work out very well, we have seen how the Mennonite
Mission decided that they should start their own school. We
have also seen how that decision was not backed by the
pastors and the churches, how they got sidetracked with
Mission-Church relationships, and how the proposal eventually fell through. But that was not the end of the story.
The pastors and missionaries were agreed that some kind of
training was necessary. We have already seen how there were
a few attempts here and there at what was called "lay training." This was not an effort to produce pastors. It was
directed more toward producing a greater number of trained
laymen. The efforts were local rather than conference-wide
as a Bible school would have been, but several churches
experimented along these lines.

The most extensive experiment was that undertaken by the
Kobayashi Church. We are fortunate to have a fairly good
record of their attempts at this in a small book called
Experiments in Church Growth: Japan, by Neil Braun, Paul W.
Boschman, and Takashi Yamada (Boschman 1968). The latter
two were both related to the Kobayashi Church at the time.
As their book is now out of print, I would like to simply
introduce here the pages relevant to the matter to give us
an idea of what they did, how they did it, results, future
plans and so on. Takashi Yamada relates their experiment as
follows:

That we were able to begin a Laymen's Bible School
in Kobayashi in May of 1962, we are convinced, was the
leading of the Lord. It goes without saying that this
was but a tiny, imperfect beginning. Nevertheless, we
believe it has contributed much to our church during
this time. We wish to take this opportunity to review,
re-examine and assess this Laymen's Bible School which
has been the center of our lay training program in

Kobayashi. From this we also wish to consider or project the future direction of our lay training keeping in mind the present situation and needs of our congregation. If this report can be of some benefit to fellow workers and the churches they serve it will have been worth the effort.

ITS BEGINNING

In the afternoon of May 20, 1962, at the Kobayashi Mennonite Church, our Laymen's Bible School was begun. According to the registration records still at hand we began with 9 students (2 men, 7 women) and one auditor (woman). According to the original application records, each student put his signature and seal to the following statement: "I whole-heartedly support (agree to) all the emphases and purposes of this Laymen's Bible School, and hereby desire to be accepted as a student. If I am accepted I promise to obey the regulations and as a faithful student I promise to be diligent in my studies." It is regrettable that a record of these regulations is no longer available. As I recall, the purpose of the school was to train in discipleship and build up a vital Christian fellowship; the main emphasis was to be on practical witness and the mature life of faith.

Of the original 9 students and auditors, 4 students are still studying with us, 4 others have left the community and 2 have discontinued. However, we still have a membership of 9 which includes the first four and as at the time of organization we have 2 men and 7 women.

When we began the Laymen's Bible School it was just one year after our group had reached a crisis and begun anew as a church body. Among our students too there was a renewed dedication and sense of calling.

In the first year of operation we met twice a month, once on Sunday afternoon from 1:00-3:00 at the church and once at Kyomachi, Kakuto, and Nojiri at the time of our regular weekly meeting. Since then however, we have been meeting on the third Sunday of the month only from 1:00-3:00 in the afternoon.

CURRICULUM

The main subjects were as follows:
A Course - Taught by T. Yamada
   1. Bible Survey
      a) General Introduction
      b) Old Testament Survey
      c) New Testament Survey
   2. Bible Study Methods
      a) Analytical Method
      b) Inductive Method
   3. Church History
      a) Outline of Church History
      b) The Reformation - difference between Catholics
         and Protestants
      c) Japanese Church History - reception of
         Catholic Missions, opposition and persecution
   4. Evangelism - (Christianity and Culture)
      a) Reception of the Catholic Faith and Group
         Conversion
      b) Entrance of Buddhism into Japan and its
         Process of Indigenization
B Course - Taught by Paul W. Boschman
   1. How to Study the Bible and Enjoy It (Acts 1-12)
   2. Principles of Evangelism - the growth of the
      Church as seen in the book of Acts (Acts 13-21)
   3. Purpose and Mission of the Church (Book of
      Ephesians)
   4. Witness, Its Content and Experience
   5. Sharing of Practical Experiences in Evangelism

Note - When we put on paper, as above, the courses
taught, it appears as though we had a well-rounded
curriculum. However, being a very busy church, it was
not always possible to have printed lessons ready in
time. Even when we did, there was only time to look
over the main points and then go into discussion of the
subject at hand. Our teaching material was very simple.
Under No. 1 above (Bible Survey) we were able to study
only about one half of the material. As a whole it was
very difficult to continue in a well organized manner.

Now, after six years, as we re-examine what we have
tried to accomplish through our Laymen's Bible School,
we realize that in curriculum, study hours, preparation
and review, we certainly lacked thoroughness and com-
pleteness. Part of this was due no doubt to the fact
that students were limited in time because of regular

employment and household duties. Nevertheless, we must recognize that students were helped in the following areas:

1. Study habits and attitudes were developed.
2. The mistaken attitude that only professionally trained Christians are capable of witnessing effectively was rectified.
3. Through a wider and deeper perspective, they were helped to discover what one's personal life of faith and the life of the church should be or should become.
4. In a natural way, the laymen became deeply conscious of their personal mission in life.
5. In addition to the above, by having a laymen's training school such as this, the pastor and missionary are greatly encouraged. It has helped them to feel more at one with the laymen of the church; this certainly has been another significant "plus."

LESSONS LEARNED

Let me here enumerate some of the lessons we have learned through this six-year experiment in lay training.

1. For effective evangelism and church extension, it is of utmost importance for church leaders to recognize that Christian education must take place within the local church.
2. Keeping in mind the needs and maturity of the local church as well as the society surrounding it, one should plan a simple, practical training program and begin with the resources available.
3. It is important that such a training program include not only a selected group of baptized laymen but people, seekers and baptized, who are already doing meaningful service both inside and outside the church. The program should take into consideration the needs of these people and therefore should be student and need centered.
4. A rigid curriculum, set up primarily to satisfy the intellectual demands of students and teachers, is not only useless as lay training but could possibly do much harm.
5. A practical, existential curriculum should by all means not neglect that which teachers and students have to contribute from their own experience of teaching and learning in their active life of witness and faith.

6. Since the number of class sessions is limited, the effectiveness of this program depends greatly upon home study and preparation of both teachers and students.
7. Discussion sessions seem to be quite effective and worthwhile.

THE FUTURE OF THE LAYMEN'S SCHOOL

In speaking of the future of the Kobayashi Laymen's Bible School, I would like to stress something which I have been experiencing in these recent years. What I want to say goes somewhat beyond the present training program for it grows out of what I as an evangelist and as a Christian have experienced and has now become a firm conviction with me. In a few words it is this: It is of utmost importance that we take care never to lose the freedom, already given by the Holy Spirit to each believer individually and to the whole body, the freedom to witness spontaneously and freely. ...

That is precisely why training in the Laymen's Bible School, or in any other disciplines in the church, must never be allowed in any form whatsoever to suppress, or restrain spontaneous, independent, and creative activities and joy in the heart of the laymen. Rather, training must develop and contribute toward a right and proper expression of the spontaneous and creative witness of the laymen. It must assist and not restrain. We have seen many times that new converts, filled with life and joy, are powerful communicators of the Gospel. To our sorrow we have also seen some of these same converts, as they grow older in their Christian life, lose their zeal for witness, a problem which greatly hinders the expansion of the church. On the other hand this is precisely the point where lay training takes on real meaning. As mentioned above we must not suppress spontaneity in witness. ...

... I would like to emphasize that the key in lay training lies not in dispensing additional knowledge but in seeking, discovering, drawing out and developing what God already has placed in the laymen's heart. In other words it must develop what is already there; this is the purpose of lay training. This is what I have often been led to think during these last six years as I have struggled with the meaning and purpose of our lay training program.

I think it is well to proceed with the present program with some curriculum adaptation to meet changing needs. This change is indicated under A below. In addition to the present program I see the need for a concentrated, short term course as outlined under B below.

A - *Curriculum Adaptation of Present Program*

Since the Kobayashi Mennonite Church works on the larger parish system that includes Kobayashi City, Nishimorogata County and Kagoshima City, we must work out a plan that will meet our changing needs and then take steps to fulfill such a plan. Our strategy for evangelism must include a kind of lay witness that will be both effective and fruitful. To find answers to these questions we will use the group study approach touching on the following patterns of witness.
1. Patterns of Church Growth
2. Patterns of Lay Witness
3. Patterns of Group Conversion
4. Patterns of Group Witness

All of these patterns touch on social structure in evangelism and group activity.

B - *Concentrated Bible Training Course*

Up to this point we have dealt with the basic issue of how we might bring to fruition the laymen's spontaneous desire to witness, how to permit and foster active on-the-job training. To this we must now add the wider dimension of intellectual discipline. In order to do this we propose the following:
1. To arrange for a concentrated training period in either Spring or Fall, during the slack season, twice a year. As to the time in the week we see two possibilities.
   a) Continue every week for one month beginning Saturday evening and ending Sunday afternoon, not including the worship services. This plan would allow for 20 to 23 hours of instruction.
   b) Meet every evening for one week, from 7 to 10 o'clock. This would allow for 21 hours of concentrated instruction.
2. Content of instruction would center around Bible, Christian faith and evangelism. We would choose material for instruction that would be immediately

applicable in our commitment to evangelize in our
parish. Our plan would be to complete one or two
units of study in one short term period.

3. It should be possible to complete basic courses
in three years. For students that find it
impossible to adjust to this kind of plan we
would make arrangements to have them finish their
assignments by correspondence or special classes.
Taking into account personality, spirituality
and actual witness activities, students who
finish the concentrated unit of studies would be
recognized as qualified lay evangelists. Those
who in this way become lay evangelists, and are
then willing and able to pursue further outlined
courses of study, and who during practical experience have felt the direct call of God into the
ministry, could then, upon the recommendation of
the home church and the Church Conference, be
fully ordained by the board of elders into the
full-time ministry. Depending upon circumstances,
this could be either the salaried or self-supporting ministry.

For those who find this type of training impossible
we will need to think of other ways to achieve lay
training in the local church.

In September, 1968, 18 laymen were appointed as local
lay leaders (evangelists). This responsibility will
include the following: 1) Make earnest efforts to win
new people to Christ. 2) Open and lead new house meetings or other group activities. 3) Encourage and counsel
new converts and fellow church members. In addition to
the above each one personally subscribes to the following disciplines. 1) To live a consistent Christian life
of service. 2) Attend the lay training sessions. 3) To
read and report on a selected number of books.

We hasten to say that this is indeed a venture of
faith for this is a new dimension in our training
experiment. It is our hope and prayer that in years to
come, winnable people will have been found and the number
of seekers and baptisms greatly multiplied to the glory
of God (Boschman 1968:122-132).

The Kobayashi experiment began in 1962 and continued for
about 10 years. During that time, several other churches
also made attempts at having their own lay training programs.

In order to give an overall picture of the various attempts
that were made, I have compiled a Lay Training Program Chart
(see Figure 2.1). The information contained in this chart
comes from church questionnaires filled out primarily by the
pastors serving the various churches. In addition, some of
them were filled out by laymen, missionaries, or a combination of the two. (See Appendix G for the Church Questionnaire, and details on who filled it out for each group.)

The churches on the chart have been arranged in chrono-
logical order, that is, in the order in which they were
founded. As indicated earlier, all of them are located in
Miyazaki Prefecture except the Oita Church which is in Oita
Prefecture, and the Baba Cho Church which is in Hyogo Prefecture. Seven of the churches were started in the 1950s.
Three in the 1960s or early 1970s. Their present active
membership (1974) totals 229, giving them an average of
about 23 active members per church. When asked how many
"potential lay leaders" there were in the churches, the
total came to over 40, or slightly over four per church.
One observation that is very striking is that the number of
potential lay leaders is almost the same in each church,
rather than in direct proportion to the size of the congregation. We will have more to say about that later. What
concerns us now is whether or not they have had any lay
training programs.

When asked if they have had any lay training program in
the past, five churches said they had; five said they had
not. In other words, half of them did and half of them did
not. As pointed out before, Kobayashi's was by far the most
extensive program. Next would appear to be Miyazaki, having
had at least several different courses such as doctrine,
church history, social problems, preaching, and nonresistance. The other churches which had programs seem to have
had only one or two courses at the most, and in some cases
it was not clear what the courses were. In all cases the
courses were taught either by the pastor or missionary, or
leadership was shared by them or with the church board.
They varied in length anywhere from three days to three
months, from a week to a year. The number of students
ranged from three to 13, with an average of six or seven.

When asked if they felt the program was worthwhile, all
of the churches which had it replied Yes. When asked if
there were any special problems, one of the churches said it
created some tensions between those who participated and
those who did not; another said it was difficult for some of

Figure 2.1

LAY TRAINING PROGRAM CHART (1974)

Name of Church	City	Year Founded	Present Active Memb.	Potential Lay Leaders	Lay Tr. Program in Past?
Baba Cho Christian Church	Kobe	1952	11	5	No
Oyodo Christian Church	Miyazaki	1952	52	4	Yes
Namiki Christian Church	Miyakonojo	1953	21	5	Yes
Aburatsu Christian Church	Nichinan	1954	35	5	Yes
Hyuga Christian Church	Hyuga	1955	12	2	No
Kirishima C'n Brotherhood (Kobayashi Church)	Kobayashi, Ebino, Kagoshima, other	1955	30	5?	Yes
Atago Christian Church	Nobeoka	1959	31	3	Yes
Takajo Christian Church	Takajo	1965	13	2?	No
Oita Mennonite Christian Church	Oita	1967	21	5?	No
Kirishima Christian Church	Miyazaki	1972	21	5	No

Figure 2.1

LAY TRAINING PROGRAM CHART (continued)

Courses Taught	Length	Teacher	Number of Students	Worth-while?	Lay Tr. Program Now?
					No
Doctrine Ch. History Soc. Prob. Preaching C'n Non- 　resistance	6 months 3 months 1 year 3 months 3 months	Pastor " " " "	13 10 8 5 ?	Yes[a]	No
Bible Study Methods	6 months?	Pastor/Miss.	3-4	Yes	No
(Lay Tr.)	1 week 3 days	Pastor "	5 ?	Yes[b]	No
					No
Laymen's Bible School (see page 90)	10 years	Pastor/Miss.	many	Yes	No
Church Officers Training	3 months	Ch. Bd./Pastor?	4	Yes	No
Special Problems? [a] It created a few tensions between those who participated and those who did not. [b] There were cases where the people enrolled could not continue due to their work.					No No No

the participants to take in all the sessions due to their
work; three of the churches said they had no special
problems.

Thus five of the ten churches have had some sort of a
program at one time or another. They all felt it was beneficial. But when asked if they have any lay training
program at present, all of them answered No. This causes us
to ask, as we did in the case of the proposed school, what
happened? Why did not at least some of these programs continue? That is a question which is difficult to answer here
with any degree of certainty, because it was not asked and
answered on the questionnaire. If one were to inquire, however, I expect that there were a number of factors involved.
One perhaps was time. It takes a lot of time to prepare and
teach such classes. Another may have been interest. It is
sometimes hard to maintain the motivation or the original
enthusiasm for such a program. There is also the fact that
in most cases, with the exception of Kobayashi, and perhaps
Miyazaki, there was no overall plan to the program. It is
no doubt difficult to keep a program going without long-
range objectives. These may have been some of the reasons
for stopping.

But whatever the reasons, the thing that should concern
us most, I believe, is that while the programs were all felt
to be worthwhile, they benefitted only a few of the churches.
They were almost entirely local in nature. Some churches
had no program at all, depending on the interest of the
pastor or missionary in this sort of thing. This is perhaps
another reason why the programs died out. They were local,
and when local interest waned for one reason or another,
there was nothing to spur them on. That may have had its
good side as well, in not perpetuating something in which
there may not have been all that much interest. But it
seems to me it is regrettable that not more churches prof-
ited from the training programs that were held. This is
especially true of the newer churches, those begun after
1960, which apparently have had nothing at all along this
line.

It was no doubt the negative influence of factors such
as these, as well as the positive influence of the
Kobayashi experiment which was in progress at the time, that
caused the churches to increasingly feel the need for some
kind of a joint lay training program. The interest in such
a project peaked around 1969, but as this is the topic of
the next section, we better leave it till there.

WHATEVER HAPPENED TO OUR OWN SCHOOL IN 1970?

"That we establish [a] Lay Bible School to supplement the lay training programs already operating in all the churches. Further, that we appoint a committee to prepare the curriculum, select instructors, and take responsibility for all preparatory and administrative matters, so that the school can be opened by April, 1970."

The above decision was made at the 1969 annual Church conference. It was made by the official delegates from the various churches which included pastors, laymen, and missionaries. But what happened to this decision? That is what we want to try to find out.

In the second section of this chapter, we considered a similar question, Whatever happened to our own school in 1963? To do that, we looked into the minutes and reports and some correspondence related to the matter. We want to take a parallel approach here, and once again let the material speak by itself before commenting on it. One thing to keep in mind, however, is that whereas Mission and Church were separate during the period covered before, in 1964 they became one organization. Therefore all the decisions made from then on were joint decisions. So the second section took us up to 1965. In this one we want to continue from there. As before, we will first of all allow the record to speak for itself. (Note: Unless otherwise indicated the following references from 1965-1970 all pertain to the Japan Mennonite Christian Church Conference.)

1965 Regarding enlarging the area of responsibility of the Church Conference:

> Concerning the various kinds of activity which have been carried on only by the Mission outside the Church Conference, in the spirit of integration and unity and in the name of the Church Conference, we make the following request: "We request that the Church Conference shall join decisions regarding placement of missionaries, and various institutions such as the kindergarten, bookstores etc." (Joint Executive Committee, October 5, 1965:3).

Resolved that the calling and placement of missionaries be done in consultation with the Executive Committee of the Church Conference.

Resolved that for 1966 we function without Education
and Evangelism committees (GCMM, Resolutions 1,3,
Annual Conference, October 1965:3).

Resolved that the mission Executive Committee decide
all kindergarten matters related to the mission.

Resolved that we take steps to set up a board of
directors for the operation of Kei-Ai [Grace-Love]
Kindergarten.

Resolved that the literature committee take steps to
form an advisory committee for the operation of our
bookstores ... (Resolutions 4,15,19, 1965:4,7).

1966 First, the radio worker (Yamada) presented a report of
the radio work for the first nine months of 1966. For
the period of October 1965 to September 1966 the
following responses have been made to the radio broadcasts and to the correspondence course:

Responses to the mail pull:	177
New applications for the correspondence course:	88
General inquiries:	68
Number taking the regular correspondence course:	126
Others (inquiries through the churches):	36
	495

... Prior to the opening of this conference the problem of whether or not to continue the radio ministry
next year was discussed at the Executive Committee,
but no concrete proposals were set forth. ...

That we discontinue the radio ministry, and instead
seek to do audio-visual evangelism (Decision 8, Annual
Conference, October 1966:9-10).

The items occurring in the usual budget under education came up for review one by one. The following
decisions were made:
1. That we continue the Pastor-Missionary Fellow-
    ship next year.
2. That we have one Workers' Retreat next year in
    conjunction with one of the Pastor-Missionary
    fellowships. Those attending would include:
    pastors, missionaries, bookstore workers,
    kindergarten workers, as well as all church
    delegates sent to the Church conference. ...

3. That we have one fellowship for pastors and their families.
4. That we continue the pastors' book fund next year on the same basis as this year (6,000 yen [$17] per pastor).
5. That we provide budget money for special meetings to train lay leadership, leaving exact amount of money and other details up to the Executive Committee.
6. That we make another financial contribution to T.C.C. (Tokyo Christian College).
7. That we continue to extend financial support to our Bible students (in this case, our students at T.C.C.).
8. That we provide funds for and hold another Pastors' Seminar next year.
9. That we hold another Sunday School teachers' meeting next year. ...
10. That we continue sending a delegate to the meetings of the permanent standing committee (Jōchiin) of T.C.C. (J.C.C. -- Japan Christian College -- has been authorized to become a Christian Junior College or a Christian Short-Term University, "Kirisutokyō Tanki Daigaku," and has been re-named the *Tokyo Christian College*) (Decision 11, 1966:16).

Looking back at the minutes of the church conference of two years ago, we find that the conference was evenly divided on the issue of whether or not we should choose J.C.C. (the present T.C.C.) as the school with which we would closely cooperate and which we would recommend to our students. (In actuality, for all practical purposes, T.C.C. has become the only institution receiving our support.) Only the chairman's vote broke the tie which determined that we would cooperate with T.C.C. Then, on the basis of this decision, it was further determined (by a vote of 12 to 1) that we would send a representative to the standing committee meetings. This, however, is recorded very briefly in the minutes of that conference. More reflection was called for on the matter of our having chosen T.C.C. as the only institution we are supporting and recommending to our students. This is not because we consider T.C.C. as an unsuitable school, but because we feel that our students should be offered more choice, with T.C.C. as one of the schools of a wider selection.

With this as a background, the following recommendation was made and brought to a vote:
  a) That we do not make T.C.C. the only school we
     support and recommend to our students, but that
     we continue sending a representative to the
     standing committee meetings. ...
  c) That we appoint Pastor Takarabe as our commit-
     tee member and send him to the meetings two
     times a year (1966:17).

1967 Budget:
  13. Lay Leadership Training @   80,000 [$222]
  14. Contribution to T.C.C. @@   30,000 [$ 83]
  15. Aid to Bible Students #   150,000 [$417]

  Footnotes:
  @   To be adapted to the circumstances of the vari-
       ous churches, given upon request as the need
       arises, within the framework of the budget.
  @@   It was discussed as to whether or not we should
       make a financial contribution to T.C.C. in view
       of the fact that we have decided not to make
       T.C.C. the only school we recommend to our stu-
       dents. However, for the time being, since we
       have a number of students there, it was decided
       to make this contribution.
  #   The matter of an allowance for pastors wishing
       to take university work by correspondence was
       also discussed, but since there are many ways
       in which one might wish to pursue further
       studies, and since this problem is related to
       the whole matter of pastors' education, no con-
       clusion was reached, and no special budget was
       set up (1966:22).

1967 Pastor Takarabe, the T.C.C. representative, gave a
      brief report of the T.C.C. council meetings. ...
      Lively discussion centered around what kind of pastors
      we actually need in our church now, and what kind we
      will need in the future, and whether T.C.C. really
      meets our needs. Our goal is church growth, and for
      that reason, as well as in view of the actual condi-
      tion of our various churches, it would seem better to
      have various types of pastors. Even if we entertain
      an idea of the "ideal" pastor, it may finally turn out
      that this idea is not correct. T.C.C. is by no means
      perfect, but it was decided to continue recommending
      it to our students as we have until now.

That we again budget 30,000 yen [$83] as a contribution to T.C.C. for next year (Decision 17, Annual Conference, October 1967:10).

After examining the state of the budget for lay leadership training, and noting to what extent the funds had been used in the past, it was suggested that the budget for next year be placed at 60,000 yen, or 20,000 yen lower than this year. However, because of the high importance of lay leadership training, the opinions of those opposing the lowering of this budget prevailed. Moreover, Pastor Yamada reported on the Kobayashi Church lay leadership training school, stating that it was the purpose of this school to train qualified lay evangelists. In response to this the opinion was voiced that until this kind of lay leadership training school becomes the model for the Church Conference, we should strive to put more effort into such a program.

That we again budget 80,000 yen [$222] for lay leadership training for next year (Decision 22, 1967:10-11).

1968 – Lay training is vital. ...
– Heavy stress should be laid on lay training, both on the local church level and on the church conference level (Annual Conference, October 1968:7).

1969 Budget:
  14. Lay Training   100,000   [$278]
      (Includes 15,000 yen for S.S.
      teachers' rally) (1968:11).

1969 The other day at our Pastor-Missionary Fellowship opinions were expressed to the effect that we need to deepen our "group consciousness," or "Conference consciousness," and that our failure to bear our share of financial contributions to the conference treasury demonstrates how shallow this consciousness really is. ...
Things that might possibly lead to a deepening of our group consciousness:
  1. Publication of a Conference paper -- exchange of information. ...
  5. Greater emphasis on lay training in all local churches.
  6. Create a systematic lay training program as a Conference.
  7. Pastor-missionary pulpit exchanges.

Discussion:

1. Conference publication: information exchange
   -- our past experience shows that budget and a
   person who will take responsibility for this
   have been formidable obstacles (Executive
   Committee, February 2, 1969:5-6).

T-san: I would like to ask for your reactions to some
of my proposals at the last regular meeting of the
Executive Committee. First, concerning the pro-
posed annual goal: "A MORE ABUNDANT HARVEST ...
THROUGH STRENGTHENING OUR CONSCIOUSNESS OF BROTHER-
HOOD."

J-san: Brotherhood consciousness seems to me to be
turning inwards upon ourselves rather than outwards
to evangelism. What connection does brotherhood
consciousness have with a great harvest?

T-san: A strengthening of brotherhood consciousness
is being used in the sense that we strengthen
cooperation between the churches. By greater
cooperation between all churches in various ways,
we should be able to strengthen our evangelistic
outreach and thus gain a greater harvest.

My other personal thoughts on recommendations were
formulated in the light of this. For example, how
about a unified program of lay leadership training
in our Conference? Here we might think in terms of
a unified curriculum, determining responsible personnel for each subject, sending them around to all
the churches, etc. Of course, it might be difficult to come up with specific recommendations to
this year's annual conference due to the brevity of
the remaining time, but we might appoint a committee at this year's annual conference to study the
matter and come up with concrete recommendations
for next year's conference.

M-san: That would mean that this plan would not be
realized until the year after next, which in my
opinion is too long to wait.

O-san: I think it would be better to elect a committee at this year's annual conference and ask this
committee to make preparations to launch a unified
lay training school no later than April of next
year (Executive Committee, September 7, 1969:2-3).

The school [T.C.C.] strongly recommends that local churches confirm the call to service claimed by new applicants. It is seen as highly desirable that students have a preparatory period of service (at least one year) in local churches to test their call (Annual Conference, November 1969:2).

At last year's annual conference a Confession of Faith and a Conference Constitution were adopted, but the laymen have not become very familiar with these. To emphasize our unity in faith and organization, how about preparing a handbook for laymen that would include the Confession of Faith, the Constitution, and an abbreviated Anabaptist historical sketch showing our spiritual heritage? Since the first two are already officially in existence, we recommend the appointment of a group to study what should go into an article on Anabaptist history and our spiritual heritage, and then appoint someone to write the article.
...

THAT WE PREPARE A HANDBOOK FOR LAYMEN WITH THE FOLLOWING CONTENT: 1) CONFESSION OF FAITH 2) CONFERENCE CONSTITUTION 3) AN ARTICLE ON ANABAPTIST HISTORY AND OUR SPIRITUAL HERITAGE (Decision 2, 1969:7).

This [a Laymen's Bible School] would provide for a basic unified curriculum of instruction, the appointment of a special instructor for each course, and a uniform, adequate Bible school for the training of laymen in all churches, and that for this purpose we create a committee to make the necessary preparations so that the school can be launched by April, 1970. Several years ago at an annual conference the idea was expressed that we should have a unified lay training school, using the pattern Yamada sensei is employing in Kobayashi. All the churches have their own special characteristics, but areas of common need are also numerous. Also, in a number of churches there is almost no effective program in operation. A lay training school should be opened everywhere with as adequate a curriculum as possible. If one pastor undertakes to instruct all courses, the instruction necessarily becomes shallow. Where possible, laymen can be employed as instructors. If we have the will to do it, I believe we can open such a school by April, 1970. Discussion ...

- This should be a school based on a clear understanding of the direction in which we wish to move
  as a conference, and the methods we wish to employ,
  and one that would act as a tool assisting us in
  reaching our goal.
- I would like to aim for a school that does not stop
  with the mere impartation of knowledge, but one
  that gives practical training in making evangelists.
- Making evangelists of all the laymen is certainly
  an ideal, but the danger is that it will end up
  simply as one more Bible study group. Would it not
  be better to aim clearly at training lay leaders?
  What are you doing in Kobayashi?
- I think one of the most important points is what we
  consider as common areas and what we leave flexible
  in the program for each church. The more the organization grows, the more difficult it becomes to
  develop individual personality. There are areas
  where organization should grow, and also areas
  where it should not. We talk about lay training,
  but we need to clarify just what we mean. In
  Kobayashi we have adopted a progressive lay service
  organization. This is different from the whole
  pattern of churches that retain the professional
  pastor.
- The secret of success is the relation between the
  pastor and the laity. It would seem that this
  would be a loose relationship at best where
  instructors itinerate among the churches.
- We do not aim at doing away with present lay training programs in local churches. There are surely
  common areas of interest. This is just to supplement local programs already in operation.
- It would be best to decide clearly to train lay
  leadership. We must put our emphasis on essentials.
- Is lay leadership training something that really
  raises the level of the whole church?
- Wouldn't it be good enough to simply have local
  churches invite special speakers as they desire
  rather than itinerate?
- At the annual conference in 1963 we decided to give
  special instruction to non-professional Christian
  workers (leaders, elders, deacons, etc.) and asked
  the Education Committee to suggest ideas to carry
  this out. If we really want to carry out this
  decision, then we need to decide our goal clearly.
- If our goal is to move in a direction where certain
  laymen can occasionally fill the role the

professional pastor usually takes, then I am glad
to serve. However, if we continue in the present
direction where the pastor plays the leading role,
then the position of the layman is greatly threatened. We have talked about this for many years,
but so far nothing has become of it. The pattern
(structure of the whole) is our problem. I would
like to hear opinions related to the changing of
the form and structure of the church, even concerning lesser points. Then, if there is anything we
wish to try, we can share our concerns on the local
level. This should permit communication between
churches that have a totally different structure.

- Even if instructors don't itinerate, how about
  creating a budget that will allow those that can
  serve in other churches to do so, as a first step?
- It seems we all have slightly different ideas about
  this, and I think there are both good and bad
  points. The Kirishima group would like to express
  itself in favor of the project because we would
  like to learn to know the pastors and receive the
  instruction they can give.
- It is easy to get locked in by the limited bounda-
  ries of our own creation, and simply continue our
  lay training school as we have in the past. Itin-
  erating instructors will themselves be richly
  taught, and with widening horizens their own sense
  of group unity will grow.
- The thought pattern of one-church-one-pastor is
  deeply rooted in our consciousness. As the leaders
  of the early church itinerated freely, so can we,
  and I'm convinced that a deep group consciousness
  will develop.
- A perfect Bible school will, of course, be impossible from the start. But even if imperfect, and
  even if our start is small and weak, if it is vital
  to our needs, it will gradually become more perfect.
- The main problem in this recommendation is
  "uniform." We need to respect the individual
  characteristics of the local churches.

THAT WE ESTABLISH [A] LAY BIBLE SCHOOL TO SUPPLEMENT
THE LAY TRAINING PROGRAMS ALREADY OPERATING IN ALL THE
CHURCHES. FURTHER, THAT WE APPOINT A COMMITTEE TO
PREPARE THE CURRICULUM, SELECT INSTRUCTORS, AND TAKE
RESPONSIBILITY FOR ALL PREPARATORY AND ADMINISTRATIVE
MATTERS, SO THAT THE SCHOOL CAN BE OPENED BY APRIL,
1970 (Decision 3, 1969:7-9).

THAT FROM NOW ON WE SEEK TO CHANGE THE STRUCTURE OF
THE CHURCH FROM ONE OF OVER-DEPENDENCE ON THE PASTOR
TO ONE EMPHASIZING THE PRIESTHOOD OF ALL BELIEVERS,
AND THAT AS ONE STEP IN THIS DIRECTION, WE ESTABLISH
A LAY BIBLE SCHOOL IN 1970, AND THAT WE PROVIDE A
CURRICULUM AND APPOINT INSTRUCTORS, DESIGNED TO HELP
INDIVIDUAL CHURCHES TOWARDS PERFECTION. FURTHER, THAT
WE CREATE A PREPARATORY COMMITTEE AND AIM TO BRING
THIS PROGRAM INTO OPERATION BY APRIL, 1970.

THAT THE LAY EVANGELISM FELLOWSHIP EMPHASIZE LAY
LEADERSHIP TRAINING, AND THAT THE BIBLE SCHOOL PRE-
PARATORY COMMITTEE ACT AS AN ADVISORY BODY TO THE LAY
EVANGELISM FELLOWSHIP (Decision 7, 1969:15).

*Laymen's Bible School Preparatory and Administration
Committee:*
    Yamada Takashi, Yanada Hiroshi, Katsuragi Takashi,
    P. Derksen, R. Ramseyer

Laymen's Handbook Preparation Committee: [Same
members as above]

1970 Budget (Education)

Laymen's Bible School[a]	60,000	[$167]
Lay Training Assistance[b]	30,000	[$ 83]
Lay Evangelism Fellowships[c]	40,000	[$111]
Laymen's Rally[d]	30,000	[$ 83]
Pastor's Library Fund[e]	60,000	[$167]
Laymen's Handbook[f]	20,000	[$ 56]
Contribution to T.C.C.[g]*	30,000	[$ 83]

[a] Preparatory comm., speaker itineration
[b] Assistance for all local church programs
[c] 10,000 yen X 4
[d] One rally
[e] For the purchase of new books by pastors
[f] Stipendium for writer, preparation, etc.
[g] Gift offering

* *Contribution to T.C.C.* - Is this item really
necessary in view of the direction we are
moving, namely away from the specialized
pastoral ministry?
- We cannot say that the specialized pastoral
ministry is not necessary.
- Well-trained pastors are necessary. I believe
future pastors should be encouraged to pursue at
least a regular university and seminary course.

- Perhaps we should pass this item this year and
do some more solid thinking about the important
problem of training pastors to meet our future
needs (1969:22-23).

According to the recent Church Conference decision,
the object of the Laymen's Training School is the
average layman, and the purpose is to raise the level
of the laymen, but at our committee meeting there was
a thorough discussion of these points. Especially
with regard to the purpose, it was strongly felt that
it did not have much meaning if it was merely to raise
the level of the laymen, and that we must rather aim
at training leaders.

With regard to the content of the teaching materials,
Bible doctrine, history, Christian ethics, sociology
and so on were taken up, but in order to make the content a little more concrete, it was decided to present
the following subjects and continue the discussion
again at the next meeting on the basis of the various
reports.

Yanada: prepare a manual on "How to Read the
          Bible" for the Lay Bible School
Ramseyer: prepare a manual on "Sociology" for the
          Lay Bible School
Derksen: prepare a manual on "Bible Interpreta-
          tion" for the Lay Bible School

There was discussion concerning the Mennonite history
section of the Laymen's Handbook. It was decided to
ask Yamada san to think about the content by the next
meeting (Lay Bible School Administration Committee,
December 12, 1969:1J).

1970   How goes the language study by this time? ...

At the last meeting of the committee planning curriculum for training of church members we decided to ask
you to take a little time off from this and give us a
little help in a rather far removed area. One of the
areas which we want to cover in training classes will
be a unit on Anabaptist-Mennonite origins and their
relevance to the church here in Japan. Pastor Yamada
is taking overall responsibility for this. However we
would like to ask you to write kind of an interpretive
article on the Anabaptists covering the period from

their beginning until about the time when the last of
the first generation leaders passed from the scene.
This would include background materials as to why the
Anabaptists arose. ... The idea is to make clear or
bring out what precisely the contribution of the Anabaptists is. ...

We would like to have this at the latest by the time
of the pastors' seminar in Tokyo the first week in
May. ...

Just remember that this is for lay church people here
in Japan. Whatever you think they ought to understand
about the Anabaptists will be fine (Robert Ramseyer to
author, February 20, 1970:1).

Needless to say, I was surprised to hear from you and
your committee. I really don't know any more about
this committee and its function than what you told me
in the letter. ... I had a lot of questions after I
read your letter. The main ones seemed to have to do
with how the material was to be used. Is it simply to
be translated into Japanese for the laymen to read?
Is it going to be a part of a text? Is it going to be
coordinated with some kind of workbook? You suggested
that it should be an "interpretive article" but I
wasn't sure how it was to be used. Anyway, you can
sense I'm sure that I am not quite clear on the whole
thing. ...

I appreciate your committee's vote of confidence in
asking me to write up something on the Anabaptists.
The only problem is, I just don't see how I could give
any time to it until our vacation in August. [Dr.]
Brannen made it quite clear that we are at school to
learn. We are not supposed to take on a lot of other
responsibilities. Right now I feel that number 1
priority is getting the language. ... If you can wait
until fall, I could try to get something out this
summer. But I have never had any course on the Anabaptists, and to write an "interpretive" article I
would want to do a lot more reading. I am wondering
though, if maybe there isn't something in print
already that could be used. Hokkaido [Mennonite Con-
ference] has a laymen's program. Have they written
anything? That might be the best bet if you want
something by the first week in May. I just don't see
how I could have anything ready by then (Author to
Robert Ramseyer, February 24, 1970:1).

Since there was communication from Mr. Sprunger, who was requested to write a brief history of the Anabaptists (mainly historical facts), to the effect that due to various circumstances he cannot comply with our request, we talked about other possible writers, but did not reach any conclusion. After this, there was an introduction somewhat as follows from the committee in charge concerning a recently published book (*The Anabaptists: Radicalists of the Religious Reformation Period* by Akira Demura, Publication Department of the United Church of Christ in Japan).

1. Because it is written from an objective point of view there are many things to make one think, especially for persons living within that tradition.
2. If the teachers would digest the contents and explain it in a suitable way, it could be used as a text for the Lay Bible School.

The first draft of the first chapter of the manual on "How to Read the Bible" was presented by the committee in charge. In this chapter, while touching on the literary nature and canonicity of the Bible, the question of, In what sense is the Bible the Word of God? is also spoken to. After the manuscript was read aloud, there was a rather heated exchange of opinions among the committee members concerning this approach.

As for chapter one, the plan is to mimeograph it by the next meeting without losing any time, including revision of some of the phraseology, distribute it for use in the Lay Bible School, and continue by beginning work on chapter two and following (Lay Bible School Administration Committee, March 5, 1970: 1J).

At the time of the recent MCC (Mennonite Central Committee) consultation meeting May 7, 1970, in Tokyo, we learned that in Hokkaido, Tokyo and so on translation of Bender's *Anabaptist Vision* and other basic literature is proceding. There was a growing feeling that from now on the introduction of Anabaptist related research and materials should be promoted within the wider Mennonite fellowship. ...

Part of the revised manuscript of the manual on "How to Read the Bible" was printed up and distributed by the committee in charge, and as the result of an

examination of the contents, it was decided to continue the work while trying to keep it simple enough
to understand.

The committee in charge of the "Sociology" manual
talked about the possibility of using the manuscript
of a previously worked out series of three lectures
(I. Man, Culture, Society; II. Anthropology and the
Proclamation of the Gospel; III. Bible and Sociology).
The committee desires that it be revised and a number
of corrections made so it can be used as a manual. As
there are a number of technical problems connected
with printing and publishing, there was no definite
conclusion at this time. With regard to the manuals
for "Biblical Interpretation" and "Methods of Teaching," the various committee members have been decided
on, but there was no special report (Lay Bible School
Administration Committee, May 30, 1970:1-2J).

Our aim for next year will again be "A greater harvest
through aggressive action by laymen."

A fund for the training and retraining of the professional clergy will be established. The executive
committee will work out details along the lines of our
discussion (Decisions 2,3, Annual Conference, October
1970:1).

It is thought that the Laymen's Handbook can be
finished within the year. As for the administration
committee, it is continuing the task of preparing
teaching materials. ...

- The whole year seems to have been spent in making
  adjustments within the committee.
- The main task of the committee was choosing the
  curriculum and the lecturers for the year.
- The main task of the committee was recognized as
  being important and it is good to have gotten it
  done.
- When a committee's work is done it is better to
  dissolve the committee.
- It is requested that all the assignments which
  have been made be completed.

The present members of the Lay Training Administration-
Laymen's Handbook Preparation Committee will continue
for 1971. These are Yamada, Yanada, Katsuragi,
Derksen, and Ramseyer (Decision 17, 1970:21J).

1971 Budget (Education)

Laymen's School	50,000	[$139]
Laymen's Training Aid	30,000	[$ 83]
Laymen's Handbook	20,000	[$ 56]
Aid to TCC	30,000	[$ 83]
Aid to Theological Students	100,000	[$278]

(1970:33-34J).

This brings us to the end of the minutes, letters, and reports bearing on the question, Whatever happened to our own school in 1970? As we have seen, from 1966 on the workers' retreats, pastors' seminars and so on continued to be held. Students also continued to go to Tokyo Christian College, although it was decided not to make it the only school we support and recommend to our students. In 1967 there was talk of having several types of pastors instead of only one. There was also considerable interest in lay training and the Kobayashi Laymen's Training School, and it was even suggested that it might become a model for the Conference.

In 1968, interest continued to run high in lay training on a local level, and there was also discussion of trying to start something at the conference level. This culminated in 1969 with a decision at the annual Church conference to establish a unified Lay Bible School to supplement the programs already operating in some of (not "all of," as the minutes imply) the churches. It was hoped to open the school in the spring of 1970, and a committee was appointed to make necessary preparations to that end. It was also decided to put together a Laymen's Handbook consisting of the Church Conference Constitution, the Conference Confession of Faith, and a brief introduction to Anabaptist-Mennonite history. Actually, the decision to prepare the handbook preceded the decision to open the school.

The committee that was appointed to carry out the above mentioned responsibilities met once in December 1969, and several times before the next conference in the fall of 1970. The committee felt the objective of the Lay Bible School should be not just training laymen, but training laymen to be leaders. It spent most of its time working out a basic curriculum and trying to get together some teaching materials. This was easier said than done. There were some others perhaps, like myself, who could not help them out at the time. Consequently, they had to try to find someone else to do a certain job. The objective was to start a Lay Bible School, but in fact, almost all the committee's efforts were put into curriculum and materials.

At the annual meeting in 1970, they reported that the Laymen's Handbook was expected to be finished by the end of the year. It was requested that any unfinished assignments be completed. It was decided that the same committee should continue for 1971. To the best of my knowledge, however, nothing more was ever done and the whole project was dropped almost as suddenly as back in 1963. It seems that even the Laymen's Handbook was never finished up. There is nothing more about the school in the minutes. As a case in point, at the Annual Conference in 1974 there were reports from the Executive Committee, the Publicity Committee, the Camp Committee, the Kindergarten Committee, the Bookstore Committee, reports from each of the churches, and discussion of future evangelism but there was nothing regarding the Lay Bible School. In fact, the only reference to "lay training" was in the budget for that year where 50,000 yen ($170) was budgeted for lay training, supposedly for any churches which wished to conduct something locally (JMCCC, February 1974:2).

As with the previous proposal in 1963, we have to ask about this one, what happened? What went wrong? Where was the breakdown? Was it the same as before? Could anything have been done about it? We saw earlier in the case of the 1963 school proposal that the main reason it failed apparently had to do with Mission-Church relationships. The pastors and the churches were not behind the missionary decision to begin a school. But we cannot say that here. For as you will remember, the Mission and the Church merged in 1964 to form a single organization. From that point on, all decisions were joint decisions. Therefore we cannot lay the blame on Church-Mission relationships this time.

The decision to begin a Lay Bible School was made jointly. It was a unanimous decision, with 13 voting for it and no one against it (JMCCC, Annual Conference, 1969:9). And it was made not only once, but twice! It was made first in connection with the need for training laymen. It was made again, at the same conference, in connection with a discussion about the possibility of restructuring the churches to get away from overdependence on the pastor to reemphasizing the priesthood of all believers. As we noted, a committee was also appointed to carry out the decision to begin the school. But while the committee began its work in earnest, after about a year it unexpectedly disappears from the scene. Once again we are caused to ask, what happened this time?

There were no doubt various factors behind its demise,
but according to a personal letter from Hiroshi Yanada (and
Robert Ramseyer), who were both members of the committee,

> There were two basic reasons, lack of enough input
> and theological disagreement. The one who was pushing
> the project most ... got interested in some other
> things. And he and a few other members ... could not
> reach agreement on some issues theologically. This is
> all we remember for sure (Yanada 1975:1).

Insufficient input and lack of theological agreement seem to
have been at least two of the factors involved in the
committee's downfall. There were also the problems of
curriculum, materials, teachers and the like. But one wonders if perhaps another reason it fell through this time was
that no one person had been appointed to be responsible to
see that the program was carried out. After the committee
felt it had finished its basic work, no one assumed the responsibility to carry the decision through to its completion.
In other words, the decision may have simply died a committee death. Such things have happened before. The Conference Executive Committee should have been the group responsible to see that the decision was actually carried out, but
in reading the minutes we see that from 1970 on they got
sidetracked with other matters, especially that of becoming
incorporated as a Religious Juridical Person, and had little
time or energy to give attention to much else.

As pointed out, at the yearly meeting in 1970, it was
decided that the same members of the Laymen's Bible School
Committee should continue for 1971. But that appears to be
the end of the matter. We have seen how during the year of
operation they ran into problems deciding on curriculum, and
on finding suitable teaching materials, that there was lack
of input and theological disagreement, but while these were
serious problems, they were not the only factors responsible
for the failure of the resolution. There is also the matter
of budgeting. In 1969, 60,000 yen ($167) was budgeted by
the Conference for 1970 for the Laymen's Bible School,
30,000 yen ($83) for lay training assistance, and 20,000 yen
($56) for the Laymen's Handbook, a total of 110,000 yen
($306). This was a little more than in previous years, but
not much. In 1967, for example, the budget for lay leadership training was 80,000 yen ($222). In 1968, it was the
same. In 1969, it was 85,000 yen ($236), excluding 15,000
yen ($42) for a S.S. teachers' rally. So for 1970, it was
only a total of about 25,000 yen ($70) more than the year

before, including the handbook. Without the handbook, it
was only 5,000 yen ($14) more! One wonders how serious the
decision was to begin a Lay Bible School with no more budget
than that.

Still, I do not think this was the main factor that
caused the proposal to fail. If there is any one reason why
it failed, I believe it was the fact that no one was ever
appointed as the responsible person to see that the decision
to begin a Bible school was followed through to completion.
If there had been some one person responsible for seeing
that the decision was actually carried out, it is quite
possible most of the other problems would have eventually
resolved themselves. But there was no built in accountability to ensure the success of the program. There may be
other opinions about this, but personally speaking, I feel
this was likely where the major breakdown occurred.

What would have happened if the school proposal had been
followed through on? That, of course, is purely a matter of
conjecture. The fact is, it was not. For the second time
within 10 years, a badly needed and carefully proposed
school never got off the ground. Like the first one, it
died before it was ever born. It would help us little to
speculate about what might have happened had it been carried
out. About all we can do at this point is try to summarize
the major problems that have been encountered in the training of pastors as well as laymen, and then move on to see if
there is not some way by which we might do better.

SUMMARY OF PROBLEMS THAT REMAIN TO BE SOLVED

What we want to do now is try to sum up the various
problems that we have encountered in this chapter. But
before that, there is one other matter that ought to be
clarified. So far we have been talking of training programs
without distinguishing too carefully between lay training
and leadership training programs. To some extent, of course,
we have made a distinction between them. For example, in
sections one and two we dealt primarily with the training of
pastors, that is, with leadership training. In sections
three and four, we dealt largely with the training of laymen,
that is, lay training. There is naturally a certain degree
of overlap between lay and leadership training. But for the
sake of clarity, I think it would be helpful to separate
them as we attempt to summarize the problems that need to be
resolved. And if we are thinking of leaders and leadership
training, the problems that we have faced and continue to
face today fall into roughly six categories.

First, the problem of testing a person's call. Most of the students we have sent off to school have gone with little or no practical experience in a church. Some of them have gone straight out of high school. And a number of them have undoubtedly been uncertain of their call. This has surely been a contributing factor to the numerous dropouts experienced by many churches and missions in Japan who have sent young people away to study. It has been not only a serious loss to the church, it has meant a needless losing of face for many students, for it has become obvious that some of them were never called to the ministry to begin with. This is a problem not only for the churches, but also for the schools. For as we saw in the Church's Annual Conference minutes of several years ago, it was noted that

> The school [TCC] strongly recommends that local churches confirm the call to service claimed by new applicants. It is seen as highly desirable that students have a preparatory period of service (at least one year) in local churches to test their call (JMCCC, 1969:2).

Second, the problem of support while in school. This has been a problem from the beginning, as evidenced by the minutes, reports, and letters. As a result, parents, churches, and the Conference have tried to help as much as possible. But even with the aid they have gotten in this way, most students have had to work part time to help cover their expenses at school. This has meant less time for study, which is why they went to school in the first place. And it has made it almost impossible for families, that is, married men who feel called to the ministry, to leave and go to school somewhere with their families. One or two have done it, but it has been difficult. Interestingly enough, however, when the pastors were asked in a questionnaire what the most difficult problem was they faced when they were in school, not one of them mentioned finances. (See Appendix I for the Pastor Questionnaire.) Perhaps things are better now and they have forgotten what it was like before. But the references cited earlier make it clear that many students had to work, and finding a proper balance between work and study was a big problem.

Third, the problem of undesirable influences. By this is meant mostly teaching influences, although this problem does not seem to have been as serious as some of the others. And this does not necessarily reflect on any particular school. It is something that could happen anywhere, in denominational

as well as interdenominational schools. But one area, for
example, in which there seems to have been considerable
influence is in the concept of the church. Students have
absorbed a very traditional view of the church and its
ministry. This has probably taken place more or less unconsciously, on part of both the teacher and the student, but
it has nonetheless had a definite impact on our work.
Related to this is the fact that the students did not get
exposed to Anabaptist-Mennonite studies in school, which
might have served as something of a corrective. That is no
doubt due in part to the fact that there has been no
Mennonite on the faculty of the various schools to which
our students have gone. This problem of influences is
largely a matter of emphasis. For instance, one of the
pastors mentioned that for him the most difficult problem
when he was in school was an "imbalance between the intellectual, spiritual, and practical training." As said before,
these influences were likely unconscious rather than intentional, but still they were there.

Fourth, the problem of not coming back. This has been
one of our most serious problems. It is part of the reason
we are short of pastors. As we have seen, four of the first
five students we sent away did not even finish school.
Later on, too, others dropped out, some went abroad to study,
and a few decided to serve non-Mennonite churches. Their
education was subsidized by the Mennonite churches while
they were in school, but after graduation, for various reasons, because of greater opportunities and so on, they did
not return to serve the churches from which they came. This
has naturally been a disappointment to the churches, but
actually, we have not lost as many pastors this way as I
thought when I first began the study.

According to a questionnaire sent out to the churches,
about 10 or 11 pastors have come out of the churches, and of
those, about seven of them are still pastors, and six of
those seven are serving our churches. In other words, about
50 percent of the pastors who have come out of the churches
are serving the churches, which may not be such a bad record
after all. In fact, considering that several of the pastors
who came out of the churches are not pastors anymore, one
would have to say it is indeed a good record. The loss due
to non-return may not be as great as sometimes imagined.
Two of the pastors are even serving their home churches.
There are many others, of course, who went off to Bible
school but did not finish or become pastors and are doing
something else. In a letter from Donald Hoke, former president of Tokyo Christian College, he states that

> ... as far as students from the General Conference
> Mennonite churches, we have record of eleven men and
> four women having graduated from the College. Probably
> another 50 percent greater number have enrolled for
> study without graduating (1975b:1).

This would seem to confirm my own findings. There are three
or four students in Bible school or seminary now, but
whether they will come back or not remains to be seen. In
any case, rather than lamenting the shortage of pastors, it
seems to me we should consider ourselves fortunate to have
as many pastors as we do under the circumstances.

Fifth, the problem of readjusting to their own society.
As we have just pointed out, there were some who did not
return. On the other hand, adjustment was a big problem for
those who did. Even though it had been hard making ends
meet in school, it could be doubly difficult if a student
got married, returned to a small church, and had to live on
what the church could supply. Most of the pastors could not
be adequately supported and had to do part-time work. But
that was something of a problem, too, for most of them were
expected to be full-time pastors and had given up their
secular jobs when they had become pastors. If they went to
Bible school right out of high school, they had not had time
to learn a trade or special skill, so many of them were
limited to tutoring pupils in English, math, or some other
subject they had taken in school.

But another adjustment for them, and for their people,
was that they were expected to be the "*sensei*," the learned
teacher, at age 22 or 23! The adjustments were not easy.
Reentry could be a traumatic experience. It was hard for
young men trained in the city to find they were not really
trained for ministry in the country, or elsewhere for that
matter. One result is that today the pastors are encouraging young men to first get a university education if they
can, then go on to Bible school or seminary. Or instead of
university, to go to Bible school, and then on to seminary.
This advice no doubt grows out of some of their own training
and experience as pastors.

Sixth, the problem of continuing education. Education is
highly treasured in Japan. And while the schools the
pastors went to were undoubtedly good schools, most of them
were undergraduate schools rather than graduate schools.
They were Bible schools rather than seminaries. Consequently, the pastors seem to feel a need for further study.

One of them has taken his university work by correspondence,
by spending several summers in Tokyo and studying at home.
But it is difficult for a man with a family to go back to
school, even if he wants to. For many, financially, it is
impossible. Yet there is a desire to continue their education.

From the questionnaire which the pastors filled out, we
learn that three of the six pastors have had Bible school
only; one has had Bible school and some university; one has
had university and seminary both; and one is self-educated,
not having had any formal schooling beyond high school, but
having taught and observed some classes for several months
as a churchman-in-residence at the Mennonite Biblical
Seminary (AMBS) in the United States. Of the five who went
to school, only one of them felt his education was adequate
for his work. The other four said it was not. And when
asked if they would like to continue their education, all
five of them said Yes. (As this is being rewritten three of
them have done so already for a year each, also at the
Mennonite Seminary, under a new "Overseas Church Leaders
Study-Service Program," sponsored by the General Conference
Mennonite Church.) The sixth one said he is "always studying." There is a definite interest in furthering their
education, and this, like the other needs, ought to be met.

Another problem we have had is what to do with someone
who feels called to the ministry, but because of job or
family or failure to meet entrance requirements cannot leave
home and go away to school. This brings us to the matter of
laymen and lay training.

We have seen how various attempts have been made at
training laymen, but we have also seen that there is little
if any lay training being done at present, at least not
formally. In fact, there is less lay training being done
today than there was 20 years ago, when the spring Bible
schools were held from 1957-1959. It was about the same
time, in 1960, when over 1,000 people were enrolled in the
Bible correspondence courses! That, of course, was primarily for unbelievers rather than believers, but that too
was eventually discontinued. So there is not much if anything formal being offered at the moment in the way of
training for laymen. This might not be so regrettable if
all of the churches had pastors, and adequate pastoral care.
But the fact is, they do not. To look at the situation this
way, however, is to view it negatively. That is, that we
are short of leaders. It seems to me we might do better to

look at it positively. In other words, we need to recognize
not only the fact that we are short of leaders, but that
there are a large number of potential lay leaders in the
churches.

When we were considering the various lay training programs in the churches, the churches reported that there were
about four or five people in each church who were considered
potential lay leaders. This means that there are 40 or more
such people within the ten churches! Which suggests that
the statement that we are short of leaders may be something
of a myth -- unless we think only in terms of pastors and
missionaries as being leaders. If we think in terms of full-
time national pastors, then it is true we are short of
leaders. But is there really a shortage of leaders? It all
depends what you mean by "leader." If mature laymen can be
considered as leaders, then there are a tremendous number of
potential leaders in the churches already, and this *regardless of the size of the congregation.* Whether a church had
15 or 50 members, it was said there were a few such leaders
within each group. That in itself may be highly significant as to the kind of leaders we need and where to begin.
For the leaders are there, if we can see them. The problem
is not that we are short of leaders. We are simply short of
trained leaders. The leaders are right there, inside the
churches themselves, and more than anything else we need to
tap this potential.

To illustrate this a little more clearly, in May of 1974
a questionnaire was distributed to church members. (See
Appendix H for the Church Member Questionnaire.) One of the
questions asked was whether or not they had ever participated in a lay training program, not counting Bible study,
women's meetings and so on. Of the 115 responses, only 13
said they had. Of these 13, as might be expected, nine
were from Kobayashi, which had a rather extensive lay training program several years ago. This was about two-thirds of
the respondents from that particular church. Three others
were from Miyazaki, which also has done some lay training.
One was from Aburatsu, which also has had a little along
that line. But those 13 were only slightly over 10 percent
of the total. Almost 90 percent have had no formal lay
training whatsoever. There may be others in the churches
who have had some training, but did not answer the questionnaire. Likely there are. There were two or three who had
studied in lay training programs elsewhere, one as far away
as Hokkaido. There was another who had studied in a small
Bible school in Kyushu for about three years. But these

were exceptions, and I believe the survey is quite representative of the overall pattern in the churches.

The 115 who replied made up just over 50 percent of the
229 present active members. In one church, the response was
a little less than 25 percent of the believers. In another,
it was over 90 percent. In most cases it was about 50 percent. Thirty-eight of the total number were men, 77 were
women. Fifty-four were single, 57 married, and in four
cases it was not clear if they were married or not. Twenty-
eight or almost half of those married said their partner was
also Christian, so there are many Christian families represented also, although there may be some overlapping here.
Occupations ranged from housewives to nurses, students to
teachers, farmers to pharmacists, bill collectors to bookstore workers, mushroom raisers to market researchers, and
company employees to the unemployed. As said, I feel this
is quite a representative sample of church members. Perhaps
a simple diagram of the age spread (Figure 2.2) will help to
visualize the potential a little more.

Figure 2.2

CHURCH MEMBER AGE SPREAD

Age:

Age	
66+	2
56–65	15
46–55	28
36–45	14
26–35	29
15–25	27

Look at the tremendous potential! Between the ages of 26
and 65 are eighty-six people. And those are from only about
half of the active church membership. Surely some of these
would have leadership gifts. Surely some of these would
like to be trained. Surely there must be an effective way
to train them. In light of this, to say that we are short
of leaders is to overlook the tremendous lay potential
within the churches. Part of the reason for so often tend-
ing to do so may be the distinction commonly made between

laymen and pastors. Might it not be helpful to make a distinction such as pastors and lay pastors, full time and part
time, professional and nonprofessional, or something like
that, or do away with the term "leader" altogether?

In any case, any training program that might be established in the future must try to solve not only the problems
connected with the training of pastors, but seek to tap
potential lay leaders within the church itself. Attempts
that have been made to that end were good. But too many of
the laymen were left untouched. The programs benefited only
the churches which held them. It is hard to see how the job
could be done by any one church alone. The churches need to
work at this together. What is needed is a program which
grows out of all the churches to meet the needs of all the
churches. Any such program must promote the continuing
education of the present pastors; it must prepare for the
training of future pastors; and it must provide for the
training of lay leaders as well. In short, if it is to be
effective, it must deal with both the problems that have
been encountered in exporting men to the city, and experimenting with lay training at home.

Is there any model, then, which might help us to formulate a program to meet the specific needs of our churches?
I believe there is, and that one solution may lie in the
recent efforts made in the area of Theological Education by
Extension, better known as TEE. We want to take a look at
TEE in the next chapter. In so doing, we will be turning
our attention from problems to possibilities, to see what
has been found successful elsewhere, and what might apply to
us if we were to try to formulate a program of our own.

3

Theological Education by Extension as a Model Leadership Training Program

"Theological Education by Extension" has been called "the most significant development in theological education in the Twentieth Century" by Milton Baker of the Conservative Baptist Foreign Mission Society (Winter 1969:139). But what is it that makes TEE so significant? How is it different from traditional theological education? How might it help us solve some of the problems we face?

Actually, as a method, Theological Education by Extension is just what it says it is. It is a program of theological education, just like you would find in a Bible school or seminary. But in contrast to the traditional method of study where the student goes to the school, in TEE the school comes to the student. Indeed, one of the first articles written about TEE was entitled, "This Seminary Goes to the Student" (Winter 1966). The school goes to the student by means of the professor, who meets in person once a week or so with the student. In other words, with TEE, a genuine theological education program is extended to where the student lives and works. The student is thus afforded an opportunity to receive theological training without having to go away to a school to study. This type of study takes place largely when and where a student is free, and the student can proceed at his own pace.

Now lest this sound like a rather haphazard way of study, it should be pointed out it has been done for years already in secular fields with considerable success. It is, to be sure, a rather recent innovation in the field of theological

education. But while TEE involves some new methods of study, it is far more than mere methodology. One of the reasons it is so significant is that "The extension approach to theological education is focused primarily on the men that are, in fact, serving the church" (Ward and Rowen 1972:22). That is, its great significance lies in the fact that it makes it possible to reach more of the real leaders of the church.
In any case, in this chapter we want to take a look at
   where it all began,
      some of the concepts that underlie it,
         how it actually works, and
            how the movement has become a worldwide phenomenon.

A NEW BEGINNING IN GUATEMALA

Guatemala is a small country located in Central America. Many people, like myself, would probably have to look at a map to see exactly where it is. In area it is only slightly larger than the state of Ohio, but it should not be judged by that, for as we say, "Great things have small beginnings." And the beginning of the whole TEE movement, which has grown so rapidly, took place in the little country of Guatemala back in 1963. Much of the information which follows is taken from an article called "The Presbyterian Seminary in Guatemala Three Years Later, 1966" (Winter 1969:86ff.), by James H. Emery, who, along with Ralph D. Winter, was one of the pioneers of Theological Education by Extension.

The Presbyterian Church has been working in Guatemala for about 80 years. They have 65 or so churches, and perhaps twice that many mission congregations, with a total membership of around ten thousand. Since 1938, the Presbyterians have had a seminary, the Evangelical Presbyterian Seminary, in Guatemala City, the capital, to prepare leaders for their churches. The enrollment, however, has not been very great, averaging only six to 20 students per year up until about 1960. Students came from both city and country, although the majority of them have been from the country. The Presbyterians have also had a rural training program, where students studied at home, followed by an examination upon completion of their studies. So some of the leaders in the Presbyterian Church have been trained in the seminary, and others locally. The seminary was able to meet the needs of the urban churches fairly well. But most of the Presbyterian churches are rural, and as indicated, most of the students have come from the rural areas. One of the problems they have had is that many of the rural students do not want to return home after graduation. The result is that there has been a chronic shortage of leaders, especially in the rural churches, and the real leaders were not being reached. There were "churches without pastors" and "pastors without churches."

In order to remedy this situation, it was decided in 1960 to move the seminary to a rural area, in hopes of solving some of the problems they had. So the seminary was moved to the small town of San Felipe, about 200 kilometers (125 mi.) from the capital. A couple of residences, a dorm, and a dining hall which also served as a classroom were all constructed. This put the school more or less in the geographical center of the largest concentration of their churches. It was hoped this move would make it easier for the rural students who wished to enroll to come to seminary. To everyone's surprise, however, they soon learned that rural students could not come even that far to go to school. Prospective students were mostly married, had jobs and families, and simply could not afford to leave home to go to school -- even just a few miles. So ingenuity was once again called for, and those responsible decided that if the students could not come to where the school was, then the school would have to go to where the students were.

The new program, then, initiated in 1963, was in essence a decentralization of the seminary. About 10 extension centers were set up, anywhere from 13 to 240 kilometers (8 to 150 mi.) from the school. The centers were usually church buildings, and each one had a small library. About once a week a professor or two would go to teach at each of the extension centers, and meet with their students. One teacher could generally handle several weekly meetings. The number of teachers has varied from about six to 12, with roughly half of them being missionaries and the other half nationals. The extension program was an extension of the seminary, but the residential program also continued as before, with up to about a dozen students. Classes still met at the central school three days a week, but the seminary now had both a residential and an extension program. Two days a month, all of the students, both extension and resident, came together at the seminary for a monthly meeting. This meeting was used for exams, sports, special lectures and so on. But it gave the extension students the feeling that they were also a part of the school. The seminary payed the student's travel to the monthly meeting, but the student bought his own books and payed a small fee for each course.

The extension students, just like those in residence, followed the regular curriculum which consisted of 15 year-long courses. The only difference was that it generally took the extension students longer to complete the whole program. A resident student, for example, could complete the program in three years by studying full time and taking five courses a year. But an extension student, who would probably be studying only part time, might take anywhere from three to 15 years, or even longer, to finish the program. But this was not especially a big concern, for the aim was to try to reach more of the real leaders of the church, even if it took longer. The attempt was made to reach students when and where they were free, and to let them study at their own speed. This might include nights, weekends, or vacations. In other words, they tried to start with the student rather than the school. And the results speak for themselves. F. Ross Kinsler, another one of the trio who pioneered TEE, reports that under the old program, there had been only five resident students in 1962. But when the new extension program was begun, enrollment jumped from 5 to 50 in 1963, 88 in 1964, 90 in 1965, and 143 in 1966 (Winter 1969:117).

As might be expected, with any new program of this nature, there were bound to be some problems. One of these was that because student-teacher contact was so infrequent, the students had to study at home. Each course required about one hour a day of home study. But many students were not prepared for this, and it was difficult for them to use traditional textbooks. This made it necessary to prepare some workbooks to use with the textbooks, or self-study materials that the student could use at home. Some of these took the form of semi-programmed texts, that is, texts that were geared for self study. But getting suitable materials was one of the biggest problems they had to begin with.

Another problem that came up was how to meet the needs of students who came from such varied backgrounds, socially and academically. There were numerous Indian subcultures on the one hand, and Spanish-speaking Ladinos on the other. There were students from the city, and those from the country. There were junior high graduates and university graduates. For some who wished to study it was even necessary to provide "pre-theological" training in order to meet the sixth grade entrance requirement. This great diversity meant that it was impossible to try to teach everyone on the same level, because it would be too high for some and too low for others. It also meant that not only did they have to

prepare new materials, but it was necessary to prepare them
on several different levels. That is how the program became
multi-level, four levels in all, with different diplomas for
each of the different levels. But this development also
made it possible for a person to start on a lower level, and
later on upgrade his education simply by meeting the additional requirements for the next level. This would include
those who were already serving as pastors. Anyway, these
were just a few of the problems they had to work out as they
went along.

At the same time, there were also some "unexpected dis-
coveries," as Winter calls them, which are summarized
briefly as follows (1969:308-309):

1. Students and faculty they had never noticed before
   popped out of nowhere.
2. They were able to reach higher as well as lower
   academic levels than before.
3. They could train men right where they were, in their
   own environment.
4. Extension studies gathered men who had both talent
   and personal discipline.
5. There were more young men than ever, despite a higher
   average age.
6. The curriculum was the same, but the new students did
   better work.
7. The program cost far less per student.
8. With no increase in personnel or funds, enrollment
   increased from 7 to 200+.
9. Extension studies can also handle students not studying for ordination.
10. Extension studies take longer, but keep a man study-
    ing seriously.
11. Students can teach laymen, and potentially reach any
    laymen in the church.
12. There is the possibility of sharing weekly meetings
    with other denominations.

It has been over 15 years now since the Guatemala experiment began. In the early stages, there were some critics
who were opposed to it because they were afraid it might
lead to "degrading the ministry," or "closing the seminary"
and the like. But as it became clear that such fears really
had no foundation, and the church became convinced of the
program's value, it was there to stay. At the time it may
have seemed like an insignificant experiment, but the idea
has really caught on and today there are literally thousands

of students all around the world getting their theological education by extension. Exactly what shape TEE may take in the future is hard to say, but it is with gratitude that we may look back to those who pioneered and promoted it.

TEE IN THEORY

Next we want to look at TEE as a concept, at some of the thinking underlying it. As we have already seen, however, it did not begin as a concept but rather with a need. It is said that "Necessity is the mother of invention," and in this case, it was certainly true. TEE did not begin originally as a theoretical study. It was instead the response to an urgent need. The extent of that need, not only in Guatemala but throughout Latin America, is brought out by Winter in an article written several years after the movement began. He says:

> In Latin America there are by the latest estimates 74,953 Protestant congregations. Since there are an average of at least two (perhaps three) "preaching points" for each of these congregations, this means there are a minimum of 150,000 men of pastoral gifts, probably 90% of which seriously lack further training. But if only 100,000 of them need ministerial training, this is a massive, urgent challenge. To meet this challenge, there are sixty seminaries with a total enrollment of one thousand plus 300 Bible institutes with a total enrollment of some 12,000. Even assuming these students were all to become pastors, or better still, were mainly men in the group of 100,000 who are already on the job, we would still be backlogged for fifteen years in meeting the need by conventional methods. And this assumes that the movement would stand still, needing no more pastors than it needs right now (1967a:13).

But while TEE began as the practical response to a pressing need, there are certain basic concepts or presuppositions that underlie it. These have perhaps not been spelled out in detail, but nevertheless I believe they are there, and would like to attempt to elaborate on what several of them are.

First, there is the conviction that churches need adequate leadership. This could perhaps be left unsaid, as it underlies not only TEE but all theological training. And yet, I think it needs to be mentioned because it was one of

the reasons behind the development of TEE. As we have
already noted, there were many churches without adequate
leadership. There were churches without pastors. There
were pastors with little or no training. There existed a
tremendous need for more and better trained leaders, a need
which the traditional schools simply could not meet. What
those schools were doing was good, but it was not enough.
This is not in any way a judgment on such schools or on
those who have received training at such schools and are
already in the ministry, faithfully serving churches. But
the simple fact was and is that in many situations there is
an enormous shortage of trained leaders, especially pastors
-- pastors needed to shepherd flocks of believers, pastors
needed to combat heresy, pastors needed to preach, teach,
and baptize. It was out of this desire that not only some
but all churches have adequate leadership that TEE emerged.

Second, there is the belief that leadership is a gift.
We have already stated that the church needs leaders, but
this raises the question, where do these leaders come from?
What is it that makes a person a leader? How does a leader
differ from a non-leader? To begin with, the word "leader"
itself suggests that not everyone is a leader. Some are
leaders and some are followers. The Bible would seem to
affirm this inference. To be sure it says in I Corinthians
12:7, in speaking of spiritual gifts, that "To each is given
the manifestation of the Spirit for the common good." The
implication is that each person has a gift, and Paul goes on
to enumerate some of those gifts in verses 8 to 11. But at
the end of the chapter, in verses 27 to 31, he implies that
not everyone has the same gift. Some are "apostles," some
are "prophets," some are "teachers" and so on -- but not all.
While everyone has a gift, not everyone has a leadership
gift. There are a great variety of gifts. In addition to
those mentioned in I Corinthians 12, there are those in
Romans 12:3-8, and others listed in Ephesians 4:11-12. It
is especially in this latter passage that Paul sums up what
we might call the leadership gifts:

> And his gifts were that some should be apostles, some
> prophets, some evangelists, some pastors and teachers,
> for the equipment of the saints, for the work of
> ministry, for building up the body of Christ, ...

It would seem from this then that while all Christians are
given gifts, not all are given the gift of leadership. Not
all believers are leaders. Each one has a gift, but God
calls people to different ministries, and when He calls them

He gives them the necessary gift to carry out that particular ministry. Leadership is only one of these gifts, yet the Bible makes it plain that churches do need leaders, and that God gives the Church the leaders it needs.

Third, there is the concern that many leadership gifts are not being developed. That is, in addition to the pastors and other leaders we already have, there are many potential leaders within congregations whose gifts have not even been discovered, let alone developed. Many gifts are being overlooked. Many gifts are not being used. This is not necessarily intentional. It is more due to a misunderstanding of spiritual gifts. Part of the reason for this situation is also no doubt the existence in most places of a professional ministry. Where there is a professional ministry, people tend to think more in terms of the gifts their leaders have rather than their own. They expect their leaders to be gifted, and to make full use of their gifts. But they are apt to forget that "to each is given the manifestation of the Spirit," and that while not all of them will have leadership gifts, there are no doubt some others in their congregation who do.

Like Paul's reminder to Timothy to "rekindle the gift of God that is within you" (II Tim. 1:6), perhaps that is what is needed here. To the extent to which we neglect to do that, the church suffers. It is a loss to the individual, and to the church, for all gifts are given "for the common good." This means that if some of these latent leadership gifts within the congregation were developed, it might go a long way toward solving the leadership problem. There are undoubtedly many people within the church whose gifts have never been tapped. They may be young or they may be old, but whoever they are, something must be done to try to help them discover and develop their gifts. Many gifts, of course, have already come to light, but we must recognize the fact that there may be many more to be uncovered and used.

Fourth, there is the recognition that training must be added to these gifts. The gifts are already there. God has put them there. But in order to develop and use the gifts as God intended them to be used, some training may be beneficial. Traditionally, we have sent young men off to seminary for training, without necessarily having evidenced any gifts. As time goes on, it becomes clear that some have leadership gifts and some do not. We expect the school to train the students to be leaders. The problem is, it is difficult to do if the student does not already have a leadership gift. In many cases, students graduate from seminary and take churches without ever having demonstrated that they have any leadership gifts. TEE, on the other hand, suggests that "Learning is more easily added to gifts than gifts to learning" (Winter 1969:388), that it is easier to add "training to gifts" than "gifts to training."

C. Peter Wagner, an extension advocate, points out that

> Theological educators are now coming to recognize that the task of the seminary is not to *make* leaders. ... The calling of the seminary is to *train* the leaders that God has already made (Covell and Wagner 1971:7).

This is also partly the task of the pastor. He is to "equip the saints for the work of ministry." His gift is an enabling one. He is to help others discover and develop their own gifts for the good of the church. His own gift is but one among many. Theological training then, whether it takes place in a seminary or the local church, should become more and more "gift-centered." As J. Allen Thompson, General Director of the East Indies Mission puts it, "The church will progress more through a formally untrained, but gifted ministry than through a formally trained, but ungifted ministry. The desired goal is to have a trained gifted ministry" (Winter 1969:273).

Fifth, there is the idea that the best way to add training to gifts is by extension. Actually, most students who would fall into the category of extension students really have little choice between studying in residence or by extension. Most of them are married, have jobs, families, homes, and other responsibilities, which they could not leave to go to school even if they wanted to. Thus they really do not have much choice about the place of study. But even if they did, it is felt by the followers of extension that this is probably the most effective way to train such people.

There are many reasons for feeling this way. One of them is simply that it keeps the person in his environment. It avoids the problem of someone going away to school, and when he comes back, not fitting in anymore. A man is not separated from his people. Another thing is that the student is required to immediately put into practice what he learns. This is, of course, one of the weaknesses of traditional theological education, where the training is largely "pre-service" rather than "in-service" as with extension. In extension, a person has an opportunity to apply what he learns as he goes along. The theoretical and practical aspects are integrated. It has been well said, "The best training for ministry is training in ministry" (Winter 1969:497). One more advantage of this type of education is that it reaches more of the real leaders of the church. It reaches men who are already the natural leaders of the group, the "elders" of the church. As Winter has noted, "the Extension Seminary ... is designed to train those men whose gifts come to light in the normal dynamics of the local fellowship of believers" (1969:386). For most of these people, education by extension is not only the best way to train them. It is probably the only way they will ever be trained.

Sixth, there is the confidence that an extension education is just as good as a residence education. Such a statement is not meant to depreciate in any way the contribution of residential schools. It is not intended to suggest that those who have received their education at such schools received an inferior education. The proponents of TEE also recognize the importance of residential schools. For any kind of specialized research, for training professors and scholars and theologians, residence schools are indispensible. In fact, without residence schools or some authority to relate to, it would be impossible to have extension programs. But it must also be kept in mind that one of the greatest needs of our day is not for more professors, but for more pastors, and that traditional seminaries are not and cannot meet that need sufficiently.

This is where extension comes in. It extends the school to where the student is. It gives him or her a chance to get theological training without going away. It also makes it possible to offer theological education on several different levels, rather than just one. In most cases, the level of training would be exactly the same as that received at the school. In others, it may be somewhat lower, depending on a person's academic background. But while there may not always be a formal equivalence in every case, extension can at least provide a man with a functionally equivalent education. It can teach him what he needs to know.

Those already in the ministry can also raise the level of their education if they so desire. Extension education is extremely flexible. It can train "tentmakers" or full-time pastors. It can reach more of the real leaders of the church. It can meet the needs of both city and country churches. But as said before, it does not seek to compete with more traditional schools. It rather seeks to complement them. And although TEE is an extension of a residential seminary or Bible school program, it is in no way inferior to it. In fact, indications so far are that education by extension is every bit as good as or better than education in residence.

These then are some of the concepts underlying the entire TEE movement -- churches need adequate leadership; leadership is a gift; many leadership gifts are not being developed; training must be added to these gifts; the best way to add training to gifts is by extension; and, an extension education is just as good as a residence education.

TEE IN PRACTICE

Up to this point we have explored the beginnings of TEE, and also some of the theory which lies behind it. What we want to do now is take a look at how it actually works. But before we do that, perhaps it should be mentioned that TEE can take many forms. There is no one way of best doing TEE. There are many ways.

There are also many definitions of TEE. It can be defined in broad or in narrow terms. Ralph Winter, for example, states that "Any method that allows a person to continue as a member of society, earning his support, is an extension method, by our definition" (1969:389). That would not necessarily be TEE, but he does go on to say, in another article, that "The simplest possible situation is where an existing institution opens up an Extension Center in its same building " (1969:437). Wayne C. Weld, however, author of *The World Directory of Theological Education by Extension*, does not include "short term courses and evening schools which depend largely on the lecture method" in his survey. He says that the term

"Extension" is reserved for those programs in which the student masters and applies the subject content during the week and meets with a professor and other students periodically for sharing and discussion (1973:74).

Winter defines TEE broadly; Weld, narrowly. There is also some debate as to whether TEE can exist without an institution or not. Some seem to feel it might, and others are not so sure.

In light of these various definitions, I would like to add another, not to confuse things any further, but hopefully to clarify the kind of program we are talking about. As TEE represents a very distinctive kind of education, it would seem fitting that we define it accordingly. Therefore I would like to propose that we define TEE as *the geographical extension of the program of a recognized theological training institution.* (By "recognized" is meant an institution which is recognized at least within theological circles, and that would qualify a person to go on to more advanced levels of training if so desired. This is apart from any additional recognition which an institution may or may not have from the government.) That is, TEE involves basically two things. The first is the existence of a recognized theological training institution. The second is the geographical extension of the program of that institution. The institution could be a Bible school, a seminary, an institute of some sort, but whatever it is, unless it extends itself geographically, I do not feel we are justified in calling it TEE. This may seem like a rather arbitrary definition to some, and to a certain degree it is. But for the sake of a working definition of the kind of program we are thinking about, I believe it would be helpful to define TEE as suggested above. We will hence be assuming this definition throughout our study.

While there may be different definitions and different forms of TEE, the average TEE program would have a number of characteristics in common. One of these would be extension centers. As we have said, TEE is an extension of a recognized institution. The institution sponsors the program, and serves as the headquarters. But while there is this base institution, according to our definition, the only way it can conduct a TEE program is by geographically extending itself. The distance is not so important. It might be ten kilometers or it might be a thousand. What is important is that the program of the institution be extended to where the student lives and works.

The extension center is simply the place where the extension classes meet. It might be a church, a school, a rented room somewhere. But wherever it is, it represents the school. It is just as if the school were there, or the student were at the school. And as some schools reportedly do, it is probably a good idea to put a sign above the

entrance of the extension center to remind the student that
when he enters that door, it is as if he were entering the
school itself. Depending on the size of the program, a
school might have few centers, or many. But in order for
the type of program we are talking about to exist, there
must be one or more extension centers away from the school.
An extension center is usually located where it is most convenient for the majority of the students.

An extension center does not require extensive facilities.
About all that is really needed is a room that is suitable
for classes to meet in. A center also usually contains a
small library for students to use. The main library, of
course, is located at the sponsoring institution. Someone
is also needed to coordinate the program, and he or she is
usually called the director of the extension center. It is
this person's responsibility to arrange classes, secure
teachers, register students, keep track of attendance, pay-
ments, tests, credits and any other necessary records. In
short, the director acts as a middleman between the school
and the extension center. It could be a pastor, missionary,
or someone specially appointed to the task, but whoever the
person is, he is responsible to oversee the whole program.
In many cases, this might be only a part-time position, or
could possibly be the same person as the teacher, depending
on the size of the center. But someone must take care of
such mundane matters, and see that everything runs smoothly.
There may be cases, however, where it is felt that a
director is unnecessary.

One of the most important components of the extension
center we have not even talked about yet, and that is the
extension student himself. No school can operate for long
without students, and TEE is no exception. But since the
school is extended to the student, and the student is not
compelled to go off to the school, the chances are that it
can reach many more students this way. Just as a residence
program is open to anyone who can meet the entrance requirements, so an extension program also is open to anyone
interested in serious study. One of the differences,
though, between residence and extension studies, is in the
kind of students attracted to an extension program. The
traditional seminary generally gets students who are young,
unmarried, and inexperienced. In an extension program, on
the other hand, the average student tends to be older,
married and with a family, and have experience in both
secular work and church work. In short, students studying
by extension are as a rule more mature than those in

residence programs. Their motivation may also be higher if
they are actually in service and have a clear-cut call to
the ministry, which resident students often lack. Even
those who do not especially feel called to the ministry will
no doubt do their best to prepare themselves for responsibilities they may already have in the church.

Since an extension program is part of an institution,
classes taken by extension are basically the same as those
taken in residence. Extension classes are part of the same
curriculum, have the same content, requirements, credits,
and may follow the same school year as residence classes.
The school sets the standards for extension work, just as it
does for residence work. The standards are the same. Extension work is recognized just like residence work. Both
programs are fully accredited by the school. The only
difference is that in extension, the learning takes place
away from the campus. Classes are less frequent, and the
student must do most of his study at home. Since each
course requires an hour or so of homework a day, it means
that the student must discipline himself.

Another difference is that whereas a resident student may
take five courses at a time, an extension student will
likely take only one or two, depending on how much free time
he has. If he could study full time, as the resident student does, he could conceivably complete the course of
studies in the same amount of time. The extension student,
however, as he is probably working while he studies, will
usually take longer to finish. If the program consists of
a total of 45 courses, and a student takes only one course
a term, with three terms a year, it would take him 15 years
to finish.

But even though it might take longer, it keeps the student studying, and allows him the opportunity to apply what
he learns. In fact, there are those like educator George
Patterson who make a strong plea for an "obedience-oriented
education," that is, one in which priority is given to
actually doing the commands of Christ as the heart of training, with doctrine, history and other matters being built
around that. The possibilities of "student-workers" being
used to multiply churches through the creation of "extension
chains" (mother-daughter-granddaughter churches) is seen too
as an integral part of such a setup (1978:1-19). But with
extension it is also possible to offer special courses a
student or students might be interested in, as well as
seminars or concentrated courses. Or it is even conceivable

that a student may want to move back and forth between
extension and resident studies. In any case, the method
would allow for such an option.

One of the distinct features of extension education is
that courses can be taught on different levels. That is, a
typical residence program usually operates on a single
level. But an extension program can function at more than
one level, depending on a person's educational background.
In other words, courses can be taken at different levels.
One level might be for junior high graduates, another for
high school graduates, and a third for university graduates
and so on. This may sound a little complicated, but the way
it is generally done is to give students different assignments. For instance, the students on the first level may be
dealing primarily with objective material. Those on the
second level would use the objective material too, but also
be responsible for book reports or something like that. And
the students on the third level would then be responsible
for the objective material, the book reports, plus some
thought questions or an essay or an assignment of a more
subjective nature. In this way, the training program of an
institution can be adjusted to meet different social,
cultural, and academic backgrounds. It can meet the needs
of laymen, lay pastors, or full-time pastors.

But regardless of what level the work is taken on, the
unique thing here is that an attempt is made to keep students on different levels in the same class. The more able
students, rather than going faster in a given class, are
urged to take more courses, and thus the students in any one
class more or less stay together. Probably not all students
will take all of the classes offered. Or if a student does
not complete the work for a course, he naturally does not
get credit for it. But a student who completes the work
always receives credit according to the level his work was
taken on. This feature means that later on, if a student
wants to upgrade his education, he does not have to start
all over from the beginning but can simply do the extra work
required for the next level. The students, of course, all
pay tuition for the classes they take, just as they would if
in residence. As with anything else, people usually value
more what they pay for.

Another unique feature of TEE is the use of self-study
materials. Because the student meets only occasionally wit'
his teacher, the effectiveness of the program depends to a
large degree on what the student does at home. For some,

home study is easier than for others. But as we saw in the
case of Guatemala, one of the biggest problems they faced
was getting adequate materials for their students, and they
ended up largely writing their own. This was a very difficult task, but something that had to be done. One of the
methods that has been used quite successfully for this
purpose is the use of "programmed instruction materials"
(PIM). The technique of "programmed instruction" (PI), like
extension education itself, is borrowed from secular education. Programmed instruction material is material that is
geared for self study. In programmed instruction, a short
paragraph of information is presented, followed by questions
on it which the student must answer, and immediate confirmation as to whether the answer was correct or not. Below is
a brief example of one of the ways in which material can be
programmed (Winter 1967b:14):

Answer 62	Information	Question 63
a) They lived in different epochs.	The first books were written some 1,500 years before Christ. The last one was written almost 100 years after Christ.	Approximately how many years passed from the time the first book of the Bible was written until the last one was finished? (a) 50 (b) 66 (c) 500 (d) 1,600

In contrast to traditional methods where a student often
reads a book passively, this technique forces a student to
study actively. And he constantly knows how he is doing,
and whether he is understanding or not. A programmed text,
then, is sort of a combination of a regular text plus a
workbook and an answer book, all in one. In some cases, the
material must be worked out from scratch. In others,
materials already in existence can be adapted to programmed
methods, thus coming up with semiprogrammed texts, which
take a student through a regular textbook in a programmed
fashion. In any case, programmed instruction materials are
based on very clear objectives. They begin with the student
rather than the subject. An attempt is made to determine
where the student is, where we want him to be, and how we
can help him get there. The important thing is that the
material enables the student to study on his own. (For a
more extensive sample of programmed material, see Appendix
E on "The Mennonites in Japan.")

As indicated, the writing of PIM is a tremendous undertaking. If a student studies one lesson a day, five days a

week, that means 50 lessons for a 10-week term. Or if the
course runs all year, it would mean 150 lessons -- for just
one course! Writers need to be found to write this type of
material. Once it is written, it must be tried out and
revised before ever being published. It is said that it
takes up to 10 times longer to produce a programmed text
than a regular one. It takes time. It takes work. It
takes money. Not everyone can do it. It takes a special
kind of person. In order to find and train such persons, a
number of PI workshops have been held in different parts of
the world. That is a good beginning, but much more needs
to be done.

The original production cost of programmed materials is
one of the most expensive aspects of TEE. This means that
wherever possible it is desirable that different groups
involved in TEE cooperate in the production of basic
materials. This has been done to some extent in Latin
America already. Various schools with TEE programs are
seeking to produce materials jointly. Such texts are
usually produced in a preliminary edition, which is then
sent out for approval, and the names of the cooperating
groups who approve it are printed on the title page in the
next edition. An attempt is being made to write the books
in relation to each other, to produce an integrated, comprehensive curriculum. Supplements to these texts can also
be written to cover denominational emphases. The name given
to these texts is "Intertext," primarily because they are
"inter-institutional, interdenominational and international"
(Winter 1969:532). It will take many years for materials to
become all that is desired, but such efforts are to be
commended. In the future, students who have already taken
a certain course may make some of the best writers.

Some attempts have also been made at translating materials, but this has not been too satisfactory. It is felt
that it is best to try to write materials which fit the
culture in which they are going to be used. PI is said to
be a good way of learning. At the same time, it is important to remember that each situation is different, and that
while this technique is effective in many situations, it may
not be essential in all. As students get more advanced, and
are able to study more on their own, it is probable that
there would be less need of PIM and more use of materials
already in existence, although perhaps in a semi-programmed
format. Missionary-teacher Edwin Brainerd asserts that, at
least in some cases, the ideal may be "programmed introduc-
tions to standard textbooks, so that each worker indeed

learns to study on his own" (1974:223). It might also be added that PIM can be used in residence as well as extension studies.

Another important component in extension education is the extension teacher. As has already been indicated, where programmed materials are used, "the text is the teacher." The text rather than the teacher provides the necessary input. There is little lecturing in TEE, partly because of time limitations, but also because it is felt that the lecture method is in many cases not the most effective way to learn. Commenting on methods of theological teaching, Professor E. E. Harvey states that

> The lecture method has scarcely been modified since the fourteenth century. This method originated before printing when there was no thought of turning a student loose in a library. This method is the easiest, the cheapest way of imparting the maximum information with the minimum of emotional strain and exact preparation. In this method the teacher does all the thinking for the students. He recites the fruits of his own research and reads it for the student to copy or outline (1970:74).

To help remedy this situation, in TEE the teacher is not seen as a lecturer. His function is rather to be a catalyst, an enabler, a facilitator, a guide, a resource person. In fact, in some situations, the terms "student" and "teacher" have been done away with, and the terms "worker" and "leader" or substitute words are used instead. Since the teacher does not need to be a lecturer, it could be almost anyone who is well acquainted with the subject matter and has a gift for teaching. It might be a professor from the sponsoring school. Or, as suggested before, it might be a pastor, missionary, or someone like that who may also serve as the center director. Preferably it would be a national, but need not be limited to nationals.

There are cases also where students may do some of the teaching. That is, as part of his assignment, a more advanced student may be asked to teach what he is learning to a group of laymen in his church. The school then gives the laymen a test at the end of their course. If they pass, the student passes. If they fail, the student fails! This is in line with Paul's exhortation that "what you have heard from me ... entrust to faithful men who will be able to teach others also" (II Tim. 2:2). Some of those who

graduate from an extension program may also become some of
its best teachers. A teacher need not always be a professional in the sense of having a Ph.D. or Th.D., but he
should at least have the gift of teaching, of drawing out
the best that is in the student.

The teacher meets with his student or students on a
weekly basis. The time of the meeting could be anywhere
from early in the morning to late at night, whatever time is
mutually agreeable to all concerned. The teacher naturally
tries as much as possible to fit into the student's schedule,
but the teacher also has a schedule which must be taken into
consideration as well, especially in terms of days of the
week he is free. But the general pattern is to have a
weekly meeting between the student and teacher. This is
sometimes called a weekly seminar. Time is allowed for
about two different classes to meet. Each one meets for an
hour or so. Usually there are only one or two classes
being offered any given term, so this time is generally
adequate. But the class time, rather than being used for a
lecture, is used differently than in the average residence
class. Ted Ward and Samuel F. Rowen point out that educationally these seminars can be compared to a two-rail fence:
"the upper rail represents the cognitive input, the lower
rail represents field experiences, and the fence posts
represent the seminars" (1972:24). They go on to say that
the seminars are the place where cognitive input (information learned through books, lectures, tapes, films, PIM,
etc.) and field experiences are integrated through sharing
and discussion.

D. Leslie Hill, in his book on *Designing a Theological
Education by Extension Program*, suggests that the weekly
meeting be structured somewhat as follows. The first 20
minutes would be a "Joint Opening Session" of worship. The
next 10 minutes would be used for "General Housekeeping
Procedures," taking care of accounts, making necessary
announcements and so on. This would be followed then by
two seminar periods of 60 minutes each, with a 10-minute
break in between. The seminar meetings would consist of a
10-minute "Review Exam of Week's Work," "to encourage the
students to keep up with their daily work and to review."
The next 45 minutes would be for "Discussion and Application," where the "student's work is checked and explanation
made where necessary. The material learned is applied to
actual life situations." The last five minutes would be
used for a "Preview of Coming Materials," "to be sure that
the next week's lesson is clear" (1974:185-186). According

to this plan, the basic format of an extension class would be review, discussion and application, and preview.

As hinted earlier, the teacher's role is not so much to teach. He is not a lecturer. His function is rather to check to see that the student has done his work, to answer any questions he may have, and to encourage him on. Since the student knows that his teacher will be checking his work, there is a certain accountability built into the process. On the other hand, with this type of class, there is the danger that the teacher might not feel he is teaching, and the student not feel that he is learning. While in extension there is greater concern with what the "learner learns" that what the "teacher teaches," it is important that both student and teacher understand the purpose of the weekly meeting, and seek to make the best use of the time they have together. The student does not spend as much time with the teacher as he ordinarily would in the classroom in a residence situation. But the chances are that the quality of the time together may be much higher -- that the student will get to know his teacher better, and the teacher his student.

It is also extremely important that the student attend all of the weekly meetings. In fact, in many cases, the student's grade is based not only on the work he does and his scores on the exams, but on his attendance as well, to give him greater incentive to be there. It is also important for the teacher to be there. He represents the school, and where the teacher is, the school is. In extension, as we have said, the teacher goes to where the student is. And while this makes TEE possible, it is also one of the most costly parts of the program. The teacher spends less time in preparation, but more in travel, and one of the biggest expenses is in getting to and from the weekly meetings. One teacher, however, can normally handle several weekly meetings, as long as they are not all on the same day.

Besides the weekly meeting, there may also be a monthly meeting or seminar. For the monthly meeting, all the students from the various extension centers in an area meet together at one of the centers or at a regional center. The nature of these meetings is somewhat different from the weekly meeting. The monthly meeting can be used in many ways. It can be a time for Bible study, recreation, fellowship and the like. Winter mentions several values the monthly meeting had for them in Guatemala (1969:432-433):

1) Larger-group fellowship.
2) Cross-cultural fellowship.
3) Special types of training (English, music, etc.).
4) "Recognition" as seminarians.
5) Mid-term exams.
6) Contact with theological specialists.
7) Development of research library skills.
8) Spiritual inspiration.

Thus the monthly meeting can serve many purposes. In some cases, it may not be every month. Perhaps only bimonthly, or only at the beginning and end of a term. Or in situations where some of the students have responsibilities on weekends, it may be necessary to hold two monthly meetings, one for those who can come during the week, and another for those who are free on weekends. It may also be desirable to meet for two or three days instead of one. The variations are endless, and it will need to be determined what is best in each case.

In addition to the weekly and monthly meetings, there is also an annual or yearly meeting at the headquarters of the sponsoring institution itself. As we have seen, the only difference between extension and resident students is that one is resident and the other is not. But occasionally going to the school itself gives the extension student the feeling that he actually is a part of the school. It is recommended that as many as possible attend the graduation ceremonies. This may vary according to distance from the school. It is especially important that those who will be graduating attend, for this is the time when they are recognized for their work. Just as students were able to take courses on various levels, so graduation also takes place on various levels. In Latin America, for example, nearly all institutions which have extension programs graduate people according to the following academic divisions (Covell and Wagner 1971:85):

Name of level	Academic prerequisites for beginning the course
Licentiate (B.D.)	Two or three years of university
Bachelor	High School diploma
Diploma	Primary School diploma (six years)
Certificate A	Two or three years of primary school
Certificate B	Little or no formal training, but functional literacy in vernacular

The degrees offered and the necessary prerequisites would, of course, vary somewhat from country to country and continent to continent, depending on the average academic level of the people. But from the above scheme it can be seen that extension is able to reach people of both high and low academic standing. It can be multi-level, meeting the needs of people on varied levels, and leading to a multiplicity of degrees. But since it takes some of the students as long as 15 years or more to graduate, there are also some schools which have graduation in stages. In other words, a student might "graduate" every five years or so, until he completes the entire program. Part of the reason for this would be to keep him from getting discouraged after several years of study without graduating. But the annual meeting is where all the students, resident and extension, have a chance to get together with each other, and with the entire faculty. This really is what ties the program together and where the extent of it becomes more visible.

As defined, the extension seminary or Bible school is the extension of the program of a recognized theological training institution. It differs from residence studies, however, in not extracting a person from his environment for long periods of time. It extends rather than extracts. It is "extension" rather than "extraction." At the same time, even extension studies extract people for shorter periods of time, in order to achieve their goal. This is brought out quite clearly by Ralph Winter's diagram (Figure 3.1) of the overall pattern of the extension seminary (1969:428).

Figure 3.1

PATTERN OF AN EXTENSION PROGRAM

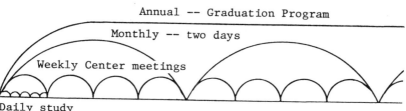

From this we can see that it involves daily study, as well as weekly, monthly, and annual meetings. Theological education is extended to the student, but the student is also extracted from his daily routine for various lengths of time. And while a student eventually graduates from an extension program, he in a sense never graduates. He has taken his studies over a long period of time, has cultivated the habit of study, and there is always more to learn. Hopefully he will continue studying, and learning will be a lifetime process. "Lifetime learning," not just graduation, should be our goal. Extension studies are designed to instill such an attitude.

This is in general, then, what TEE is all about. As we have seen, there are many advantages to such a program: it reaches more students; it reaches them in their own environment; it avoids the support problem; it costs less per student; it can be multi-level; it uses creative teaching methods; it reaches more of the real leaders in the church; it gives them an in-service training; the student can go at his own pace; it creates habits of lifelong study; one teacher can handle many students; and the program is fully accredited.

There are also some disadvantages: there is infrequent contact between student and teacher; to a great extent learning depends on the student; only a limited number of courses can be taught each year; there is a lack of good programmed materials; it takes longer to finish; resources such as a library are limited, and so on. But when one compares the advantages with the disadvantages, I think we would have to fairly admit that the former far outweigh the latter.

I believe it is also important to underscore the fact that TEE is not just a glorified lay training program. In the typical lay training program, for example, little is expected of the student; TEE expects a lot. The content is mainly Bible; TEE offers a comprehensive curriculum. There is heavy reliance on the lecture method; TEE stresses creative instruction. The class meets weekly; the TEE student studies daily. The program is for the whole church; TEE aims mainly at the development of leaders and leadership gifts. These are only a few of the differences between TEE and lay training.

But if TEE is not a typical lay training program, neither is it a correspondence course. In a correspondence course, the student must send in his material to have it checked; in TEE, there is instant feedback. The student never meets with a teacher; in TEE, the student meets weekly with his teacher. There is only one level of instruction; in TEE, there can be many levels. The program usually does not lead to a degree; a TEE program can offer various degrees.

It has no relation to the local church; TEE is church-centered. These are but a few of the differences between TEE and correspondence. There are many other points at which TEE differs from either a lay training program or a correspondence course. But perhaps the most significant difference is that generally neither of them is tied to a recognized institution, whereas TEE is. These comments are not intended to play down any contribution these other programs may be making, but rather to stress that in every way, TEE is more, much more.

In summary, TEE is just what the words say it is. It is theological education. The method is extension. It is a theological education program which is extended to the student. In short, we might call it a decentralized seminary or Bible school. As we have indicated, it is not just a general Christian education program for the entire church, although the entire church can benefit from it. It aims more specifically at leadership, at training men and women who are gifted but have never had the opportunity of getting a theological education. And yet, while extension and residence programs differ in methodology, TEE recognizes the need for residence schools. It does not suggest that all Bible schools and seminaries close their doors. It does not seek to "exterminate," but rather to "extend" traditional residence schools. In fact, as we have said before, TEE itself cannot exist without being connected to a base institution or relating to some authority. If all institutions were to disappear, so would TEE. The institution is what gives TEE credibility.

Promoters of TEE do feel, however, that traditional schools cannot do all that needs to be done. The job is too big for residence schools to handle alone. So TEE seeks to supplement rather than supplant what is already being done, to reach out to students who otherwise would not be trained, to try to provide them with a solid theological education. And it is not just a gimmick. One of the basic principles of the extension method is that "form follows function" (TEF 1972:36). As the function of theological education is to train believers for ministry, TEE is a serious attempt to take such training to the student, to educate him at a "time, place and pace" convenient for him. It seeks to provide students with a first-class theological education, an education that can lead to ordination, and is not inferior in any way to residence education. In fact, in many ways, as we have noted, it may be superior. It may still take many years for TEE to prove itself, but it looks promising

as a way of providing churches with leaders who are both
gifted and trained. There is no need though to pit extension against residence, or residence against extension.
They are both needed. Both are full-fledged theological
education. Both should be recognized for what they are.

A MOVEMENT GAINS MOMENTUM

We have seen how the TEE movement was born, some of the
theory that underlies it, a little about how it works in
practice, and lastly we want to take a look at how the movement has spread. As we saw, it all began as a rather
isolated experiment with about 50 students in Guatemala.
That was in 1963. For the next three years, it was confined
to just that one program. In 1967, however, which has been
called "the year of the breakthrough," several groups in
other countries began extension programs. From that point
on, the movement grew rapidly. It spread not only into
other parts of Central and Latin America, but into other
parts of the world -- Africa, Asia, and North America.
Numerous workshops have been held throughout the world to
promote the idea of TEE, and many have caught the vision.
Truly it was "an idea whose time had come."

Figure 3.2

TOTAL OF EXTENSION STUDENTS
1962-1972

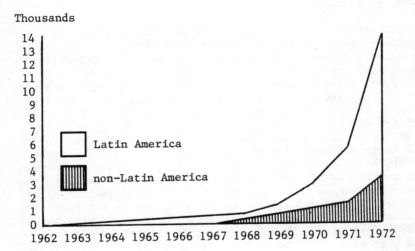

The chart (Figure 3.2) by Wayne Weld (1973:40) helps to visualize the amazing growth of TEE a little better. According to Weld's chart, there were about 14,000 students studying by extension in 1972. The chart is also instructive in pointing out where most of the students are from. As might be expected, the majority are from Latin America where the movement began, and are represented by the white area. The crosshatch area is to indicate those students from outside Latin America.

According to another of his charts, the regional distribution of extension students is roughly Latin America 73 percent, North America 8 percent, the Caribbean 7 percent, and Africa and Asia about 6 percent each (1973:44). His chart on the distribution by academic levels is also striking, especially in Asia, where the academic level appears to be considerably higher than in other areas. Several factors he suggests to account for this difference are that the general academic level of leadership in the churches may be higher; several institutions have begun their extension programs first as continuing education for pastors; and some programs have started with the use of materials in English, which may have limited the student body to the higher academic levels (1973:45-46). In any case, the point worthy of attention is that TEE has caught on, even in Asia. Latest statistics available show that there are now over 35,000 extension students enrolled in 279 institutions in 55 different countries. Over 12 percent are in Asia (*Extension* 1977:3). This means the movement has grown from just 50 to over 35,000 in only fourteen short years!

As far as the General Conference Mennonites go, they are involved in programs in Columbia, India, Taiwan and so on, if not always as a sponsoring group, at least as participants. They do not have any programs of their own, but they are cooperating with others. This includes cooperation with other Mennonites, such as the Mennonite Brethren, as well as with many non-Mennonite groups. A good example of such cooperation is the United Biblical Seminary (UBS) of Columbia, which was reorganized into four divisions in 1969 -- a continuing residence division, and three extension divisions. In addition to the two Mennonite groups mentioned above, the Christian and Missionary Alliance, the Evangelical Covenant, the Inter-American Missionary Society (OMS), the Latin America Mission, and Overseas Crusades were among the other groups cooperating in the new venture. The enrollment of the newly structured UBS, by the way, jumped in one year's time from 19 in the original residence school

to 156 in the four divisions (Winter 1969:210-216)! More of
this kind of cooperation is needed.

As far as Japan goes, there are no TEE programs here yet.
Nor do there seem to be any in nearby Korea. The closest
program to Japan would appear to be what is being done in
Taiwan. So we want to take a close look at that, and see if
there are not some things we can learn from it. The case
study on TEE in Taiwan which follows was done in June 1974.
It is not presented as a perfect example of what a TEE program ought to be like. But it does reveal, I believe, some
of the basic features and gives us a good look at the relationship between resident and extension programs. The study
deals primarily with the China Evangelical Seminary,
although in it we are also interested particularly in the
Mennonite relationship to it. As you will see, however, the
Mennonite churches as such are not really very actively
involved in the TEE movement there. But that may say something too. Something about the movement, and something
about the Mennonites. In any case, the study is offered in
hopes that we can learn something of value from it. Some
minor changes may have taken place since the study was made,
but as far as I know the program remains basically about the
same. Following the study is an evaluation of the program
by way of some observations.

CASE STUDY: TEE IN TAIWAN

(Based on an interview with Hugh D. Sprunger, June 3-4, 1974,
and a letter of November 24, 1974.)

"TEE work began in Taiwan in the fall of 1971," according
to the May 1974 report on that work (Sprunger 1974c:1). The
same report notes the growth that has taken place during
these past three years. In the 1971-72 school year, three
classes were held in two regional centers (Kaohsiung and
Hsilo) with a total of 20 students. In the year 1972-73,
three classes were held in three centers (the above two plus
Taichung), with a total of 34 students. In 1973-74, 12
classes were held in two centers (Taichung and Taipei), with
a total of 132 students. Thus during these three years a
total of 18 classes have been taught to 186 students. It
should be noted, however, that "The 186 students do not
represent 186 different persons; some students enrolled in
their second course are counted twice" (1974c:1). Five
different courses were taught: Jeremiah, Church Growth,
Mark, Christian Theology, and Homiletics.

From this it can be seen that the number of classes, the number of students, and the number of courses offered have all increased. So have the number of persons involved in running the program. Hugh Sprunger is the Executive Director. There is also a Materials Production Coordinator, and a Taipei Regional Center Coordinator who is also serving as Assistant Executive Director. The faculty is composed of both nationals and missionaries, and the above mentioned report says that "A total of seven Chinese teachers and six missionary teachers have helped to teach TEE classes" (1974c:1). It also indicates that the TEE budget is getting bigger, the program is coming to have a more important place in the China Evangelical Seminary (CES), plans are being made for more courses and more textbooks and study guides, and further training for staff members. But while the work has grown, it is stated too that the TEE work needs greater support -- more prayer, more giving, more students, more teachers, more encouragement. It needs the wholehearted backing of both missions and churches.

One of the factors that created an interest in TEE and resulted in TEET (Theological Education by Extension in Taiwan) were some workshops on the subject held in 1968 and after, especially the one held in the fall of 1970. There was one in Taipei in Chinese for pastors. There was another one in Taichung in English for missionaries. Another factor was the decision to establish the China Evangelical Seminary, an interdenominational school at the graduate level, in Taipei. This opened in October of 1970. It was felt that perhaps an extension program could be combined with the new seminary. So a committee was formed with a representative from each of the four other schools that pledged to cooperate with CES in experimenting with TEE. These were the Taiwan Conservative Baptist Seminary in Hsilo, the Central Taiwan Theological College (OMSI) in Taichung, the Holy Light Theological Seminary (Free Methodist) in Kaohsiung, and the Taiwan Nazarene Theological College in Taipei. The president of each of these institutions served as their representative, plus David Liao, who has been active in the church growth movement and inter-church activities, and Hugh Sprunger, who was later asked to serve as Director of the program.

Following the workshops referred to above, a statement on TEE in Taiwan was drawn up. It was in the form of a paper called "Planning for an Extension Seminary Program," and included "basic presuppositions, purpose, principles, and first steps in implementation." The statement was written by Sprunger and Liao at the request of the consultative committee, and was then subject to their discussion, suggestions, and final approval. But it is very well done, and as it is foundational to their whole program, I believe it is worth including here in its entirety as follows:

PLANNING FOR AN EXTENSION SEMINARY PROGRAM

BASIC PRESUPPOSITIONS

As participating churches, schools, and other groups we are:

1. Thoroughly committed to the principle of more rapid and extensive church growth which creates a need for many more theologically-trained church leaders and ministers. When this kind of rapid church growth takes place at all levels of society and in all geographical areas, leaders will be found at all educational levels and must be given theological training.

2. Persuaded that multi-level theological training is a necessity (college graduate, senior middle school graduate, and junior middle school graduate and below, at least three levels). Multi-level theological education should utilize the same general course of studies, but the amount of material covered in any one course will differ according to the educational level.

3. Aware that, although there are presently existing schools which give theological education at several levels, there is a need for an additional program. This additional program is an extension seminary program to bring theological education to persons who cannot, or perhaps should not, be a resident student in an existing theological institution.

4. Ready and willing to recognize the theological education of all levels by giving those persons so trained additional opportunities for responsibility in churches and developing groups.

5. Wholly convinced that a cooperative and centralized approach to an extension seminary program is essential to achieve maximum impact and effectiveness due to the financial and personnel needs of such a program. Under the present situation, China Evangelical Seminary is a logical institution to coordinate such an effort.

PURPOSE

The purpose of an extension seminary program is two-fold: first, to strengthen existing churches by helping present church leaders/ministers with limited training to gain additional theological education needed to make them more effective without taking them away from their present work; second, to make possible the rapid opening of many new churches, at all levels of society, which are self-supporting, self-governing, and self-propagating. Thus the persons who should be enrolled in the extension seminary are the *present leaders* (full-time or part-time) and the *potential leaders*. Present church leaders include ministers, evangelists, elected or appointed church officers (deacons, elders, committee members, Sunday school superintendents, youth group advisors, etc.) who are recognized as leaders both by virtue of their position in the church and also by experience in society (secular jobs, etc.) *and* who cannot leave home, family, job to attend a regular residence seminary.

PRINCIPLES

1. Theological education. The extension seminary program at all levels is to be recognized as a standard theological education and not as a correspondence course or an ordinary laymen's training course.
2. Multi-level theological education should be carried out at three levels, graduate, undergraduate, and diploma levels. While the graduate and undergraduate extension programs can be developed eventually under CES, there is an urgent need now for developing a diploma extension seminary program which should receive priority.
3. Qualifications for enrollment. Those enrolled for extension seminary courses at the graduate and undergraduate levels should meet the same general qualifications of students enrolled in residence programs of the cooperating institutions. Those enrolled in the diploma course level will not be required to present any graduation certificate but must be at least 17 years of age, pass a qualifying examination (covering general knowledge, Chinese, and Bible), and have a written recommendation from their pastor certifying that they are Christians and already active in the church program of their local congregation. While entrance qualifications

for the diploma course are open-ended, it is likely
that some students may drop out before graduation
if they do not have the necessary motivation or
ability to cover the required courses and examinations. Only those who pass a standard examination
will receive credits toward eventual graduation.
This will ensure that *graduates*, not all enrolled
students, are qualified to be considered seminary
graduates.

4. Programmed texts. The only real solution to an
   extension seminary program is self-study by students
   with programmed texts which involve only a limited
   teacher/faculty supervision. Initially, a semi-
   programmed approach can be used by preparing workbooks for use with the currently used conventional
   textbooks. The programmed texts for the diploma
   course will be written in Chinese using vocabulary
   which can be generally understood by anyone who has
   completed at least primary school. While the
   language of the texts will be simplified, the contents will not be simplified.

5. Academic recognition. Diplomas for extension
   seminary graduates should be issued by the China
   Evangelical Seminary and signed by the chairman of
   the Board of C.E.S., the C.E.S. president, and the
   dean of the regional center where the student is
   registered. The diploma for graduates of all levels
   should be similar in appearance but have different
   wording suitable for the course level.

6. Organization. Organizationally the extension
   seminary program should be parallel to the resident
   C.E.S. program. The extension seminary committee
   should be appointed formally by the Board of
   Directors of C.E.S. This committee should include
   the principals of the four schools (Nazarene, Free
   Methodist, O.M.S., and Cons. Baptist) which are
   related to C.E.S., plus the C.E.S. president, who
   would be chairman of the committee, and two or
   three others from interested groups. The Central
   Faculty of C.E.S. would be a principal advisory
   group to assist the C.E.S. president in overseeing
   the development and maintaining the standards of
   the extension seminary program.

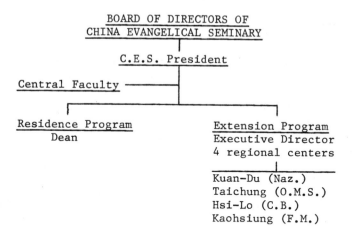

Regional centers would be set up at the four cooperating schools carrying signs that they are regional extension seminary centers of the China Evangelical Seminary (in Wade-Giles Romanization, Chung Hua Fu Yin Shen Hsueh Yuan _____ Fen Pu).

FIRST STEPS IN IMPLEMENTATION

1. Consultation with church/mission leaders of interested groups to inform about plans for extension seminary and about the background, goals, etc. of this program and to inspire participation in the program (encouraging leaders to enroll, utilizing enrolled students, recognizing graduates, etc.).
2. Appointment of Extension Seminary Committee (as an executive committee) to make and oversee decisions on appointment of personnel, goals, curriculum, preparation of texts, standards, priorities, etc.
3. Selection of an executive director to carry out the decisions of the Extension Seminary Committee, coordinating and administering the programs.
4. Financial support must be provided (Sprunger and Liao 1971:1-5).

There are many comments one could make on this statement. Just note how it incorporates not only extension concepts, but how permeated it is with "church growth" thinking, especially the sections on Presuppositions and Purpose. It is concerned not only with providing adequate leadership

for existing churches, but with opening new ones. The
sections on Principles and Implementation are more practical
in nature, but it is obvious that the overall plan was carefully thought out. And it was implemented as planned.
What we need to do now is to see how closely the current
program, or the program as it has actually been carried out,
resembles the program as originally conceived.

As pointed out in the paper, there are many other theological schools existing in Taiwan, over 20 in fact. But
only about 12 of these are recognized by TATE (Taiwan
Association for Theological Education) as being certified
theological training institutions. For example, the Presbyterians have two schools, the Taiwan Theological College
in Taipei to the north, and the Taiwan Theological College
in Tainan to the south. These schools offer a six-year
course which is a combination of both college and seminary
together. Students who enter this program receive a M.Div.
degree on completion of the work. If they have taken three
years of college elsewhere, with four more years of theological study, they can get the same degree. But if they
have already had four years of college (Taiwan has both
three and four-year colleges), they would need to spend only
three more years to graduate.

By comparison, CES is a graduate school only, and offers
a three-year program beyond college, leading to a M.Div.
A college or university degree is required for admission.
Three majors are offered -- Missions, Pastoral Studies, or
Christian Education. A total of 90 hours is required for
graduation. Previously the school also offered an M.C.E.
(M.R.E.) for two years of work in Christian education, and
a Diploma in Christian Studies for one year's work, but now
it is said to offer only the M.Div. degree. While the
faculty and library and so on are not yet adequate, the
school seems to be drawing a higher number of college graduates than the other seminaries are. The first class of
seven graduated in 1973. Some denominations (not including
the Presbyterian) support CES and have a program of their
own at the Th.B. level. The Th.B. would be equivalent to
four years of Bible college with a Bible major. There is
some talk of merging at this level because most such schools
have too few students and too many faculty. Yet even with a
graduate school like CES, it is still important to run some
of these lower level programs to meet various educational
needs.

When it comes to their extension program, CES hopes to
eventually operate it on three different levels. One would

be the graduate level, for college graduates, leading to the M.Div. degree.   Another would be the undergraduate level, for senior high school graduates, leading to the Th.B. degree.   The third would be the only level they are operating on at present, the diploma level, which leads to a diploma rather than a degree and is mainly for junior high school graduates.   They say that the extension program as it is now is aimed at laymen.   It is not a continuing education program for pastors, although a few of them are enrolled simply because it is a "new way of studying."   Be that as it may, the basic purpose is to equip laymen for their ministry, to provide them with a theological education functionally equivalent to that of a residence program.

To enter, they are supposed to have the minimal equivalent of a junior high school education, but according to Sprunger, over 70 percent of their students are either college students or graduates.   Most of the remaining ones are in the senior high category, which means that while the current program is supposedly on the diploma level, they are actually operating at the undergraduate level because of the type of students enrolling.   They are attempting to keep the extension program at a standard theological level, since it is not an ordinary correspondence course or lay training program.   As yet, however, they say they are not teaching extension courses at the graduate level in terms of the amount of collateral reading required.

There also seems to be a rather high dropout rate. According to the May 1973 report on TEE in Taiwan, only 17 out of 32 enrolled in two different centers completed the course they were taking (Sprunger 1973:1).   That is almost a 50 percent dropout rate.   The composition also varies from place to place.   The same report notes that

> In the Kaohsiung classes some of the students have been ministers of mountain or rural churches while others are laymen, but the general educational level is not very high.   In the Hsilo classes most of the students have been military men, many of them retired soldiers, so the average age of students there is higher than elsewhere.   In the Taichung class all of the students are below the age of 30 and all are either college graduates or college students (1973:1).

In the "Taipei Regional Center Report" of May 1974, there are statistics on the second semester of the 1973-74 school year (Chen 1974:2).   A total of 78 students were

enrolled in six different classes. Of these, 47 percent
were men, 53 percent were women; 67 percent were between the
ages of 20–35, 10 percent were in the 36–50 bracket, and 23
percent were 51 or over; 76 percent were either college
graduates or college students, 10 percent were senior high
graduates, and 14 percent had less than senior high or it
was not clear; 14 percent were pastors, 74 percent were
deacons and elders, youth group leaders, Sunday school
teachers, or youth group officers, and 12 percent had other
positions in the church. These students came from at least
thirteen different churches or denominations, led by
Lutheran (20), Presbyterian (9), and followed by Baptist,
Covenant, and Independent churches with 7 each, the others
with less.

The extension program is also open to the regular CES
students. The classes at present do not meet in the CES
buildings. One meets in the Bible Baptist Church. Another
near the National Taiwan University. A third in the
Lutheran Church, with all of the students in that particular
class being from that congregation. But with this setup it
is possible to have a junior high graduate and a university
graduate, plus perhaps a pastor or two, all in the same
class. While the aim was to be narrower, in actuality, the
students are multi-level. In light of this, Sprunger
remarked that "we should be aiming like a rifle, but instead
we're shooting like a shotgun."

CES does not feel bound to follow the format used in
Latin America. The situation in Taiwan is thought to be
quite different. Most of the churches already have pastors
with some formal theological education. The majority
probably have at least senior high education plus some
Bible school. So the aim is not to train pastors but to
equip laymen to serve the congregation. Five percent of the
Taiwanese are Christian. This is a tremendous potential for
outreach if trained and used. It usually takes several
lessons for people to get used to the approach, but if the
pastor recommends it and the people get going, many of them
stick it out. Some of the pastors, as might be expected,
feel threatened by this new system. They say it is a
"cheap way" to get a theological education. But as inferred
earlier, that is simply not true. It takes at least four or
five years, perhaps 15, to complete the basic course and get
recognition for it. Classroom hours may be less, but outside study hours are much greater than in the usual residential training program.

The curriculum is divided into three categories --
Biblical, Theological/Historical, and Practical studies.
The diploma level is heavier on practical subjects than are
the other levels. Biblical languages are also not required
at this level. Courses are worth from two to six credit
hours (most of them are three, six for two semesters), and
it takes a total of 96 hours to graduate. With 24 hours a
year as a maximum, that means it would take a minimum of
four years to complete the course, if one studied full time.
For part-time students it would of course take longer. The
school is on semesters now, but is also considering summer
courses. Whatever the length, the school sets the standards
for each course, and whether it is completed in a month or a
year, the student gets credit. By 1977, they want to have
the basic course (32 hours) fully developed, including study
materials, the various courses to be offered on a three to
five-year cycle. They hope to have the full theological
course developed by 1980, at a Th.B. or M.Div. level.

Tuition is currently $1.25 (NT $50) per credit hour,
which is paid at the time of registration. But this will
likely be raised in the near future to two or three times
that much. The printing of materials is one of the most
expensive items, as the texts must be printed for more than
just CES. It is felt that programmed texts are helpful.
They make the target group clear. They determine what a
student will do, where he should be at the end, and must be
engineered to get him there. They must include all the
information necessary to meet the minimal requirements for a
course. If the student does not reach the goal, then the
text must be examined to see whether the fault lay there or
somewhere else. It is a costly business in time and money.
So far the basic method has been to use texts with a study
guide already available. It will take a long time until the
texts for the extension courses are what they ought to be.
But still it is felt it is worth the effort. Men who know
the content will have to develop the courses applying programming techniques. Several workshops have been held to
train writers to produce such materials.

Under this type of program, each day the student studies
at home with his workbook and text. Each week he meets at
the extension center with his professor. When he completes
a course, he gets credit for it. When a student graduates
he gets a diploma. If he wishes, he may transfer his
credits to an undergraduate residence program. But the
school does not emphasize the degree. They tell their students, "If you want to serve Christ and His Church, we can

help you get better tools to serve Him. Your reward will be
when your church gives you more responsibility." Other
schools say they may give credit for CES work. If a student
transfers to another theological school, he is given a transcript, and each school evaluates it and may grant credit in
accordance with its own standards.

As originally envisioned, the extension program was to be
parallel to the residence program. An extension seminary
committee would be appointed by the board of directors, and
include the principals of the four cooperating schools and
the president of CES. (Later on a national from each
cooperating organization was invited to be on too.)
Regional centers would then be set up as part of the CES
extension program. Everything was to be under the umbrella
of CES.

In the beginning, however, CES did not pay for any
needed personnel or provide office space or anything like
that. It simply acted as a convenor in bringing the TEE
committee together. But after a couple of years, when it
became clear that the other supporting schools would not be
able to supply all the funds and personnel necessary
(because of the great expense involved in also financing
their own residence programs), CES began to support a full-
time and a part-time worker, as well as furnish office space
and some equipment and supplies. In short, it underwrote
the TEE work. The other institutions also all contributed
something toward the undertaking in terms of giving some
help with personnel or paying for the production of materials and so on. But there were many problems to be dealt
with. The main ones appeared to be men, materials, and
money. As Sprunger said, with an expanding program as they
have had, "the greater the success, the greater the financial problem." Without more financial support, especially
for personnel such as regional center coordinators, the
program could not be expanded much further.

The result of all this was the need to restructure the
whole program, which has been done. Under the new structure
(from July 1974), TEE is being integrated into CES as one
department of their program, rather than being parallel to
the residence program as before. Its budget will be part of
the total CES budget. CES will conduct extension work only
in Taipei. They will turn their night school program over
to the extension department. But there will be no CES
regional centers outside of the Taipei area. A TEE committee will continue to coordinate and counsel the various TEE

programs. CES will pay a full-time person to work on books and materials which the others may also use, but they will not be able to provide teachers and pay their salaries for all over the island. Previously, for example, CES had several classes in Taichung. Now the OMS school or some other institution will be carrying most of the responsibility. Any regional centers will be called the Central Taiwan Theological College Regional Center, or the Taichung Regional Center and so on. Once a month or so, CES may be able to send someone to check on how the various regional centers are doing, but more and more the local schools will be supporting their own TEE programs. In some cases, they may need to release a teacher or two to teach outside their regular program, but it is felt that such an arrangement could be workable.

CES itself has grown considerably since its inception several years ago. According to the school's January 1974 *News Bulletin*, they now have 20 full-time resident students, 30 in part-time studies, and 44 in the TEE program; they also have five full-time and five part-time faculty members (1974:2). It is interesting to read in the same report that at present almost 70 percent of the CES budget (US $30,960) comes from contributions of Chinese churches or individuals in North America and Southeast Asia (1974:3). Local support is increasing, but the school needs to develop a broader basis of support among local churches. One would hope that churches would increasingly realize that such schools deserve support, too. For as CES President James H. Taylor Jr. says in the bulletin referred to above, "the Seminary's only reason for existence is to serve the Church" (1974:4). Sprunger feels it is a matter of conviction: "Teachers need remuneration at least for their expenses. If all the pastors in a denomination agree they want to train laymen, they should be willing to contribute something toward that end. What is needed is support at the local level." There are many groups which want TEE, but what CES hopes to encourage from now on are self-supporting regional centers.

What we have done so far is to give a brief report on what has been and is being done with TEE in Taiwan. We have seen that in spite of having carefully worked out a plan for an extension program that at certain points it has had to be modified, and it is commendable that CES has felt free to make the necessary changes. CES would someday like to see a TEE center in every major city. Exactly what shape the program will take in the future, we cannot say. But what we

want to do next is to see how one particular group, the
General Conference Mennonite churches of Taiwan, have been
affected by the program up till now.

There are 13 General Conference Mennonite churches in
Taiwan. Together they are called FOMCIT, or the Fellowship
of Mennonite Churches in Taiwan. The Mennonites first came
to Taiwan in 1948 at the invitation of the Presbyterians.
The Mennonite Central Committee, a combined Mennonite service organization, was invited to come and do relief work,
which they did. The first Mennonite missionaries arrived
later on in 1954. As churches were formed, there was of
course a need for leadership, but they never had enough men
to have their own school, and there was no one highly
enough trained to teach, so they sent them to other schools.
Today (in 1975) 11 of the 13 churches have their own
pastors. Six of them were trained in Presbyterian schools,
three in Baptist, and two in Holiness. In spite of doing
things this way, there has not been a problem like in Japan
of sending men away for training and then not returning.
Part of the reason for that may be that the schools in
Taiwan are at most only a couple of hours away by train.
Anyway, the system has seemed to work fairly well. In 1974
there were two graduates from Presbyterian schools, and five
others were enrolled.

While the students are in school, they are supported
basically by tuition scholarships, living allowances, and a
modest subsidy for books. A student applies for aid through
the education committee of FOMCIT. The support is minimal,
and some of the students have also done part-time work.
Examples would be publishing books, raising canaries, or
serving as translators. One problem is that parents with a
son who qualifies to go to university are often unwilling to
send him to seminary to become a minister, unless they are a
devout Christian family. Even if they have the resources,
most parents will not support their child in seminary
because in Taiwan seminary is considered as "training"
rather than education. The government makes this distinction. The seminaries are not recognized as academic schools.
They have no standing with the Department of Education, but
only with the Department of Interior as a religious organization.

There does not seem to be any special problem with the
graduates of these schools fitting into Mennonite churches.
There are naturally differences of emphasis at some points.
For a while, the Mennonite churches tried to supplement

their pastors formal education with Anabaptist and Mennonite studies, introducing the peace position and so on. But there was a shortage of missionaries, and none of them felt adequate enough in the language to lecture well, and they could not keep it up. There was a time, too, when they required their pastors to write a thesis after graduation on a Mennonite theme, but that has been dropped. The pastors, of course, can also read on their own if they have the time and interest.

More recently (1973-74), Henry Poettcker, then president of the Canadian Mennonite Bible College, lectured for several months at two different seminaries in Taiwan. The students, especially the Mennonite students, seemed to appreciate that very much. It did something to bring them together, and as such was a valuable experience. Sprunger has suggested in an article elsewhere that it might be well to have a Mennonite professor on the staff of one or more of the schools, not only for the sake of the Mennonite students, but that "This would also make the Mennonites contributors to as well as recipients and beneficiaries of theological education in Taiwan" (1974d:E-3).

According to Sprunger, in Taiwan, small as it is, everyone is everywhere. If all the missionaries pulled out, there might not be a uniquely "Mennonite" Church. Nor would there be a "Baptist" or any other church. All are pretty well blended together. There are though some basic Catholic and Protestant differences. In fact, it is interesting that in Taiwanese there is no one word for Christianity that includes both Catholic and Protestant. The distinction that is usually made is between the Catholic or the "old" religion and the Christian or the "new" religion. But differences among Protestants themselves are not felt to be that great. Interdenominational theological training may have something to do with that. At some points, however, it is clear that the Mennonites have been influenced by other traditions. For instance, the case of the pastor who at a child dedication service said that this was "child baptism without water." In that case it may have been a functional substitute for some of his people. But for the most part, it is felt that pastors trained in non-Mennonite schools fit well in the Mennonite churches.

Although there are many similarities between the Mennonite Church and other Protestant churches in Taiwan, it was suggested that there are also some distinctives. One of these would be that it is different from any other blend.

There are other churches which practice believers' baptism.
In the Presbyterian Church too adults are baptized, but
they also baptize infants which the Mennonites do not do.
There are other groups which believe in nonresistance. But
the Mennonite blend is just a little different. There is
also the Fellowship of Mennonite Churches which grows out of
the local churches and enables them to do some things
together which they could not do independently. But the
churches remain autonomous.

As far as the use of the word "Mennonite" goes, it was
said there was no pressure from the home board to use it,
but the missionaries were encouraged to emphasize distinctive Mennonite beliefs. For the sake of identity, of having
a "family" to belong to, it seems that the churches have
chosen to use the word *Mennonite*. They have also chosen to
use the General Conference Mennonite symbol (Figure 3.3), and
many of the pastors and missionaries have it on their name
cards. But while some attempt has been made at teaching
Mennonite beliefs, the emphasis has been more on making
Christians first and Mennonites second.

Another distinctive is the presence of elders and deacons
in the church. Most churches start with deacons, and add
elders later on. The deacons are "people who serve"; the
elders are "people who assist the pastor with the spiritual
oversight of the church." Both deacons and elders are
elected. The people wanted to have them because they had
them in the Bible. At one point, an attempt was made to
also introduce the word "trustee" into the churches, but the
people said, "no, it's not in the Bible." So they do not
have trustees, but they do have deacons and elders. They
can be either men or women. One difference from the Presbyterian Church, however, is that whereas they ordain elders
and deacons for life, in the Mennonite Church it is only a
three-year appointment. Upon their election, deacons and
elders are formally installed to their particular offices,
but they are not ordained as such. (Only ministers are
ordained.) When their term expires, they must wait at least
one year before being eligible for reelection. The Presbyterians also elect people to these offices, but they can be
reelected indefinitely.

Figure 3.3
GCMC SYMBOL

The symbol of the General Conference Mennonite Church
is described by originator Robert W. Regier as follows:
"The cross and orb design is a contemporary variation of a
symbol with a long tradition. While the new symbol is intended to be flexible in meaning, historically the cross
and orb design has signified the sovereignty of Christ in
the world and in life to come. The symbol also suggests
the inseparable relationship between faith (the cross) and
life (the world). The line below the cross suggests the
concept of a foundation. Our faith, as expressed by the
meanings derived from the cross and orb, rests on a sure
foundation" (*The Mennonite*, 1961:574-575).

While no attempt is being made here to pit one system
against another, the Mennonites seem to feel their system
has certain advantages. It not only gives an opportunity to
rest for those working hard, but it also makes possible a
larger number of persons trained in church leadership if
some move away, and provides for a way to get a person out
of office without a trial if he or she is involved in
immoral living or heresy or simply does not take the responsibilities of the office seriously. In cases of flagrant
sin, of course, a person could be removed without waiting
for his term to expire. Sprunger also points out that

It is customary that deacons may be elected as elders
but that elders can only be elected again as an elder
but not as a deacon (this would be a demotion, since
the eldership is generally conceived to be a higher
office) (1974b:3).

A third distinctive is social service. This is primarily
through Mennonite Christian Hospital in Hwalien, an out-
growth of the MCC work. There is also a Mobile Clinic work
related to the hospital. Then, too, there have been work-
camps and Poverty Fund projects, especially to help the
mountain people get on their own feet. There is also a
social concerns committee under FOMCIT. It is felt that
this kind of service is worthwhile, but it is sometimes hard
to implement it.

A fourth distinctive that was not mentioned, but I consider is also noteworthy, is the active involvement of the
Mennonites in the Church Growth Society of Taiwan. Of the
thirty or so workers the General Conference Mennonites have
in Taiwan, only five couples and one single worker are
involved in church planting. But at the time this interview
was conducted, one of them, Sheldon Sawatzky, was chairman
of the society, and Hugh Sprunger was responsible for pro-
motion. Both of them are Mennonites, and both have studied
at the Fuller School of World Mission and Institute of
Church Growth. The society publishes the *Taiwan Church
Growth Bulletin.*

As said before, the Mennonites do not have a school of
their own, and they say they do not intend to. Financially
it would be difficult with the hospital already absorbing
most personnel and funds available. It is felt that to have
two competing institutions would not be wise. Besides,
there are a number of good theological schools in existence.
There was a time back about 1967 when they tried to start a
lay training program using correspondence materials. Some
took several courses. The people felt they needed it. But
there was no one to push it, and the program died out. It
was stressed that you need the right person. If the pastor
does not pick it up, no one else will. The pastors who
were enthusiastic and pushed it had some results. Those who
did not, it never got going. It was emphasized that a program like this will not start by itself. No matter how much
we talk, we have to find the right man who gets on fire, and
has enthusiasm about it. That is the key. "The right man
introducing the right idea at the right time."

The Mennonite pastors are all supported by the churches, although some have other sources of income. FOMCIT has set a minimum living standard including so much for parsonage, fringe benefits, and salary based on the size of the family. If the local church cannot meet the standard, the Fellowship subsidizes it. Of the 11 pastors, seven are currently receiving subsidy. Others are raising dogs or doing translation work or other part-time work. Some wives work. All of the churches have buildings, but these have all been subsidized to some degree from the States, and some churches are now paying back the loans they received on a matching basis. This also makes it harder for them to meet the standard set for supporting the pastors. Some of the pastors have over the years developed a gift for teaching, but nothing has been done in the area of leadership training. A little has been done in the area of lay training, but nothing systematic.

The question to be faced is, if lay training is a need in the Mennonite churches, which those I spoke to feel it is, how can that need be met? Is there any way that TEE can fit in here? The answer to that, I believe, is yes and no. In its present structure, TEE is not meeting the lay training needs of the Mennonite churches, primarily because no Mennonites are enrolled. There are four Mennonite churches in Taipei where there have been TEE classes. There are six Mennonite churches in Taichung where there have also been TEE classes. But out of over 100 students who have been enrolled in those programs, only one has been a Mennonite, and he dropped out. He was a deacon in one of the churches, a primary school teacher who wanted to do evangelistic work after he retired. But he felt the study required too much of him. For others, it might not be too difficult. But as long as students do not enroll in the program, it cannot do them any good. If the Mennonites plan to open more new work in the cities of Taiwan, as they are doing now in Taipei, whether they are house churches or more formal congregations, they will need many well-trained lay leaders, and one would think that TEE could be very useful for training them.

Another reason for not enrolling may be that there is some confusion about who the TEE classes are for. Supposedly, they are for everyone. But according to the "extension catalog," the stated purpose of the Diploma Course is "to train full-time ministers" (CES 1972:4). There seems to be a distinction made in the Mennonite churches between "lay" and "leadership" training. The former is primarily biblical knowledge, and for the layman. The latter is

considered to be more of a professional training for those
who want to become pastors. If there is confusion at this
point about the purpose of TEE, that might be one reason
some church members are reluctant to enroll. Also, the
length of time it takes to complete the course. It may take
from five to 10 years at least, and most people may not have
that much incentive to begin. It was suggested that rather
than try to get people enrolled in the TEE courses, it might
be better to just have a "school of prayer" or some such
course for six weeks or so. It might be more realistic and
easier to make a commitment to a shorter program.

But the main reason for not taking advantage of the TEE
classes so far may lie even deeper. Sprunger says he has
not pushed the program among his own group, the Mennonites,
because they are not so sure of CES yet. They were invited
to be on the school board at one time, but declined. Part
of the reason for that is that the school uses Mandarin, and
addresses itself to the Mandarin-speaking community, rather
than the Taiwanese-speaking community. The Mennonites are
largely made up of Taiwanese-speaking people. That is why
they lean more toward the Presbyterian and other schools,
because they use Taiwanese. It is not that they are against
CES. It is rather they are looking askance. There is one
Mennonite student in CES now, but the church as a whole is
taking a wait-and-see attitude. The Mennonites have no
direct relationship with CES, and as long as their people do
not enroll in the CES or other TEE classes, it will not
benefit their churches. On the other hand, if they do gain
confidence in the school and encourage people to enroll, or
if they set up some kind of a TEE program of their own
(perhaps in Taiwanese) in conjunction with a recognized
school, it may be able to help them meet their anticipated
need for more trained lay leaders. Sprunger hopes that the
work he is doing will eventually come back to the Mennonite
Church.

In closing, I would like to share some of Sprunger's
words that grow out of his experience with TEE:

TEE work is costly. It takes the investment of time
and money if it is to succeed. God has been blessing
the TEE work already and the TEE work must benefit God's
work and His churches. The goal of TEE work is to equip
Christian men and women with all the basic tools and
training needed to serve as ministers of the gospel.
As men and women are equipped and trained to serve, God
will call some to give more and more time to His work,

and local congregations should recognize and appoint such trained servants of God as leaders in congregations and outreach programs. The aim and goal of TEE work is to give equivalent training for ministry just as residential seminary programs do. The TEE program is not a competitor to resident seminary programs, but a complement. It is a co-worker in training the many leaders which local congregations, evangelism programs and missions need. Recognition of the goal and role of the TEE work should result in strong support for *both* types of training programs (1974c:2).

Observations: TEE in Taiwan is still relatively new as it has been operating for only a few years now. But it has grown steadily, with both the number of students and the number of classes increasing. The whole program is tied to the China Evangelical Seminary but is interdenominational in breadth. Classes have been held in several different centers. The students are approximately half men and half women. A large percentage of them are university graduates or students and young, but there are also a considerable number of older people enrolled. Almost all of the extension students have positions of leadership in the church already. Credit is given for work completed and credits can be transferred to other institutions if desired. The teaching staff includes both nationals and missionaries. Work has also been started toward producing their own programmed materials. The overall approach was carefully thought out and written down before anything was begun. The plan incorporated "church growth" thinking, with stress on the importance of planting many new churches and providing leaders for them. The long-range plans include offering extension education on three different levels, but they started off on a smaller scale with only one. And when it became clear that some modifications were in order, the program was flexible enough that necessary changes could be made.

On the other hand, there are also some problems. Among them are the need for men, materials, and money. That is, more teachers and regional center coordinators, better programmed materials, and greater local support by churches, pastors, missions, missionaries and cooperating schools. Some classes have already been dropped or cut back because of lack of personnel. There is also the question of whether there is really a place in the churches for people trained

under this system. Are they in fact being given more leadership? Is there actually a plan to plant numerous new
churches where they can be used? And what about the groups
like the Mennonites which are not yet involved? This, of
course, is not necessarily the fault of the school. But is
there any way such groups can be encouraged to participate?
Would it be feasible to have some courses specifically in
the Taiwanese language for them? Also, is it really clear
on the part of the students who this program is for? Also
on the part of the pastors? Some pastors feel threatened
by the whole thing. It may be that a program of continuing
education for them should be initiated as soon as possible
to acquaint them with the advantages of the program first-
hand, and enable them to stay ahead of their people. The
goals for the future appear to be clear, but it is going to
take a lot of effort to achieve them. It will take time
for the program to receive the recognition it deserves.

There is also a minor point related to the statistics given
in the reports. Does the total number of students really
reflect an accurate picture when some of them are counted
twice? It would be helpful if a more precise figure could
be given.

4

Theological Education by Extension in Japan

In the last chapter we looked at TEE in general, and then at a case study of TEE in Taiwan. Now we want to turn to a study of TEE in Japan. As indicated, however, there are no TEE programs as such in Japan. This means that as far as actual TEE programs go, there is not much to look at. That simplifies our study in a way, although there have been some TEE workshops in Japan, and we want to begin by considering those.

TWO WORKSHOPS BEAR LITTLE FRUIT

Two workshops on TEE were held in Japan in 1971, one in Osaka (Sept. 13-14), and the other in Tokyo (Sept. 15-16). Both of these were sponsored by the Japan Association of Evangelical Theological Schools, together with CAMEO (Committee to Assist Missionary Education Overseas). Wayne Weld summarizes the CAMEO Reports as follows (1973:148):

Osaka: A general introduction to TEE was given. Because of strong professional ideas of the clergy and pride in academic attainment the idea of extension training for pastors was not readily accepted. It had been mistakenly translated as lay training (CAMEO 1972:18-19).

Tokyo: It was felt that the two day presentation (some were not present the first day) was too short to give an adequate explanation of TEE. The delegates may be classified as follows:

missionaries 17, pastors 26, laymen 18, and
seminary students 110. Greater interest was
shown on the part of the missionaries than
among the pastors. The older leadership was
not enthusiastic but would investigate the
possibilities (CAMEO 1972:16-17).

These reports speak for themselves. To say the least,
TEE does not appear to have received a very enthusiastic
welcome in Japan. Part of the reason for this may be that
it was mistranslated as "lay training" in the publicity
materials, and if so, it is easy to understand why it might
not be considered suitable as a method for training pastors.
Education is highly valued in Japan, and if TEE was thought
of as just another lay training program rather than real
theological education, it is understandable why there would
be little interest in it. It is hard to say to what extent
the possibilities of TEE may have been investigated by now,
but the fact remains that there still do not seem to be any
TEE programs in Japan that meet the major requisites of our
definition of it.

This does not mean that there are not any programs which
have adopted some principles used in TEE. The Covenant
Seminary in Tokyo, for example, is listed along with many
other schools in Weld's directory of extension programs.
The reason for this is that the seminary does offer some
morning and evening classes for students who want to get
some theological training while staying at their jobs.
Under this system, all of the core courses are taught at
night as well as during the day, and a student may progress
according to his or her own time and ability. No distinction is made between day and night classes, and all of them
are taught at a university level requiring a good deal of
self study. Of those enrolled in the program so far, most
are said to be university graduates who have felt God's
pull toward the ministry (Peterson 1973:11). Admittedly,
this is a kind of extension into the lifestyle of the student and ought to be encouraged. But according to the way
we are defining it, it is not TEE, for it is not a
"geographical" extension of their program. Weld would seem
to agree with this when in speaking of Japan, he says that
"there is no genuine extension program there" (1973:43).

Another program, which is not listed in the directory,
is that of the Eastern Hokkaido Bible School in northern
Japan. This school is sponsored by the Mennonite Church
(not the General Conference Mennonites), and is essentially

a decentralized Bible school. It goes to the student, it
meets in several different centers, and it operates on three
different levels. Some of these characteristics make it the
closest thing I know of to a TEE program in Japan. But
again, according to the way we have defined it, it is not
TEE as it is not connected to a "recognized" institution.
An example of such an institution might be one of those
recognized by an organization like the "Japan Association of
Evangelical Theological Schools" (Hoke 1963b). There may be
some other programs which I am not aware of that incorporate
TEE principles. But according to our definition of TEE as
*the geographical extension of the program of a recognized
theological training institution*, there is not yet any
authentic TEE program anywhere in Japan. Defined broadly,
we might say yes. Narrowly, we must say no.

Be that as it may, in this chapter we want to take a look
at three different schools in Japan. The first is Tokyo
Christian College, where many of our Mennonite students have
gone. The second is the Hitoyoshi Bible School in Kyushu,
on the other side of the island from where we are working.
And the third is the Eastern Hokkaido Bible School, which
has already been referred to. While there is no TEE in
Japan, and while these schools do not offer extension programs, there may be points at which they apply TEE principles and I believe we can learn something from each of them.
These three case studies were all done in May 1974, and to
my knowledge their programs remain basically the same as
reported here. As in the case of Taiwan, following each of
these reports there will be a brief evaluation in the form
of some observations.

CASE STUDY: TOKYO CHRISTIAN COLLEGE

(Based on an interview with Morris B. Jacobsen, May 7, 1974,
and a letter of October 22, 1974.)

Tokyo Christian College originally began in 1950 as the
Domei (Alliance) Bible Institute. ("Domei" is the national
organization of TEAM.) In 1955, it became officially known
as Japan Christian College (JCC), and later on, in 1966, was
accredited by the Ministry of Education as a three-year
junior college, and the name was changed to Tokyo Christian
College (TCC). In 1969, an additional year was officially
"recognized" by the Ministry of Education as an extension of
their program. The school moved to its present location in
the suburbs of western Tokyo in 1961.

According to a brochure on the school, the motto of the
college is, "To know Christ and to make Christ known."
Since 1950 there have been over 350 graduates of the school,
who are now serving Christ in various areas of Japan, as
well as in South America, Southeast Asia, Africa and elsewhere. The purpose of the school as stated is

> To train Christian men and women as pastors,
> evangelists, and other Christian workers, building
> on the foundation of an evangelical Christian faith.
> To that end, spiritual, academic, and practical train-
> ing are all emphasized (TCC n.d.).

As far as the curriculum goes, it includes both general
courses and more specialized biblical studies. The students
can choose between a two-year program of studies specially
arranged for them, or a basic three-year theology course,
followed by a fourth year of special study. While the
school is accredited as a junior college, it is best described as offering a two-year liberal arts course with a
Bible major. Courses are taught at approximately a seminary
level, with Greek and Hebrew also required. Students are
also required to take two years of English or its equivalent.
In addition, the school has an English academy in the evenings which is open to the public, in which a total of 70 or
80 are enrolled. Church is also held on campus on Sunday,
which many young people are said to attend.

Admission requirements for the regular students include
high school graduation, an exam in English and Bible, a
short essay, a recommendation from a church or pastor, and
an interview with evidence of a clear-cut call to the
ministry. According to Morris Jacobsen, they are not so
strict on the latter, recognizing that some may be "called"
in the course of study. The students planning to be there
just a couple of years need have only the interview. A high
school diploma or transcript from the previous school is
also required of all students. At present (1974) there are
57 students at TCC. Fifty-two of them are full time; five
are part time. Enrollment has been increasing slightly.

The students are taught by 11 full-time professors,
including Donald E. Hoke, the school president, plus 10
part-time instructors. With 57 students and 21 teachers,
the student-teacher ratio is about three to one. About 80
percent of the faculty are Japanese; 20 percent, American.
(Note: Dr. Hoke is now serving as Coordinator of the
Graham Center at Wheaton College, U.S.A., rather than at
TCC. The new college president is Mr. Shimpei Higuchi.)

On weekends and vacations, the students have practical
work assignments which are under the supervision of a pastor
or missionary. Dr. Jacobsen is Professor of Practical
Theology, and he said that in addition to students teaching
Sunday school and preaching in churches, TCC has an "eight-
phase" practical work program for them as follows:

1st	semester:	:	learn how the church works
2nd	"	:	personal work
3rd	"	:	family-size evangelism
4th	"	:	open-air evangelism
5th	"	:	community survey
6th	"	:	camp counseling
7th	"	:	conducting home meetings
8th	"	:	hospital evangelism

Such practical training is to prepare them for future
pastoral and evangelistic responsibilities.

There is no special recognition given a student who takes
only two years or so. But when a student has completed the
three-year program, he receives a junior college diploma,
which would perhaps be equivalent to an Associate of Arts
degree in the States. If he completes the four-year course,
he receives a diploma and also participates in the graduation ceremony. Most of the graduates enter the pastorate,
or some go on to graduate-level studies. While courses are
taught on a high academic level at TCC, it is not a seminary,
and that is perhaps why some students want to go on for
further training. In any case, there is no M.Div. equivalent in Japan, and transfer of credits to other schools is
always somewhat of a problem. The problem is not so much
one of accreditation or lack of it, but whether work taken
elsewhere is applicable or not.

As pointed out, the first three years at TCC are accredited. The fourth year is "approved," but not accredited. To
accredit it would make TCC a full university. But accreditation is a very difficult process in Japan. To get its
present accreditation, the school had to go through several
years of probation. Having received partial accreditation,
the school now receives six or seven million yen (approx.
$20,000) a year from the Ministry of Education as a junior
college. If the school wanted to become a university, it
would have to go through six or seven years of probation
again, and during that time would lose those funds. You
also need a required number of qualified teachers in order
to become accredited, and it was due to a lack in this area
that TCC was unable to receive accreditation as a full
university. In relation to this, Jacobsen notes that

There are various routes to becoming an accredited
teacher. One is completion of the doctorate. ...The
other is working up through the ranks of teacher
assistant (joshi), lecturer (kōshi), assistant professor (jokyōju), and professor (kyōju). Elevation
here comes through a combination of experience in
teaching and publication of research (1974b:1).

Be that as it may, it is felt that perhaps it would have
been wise to go for full accreditation from the beginning.
To try to do so now would work a great hardship on the
school financially.

As it is now, TCC is accredited as a biblical-theological
junior college, but getting university graduates is a
problem, especially for those who want to attend a school
with a little more prestige. If they come to TCC from
university, it may seem to them like a step backwards,
because it is not a fully accredited institution. It
actually would not be a step backwards, though, as they are
entering a whole new field of study. At any rate, with
things the way they are, TCC does not accept university
graduates at present. Yet one of the biggest challenges it
faces is the possibility of working out a program for
university students which would be an extension of the third
and fourth-year program.

Some of the distinctives of the school are that it has
been accredited as a junior college. Along with that, while
it is a college, its purpose is specifically that of Christian education. It is said to be more "incidentally" a
college. It also has a large campus, approximately 11 acres
(4.5 hectares), on which are located the main building and
classrooms, dormitories, and some faculty residences.

One of the problems the school faces is low enrollment.
Enrollment has been steady, but it would help to have more
students. Financially, the school is also very dependent on
American churches and the Ministry of Education. Accreditation is somewhat of a problem too. Occasionally, students
have come thinking the school was fully accredited, and were
greatly disappointed when they found out it was not.
Another problem that the school faces or has faced is that
its image was bad for a while. Jacobsen mentioned that at
one time there seemed to be a "hyper-Calvinism" plus an
"anti-evangelistic philosophy" that prevailed. The result
was that students were very critical of the churches they
attended. Such trends in the wrong direction are hard to

reverse. It was emphasized, however, that there has been great improvement in the spiritual life of the school.

When asked whether anything was being done in the area of TEE, it was commented that it is on the "list of things to do." They do have "participation training" seminars for pastors. These struggle with the problems of church leadership patterns, and the involvement of the laity. The school has been thinking of having a summer school program such as some universities do. This would be like a summer course after a student has completed correspondence work during the year. Thought has also been given to the possibility of starting something at the downtown Ochanomizu Student Christian Center.

In one of the TEE seminars held in Japan a few years ago, it was suggested that the "school base" type of religious education was not as good as the "experience-plus-school base," or the "in-service" type of education. Responding to a question on whether this was true or not, it was observed that ideally an "in-service" education would be good, but pedigree is also quite important in Japan. People always want to know, "What school have you been to?" There is also the question of whether the Ministry of Education would approve an extension program as part of TCC. The problem is how to best combine the theoretical and the practical. The learning theory of TEE, the combination of theory and practice is good. But it was felt that TEE probably would be most useful for lay leaders. Japan is, of course, different from Latin America, yet TEE may be applicable here too. It might depend on our aims. Jacobsen says that as things are now, "there are more pastors produced than the churches can absorb. If they are trained to be evangelists and church planters, then we can train more. We need pioneers!"

One of the weaknesses of TEE may be that, as mentioned, the Japanese are very school-oriented. It was suggested that programmed textbooks or "intertexts" might also be a problem. That is, the kind of materials needed for an extension program. Some do not recommend translating texts. But you have to start somewhere. Who will do it? Time could also be a problem. Where can you find enough teachers with time to teach? Yet in spite of such problems, it is thought that TEE may be useful in certain situations if it is adapted to the Japanese environment, not only in producing more leaders, but in encouraging greater church growth.

As for "church growth," TCC does not have a church growth department, but it does have a Church Growth Research Center (with no direct relationship to Fuller Theological Seminary's School of World Mission and Institute of Church Growth). This was first talked about at a church growth meeting held at the school in February, 1971 (at which the author was also present), and was established some time later. One of its projects was a study made for the Japan Congress on Evangelism held in Kyoto in June, 1974. This was done for the JEA (Japan Evangelical Association). It was designed primarily to obtain a profile of the successful Japanese pastor, and to relate the believers in a given church to the pastors who had served there, to see what characteristics the pastor passes on to the people. Copies of the results were not available at the time of this interview. They were later, however, under the title of *Japanese Church Growth Patterns in the 1970's* (Jacobsen 1977). Some student profiles have also been done, such as their feeling toward certain theological words. Besides these things, I was told that the school also has a good church growth library, which should be helpful in encouraging future leaders to try to find better ways to make Japanese churches grow.

Observations: Though founded by TEAM, the school is inter-denominational in character. It has by now had a 24-year history. Its objectives seem to be clear, and it has already produced a considerable number of Christian leaders. It is accredited as a junior college, has had fairly steady enrollment, and has a predominantly Japanese faculty. It has five Ph.D.'s and one Th.D. on its full-time or contributing faculty. There is a good attempt being made to integrate practical with theoretical studies through the "eight-phase" program. The Church Growth Research Center is a plus. And the school has a large campus and good facilities. It also has an English academy that appeals more to the general public.

On the other hand, the school does face some problems of a rather serious nature. One is the small enrollment. Another is the lack of full accreditation. Along with that, it does not have a graduate-level program. As a result, it does not attract many university graduates. Most of the students are still young and inexperienced. It does not provide continuing education for its graduates, and has no training program for laymen. There is, however, a growing summer school program. The school also seems to be financially

quite dependent on the Ministry of Education and American
support. One wonders whether an extension program of some
kind might not help remedy several of these weaknesses.

(On the "plus" side it should also be added that in
September 1977, the Kyoritsu Bible School for Women merged
with TCC, and the faculty and student body moved to the
campus. Consultations are also underway for a merger with
the Japan Christian Theological Seminary, which should
strengthen the entire program. The newly formed complex of
schools will go under the name of "Tokyo Kirisutokyo Gakuen"
from the start of the 1980 academic year.)

Note: The following additional "Comments on Theological
Education by Extension in Japan" were made by former College
President Donald Hoke in connection with a personal letter
of February 13, 1975:

   From the very outset of the publication of information about TEE, I have been vitally interested in it.
In my own personal library I have all of the early
materials on it. I sought to research the matter carefully, and suggested it to those persons interested in
the tiny Church Growth Institute that we have tried to
start at TCC over the years. I have also discussed it
with other educators in the country. Interest in it
has not been strong.

   Nevertheless, I think it might be said that in my
own little circle at TCC I have pioneered in trying
to stir some interest in TEE in Japan.

   The problems in Japan are distinct from those in
South America where the system was pioneered. As I
see it, the great challenge to TEE in Japan is to give
laymen a sense of qualification and fitness which will
enable them to take a fuller role in the church. Here
laymen are second-class Christians. They are treated
as such by pastors. They feel their lack of education,
in particular. Therefore, courses in TEE which would
lead to some kind of a diploma would give the layman
a sense of confidence and "shikaku" [qualification],
which would lead them to take a more aggressive role
in the church, I believe.

   In addition, TEE, provided there is leadership
from the pastor, would enable laymen to go out and

start daughter churches, beginning with Bible classes, which I believe is the key to further church growth in Japan as early church growth studies in the country have indicated.

My conclusion is that TEE needs to be developed in Japan. It will meet much opposition from the professional clergy in some areas, I feel. But I believe it is the key to unlocking the power of the laymen here (1975b:3).

CASE STUDY: HITOYOSHI BIBLE SCHOOL

(Based on an interview with H. Dale Oxley, May 22, 1974, and a letter of November 4, 1974.)

The Hitoyoshi Bible School (HBS), sponsored by the Japan Bible Protestant Missions (JBPM) and affiliated churches, opened in the fall of 1962. Hitoyoshi is a small city of 50,000 located in Kumamoto Prefecture on the island of Kyushu in southern Japan. The stated purpose of opening such a school was that "due to the lack of any evangelical Bible School in Kyushu, we feel the need to provide a school program geared to the specific needs of the local ministry" (JBPM 1962a:1). In another notice sent out, it was to be a school "dedicated to the task of training young men in the Word of God" (JBPM 1962b:1). Up until that time, a number of young men had been sent away for training, but very few of them came back. Thus there was a feeling of a need to train people locally for local service.

In the beginning, the program was arranged in two sections. First, an afternoon session with more professional courses. This was intended for the full-time students, who would work in the morning and study in the afternoon. Second, a night session, to which laymen were invited too. The first year there were four full-time students. A boy from neighboring Miyazaki Prefecture, a girl from the northern prefecture of Niigata, and a boy and girl from Hitoyoshi. These all finished the full three-year program. The boy from Miyazaki went back to his home. The girl from Niigata to hers. And the boy and girl from Hitoyoshi married each other. As for the evening sessions, an average of 20 to 25 laymen attended from Hitoyoshi and nearby Taragi and Sashiki.

The school has changed considerably since its inception. As mentioned, there were at one time four full-time students.

But the program has been cut back, and there is no full-time day program now. The night program has been cut back too. At present it meets only one night a week, with two subjects being taught. For several years, classes were held two nights a week, and two subjects a night were offered. Then in spring, a specialist such as a Japanese pastor or a seminary professor would be brought down from Tokyo or Kobe for a week of meetings, three hours a night, which 40 to 45 attended. This was a concentrated seminary-type course, and this aspect of the program still continues. It is felt that short-term concentrated efforts are very effective, and they hope to expand this to both spring and fall. But while the full-time and part-time programs have both been curtailed, it should be noted that one of their pastors is a graduate of their school. In addition, there are about 10 laymen who have received the equivalent of a three-year Bible school education. This was taken in night courses, and most of them probably have taken 25 or 30 subjects.

The Oxleys first arrived in Japan in 1952, spent one year in language study, then moved to Hitoyoshi in 1953. Nine months after they arrived they had their first baptism. At the present, there are four churches and three Japanese pastors. The Taragi Church is shepherded by Pastor Inoue, Kumamoto by Pastor Haraguchi, Sashiki by Pastor Matsuoka (an HBS graduate), and the Hitoyoshi Church is pastored by Dale Oxley. Before having their own Bible school, the young men were sent off to the cities for their training. Inoue and Haraguchi both graduated from Japan Christian Theological Seminary in Tokyo. The former pastored the Hitoyoshi Church one year while the missionary was on furlough. The latter pastored it one year in the middle of his education. That may be part of the reason those two came back. Others did not.

For example, out of six students who went to TCC, only one of them, a girl, came back. She is now the wife of a pastor on the back side of Japan. None of the others are in the ministry. Two were sent to Osaka Biblical Seminary. Neither of them came back. Neither of them is in the ministry. Three were sent to the Covenant Seminary. One is working (and doing a study of Buddhism in the evenings), and hopes to some day work in the church, but two of them lost their faith. This means that out of 13 who were sent away to study, only three came back, and only two are in the pastoral ministry. There were also a few more who went away but did not come back for various reasons.

Oxley used to go up to Tokyo and eat and sleep with their students for three or four days occasionally, and the

students came back on vacations. But he says it is difficult. The problem is not just sending them away. It is the
whole atmosphere of the educational process in Tokyo. The
people and the thinking pattern influence those who will be
working in the country. The psychology is so different.
For example, *arbeit* or part-time work. A student may be
working in a church, too, but he earns more from his part-
time work than he gets from the church. Also, the student
may have practical work such as teaching Sunday school or
helping a missionary, and they ride around in big cars and
use PA systems and get a big honorarium and it is all very
interesting. But when they come back to the country, it is
like digging rock. It takes years to get two or three
converts. It is so different.

Another problem is that when a student is in school, it is
felt he should be there to learn. Not to preach, teach, minister, or even hold evangelistic meetings. Part of the learning is to be in a local church situation as a layman, where
he can grow as a Christian, and see the working of the local
congregation from the bottom up. But they seldom do that in
Tokyo. There they are leaders. They do everything. And when
they come down here, they expect everything to be turned over
to them too. But in the Hitoyoshi program, the students who
return are expected to participate in the church as a layman.
This is a real blow to their pride. They see that the laymen
are doing okay without them. They see that the church is not
dependent on them. Oxley feels strongly that "if you can't
be a good layman, you can't ever be a good preacher either.
A student is not a preacher." As he puts it, "not even a
junior preacher!" The need for supervised practical training
of older students is also recognized. It was stressed, however, that it should be church-oriented, and that personal
evangelism and small meetings ought to be emphasized.

Accordingly, it follows that what they say they want in
Hitoyoshi is "a training program formulated to meet our
specific needs, and the needs of a rural situation." Perhaps those trained in the country will not fit in the city.
But that may be all right, they feel, for those trained in
Tokyo, even if they get good training, have a hard time
making it in the country. It is felt that if they had
trained people locally, they could have preserved many.
They started their own school in the hopes of keeping more
leaders at home. If there were other schools, that might
also be a possibility. But there are practically no other
evangelical schools in Kyushu except the Southern Baptist
school in Fukuoka, at the northern end of the island, and a

Pentecostal school in Kurume, a couple of hours away, and perhaps another local training program or two. Almost all churches send their students away. It seems difficult to get even the cooperation of other missionaries. Each is "a law unto himself."

From the start, a rather detailed curriculum was worked out, to cover a four-year course. Several subjects were to be offered each semester. Some were to cover the whole year. There was to be an average of 15 hours of instruction per week. But this plan has not been followed too closely. No courses have been offered in Greek and Hebrew, as thought at first. Rather the emphasis has been on theology -- the Church, last things, Christ, the Holy Spirit, and Bible study methods. Many of the courses have been repeated. For a time, Mrs. Oxley taught the full-time students English, and most of the pastors can read theological books and commentaries in English quite well, but they are not teaching it now.

On credits, they say they have not been very consistent. The full-time students receive a certificate of completion of the program, in recognition of their work. Most of the lay leaders have taken the basic courses too, and while they have been given a certificate for completion of each course, there has not been any graduation yet for lay leaders. The teaching level is the same for both groups. They try to keep the requirements at about a college level. But a distinction is made between the full-time students and the laymen in the amount of homework required. A few older women just listen and do not do the homework, but they naturally get more out of it if they do it. The bulk of the students have been from the Hitoyoshi area because of the location of the school. As of the present, there is no continuing education program for the pastors who have completed the course.

The school follows the American semester system, not because it is American, but because it keeps the summer free for the church's full six-week camping program. It was also hoped this would make it easier for specialists in a given field to come and help out during their vacations. This system also makes it possible for students from other churches to go back to their own church for the summer. They always encourage their students to go back where they came from. So far, besides their own, they have had one Mennonite and one TEAM student enrolled in their school.

In the early stages, there were several requirements for entrance such as a personal experience of salvation, evidence of a call to serve the Lord, being baptized and an active church member for at least a year, graduation from high school, a recommendation from a pastor or missionary and so on. But at present, there are no specific requirements other than the spiritual qualifications. Those who wish to study are met with, and if it is felt the applicant truly desires to serve the Lord in a lay or full-time capacity, he or she is accepted. If the applicant would be a middle-aged person, and it was felt he was gifted, he would be accepted even though he might not be a high school graduate. They insist on their leaders having Bible training, but they do not feel that a formal high school education is absolutely necessary. They recognize its importance, but also consider exceptions.

As for students, some may use Bible schools as a step to college or university, then go into secular work. Oxley says that if a boy is qualified, his first recommendation would be that he go to university. After that, if he is still serious, he could go on to Bible school. The only problem is that if a student goes to university first, he probably would not want to come back to study in a local school, but rather go on to a seminary somewhere. So perhaps it would be best to concentrate on middle-aged or older men, men who have been in the business world. With young men, you never know how it will go until they marry and settle down. Ideally, we ought to try to find men whom the Lord calls, who may continue to work for a living, but at the same time be called to the ministry, to be the pastor or shepherd of a little flock. This, he feels, may be one of the keys to extension education. Over the past 12 years, there have been about 40 different students studying in their school. Out of them has come one full-time pastor. But he says there are seven men or so whom, if the Lord called, could be pastors.

Currently, a course on "Leadership Training" (*Shidōsha Kunrenkai*) is being offered on Friday nights. This includes such topics as the spirit of the ministry of leadership, leadership and the Holy Spirit, Paul's thought on leadership (I Timothy), Peter's thought on leadership (I Peter 5) and the like. An attempt is being made to get away from the authoritative, dictator-type of leadership mentality. Christ's pattern was true humility, precepts lived out in daily life. Some of the pastors are attending too, but most of those participating are laymen. The course is aimed at middle-aged laymen. Most of the students are men. A pastor's wife is coming too, but women are not encouraged to come. It is mainly for those contemplating a full-time ministry in the church. This does not mean just Sunday school teaching, but actually taking over a church for several months or a year. In addition to these courses, once or twice a year there are training sessions with the pastors only at a hotel. They are said to be eager for that sort of opportunity.

When the school first began there was an entrance fee and a low tuition fee, plus utilities and room and board for the full-time students. Now there is just a little tuition for the laymen attending night school to cover the expenses of the pastors involved in the program as teachers. This is only 500 yen ($1.70) per course, which covers the printing and teaching costs. Teachers receive nothing for the teaching itself, but do get transportation costs. The program also receives a minor subsidy of twenty-five dollars per month from the mission board for the Bible school ministry. If necessary, they help students find jobs. There are a couple of Christian businessmen in the churches who are willing to take students and gear a work program to their study program. For instance, the Niigata girl worked from eight to twelve in the morning, then studied in the afternoon and evening.

Dale Oxley does most of the theological, doctrinal, and biblical (book studies) teaching. Pastor Haraguchi teaches church history. Pastor Inoue, cults and biblical studies. Pastor Matsuoka is not teaching yet. He was ordained only two years ago. But one of the biggest weaknesses at present seems to be that there is no full-time man. As was stressed, "you have to have someone full time to keep things moving, and for study." With what they have going already, if they had a full-time person to help with the teaching, the pastors would need to teach only one or two courses a year. With three men or so it is felt they could then do the basic three-year program. In another year or two, it was suggested that the churches could conceivably support a full-time teacher. It was also said that the lines of responsibility for such a program must be kept clear. Oxley himself has done some teaching in other churches too. For example in their Kumamoto church, where he has concentrated a course into three or four sessions. Or further away in Niigata where he has spoken on specific topics such as tithing, the Lord's day, marriage to nonbelievers, and the indigenous church. But most teaching has been local.

As for facilities, originally their kindergarten buildings were used for classes, and a dormitory was erected for
the full-time students. Now the dormitory has been divided
into half for classroom use, and the other half is an apartment. If they expand, as they hope to, they will either put
a second floor on this building or construct something at
their nearby camp site.

It was mentioned before that there are now (1974) four
churches and three of them have Japanese pastors, all full-
time men. The pastors have been discouraged from doing too
much part-time work. Not only is it felt that they do not
have time to do part-time work in addition to their pastoral
responsibilities, but people want them to give full time to
the church. Occasionally a pastor may have an English
class or his wife a cooking class if it is for evangelism.
But if it is not for evangelism, if it is just for support,
they feel it should be done only where absolutely necessary.
As soon as a church can support a man full time, it is felt
that it is better to give up secular work. Most of the
pastors have had the goal of giving their whole time to the
ministry, and perhaps because of the emphasis on the laity,
the laymen know how little time they have to give, and they,
too, encourage the pastors to give full time. Today all of
the churches are fully self-supporting. Three of them have
their own pastors, all full time and fully supported. The
churches all have their own buildings, all paid for. An
attempt was made at self-support from the beginning. As
soon as they had their first converts, they encouraged them
to begin looking for land.

Sometimes, though, when the churches want to begin a work,
they support a pastor and send him out to a new area, and
let the laymen, the "tentmakers," carry on the local church
program. Then the pastor comes back to serve his former
congregation in two or three years. Oxley's conviction is
that a missionary can also be a pastor, and a pastor can be
a missionary. He must be adaptable like a missionary. Some
days he is a teacher, or a pastor, or an evangelist. Other
days he may need to begin a new work, or be a conference
speaker, or a ditch digger. Actually, their Japanese
"mission board" was born shortly after their Bible school
began. Oxley was starting a new work in Sashiki, as well as
teaching in the Bible school, and when the missionary
family in Taragi left, he had to continue the work there
too. He could not do it all by himself, so one of the
Japanese layman quit his secular job, and went to Sashiki as
a missionary under their Japanese mission board. Later, he

went to Tokyo and started a kindergarten there. After his graduation, Mr. Matsuoka, the full-time student from Hitoyoshi, went to Sashiki as pastor, and continued his education in night school before he was ordained. Presently they are considering starting a new work in Okuchi.

The four churches are independent, but have a conference relationship. Locally they are named the Obiyama (Kumamoto) Bible Church, Hitoyoshi Bible Church and so on. The conference is called the Bible Protestant Church in Japan. It is not an organizational tie, however, that forces cooperation. It is "free cooperation, not coercion." The churches would all like to have a full-time Bible school program if possible.

As for the school they do have, they do not consider it a "school" yet. It is still in the formative stages. When asked if there were any distinctives to their program, Oxley pointed out two. First, the emphasis on the laity, or lay leadership. Second, a program geared to meet the needs of a rural ministry, the local church. But what they would like to see worked out in the future is a three-year basic program locally, in conjunction with a recognized school in Tokyo. After three years here, they would insist on one year of practical work here on the field. Then they would send them to Tokyo for one or two years if a program could be worked out with a seminary up there that they approved of, and the seminary would be willing to accept a student on that basis.

It was felt that schools in Tokyo must awaken to their responsibility, recognize the realities of the situation in Japan, and be willing to meet the educational needs of rural churches. They should be desirous of making such a program available. Such a school would probably have to be interdenominational. You would have to work out the basic program with that school from the beginning, and gear the courses here to prepare them for the work up there. Those that went beyond the capacity here would then go there. The program here would have to be worked out under their supervision. There are a number of questions that would have to be worked out. For instance, whether the program here would be an extension of theirs, or if it would be independent.

When asked about accreditation, Oxley replied that TCC, for example, is accredited only in the area of its Bible major. He feels that there may be some limitations in training a man spiritually and biblically for the kind of work he is going to do, with the educational requirements they would have under the Ministry of Education. A Bible school is to train men for a spiritual ministry. For that, accreditation is not so important. In America, a Ph.D. is recognized as a Ph.D. Not in Japan. Even with a degree, a person must teach in a school so many years before he is accredited, before he is recognized as a qualified teacher. Some schools, in order to get the qualified men they need for accreditation, get qualified non-Christians on the faculty. Oxley believes that is a mistake we should try to avoid.

Also, in a program like this, it was expressed that there must be someone with a real burden for it, someone to take responsibility and leadership and push it. In a Bible school program, one of the key factors is having all men involved with the same theological orientation and philosophy of teaching. Schools have broken up where this is not true. Students are torn, too, where teachers are not agreed on things.

When asked for advice if we ever tried to start something like this, it was said that we must use the same philosophy in starting a Bible school program as in organizing a church. Do not start at the top. Start in a very practical way, meet specific needs that we have now, and refine the program as we go on. It is better to start small, and add on. It is discouraging to have to cut back. "What are the specific needs of our work? Our local church situation? What location would best meet the needs of the group as a whole? What level of training?" are some of the questions that ought to be asked. If the objectives and goals can be firmly established with relatively 100 percent agreement and backing, "Yes, this is a need, something we must do," then gear the program to meet those objectives first. With each accomplishment, confidence increases. There is nothing like success to stimulate success. But as with a church building, it is easy to talk, but until you go out and look, nothing happens. They might say, "we have no money for a building." "No, but you do for the foundation." So build a foundation. That stimulates them, and they will finish it! "Once they get the vision for it, they can carry it out better than you can. They are perfectly capable. The problem is to get them going."

Observations: The school has had 12 years of experience by now. Its objectives have been clear, and it has aimed

specifically at training a rural ministry. There have been
only a few full-time students involved, but many part-time
students have been enrolled in the program. The program has
been multi-level and flexible in its requirements. As a
result, there are several laymen with the equivalent of a
Bible school education. One pastor has come out of the
program. Many other laymen have benefitted from the school,
and it seems to be training some of the real leaders of the
churches. Specialists have been called in regularly to
supplement the program. Two of the pastors have also been
involved in the teaching. And the school seems to have good
support from the pastors and the cooperating churches.
Facilities are fairly adequate for now. Their vision for
the future is clear.

On the other hand, it would appear that the school tried to
start off too big, and it is unfortunate that they have had
to cut back. One of the biggest needs obviously is someone
to give full time to the program. There also is no tie with
a recognized school, which means it might be difficult for
their graduates to continue their education if they wished
to. And they have no continuing education program locally
for those who have finished the basic courses. Then too,
in spite of the large number of students they have had over
the years, they are still short one pastor for their
churches. It also sounds like most of the students are from
Hitoyoshi, largely due to the school's location. Perhaps it
would be well to try to decentralize a little more, if
possible, to benefit more people and more of the churches.

CASE STUDY: EASTERN HOKKAIDO BIBLE SCHOOL

(Based on an interview with Takio Tanase, May 1, 1974, and a
letter of March 30, 1975.)

The Eastern Hokkaido Bible School (EHBS) was started in
1965. Before that, the young men who came to Hokkaido from
the cities and became leaders in the Mennonite churches
often had a "Tokyo mentality." So did a few young men who
were sent to Tokyo for training when they returned. They
came back with a very pastor-centered conception of the
church. Their view of the church did not fit with what the
Mennonites were trying to do.

What they had hoped to do was emphasize the "believers'
church" concept, using lay leaders. But with a misconception

of the church, leadership did not emerge naturally from the
group. Because of these and other problems, they decided to
start a school of their own. Takio Tanase, the main
teacher, emphasized that what they were interested in was
"not beautiful facilities, not necessarily a highly trained
staff, but rather a school that would meet the needs of the
churches." It was not only negative factors, though, that
made them want their own school. There were also positive
ones, such as the ministry of Dr. Howard H. Charles from
their seminary in America, who spent a year (1961-62) teaching Bible in the various churches in Hokkaido. It was said
this really laid the groundwork for the EHBS program. It
was a good stimulus in that it made people realize that this
kind of education is necessary.

Prior to having their own school, they did have what they
called "winter Bible schools." These were said to be mostly
for Bible study, doing book studies and the like, but the
purpose was not only educational. It was for fellowship
too, and classes were held during vacations or when people
were free. Short courses and seminars were also occasionally held at summer camp. But the present program is quite
different from that. It is more organized, and aims more
specifically at leadership training. In fact, the real
impetus for the new school was when two or three of their
people came and said, "We want to study!" It was felt something must be done. The study schedule was arranged so that
students could attend without interrupting their work
schedule, and thus classes were held in the evening. The
classes were open to anyone. Most of the students were
married, but there were also a single fellow and a single
girl who later married each other. Not just lay leaders
but ordinary laymen attended too. Over a period of four or
five years, they were able to train several lay pastors
locally. As careful records were not kept of the various
students who have studied in the school since its beginning,
it is difficult to give statistics on the various years.

I did run across some additional information, however, on
their winter Bible schools and the start of the Eastern
Hokkaido Bible Institute (EHBI, now EHBS). This material
was contained in a report called a "Seminary and Bible
School Study," a rather extensive survey done by two of
their own men back in 1958 and 1959. In one of the reports
included in this study, Ralph Buckwalter, a Mennonite
missionary, noted in a written interview that

The seventh annual Winter Bible School was held in
Kushiro January 1-4, 1959. Since 1952, one year

after the arrival of the first two Mennonite missionary
families in Hokkaido, annual Bible Conferences of 3 to
4 days duration have been held for the benefit of
believers and seekers.

The schools were held in Kushiro and Obihiro alter-
nately the first several years. This was replaced by
holding a four-day session in one of the centers and
continuing the school another four days in the other
center. More recently the schools are being held
simultaneously. This year a four-day school was held
in Kushiro for the benefit of the churches in [the]
Kushiro-Nemuro area while the first longer-term school
was being held in Obihiro, reaching primarily the
Tokachi area churches, but open for all who were able
to engage in the 10-day study discipline. ...

Unfortunately, accurate records of attendance have not
been kept. High school students made up the majority
of students in the beginning. As the churches have
grown adults comprise a larger percentage of those
attending. ... An average of 15 attended the day
sessions of the Kushiro Bible School this year. Half
of these were from outside the city. About 25 attended
the evening sessions, with over 50 coming on Sunday.
Overnite guests are housed and given breakfast in the
homes of members or seekers. This practice has proved
a blessing in deepening Christian fellowship and is
one of the permanent features of the Bible School. ...

We feel that the development of a longer-term Bible
School (Eastern Hokkaido Bible Institute held at
Obihiro this year for the first time) is very timely
and urgently needed (Richards and Peachey 1959:29-30).

In another brief report in the same study, Carl Beck,
also one of the Mennonite missionaries, summarizes the
beginning of this school noting that

The first "Doto Seisho Gakuin" [Eastern Hokkaido
Bible Institute] was conducted at Obihiro from Jan.
1-11, 1959. Its purpose was to provide basic instruction in Bible, practical church work, and evangelism
for lay believers who wish to become better stewards
of the gifts entrusted to them, and who cannot leave
regular jobs for longer periods of training in one
of the big city Bible schools. Approximately a hundred persons attended two or more sessions, but only

25 persons finished the entire night course and only
9 persons the night and day courses (1959:31).

The Bible Institute came to be known several years later
as the Bible School. According to the original announcement
that went out about the EHBS program, the purpose of the
school was said to be "to conduct theological education and
give spiritual training, in order to spread the Gospel and
serve the church." Two of the special characteristics of
the school were stated as being, first, "that it would
offer training that was suitable for the work in Hokkaido,"
and second, "that it would offer education that emphasized
Anabaptist-Mennonite distinctives" (EHBS n.d.). The main
school was to be located at the church in Kushiro. A
branch school was also planned to meet at the church in
Obihiro. So it was that the school began in these two
places at the same time.

Tanase has been director of EHBS for the past three
years. He says that after the first few years of operation
it was felt that it would be well if students studied on
several levels rather than one. As a result, two years ago
they decided to offer courses on three levels. The first
level is for laymen (or for the whole church). The second
level is for training laymen who want to become pastors.
The third level is continuing education for those who are
already pastors. At the same time, they felt that rather
than bring the students to one place, it might be better to
"take the school to the students." So Obihiro, which is
located more or less at the center of things, was made the
central school, and it was decided to open four branch
schools in Kushiro, Kamishihoro, Furano, and Sapporo. In
1973 they tried to operate all four of these branches, but
found it too difficult with their limited personnel, so have
closed down three of these centers temporarily and are now
operating in only two, Kamishihoro and Taiki (a new one).
In 1973 there were about 35 enrolled. In 1974 there were
31 -- one full time (from Obihiro), 10 pastors, and 20 laymen. Pastors' wives are also urged to study in the same
class with their husbands if possible. A missionary or two
are also enrolled in the continuing education program, and
are included with the pastors in the total count above.

As for the curriculum, a number of different courses have
been taught. Originally a rather detailed plan was worked
out, including Old and New Testament studies, church history,
practical theology and so on. While the original curriculum
has not been followed exactly, many of these courses have

been taught. Anabaptist history and doctrine have also been
included among them. It was mentioned that a number of
very practical courses such as "how to build a library,"
"how to make use of time," and laws concerning a Religious
Juridical Person (legal incorporation) have also been
taught. The curriculum is flexible and normally the same
course is taught in all places at the same time. Sometimes,
as at present, they are different, depending on the situation. One problem seems to be that time in class has been
inadequate, so rather than just meeting one night a week or
so, they have recently established what they call "Monday
school." "Monday school" runs from Sunday evening to Monday
noon, and gives them more time. The students stay over in
someone's house or the church or whatever facilities are
available. At present all the students are Mennonite, but
they have also had a Baptist who took several courses.

A single course usually consists of 15 hours in class,
plus outside study. The year is divided into two semesters
(April-September; October-March), and each course is worth
two to four credits, depending on whether it is a one or
two semester course. When a student completes a course, he
receives credit for it. This is true whether it takes six
months or only a week. Some courses are even concentrated
into a week. For example, in summer 1973, Dr. Henry
Poettcker from the Canadian Mennonite Bible College [now
AMBS president] taught a one-week course on the "Life of
Christ." This was during vacation time, and the class met
morning, afternoon, and evening. All together there were
reported to be 12 or 13 who attended at least some of the
sessions. But only one or two completed the necessary work
and received credit.

When he has accumulated 60 credits, the student "graduates." There is no core curriculum at present required for
graduation, but included in those 60 credits must be 12
credits given for practical work in the church. This
involves actual pastoring or preaching among a group of
believers, and is supervised by an EHBS teacher, a pastor,
or a missionary. It would be possible for a full-time student to complete the course in three years, but most would
take much longer. Perhaps 10 or 15 years or more. When a
student graduates it does not automatically give him the
right to be a pastor, but it is felt that order is needed in
the church, and it should at least be recognized that a
person has completed this much work. The various courses
are advertised in the Japan Mennonite Church Conference
(JMC) monthly paper, *"Michi"* [The Way], containing local

reports and news. The back page is devoted to the Bible
school program, what has been done, and what is coming.

Entrance requirements are rather simple. At first it was
required that a person have a personal experience of the new
birth, that he have received a call to serve the Lord, that
he have a recommendation from a pastor or missionary, and
that he have at least a high school education. At present,
however, the only two requirements are that a person be a
Christian, and that he be a high school graduate. These are
only guidelines though as some of the students are not
graduates of high school. This means that in some classes
you might have some with less than high school, and others
who are university graduates. This, of course, makes it
rather difficult for the teacher. One way they have found
that works fairly well is to give homework on different
levels. But assignments can be something of a problem.
Also required reading. Often no single textbook is used.
Rather, the most important materials for any given course
are required.

But while there may be problems in that area, there is no
problem of support during or after schooling since the student continues to work at his regular job as he studies.
After EHBS, it is also possible to keep studying in the continuing education program, and there is little thought of
sending people off to other schools for further education
except in the case of someone interested in Christian education or some other specialty. Placement upon graduation,
also, is not a problem which the school faces. The main
reason for that is that the students are leaders who have
emerged from within a group, are still a part of that group,
and already "placed." They already have a place in the
local church. After graduation, a student usually works as
part of a pastoral team. If it happens that a certain
church does not have adequate leadership, the Conference
takes it up and makes a recommendation. The churches are
said to be quite well satisfied with EHBS-trained pastors.

On the first announcement sheet that came out about the
school there is a list of eight potential teachers -- five
pastors and three missionaries. Now the bulk of the teaching is being done by Tanase himself. In the beginning, at
one of the pastors' meetings, it was decided to ask each
person to prepare in an area of his interest, and this has
helped to discern the gifts within the church. Some of the
other pastors and missionaries occasionally teach too. Outside lecturers are also sometimes called in. But while

there may be several that can teach, it is felt that it is
important to have one person responsible to oversee the program. This is also said to be true in some of their
churches which have a multiple ministry. So Tanase's job
is to oversee the total program, and while he is not teaching full time, his financial support comes from his own
part-time teaching and from the EHBS budget. Funds are
channeled into EHBS from tuition, from the Conference, from
the Mission, and from freewill offerings and gifts. The
students pay a nominal fee of 1,000 yen ($3.45) per subject
per semester, and auditors contribute to a freewill offering.

One of the biggest problems for Tanase has been time.
With doing part-time work, there simply was not enough time
to continue the program in five different places, and that
is why it has been cut back to three. Some feel it might be
good to have a full-time Bible teacher, but when asked
whether he did part-time work "because he wanted to" or
"because he had to," he replied that it was the former. He
feels that it helps him to identify more closely with those
he teaches. Interestingly, he was originally from Tokyo,
but came to Hokkaido at age twenty-one. He was baptized at
Kushiro, but received most of his theological education in
the U.S. He spent the years 1954-55 at Hesston College, a
Mennonite junior college in Kansas. From 1955 to 1957, he
was a student at Goshen College, also a Mennonite school,
in Indiana. In 1958-59, he was pastor of the Hombetsu
Church in Hokkaido. From 1959-1969, he was pastor of the
Kushiro Church, teacher at a women's college and high
school, and also a teacher in the EHBS. In 1970, he graduated from the Goshen Biblical Seminary (a member of the
AMBS) in Elkhart, Indiana, with a M.R.E. degree.

There are 15 churches ("church" being defined as "any
group of believers with an ordained or unordained leader")
which make up the Mennonite Conference. None of these
churches have their own lay training program. What they
have locally is limited mainly to Bible study. This is
where the Bible school comes in. It serves the different
churches, meeting their various needs. As mentioned before,
support comes not only from the local churches but from the
Conference as well, yet the program is not dependent on
either one alone. EHBS is an autonomous organization under
the Conference. The Conference is mostly an advisory group.
One of the items under consideration now is whether or not
they need a full-time teacher. They have not decided yet,
but they are talking about it. Time is a big problem,

although Tanase feels he has been able to maintain a pretty
good balance between his Bible teaching and his part-time
work.

A leave of absence for the teacher to make it possible
for him tò continue his study is also something of a problem.
Until now, in the case of someone studying in America, for
example, a love offering has been taken to make it possible.
But having time to get away, let alone getting support, is
often a difficulty with this new type of program. Besides
adequate time, another problem that was pointed out is that
with this type of program, there is always a lot of experimenting, and it takes a lot of energy to make decisions by
oneself on matters such as curriculum and content. It would
be easier if the whole program were more clearly defined.
As it is, the responsible person sort of has to just find
his own way.

When asked about accreditation, that is, about not being
accredited, it was not felt that this was a problem. If a
person wants to go on after EHBS, it is not possible to
transfer credits since EHBS is not accredited or linked up
with a recognized school. But it was expressed that some
schools to get accredited have to concentrate on facilities,
faculty and so on, and often lose their purpose in the process. They get separated from their original purpose. It
was felt that "we must concentrate on the needs of our
churches, rather than accreditation." If a specialist was
needed in some area like Christian education, they probably
would send them to a school specializing in that, and then
train them at EHBS when they returned.

As for distinctives of the school, several were pointed
out. One is that they have no school building. The headquarters is considered to be Obihiro because of location,
and that is where Tanase lives. A central library is housed
there also. But there is no school building as such there
or anywhere else. The classes usually meet in a church
building. If a church has a suitable room, it is felt to be
better than a central building. This way, it seems more
that the program belongs to the churches. If there is a
central building, the program gets limited to there. It was
stressed that it is important to *not* have a building. It
was also suggested that another area in which the Mennonites
are distinctive is with regard to promoting the concept of
the "free church," in contrast to the mainline Protestant
churches of Japan. This was an area in which it was felt
the Mennonites could make a unique contribution. In fact,
my impression was that their concept of the church is basic

to their whole program, that their program grows out of the churches, which is very significant, I believe, for their program and others who might wish to begin.

When asked for advice if we ever decided to start a program something like this, Tanase mentioned two points. First, we must define our objectives. We must be very clear about our purpose. Second, the Japanese should be involved in planning and also heading up such a program. It was emphasized that both of these are extremely important.

As to vision for the future of their Bible school, it was commented simply that "if we need to expand, we can do it. We can start in more centers." The big problem, of course, is personnel. If you have people to do it, you can. If you do not, you cannot. This may be one of the most pressing issues facing EHBS. Ideally, if the various Mennonite groups in Japan were geographically closer to each other, they might be able to operate a joint program like some of those in North America. But it is about 2,400 kilometers (1,500 mi.) from Kyushu to Hokkaido, and simply is not deemed to be practical as of now. The distance is too great. Besides, even inter-Mennonite cooperation is sometimes difficult. For a while there was a Japan Mennonite Literature Association (JMLA), which published an inter-Mennonite paper called *"Izumi"* [A Spring]. But after some time, the different groups lost interest in this, and did not support it anymore. They were more interested in local concerns. So the paper was dropped, although the Mennonites in Hokkaido are continuing it for their own people.

Some of the concerns of the JMLA have perhaps been taken over by the Japan Mennonite Fellowship (JMF), a loose organization of a few Mennonite or Mennonite-related groups in Japan. But if it is hard to work together on a little paper, how much more difficult might it be to cooperate in a joint training program. Local interests seem to take priority. As Tanase remarked, "we must fit the local situation. Hokkaido is Hokkaido. Kyushu is Kyushu. Yet it is also important to sometimes get together for fellowship and study."

While in Hokkaido, I also had the privilege of attending several Bible school classes which met May 2nd in conjunction with an All-Hokkaido Mennonite Retreat. These classes met just before the retreat began, which made it convenient for some of the students to take in both. Two different classes were held. One was a seminar on "Problems that

Occur in Interpersonal Relationships in Christ," taught by
missionary Marvin Yoder. The other was on "Worship," and
was taught by two of the students in the class. One, a
missionary, presented a book review on "Worship in the Old
Testament." The other, a layman, gave a presentation on
"Worship in the New Testament." Both made their presenta-
tions to the other members of the class as part of their
assignment. The reports had been well prepared, and were
followed by a time of discussion.

There were about 20 participants in each of the two
classes, but not all of them were enrolled as students.
Some had come early for the retreat and were just sitting
in. Of the 20, five were pastors and two were pastor's
wives; three were missionaries and three were missionary
wives; seven were laymen. There were 10 men and 10 women.
In addition there were the missionary teacher and Tanase.
As an example of a homework assignment that was given, in
the "Interpersonal Relationships" class they were supposed
to read (in Japanese) *The Strong and the Weak* by Paul
Tournier. If they could read English, there were two other
books they were encouraged to read. They were also supposed
to write down their personal needs, choose three problems
they faced recently, and how they solved them. They were to
write these out mainly for themselves, but they could also
report them at the next class if they wished. The rest of
the retreat was more of an inspirational nature.

At the same retreat I was also able to distribute a
questionnaire to some of the past and present students of
the EHBS. There was not as great a response as I had hoped
for, partly because not everyone knew about it and some did
not get a copy of the questionnaire. (See Appendix F for
the Eastern Hokkaido Bible School Student Questionnaire.)
There may have been others who did not want to fill it out.
In any case, I did get 12 questionnaires back, and was glad
for each of them. I cannot say how representative they
would be of all those who have studied at the school, but
would like to share the results for what they may be worth.

The 12 were from seven different churches -- five from
one church, two from another. Ten of them were between the
ages of 26 and 45, one was younger and one was older. Seven
were men, all married. Five were women, at least three of
whom were married. Five were pastors, one a pastor's wife.
Other occupations included a public official, a housewife,
and a kindergarten teacher. All of them had been Christians
at least seven or eight years, one of them for 26 years.

All of them were active in the work of the church. For
example, 7 taught Sunday school; 11 led Sunday worship; 7
preached; 9 led Bible study; 5 led women's meetings; others
played piano, organ and so on. Several indicated that EHBS
training had helped them in doing these things. Only one
had any formal Bible school training, and he was a graduate
of Tokyo Christian College. But in response to the question
of whether they had received any Bible school or seminary
training, about half of them said they had, which seems to
indicate that while EHBS may not be recognized as a formal
Bible school, the students seem to think of it as such.

As noted above, five of the students were already pastors.
At least two were not planning to be pastors. About half
had been studying in the school for a year or less, but
a couple said they had been studying for as long as nine
years. At least seven of them were presently studying in
the school. And of those who were married, at least five of
their partners were studying also. The students lived anywhere from one to 40 kilometers from the school. Whether
most of them live fairly close to the center they attend or
not is not known by the author, but one would expect that as
a general rule they probably do. There were also a couple
of students who audited courses.

A total of 23 courses were listed by these students as
ones they had taken. The breakdown is as follows:

Anabaptist History	- 7	English	- 3
Anabaptist Seminar	- 3	Greek	- 5
Bible Study Methods	- 3	Homiletics	- 5
Biblical Theology	- 1	Life of Christ	- 2
Christian Ethics	- 3	N.T. Introduction	- 2
Christian Relationships	- 1	N.T. Survey	- 3
Church History	- 5	O.T. Introduction	- 3
Church Management	- 1	O.T. Survey	- 3
Communication	- 1	Pastoral Theology	- 4
Comparative Religion	- 2	Prophets	- 1
Ecclesiology	- 4	Systematic	
Evangelism	- 4	Theology	- 6
		Other	- 1

Just how complete this list is as to courses that have been
offered and how many have taken them is hard to say, for
some students may not have remembered all the ones they took,
and others may have been offered. Even so, it looks like
this sample might be more or less representative of the
courses that have been taught. The students indicated that

they have taken these courses in seven different places,
mostly meeting in churches. As to time spent in preparation, the replies varied from 30 minutes to 3 hours per
week. Some students listed only one course they had taken;
others, up to 15 or 16, with an average of six.

When asked which courses had been most helpful, one said
Bible study methods because it helped him "learn to use and
interpret the Bible correctly." Another noted homiletics
and biblical theology as being "very helpful for the ministry of the Word." But the course that was mentioned most
frequently (4 times) was Anabaptist history. Some of the
reasons given were that they "learned that the believers'
church pattern is the real foundation of the life of the
church today"; "learned how to 'live the Bible'"; "saw the
relevance of Anabaptist history to my own faith"; "saw how
believers were able to continue walking in the true faith in
the midst of difficult persecution." There seems to be a
strong interest in Anabaptism and Anabaptist studies. With
regard to courses they would like to take if offered, in
addition to the ones listed above, church music, lay training, and psychology were suggested as possibilities. At
least five of the students had studied with Dr. Howard
Charles when he was in Japan. Six of them had not.

When asked for suggestions to improve the school, the
following were some of the things mentioned: "make clear
the purpose of the study; enlarge the supporting group of
the school, each church being connected in some way"; "wish
the students could cut down on the time needed to earn a
living to support themselves and their families"; "recruit
dedicated people to study at the school; institute a definite curriculum"; "isn't there a simple way to get reference
books into our hands? as much as possible would like the
teachers to speak in Japanese"; "it's important for each
church to cooperate in working together." One simply said,
"nothing special."

In addition to these comments from the questionnaires,
there were a few whom I talked with who felt it might be
well if the pastors could get a little broader experience,
and along that line suggested that perhaps there could be an
occasional exchange of pastors with some of the churches in
Kyushu. Also, that rather than only having leadership training, that perhaps a more general Christian education program
could be set up for churches that were located nearest to
the centers. But while some of these suggestions can
possibly be incorporated in the future, I sensed that on the
whole the EHBS has very positive support already.

During the same trip I had a chance to talk on several occasions with Marvin J. Miller, a self-supporting Mennonite missionary, who has also been teaching part time in the Bible School. In addition to the very helpful information I received from Takio Tanase, the head teacher, I learned a few other things from Miller about the churches involved in this program. Of the 15 churches participating, about half of them are located in towns with a population of 10,000 or less. In other words, they are very rural churches, located in small towns, and some of them would have only 10 members or so. (As noted earlier, they define a church as "any group of believers with an ordained or unordained leader.") Typical of Japan, most of the churches are small, averaging about 20 active members. The largest church is said to have an active membership of around 50.

Nearly all of the churches have their own buildings. Four of them are running kindergartens, and some of them use the kindergarten buildings for their meetings. One has a multi-purpose building with a meeting room, children's room, kitchen and apartment. Another has a meeting room and abacus school (run by the pastor) downstairs, with an apartment and special room upstairs for the ashes of deceased members, and a place to display momentos of the members (such as a Bible). One of the lay pastors is a teacher of architecture, and he has helped design some of the church buildings.

According to the questionnaires returned, only one of the pastors responding indicated he had any formal training in addition to EHBS, but Miller mentioned several others who have had at least some Bible school or seminary training at one time or other. There are also said to be a good number of laymen involved in pastoring the churches. The point at which a pastor becomes distinguished from a lay pastor is "when he stops preaching only, and starts baptizing." If one counts the total number of pastors, lay pastors, and missionaries (7) serving as leaders in the various churches, the number of leaders is almost twice the number of churches. Thus in some cases, there is only one responsible person, in others, there may be several who share in a multiple ministry. One case that was pointed out which is worthy of note was where in a multiple ministry (pastoral team) situation consisting of a pastor, layman, and missionary, the layman was actually the responsible person, not the pastor or missionary!

Almost all of the pastors are lay pastors. That is, they hold a regular full-time job, and serve the church on a

part-time basis. Examples of their occupations would be an
engineering consultant, a high school teacher, a purchasing
agent, a postal employee, a carpenter, an abacus teacher, a
kindergarten principal, a city office worker, a private
English teacher, a contractor, a weatherman, a university
professor, a businessman, a Japanese language teacher, a
chicken sexer and so on. Most of them have had some professional training or experience to prepare them for their
various occupations.

They have also had some theological training to help them
with their work in the church. About two-thirds of them
have taken at least some work at EHBS. Several are EHBS
graduates. A couple have graduated from Tokyo Christian
College, or studied in seminary somewhere. At least five
have spent a year or more studying in an American college or
seminary; another one spent a year studying in Switzerland.
So most of the pastors have not only some training professionally, but some training theologically as well. And yet
they are largely supported by their work rather than by the
church. A few of them receive something from the church,
if not by way of monetary remuneration, through other benefits such as housing and the like. But as mentioned before,
even Tanase receives only part of his support from the
church. They are all "tentmakers" (self-supporting), at
least to some degree.

Some of the missionaries are also "tentmaking." In fact,
there are now (1974) three couples in Hokkaido, working with
the Japan Mennonite Church, who are tentmakers. While it
has its advantages, it also has its disadvantages, and
Miller emphasized that under this sytem when people must
change jobs or change churches, it is important to "stand
behind them with mutual aid for one another, church to
pastor, pastor to pastor, believer to believer, including
missionaries being both on the giving and receiving end."
Adequate time for the work of the church is a big problem
too, but one definite advantage of the system is being able
to identify more closely with the needs of those they minister to. They know what it is like to be a layman.

In the case of a multiple ministry, the responsibilities
shift occasionally so the load will not be too heavy for any
one man. Most of the EHBS-trained leaders seem to be satisfied with their training, although once in a while there
are said to be those who are not too enthusiastic about it,
or wish they could get further training, but they are a
small minority. A few of the pastors have helped with the

teaching in EHBS. One of them has been a missionary to
Ecuador for four years. Some of these men have also deliberately chosen their work in an area that would give them
more time for the work of the church. For example, the one
who runs an abacus school in the evenings and is relatively
free during the day.

Most of the lay pastors are called "pastor" or "teacher"
(*sensèi*) by their people although some prefer to be just
"*san*" (Mr., Miss, Mrs.). There are no women recognized as
yet, however, as pastors or lay pastors. Miller stated that

> None of the pastors are full time. None of them are
> fully supported. None of them are fully trained (is
> anyone ever??). All of them are in a part-time minis-
> try. The missionaries are the only ones full time and
> fully supported. They have also generally had more
> formal training than the pastors have. But even though
> the pastors are not full time or fully supported, and
> have not had the opportunities for formal education
> that the missionaries have had, the goal is a fully
> trained ministry, with eventually a few full-time,
> fully supported national leaders. The ideal is a fully
> trained church. That is, trained both professionally
> and theologically (1974a).

While the ideal and the real are not always one and the
same, I think it must be admitted that the Hokkaido
Mennonites have already come a long way toward achieving
their aim. Their goals are clear, and they are seeking to
make them a reality. The training program they envision
would seem to make sense in meeting the needs of their
churches. But the one overriding impression I came away
with is that part of the reason for their "success" in finding a way to train leaders that fit their churches is that
they have a clearer concept of the church than most churchmen do. That is, they have a definite concept of the church,
and what kind of leaders such a church needs, and their
training program has, in fact, grown out of their concept of
the church. To what extent that is true or not I cannot
say for sure, but that was my dominant impression.

There is one other factor, too, which was referred to
earlier and that is the "Seminary and Bible School Study"
which they did before they ever began their own Bible school.
This was done about 20 years ago, specifically for the use
of the Hokkaido Mennonite Fellowship and the supporting
mission. There were at that time approximately 60 Protestant

schools in Japan. Of these, a total of 26 different schools
were visited, or someone connected with the school was
interviewed. This included seminaries, Bible schools,
colleges and universities, some rural training schools, and
even the teaching methods of the *Mukyōkai* (Non-church) movement. The results of the study were written up, and a
number of recommendations made as to what shape a Bible
school might take in Hokkaido. Paul Peachey, one of the two
who did the study, summarized his observations as follows:

1) Almost uniformly Japanese seminaries today are
forced to look for foreign financial subsidies.
Whether, if there were no unnecessary duplication the
Japanese churches could support the necessary institutions would be an interesting question to pursue, but
it is irrelevant, given the denominational character
of the churches. A denomination cannot well exist without a school to inculcate its principles.

2) The founding of schools by missions has in every
case to cope with the serious [problem] of obtaining
teachers. A new denominational group cannot have its
own teachers for years, hence it must use teachers
from other denominations, with many men teaching in up
to four or more different schools. But to build on
teachers from other denominations militates against the
objective in the school in the first place.

3) The position of the graduate of a below-standard
Bible school or college is almost untenable. Too young
and untrained to fit the category of "sensei," and yet
being forced to seek a status in society as such, since
they meanwhile will have learned no other trade, their
status is an insecure one. The best students will not
risk the arrangement, and the quality of leadership in
the churches is thereby threatened even if in individual
cases it can be financed.

4) A school to function as a school must have a fairly
strong flow of students. This in turn requires an
expanding placement program, with adequate finance, a
condition which at this point does not obtain.

5) To set up a church which looks for the distribution of the gifts of the Spirit and the functions of
leadership through the above hazardous route, will far
more throttle the life of the young churches than it
will provide the security which is thereby sought.

6) In an Orient where the missionary from the West may
be pushed out by the forces of nationalism or revolution
(and not entirely undeservedly), to set up an institutional arrangement which makes young churches dependent
on American dollars is to place upon them a strain which
they cannot be expected to bear, once the heat is on.

7) The geographic distance separating the several
Mennonite missions and the unfortunate lack of spiritual consensus makes it appear unlikely that a common
training program can be set up in the foreseeable future.

In principle, you have the following possible approaches
to a training program before you:

1) You can send students to existing schools, selecting either a denominational one which seems most
spiritually akin, or an interdenominational or union one
which necessarily grants freedom on some points where
actually clarity is needed.

2) You could send students abroad, either to India as
suggested by some, or to Mennonite schools in America.

3) You could establish a new school a) alone; b) with
other Mennonite missions; or c) with other groups in
Hokkaido who are in the area.

4) You could build up a church approach in which the
necessary training grows out of the life of the churches
and is thus an integral part of it.

Realizing that denominational schools exist for denominational reasons, and give their training a slant
different from yours, while the nondenominational school
either leaves loose ends or, as in Japan, leads to a
new denomination oriented around the theology of the
school;

Realizing further that sending any number of people
abroad is financially out of the question and spiritually hazardous (this has nothing to do with fraternal
and supplementary exchanges of mature persons which are
much needed), a fact quite generally recognized by
solid churches and missions; ...

Realizing finally that available finances, teachers,
supporting constituency, etc., do not justify the

establishment of a new school, and that inter-group
cooperation within Hokkaido or inter-Mennonite cooperation across forbidding geographic distances is too weak
in either case, and that a new still-born school in
Japan's overstocked denominational grove would be
regrettable, both fundamentally and practically, it
appears that your soundest solution lies along line
four.

The essential features of this (fourth) church approach
would be:

a) Insist on teaching (teaching and being taught) and
service as the normal essential life of the Christian.

b) Supplement the regular teaching activities with
retreats, institutes and the like, again for everyone.

c) Persons who are called by the Spirit to special
tasks -- teachers, evangelists, elders -- should
receive apprenticeship training under the missionaries
and as soon as possible, under mature people in the
churches, such training to include supervised study.

d) Persons with special gifts and calling, who may
later be supported as teachers or evangelists should
be sent to college in the normal way, if possible to
prepare for their profession, and should then receive
supplementary Bible and theological training under the
churches.

e) Support would be restricted to teachers and evangelists serving in larger areas, while the regular
pastoral and teaching tasks within the congregations
would be in the hands of elders.

f) In time mature teachers or evangelists might well
take additional training in seminary.

g) If some day with growing unity and strength among
the Christians in Hokkaido there arises the possibility
and need for some sort of school it would come as a
natural and healthy growth, as a handmaiden and not as
a substitute for life in the churches (Richards and
Peachey 1959:36-37).

I have quoted the above at length because I feel it
reveals so clearly how perceptive these men were of the

situation they faced. In many ways they were ahead of their
time in their thinking. Their program, as it has developed,
has been a creative attempt to meet the needs of their
churches. As asserted earlier, it cannot be classified as
TEE. That is, it is not the extension of the program of a
"recognized theological training institution." But it is
surprising how much it does incorporate some of the most
important principles of TEE such as taking the school to
where the students are, teaching on several different levels,
and training mature lay leaders for local service. Many of
the basic concepts of TEE are present in some form in their
approach.

Another thing it reveals is how closely the school that
has emerged has followed the basic recommendations made in
the study. It points up, I believe, the importance of being
clear about one's goals, one's objectives, before ever
beginning. To be sure, not all of their goals have been
reached, not all of their objectives fulfilled. But they
have had something to go by, to give them direction, and
that is perhaps the most important thing. Their program has
grown naturally out of the needs of the churches, rather
than being imposed from above. They have by no means
achieved perfection, but they know what they want to do, and
they are trying their best to do it. The Bible school is
still young. Exactly what shape it will take in the years
to come remains to be seen. There may be problems along the
way. But they have a vision, and are determined to carry it
out. Marvin Miller has summed up the history of the school
in a concise way, and with his words I would like to bring
this report to a close:

> For the past nine years the Eastern Hokkaido Bible
> School has attempted to give training at several levels
> and in various locations for those men who were already
> the acknowledged leaders in their congregations, as well
> as for a number of young men who had left secular employ-
> ment for service in the churches. It has never been
> the intention of the school to remove men from their
> communities for an extended period, train them to be
> leaders and then send them back. It should also be said
> that it was not so much for theological reasons as for
> practical considerations, of the type just noted, that
> we have not urged young men to go to Tokyo or elsewhere
> to study. Some have done so and have returned to their
> communities or other locations in Hokkaido with varying
> degrees of success in terms of adjustment and basic
> usability. The school is still committed to the vision

of taking instruction to the students, where they are
at times and at academic levels suited to them, however
difficult this vision is to actualize (1974b:15-16).

Observations: The school has been operating for nine years
now. It has grown out of the needs of the churches, and is
clear in its purpose. It appears to be based on a definite
concept of the church. It has had an important part in
training pastors and lay pastors for their churches. It
began on a small scale, building on the earlier Bible training programs. There are now about 30 students enrolled,
seemingly a good cross section of the church, and most of
the students are already serving within the churches. The
school is functioning on three levels -- lay, lay pastor,
and pastor. The head teacher is Japanese, assisted by other
pastors and missionaries, depending on the various gifts.
Students are also used in teaching. There is no central
building, although there is a central library. The program
is decentralized, operating in three different centers. The
school seeks to go to the students. It is flexible, for
example the change to "Monday school." One of the unique
features is fellowship in other believers' homes. A good
variety of courses are offered for credit, and credits can
be accumulated for graduation. Support is not a problem
while in school, or after graduation. Placement is no
problem either. Before starting, a thorough study was made
of existing schools. The resulting program is geared to
meet the needs of rural churches in Hokkaido. One of the
distinctives is an emphasis on Anabaptist-Mennonite studies.
The school seems to have good support both from the local
churches and the Conference.

On the other hand, the school suffers from a shortage of
personnel. It has been necessary to cut back on their program from five centers to three. This no doubt makes it
more difficult for some students to come, and means not only
fewer students but less involvement on the part of certain
churches. It may be time to consider supporting a full-
time teacher, or recruiting others on a part-time basis.
There is also the fact that there is no core curriculum, and
conceivably a student could graduate without having had certain basic courses. Perhaps a basic course should be
required. Along with this, there has been no use of programmed instruction materials, and one wonders if that might
not strengthen the program too. Another problem is that the
school has no connection with a recognized institution,

which means that credits are not transferable, and anyone wishing to go on for further education may find it somewhat problematic. It might be worth considering having a tie-up with a larger school. That would perhaps make it easier for those who desire it to get a broader education and experience. It would also be nice if there was a way to allow the teachers to get away occasionally to study in an area of interest. One other minor point is that it would be helpful if more accurate records on the students would be kept for future reference. Who knows when another researcher might come along!

With these remarks we come to the end of the case studies. As we have seen, there is much to be learned from each of them, both "pluses" and "minuses." But keeping this background material in mind, we next must ask ourselves how all these various things may apply to us and our own particular situation.

5

A Model Leadership Training Program for the Japan Mennonite Christian Church Conference

Up to this point we have looked briefly at the history of the Japan Mennonite Christian Church Conference, its leadership training patterns and problems. We have also considered TEE as a model program, and studied three different schools in Japan. Now we want to try to formulate a model program specifically for the Church Conference itself.

In our study of the three schools, however, it was apparent that in most cases the program of the school was based on a definite concept of the ministry, and that concept of the ministry in turn grew out of a definite concept of the church. In other words, church, ministry, and training are all closely interrelated. As Ralph R. Covell has put it,

> Theological education cannot be discussed without considering the church and its ministry. The nature of the church determines the nature of the ministry. The nature of the ministry dictates the nature and form of theological education (Covell and Wagner 1971:15).

This being so, before we can propose a program for the JMCCC, I believe we must first of all wrestle with three basic questions. First, what kind of church do we want to have? Second, what kind of leaders do we need for that kind of church? Third, what kind of training do we need to produce that kind of leaders? To suggest a program without first looking at our concept of the church and its ministry is to "put the cart before the horse." Therefore, in the first three sections of this chapter, we want to deal with each of these questions, one at a time. After we have done that, hopefully we can propose something more specific, and suggest what some of the major elements of a model program might be.

WHAT KIND OF CHURCH DO WE WANT TO HAVE?

Starting with the Bible itself, the word *church* does not appear in the Hebrew Old Testament for obvious reasons. It does occur frequently in the Septuagint, the Greek version of the Old Testament, as a translation of the word "congregation." But basically it is a New Testament word, a Greek word, *ekklesia*, which means "the called out ones," the ones God has called out to be His people. Yet while the word is not there, the concept is also found in the Old Testament where God "calls out" a people for Himself. This call began about two thousand years before Christ with Abraham, to whom the Lord said,

> Go from your country and your kindred and your father's house to the land that I will show you. And I will make of you a great nation, and I will bless you, and make your name great, so that you will be a blessing (Gen. 12:1-2).

This call continued with Isaac and Jacob and his twelve sons, who became the heads of the twelve tribes. The twelve tribes formed the nucleus of the nation Israel, God's people. God took care of them, and they were the object of many of His mighty acts in Old Testament times. Moses reminded them that they were a chosen people,

> a people holy to the Lord your God; the Lord your God has chosen you to be a people for his own possession, out of all the peoples that are on the face of the earth (Deut. 7:6).

At the same time he cautioned them,

> It was not because you were more in number than any other people that the Lord set his love upon you and chose you, for you were the fewest of all peoples; but it is because the Lord loves you, and is keeping the oath which he swore to your fathers, that the Lord has brought you out with a mighty hand and redeemed you from the house of bondage, from the hand of Pharaoh king of Egypt (7:7-8).

It was not because of any greatness on Israel's part, but because of God's love that they were chosen to be His people. Being chosen was not so much a privilege as it was a responsibility. As the Lord said later through the prophet Isaiah, "I will give you as a light to the nations, that my salvation may reach to the end of the earth" (49:6). Israel was commissioned to be a missionary people. That is, God needed a people through whom He could send the Messiah. He chose Israel for that purpose. To be sure, Israel was a national entity just like the other nations around her. But until the Messiah came, Israel was to live as His people in the midst of the surrounding nations. She was to prepare the way for the coming of the Savior.

While the Old Testament predicts the Messiah is coming, the New Testament proclaims He is here. In the New Testament, we see that the promised Messiah (the "Christ," in Greek) was Jesus. Jesus was a Jew, a descendant of David, of the tribe of Judah. He fulfilled all the promises that had been made concerning the Messiah. Jesus was the long-awaited Christ. As He began His ministry, He called twelve men to be His disciples, just as there had been twelve tribes in the Old Testament. These twelve were to be the nucleus of God's people, the new Israel, the Church. Jesus said, "I will build my church, and the powers of death shall not prevail against it" (Matt. 16:18). But while this was something new, when the Bible speaks of God's people, there is also a definite continuity between the Testaments. Both Israel and the Church are God's people.

One difference, however, between the old and the new Israel is that whereas the former was national, the latter is universal. This especially became clear on the day of Pentecost and following, with the coming of the Holy Spirit and the birth of the Christian Church. It was for Jew and Gentile alike. But just as Israel had been called and chosen for a particular responsibility, so now the Church was chosen. As Peter affirmed,

> you are a chosen race, a royal priesthood, a holy nation, God's own people, that you may declare the wonderful deeds of him who called you out of darkness into his marvelous light (I Pet. 2:9).

The Church was now God's people. And just as Israel had a commission, so the Church has a commission, a commission to be a missionary people. This is best summed up in the words of Jesus Himself when He instructed,

Go therefore and make disciples of all nations,
baptizing them in the name of the Father and of the
Son and of the Holy Spirit, teaching them to observe
all that I have commanded you; and lo, I am with you
always, to the close of the age (Matt. 28:19-20).

In brief, this is what the Bible says about Israel and the
Church as God's people.

When we think of the word *church* today, we usually think
of a building, or a worship service, or a pastor and his congregation. And in English, the word has come to have
various meanings like that. But it is also good to occasionally be reminded of the original meaning of some of
these words, which D.W.B. Robinson does in *The New Bible
Dictionary*. He notes that whereas in English it may mean
"the Lord's house" or "a Christian place of worship," that

'Church' in the New Testament, however, renders Gk.
ekklēsia, which mostly means a local congregation of
Christians and never a building. ... Although we often
speak of these congregations collectively as the New
Testament Church or the Early Church, no New Testament
writer uses *ekklēsia* in this collective way. An
ekklēsia was a meeting or assembly. Its commonest use
was for the public assembly of citizens duly summoned,
which was a feature of all the cities outside Judaea
where the Gospel was planted (e.g. Acts xix.39).
Ekklēsia was also used among the Jews (LXX) for the
'congregation of Israel' which was constituted at
Sinai and assembled before the Lord at the annual
feasts in the persons of its representative males
(Acts vii.38). Whether the Christian use of *ekklēsia*
was first adopted from Gentile or Jewish usage -- the
point is disputed -- it certainly implied 'meeting'
rather than 'organization' or 'society.' Locality
was essential to its character. The local *ekklēsia*
was not thought of as part of some world-wide *ekklēsia*,
which would have been a contradiction in terms. ...

While there might be as many churches as there were
cities or even households, yet the New Testament
recognized only one *ekklēsia* without finding it
necessary to explain the relationship between the one
and the many. The one was not an amalgamation or
federation of the many. It was a 'heavenly' reality
belonging not to the form of this world but to the
realm of resurrection glory ... (1962:228-229).

The word *church*, then, really means a congregation. It
refers to people, not buildings. It is a group of God's
people, whoever and wherever they are. In the New Testament,
churches took various forms. There was first of all the
house church such as in the home of Prisca and Aquila (Rom.
16:5). Then there were the city churches, such as the
church in Jerusalem (Acts 11:22), which was actually perhaps
a cluster of house churches. There were also the provincial
churches, such as the churches of Galatia (Gal. 1:2), which
were even larger groupings. The word is occasionally used
in almost a universal sense such as the reference to the
church throughout Judea, Galilee, and Samaria (Acts 9:31).

It is sometimes used in the singular to refer to each
church (I Cor. 4:17). At other times it is used in the
plural, referring to all the churches (II Cor. 11:28). In
one case there is a reference to both the singular and the
plural, to a house church and all the churches of Asia, in
a single verse (I Cor. 16:19). It is also used of assem-
bling as a church (I Cor. 11:18). And in one or two cases,
such as I Corinthians 14:28, it almost seems to refer to
the church services or the place where the church met. In
any case, it can be seen that the use of the word *church* is
quite varied. But while it is used at least 110 times in
the New Testament in various ways, it almost always seems to
have a geographical dimension to it. The area might be as
large as a province or as small as a house, but it seems to
be there, regardless of form. The word would seem to refer
primarily to all of the believers in a given locality.

Now while the form of the church may vary, the function
of the churches seems to be similar, as might be expected.
The earliest account we have of the life of the church is
that recorded in Acts 2:42-47. Although the word *church* is
not used there, Luke tells us that after three thousand had
been baptized, and added to their number, "they devoted
themselves to the apostles' teaching and fellowship, to the
breaking of bread and the prayers" (42). These seem to
have been some of the main activities from the beginning.
The account goes on to tell of how the apostles did many
signs and wonders, of how all the believers shared their
possessions with those in need, and also of how they continued to attend the Temple together. This latter activity
is perhaps surprising to us, as we do not expect Christians
to attend Jewish services. But we must not forget that
before they were Christians they were Jews.

At this point the New Testament had not yet been written.
The Christians did have the Old Testament and their faith

in one God in common with the Jews. The only difference was that the Jews did not believe that Jesus was the Messiah, whereas the Christians did. Needless to say, that was a profound difference and, as differences became more pronounced, the Christians quit going to the Temple and held services of their own (although it is said some of them kept attending the Temple until it was destroyed in A.D. 70). To the Jews the Christians were probably considered to be a sect, but just as the Jews thought of themselves as God's people, so did the Christians. The names of the churches reveal this. There was, for example, the church of God at Corinth (I Cor. 1:2) and so on. The Church belonged to God. Christians, like Jews, were God's people. And though the forms of the church varied from place to place, the functions were much the same.

While the forms and functions of the church came to be somewhat different from those in Judaism, nevertheless there was still a unique continuity between the two. Perhaps a diagram (Figure 5.1) can help us understand that better. As you can see, Christ is the center of both the Old and New Testaments. The Old looks forward to His coming. The New looks backward to His coming.

Figure 5.1

CONTINUITY OF GOD'S PEOPLE

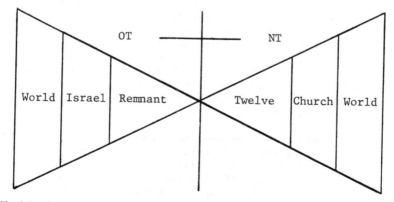

Christ is the center of the Bible. And He is related not only to Israel and the Church, but to the world.

In the Old Testament, God began with the world, then called out Israel as the people through whom He would save

the world, which later was only a faithful remnant. In the
New Testament, Jesus called out twelve, who were to become
the nucleus of the Church, whose mission it was to proclaim
salvation to the world. The Church was to carry on the
mission Israel had failed to carry out. But in both cases,
we are dealing with God's people. As Paul taught, the
Church is "built upon the foundation of the apostles and
prophets, Christ Jesus himself being the chief cornerstone"
(Eph. 2:20). The Church has a relation to the world just as
Israel did. The Church is not an end in itself. It exists
to serve the world. It is to be a missionary people. And
as we read the New Testament, we see especially in the book
of Acts that the Church was a missionary church. The
apostle Paul, of course, was the missionary par excellence.
But it was not only Paul. The whole church sought to be
God's people and not only sent out missionaries, but was a
missionary people. It was as Jesus had said, "when the Holy
Spirit has come upon you ... you shall be my witnesses in
Jerusalem and in all Judea and Samaria and to the end of the
earth" (Acts 1:8).

If the Church, like Israel in the Old Testament, is the
people of God, what is the difference between the two? The
answer to that is in their response to Christ. Israel, as
we know, expected the coming of the Messiah. But when He
finally came, most of the Jews rejected Him as the Christ,
although there were also those who accepted Him. The Church
was made up of those who accepted Him as Savior and Lord.
The followers of Christ were first called Christians in
Antioch (Acts 11:26). It was the Spirit of Christ which
made a person a Christian, a member of God's people. As
Paul declared, "Any one who does not have the Spirit of
Christ does not belong to him" (Rom. 8:9). If we do not
belong to Him, we do not belong to His people. But the
Christian belongs to Christ, and Christ to God (I Cor. 3:23).
Christ is the head of the Church (Eph. 5:23), the true
Israel of God (Gal. 6:16).

There are many metaphors used to describe the Church,
such as the body of Christ (I Cor. 12:27), the bride of
Christ (Eph. 5:25ff.; cf. Rev. 21:9), and the household of
God (Eph. 2:19). But all of them have to do with the
relationship of God to His people in Christ. The Church,
like Israel, is not to be equated with the Kingdom of God.
The Kingdom is larger than either Israel or the Church.
But in the Church, as in Israel of old, God has begun to
rule. The Church is now God's people. The Church belongs
to God through Christ. As Paul S. Minear states in *The
Interpreter's Dictionary of the Bible*,

Because the *ekklesiai* [churches] belong to Christ,
and to God, they constitute together a single reality
-- a world-wide covenant community, which is embodied
in localized form wherever a congregation exists ...
(1962:608).

The Church is in continuity with and yet distinct from
Israel. It has been called, chosen, and commissioned just
as Israel was. Israel has for the most part fulfilled her
purpose in God's plan. The Church remains under obligation
to carry out hers. We have noted that "church" in the New
Testament does not refer to a building, but rather to a congregation, to a group of God's people. It was a fellowship
rather than an institution; an organism rather than an
organization. And yet, the church took various forms --
house, city, provincial and so on. But whatever the form,
divisions seem to have been on a geographical basis. Each
local church was an expression of the universal Church.
The churches were the Church.

Today we also have geographical divisions such as local,
state, regional, national and even international. We also
have nongeographical divisions we call denominations. There
were also denominations in New Testament times, such as at
Corinth (I Cor. 1:12), which were condemned by the apostle
Paul. But as we have indicated before, looking back on
church history, it is regrettable and yet perhaps inevitable
that there are so many denominations today. While this may
be so, Christ had prayed that His disciples might all be one
(John 17:21). Such a unity of the Spirit already exists if
we are truly Christians, but it is also important insofar
as possible that our structures manifest that oneness, that
the world might believe in Christ. After all, the Church
exists for the world. The forms of the church may vary, but
its functions must remain basically the same. And the
primary function of the church, as we have said, is to be a
missionary people. As set forth in the book of Revelation,
the Church has "an eternal gospel to proclaim to those who
dwell on earth, to every nation and tribe and tongue and
people" (14:6). The task of the Church is to be "God's
people doing God's work in God's world."

In broad outlines, these are some of the things the Bible
says about the Church. Our concern here, though, is not so
much with doctrinal matters but with the more practical
question of how the churches are to carry out their mission.
While the essence of the Church will always remain the same,
the forms of the church must remain flexible in order for it

to fulfill its mission in the world. This raises the whole question of how the church should be structured. What forms should the church take in order to fulfill its various functions? What forms should it take to carry out its primary function? What kind of a church is needed in our day?

Back in 1969, there was a thorough discussion of the matter of church structure at the Annual Conference of the Japan Mennonite Christian churches. In fact, there are three pages of single-spaced typewritten minutes on the discussion alone. According to those minutes (JMCCC 1969:13-15), one of the reasons this came up was because of differences in structure and policy in the local churches, which were in turn felt to be due partially to the fact that the Conference (Mission?) never had a clear "blueprint for evangelism." Thus different structures and policies developed. It was noted, however, that the Church exists for the world. We have an obligation to evangelize the world. Churches need to cooperate through the Conference to give birth to new groups. The question was raised as to how that might best be done.

In connection with this, one of the problems pointed out was the "one-church-one-pastor" system. It was suggested that one pastor might be responsible for several churches instead of just one. It was felt that laymen need to get more involved. There was general agreement that the pattern of the church must be changed. There was talk of dividing up Miyazaki Prefecture into areas, each served by a pastor or missionary, or churches (especially those with full-time pastors) establishing other churches, or the possibilities of laymen starting groups in cooperation with pastors. It was agreed that pastors are still needed but that they should not be overly depended upon. We should try rather to move toward a true "priesthood of believers." Each church, of course, must decide what kind of church it is going to be. But it was thought that it might be well as a Conference to also develop some kind of an overall blueprint. There was talk of creating models to try out some of these ideas, and also of tying this in with the planned Bible school. The net result of all the discussion was a decision referred to before,

That from now on we seek to change the structure of the church from one of over-dependence on the pastor to one emphasizing the priesthood of all believers, and that as one step in this direction, we establish a Lay Bible School in 1970, and that we provide a curriculum and appoint instructors, designed to help individual churches towards perfection. Further, that we create a preparatory committee and aim to bring this program into operation by April, 1970 (JMCCC, Decision 7(1), Annual Conference, 1969:15).

As we saw earlier, the Bible school never got off the ground as planned. But what about the change in church structure? Was there less dependence on the pastor than before? Was there actually a move away from the "one-church-one-pastor" pattern, or has it remained basically the same? Was there more of an emphasis on the priesthood of believers or not? What happened? Perhaps that is best determined by looking at the structure of the churches as they are today (1975), and comparing them to what they were before.

In analyzing the structure of the various churches, it would appear that there are categorically three types (Figure 5.2). We might call these the single congregation, the double congregation, and the multiple congregation types.

Figure 5.2

JMCCC CHURCH STRUCTURE

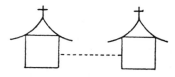

Single Congregation Type   Double Congregation Type

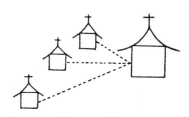

Multiple Congregation Type

First, the single congregation. It has its own local
church program. It has its own pastor (or missionary-
pastor). It has its own building. In several cases the
building also serves as the parsonage or missionary residence as well. Of the ten churches, seven are of this type.

Second, the double congregation. This is made up of two
congregations. Like the first type, each of these congregations have their own program and building, but they share
their pastor. It is an attempt to get away from the "one-
church-per-pastor" system to at least two churches per
pastor. There is only one case of this type at present.
(Note: This arrangement was terminated as of 1979.)

Third, the multiple congregation. It consists of the
mother church plus a few other groups nearby or more distant. It also seeks to move away from the "one-church-per-
pastor" system, and is a highly decentralized church. Many
of the groups meet in homes. Like the other two types, however, it also has a pastor and central building and its own
local program. There is one church of this type.

These three types, of course, all have their strengths
and weaknesses. But in evaluating them the real question
is, to what extent do these forms help us or hinder us from
fulfilling our mission as a church? Are some forms more
useful than others? Are there still other forms that might
be employed?

One of the striking things that comes to our attention
when we compare the decision of 1969 with the churches as
they exist today is that very few of them have moved away
from the "one-church-one-pastor" pattern. There has been
some experimenting with new forms. But while the desired
goal was to move in the direction of the "priesthood of all
believers," the fact that most of the churches are still
very much pastor-, program-, and building-centered is
brought out by the results of a questionnaire given to the
churches in 1974.

The churches are found in cities ranging anywhere from a
population of 14,000 to 1,300,000. Only two of them are
under 50,000. Most of them are in the 50,000 to 200,000
range. Half of the cities these churches are located in are
growing, and half are not. But the questionnaire revealed
that all of the churches have Sunday worship services. All
of these meet at the church building or in the pastor's or
missionary's residence. In almost all cases, they are led

by the pastor or missionary, although a lay leader usually
assists.

Eight of them have a midweek Bible study and prayer meeting. Like the worship services, almost all of these are
held in the church building also. Over half of them are led
by pastors or missionaries, but a few are led by laymen.
Some of the churches have other activities such as evening
worship, women's meetings, young people's meetings, young
couple's meetings, early morning prayer meetings, English
Bible classes and so on. Most of these meetings are also
held at the church, although a couple of them meet in homes.
Only two of the churches listed Sunday school as one of
their weekly activities, but I am quite sure most of them
have something along this line, and that the teaching is
shared by both pastors and laymen.

As far as monthly meetings go, there are a few home
meetings, officers meetings, fellowship meetings and the
like. But one thing that is noticeable in most cases is
that there seem to be almost no activities for people outside the church. One of the churches said they have a
monthly film evangelism meeting, also at the church building.
But otherwise, there was nothing listed! Almost everything
seems to be for the church people themselves. A number of
the churches do try to have special evangelistic meetings
once a year or so. But the evidence seems to suggest very
building-centered, church-centered, and pastor-centered
churches. The lack of activities for the world is conspicu-
ous by its absence.

What does this mean? Why has there not been more experimenting? Why has there not been more change? Have we in
fact moved away from the "one-church-one-pastor" pattern in
the last several years? Why is it so difficult to implement
the idea of the priesthood of all believers? Why are there
so few activities directed toward the world? What do we see
as our mission? Do our forms really enable us to be the
church in the world, or are we only ministering to ourselves?
Are there some viable alternatives that we ought to consider?
Many such questions come to mind.

One reason for the existence of this situation may be
that too often we have forgotten that the Church exists for
the world. Another could be that most of the churches have
had pastors, and we have failed to remember that all of us
together, and not the pastors only, are the church. Still
another reason may be that in many cases we have put up

church buildings whenever a group has gotten to a certain
size, without really considering other options. There
might be other reasons. But it seems to me that these may
be some of the basic ones. That is, when we forget the
Church exists for the world, our program tends to become
church-centered. When we forget that we are the church and
expect the paid pastor to do all the work, the church tends
to become pastor-centered. And when we have a church
building where most of the meetings are held, we tend to
become building-centered.

It should be noted though that the pastors are not
necessarily to be blamed for the way things are. In fact,
it was the missionaries who first brought these patterns
with them, which the churches continue to follow today. The
dilemma is that once a pattern is established it is
extremely difficult to change. It would undoubtedly have
been easier to make changes in our structure if we could
have started over from scratch. Unfortunately, in most
cases that was impossible to do, with the result that little
has changed. Even in the cases where the meaning of the
word *church* has been broadened, or there are two or more
"churches" per pastor, there is still just one pastor per
church. That is, there is only one person in each group
who is looked up to as the pastor, and it may be the same
person in more than one group.

But in lifting up these three problems -- the program,
the pastor, and the building -- this is in no way intended
to imply that these are not needed. We need a good program
for the church people. We need more, not less pastors.
And we need buildings to meet in, even if it is only a
house or a rented room. But the point here is that these
things may be getting in the way of carrying out our
mission, and if so, then some greater changes may be in
order.

What has just been said is also not meant to suggest that
there is no outreach or any good things going on in the
churches. I am sure there is much more than meets the eye.
Nor is it meant to suggest that all churches are exactly
alike. They are not. When we were in language study in
Tokyo, for example, we visited over a dozen different
churches just to get a feel for varied traditions. Each one
was a little different from the others. Some were more
friendly than others. Some were better singers than others.
Some used one songbook; some another. Some prayed more
than others; some all at once, and some in tongues. Some

used one translation of the Bible; some another. Some were highly liturgical; others very informal, with most somewhere in between. Some included children; some did not. In one, men and women sat separately. In another, there was a woman preacher. One church had no bulletin. Another (the largest one, by the way) had no building of their own, but rented a room in an office building instead. Still another had services in the afternoon, rather than the morning as is customary. There were many little differences.

On the other hand, almost all of them had their own buildings, their own pastors, and their own church program. While there were minor differences revealing something of the diversity of the church in Japan, there were also many similarities. And may not the fact that they were so similar in these basic ways be part of the problem. That is, churches tend to copy one another. I remember one of our missionaries engaged in church planting lamenting how he had tried to let the church develop naturally along New Testament lines, but when it got to a certain point, the members started asking for things to be done the way they were done at another church down the street. What do you do then? As pointed out before, most of the patterns used today were inherited from missionaries. But even attempts at creativity to break down the old patterns or introduce new ones are sometimes doomed to frustration or failure.

There have been, however, some creative movements in Japanese Christianity. One of these is *Mukyōkai-shugi*, better known as the "Non-church movement" or "churchless Christianity." This movement was founded around the turn of the century by Kanzo Uchimura (1861-1930). Uchimura was the convert of a missionary, but reacted to denominationalism and the westernness of Christianity. He went to study in America for several years as a young man, but on his return to Japan in 1888 determined to purify Christianity of everything which did not spring from the doctrine of "justification by faith."

The movement which he began consists mainly of Bible study groups. These are led by lay teachers, unpaid and unordained. There is a strong teacher-follower relationship, but no pastors or church buildings, the meetings taking place largely in homes. There is little organization. The movement keeps no membership lists, and does not practice baptism or communion. No one knows how many "members" there might be, but some estimates are around 50,000. Its influence is said to be greatest among the more educated classes.

The movement is based on the cell approach and is self-
perpetuating.

Probably more than any other movement in Japan, this has
been a truly indigenous expression of Christianity. Perhaps
that is exactly what it was intended to be. Paul Peachey,
Mennonite scholar, hints of this in his article entitled,
"*Mukyokai-shugi*: A Modern Japanese Attempt to Complete the
Reformation." But Peachey says that

> As Uchimura developed his vision of a "Re-reforma-
> tion" it appears that he was totally unaware of efforts
> in the "left wing" of the Reformation in the time of
> Luther to accomplish this very thing. ...
>
> Phenomenologically, the movement Uchimura initiated
> would fall somewhere between Quakerism and Anabaptism.
> Like the Quakers, though not entirely for the same
> reasons, *Mukyokai-shugi* rejects clergy, hierarchy and
> sacraments. Like the Anabaptists, *Mukyokai-shugi* is
> Bible-centered rather than dependent on the "inner
> light." Likewise emphasis is strong on the cross and
> suffering. Membership is less formal than in either
> Anabaptism or Quakerism. Baptism and communion may be
> accepted in individual cases, but only with the clear
> understanding that these are not a means to grace and
> are not bound to clergy or hierarchy.
>
> Like Anabaptism and Quakerism, *Mukyokai-shugi* lays
> great stress on its "lay" character. The church
> assumes the form of a Bible class, though it is
> insisted that even this class is non-ecclesiastical.
> Nevertheless the Biblical idea of the church (as under-
> stood by *Mukyokai* believers) is affirmed; but the
> church must always be accepted as a spiritual reality
> in Christ and not an empirical institution. The
> teachers are for the most part fairly sophisticated
> Bible scholars, using the tools of critical Biblical
> scholarship and sometimes publishing exegetical
> magazines on a purely personal basis. On the other
> hand, their approach to the Bible is marked by deep
> reverence and piety. Hence they would reject both
> the term liberal and the term Fundamentalist in de-
> scribing their own position, although they claim to be
> orthodox in doctrine.
>
> *Mukyokai-shugi* appears to make its strongest appeal
> among intellectuals, though some evangelists also do

effective work in small towns, and rural areas. One
of its major strongholds is Tokyo University, the top
educational institution in Japan. ...

... It is customary in Japan to observe death anni-
versaries, and in the case of *Mukyokai* the annual
meeting [held on the anniversary of Uchimura's death]
constitutes perhaps the only visible link among the
various teachers and classes. ...

... The point on which the *Mukyokai* brethren are
criticized most severely is that their strictures
against church organization are such as to virtually
deny the church as an historical reality. Perhaps
indeed their case is somewhat overstated or at least
misstated. And yet in the end their position is more
consistent than that of the typical Protestant distinction between the visible and the invisible church
(1961:71-72).

... Enough has been said, however, to indicate the
desirability for a deeper encounter between *Mukyokai-
shugi* and Western Christians, particularly those within
the "left wing" of the Reformation (78).

The Anabaptists, like the *Mukyōkai-shugi*, also attempted
to complete the Reformation. It would seem, as Peachey
suggests, that this movement should be of particular interest for those within the Anabaptist-Mennonite tradition.
But to what extent has it seriously been considered as an
alternative to the forms of the church we are following now?

In contrast to the *Mukyōkai* movement, which is only very
loosely organized, is the Shinagawa Church in Tokyo, which
is very highly organized. The information I have on their
program is taken from a report on the "Shinagawa Community
Center," which was part of a presentation given on the work
of this church at the annual Hayama Conference in Japan in
January, 1971. The Shinagawa Church is an inner-city church
in downtown Tokyo. It is a member of the United Church of
Christ in Japan (*Kyōdan*), and has about 160 communicant
members. Back in the early 1960s, it felt the need for concentrating more on the needs of the immediate community.
According to the report, some of the problems they faced
were

... population density, poor housing, concentration
of young and single laborers away from home, lack of

playground facilities and programs for children,
lonely aged, increase in number of large industrial
buildings, and the like (1970:1).

As a result of their study they decided that there was the
need for a Community Center building, which was erected in
1968. There were several concepts underlying their ministry.
The first one was that "Christian people are those who live
in and for Christ, in and for the Church, and in and for the
world"; the second was that "The Church is a congregation of
these committed people. The Church ... has a mission to
witness and serve in the midst of the life of the people in
the community"; the third was that "The organization structure of the Church must be arranged according to the work
that is to be done" (1970:1). A few other points were
mentioned also.

With this as a basis, their approach to evangelism is
twofold. They note it includes "evangelism in the traditional sense" where Christ's name is spoken. This would
mean activities such as worship, church school, inquirers'
classes, a prebaptismal course, door-to-door visitation and
literature distribution. The church has singing, Bible
study, discussion, and a weekly love feast following morning
worship and communion. But their approach also includes
"evangelism in the broader sense," in which Christ's name
might not be spoken but His love would be acted out in
service.

They have a rather comprehensive program along this line
for people of all ages. For the children, for example,
there are nursery or kindergarten classes, day camps, base-
ball clubs, cycling clubs, English classes, and piano and
dancing lessons. For the youth there are an inquirers'
course, Bible study, study retreats and recreational trips.
For the adults there are physical fitness courses (for both
men and women), English classes, and counseling services.
There are monthly neighborhood programs for the children,
group discussion and lecture meetings for all the local
youth, and special feature programs of interest to the
entire community. There are also spring and fall evangelistic services.

To carry out all these activities, the church staff consists of a pastor, assistant pastor, missionary, several
secretaries, a director of music, plus the kindergarten
personnel. In addition to their work at the church, the
staff is also involved in probational work, juvenile patrol,

public school P.T.A., and the Shinagawa Urban Redevelopment
Project. But the church as a whole is seeking to meet the
needs of their own community. Perhaps we should take a
good hard look at our programs and try to see to what extent
we are involved in meeting the needs of our communities.
Have we in fact been starting with the needs of the people
around us, or with our own program?

Mukyōkai then is trying to reach the world through home
Bible study and lecture meetings taught by laymen, as well
as through the witness of its members in their homes and
their places of work. The members of the Shinagawa Church
undoubtedly are also trying to be good witnesses at home
and at work, but in addition feel the need for something
more concrete like the Community Center. I am sure we can
learn something from both of them. But there is another
type of church which is still different from either of these,
and that is the "intentional community," or the various
experiments in communal living. I am not familiar with any
such groups which may exist in Japan, but there are many in
other parts of the world, including the U.S.A. There is,
for example, the Reba Place Fellowship in Evanston, Illinois,
which began over 20 years ago, or the Fellowship of Hope in
Elkhart, Indiana, which is more recent.

An article in *Christian Living* magazine (Stahl 1973)
describes what life is like at the Fellowship of Hope. The
Fellowship began in 1970 with a small group who made a
commitment to God, to each other, and to a new way of life.
There were nine members at the time. Three years later
there were 19 (as of 1980 there are over 50). Most of them
are young adults from Anabaptist and other church backgrounds. As for their reason for covenanting together, it
is simply that they are trying to be the people of God.
Part of their commitment involves a pooling of all their
resources, including wages. They try to live on a minimum
of "life's necessities." They own several homes, cars, and
appliances as common property. Since they live within a
couple blocks of one another, they are able to share such
tasks as laundry, cooking, and babysitting. Individuals
have their own clothes, books and so on, but there is no
rule regarding what belongs to an individual and what
belongs to the group. Vocational decisions too are made
within the group. Because they share many things together,
a number of them are able to work at volunteer jobs with
little or no pay. Many of the group are working at social
service or church agencies.

There is not only a sharing of income. There is also a
sharing of time. A lot of time is spent together. Tuesday
evening is for brief vespers. Wednesday evening is a
"discernment" meeting. One of the most important functions
of the group is discerning God's will for the individual, as
well as for the group. Much prayer, thought, and discussion
is given to this. At other times, during the week, smaller
groups meet for sharing and prayer. Thursday evening is a
common supper. Once a month on Friday is recreation night.
Saturday is a work day for cleaning up or doing neighborhood
jobs. Rather than sending out missionaries, they are seeking to be missionary in their own community. Sunday there
is an informal worship service, including the children.
This is followed by a time of Bible study. The morning
comes to a climax with a communal meal (love feast).

There are also special times of celebration for new
members, births, baptisms, communion, marriage and so forth.
Anyone wishing to become a member of the group may first
become an "intentional neighbor," until the person decides
whether he or she is willing to make the commitment or not.
The article referred to begins by saying that

> The Fellowship of Hope wants to be faithful to
> Jesus Christ. The members of the Fellowship are
> committed to group life, not for its own sake, but
> to being the people of God (1973:17).

It concludes by saying that

> For the members of the Fellowship of Hope, being
> the church means forgiveness, admonition, and search-
> ing together for God's will. Church means sharing
> all they have in time and resources. Church to them
> is a way of life (21).

The members of the Fellowship are concerned primarily with
"being the Church." Might not this model have something to
commend itself to churches in Japan?

Many other illustrations could be given. These are only
a few. But perhaps they are sufficient to indicate that
there are alternative models to the ones we have been following. Actually, the problem of structure that we are dealing
with here has very deep roots. In an enlightening study
document called "Church Reform and the Missionary Congregation in the 1970's," John W. Miller traces how the church
received the structures it has today. This study was

prepared under the auspices of the Council on Faith, Life and Strategy of the Mennonite Church. Miller notes that earlier in this century Mennonite scholars discovered that the founders of the Mennonite Church placed great emphasis on both discipleship and discipline, and that the church for them consisted of "a network of relatively small, disciplined fellowships" (1972:2). We might also think of this pattern as the ideal for a Mennonite congregation today.

As we look further back into church history, however, Miller points out that there were basically two forms of congregational life. The first was the "house church," with close group fellowship and discipline, which was the main form of the church in the first two centuries. The second form was the "sanctuary church," with a special building and ruled by a bishop, which came into being from about the third century on. It was especially after Christianity became a state religion under Constantine in A.D. 325 that churches began to build large sanctuaries, patterned after the Roman basilica. This pattern was dominant until the time of the Reformation, when Luther wanted to go back to the house church pattern as the basic pattern of congregational life, but he could not find the people to do it. So instead, he modernized the worship services, using German instead of Latin, emphasizing Bible reading, preaching and so on and hoped that these changes would lead to the conversion of Christians who would in turn start house churches. Unfortunately, the services became ends in themselves, and Luther (like many of the other reformers) ended up defining the church as where "the Word is preached" and "the sacraments administered."

There were some groups though such as the Anabaptists, who succeeded in establishing churches along the house church pattern, where fellowship and discipline by the congregation were again the distinguishing marks. Other groups such as the Quakers and Methodists also revived the house church form in later centuries. But while Mennonites stand historically at least within the Anabaptist tradition, Miller observes that

> The Mennonite congregations today however, for the most part, have adapted themselves to the style of the sanctuary church tradition. They are mostly large assemblies, meeting in basilica type sanctuaries, with a focus on Sunday worship services. Membership is loosely defined and poorly disciplined (1972:14).

If what Miller says is true, it means that the Mennonite
congregational ideal of the house church and the Mennonite
congregational reality of the sanctuary church are two quite
different things. They are so different, in fact, as to be
almost opposing models. He goes on to suggest that in
light of this disparity, there are at least three alternatives: the first would be to "adapt our ideals to the
reality of what is"; the second, to "seek to modify the congregations as they now exist in the direction of the house
church model"; the third would be to "encourage the founding
of house churches, while redefining the sanctuary church as
a 'cluster' assembly" (1972:10-11). Of these three alternatives, Miller feels that the last one has the greatest
possibility, and goes on to remark that

> If this is a valid suggestion, we would project as
> a goal of congregational reform a pattern where members
> would typically belong to a house church. Baptism and
> the Lord's Supper, membership and discipline, pastoral
> nurture and oversight, evangelistic outreach and ser-
> vice would be vested primarily in the house churches,
> and they would be accorded the status of "primary
> organizational units of the church," now given to the
> larger assemblies. The larger congregations would
> then become centers of cooperative activity (1972:12).

According to Miller's proposal, the "house church" would
be the basic unit of the church. The house church would be
a congregation in its own right. There would still be a
need for the larger congregations, though, to cooperate for
certain activities. But they would be "cluster assemblies"
rather than the basic organizational unit of the church.
The cluster assembly would then in a sense stand between the
local congregation and the regional conference. Miller
realizes, of course, that to implement such sweeping changes
as this would be difficult, and yet is of the conviction
that if we have the vision for it and the will to do it, it
can be done. And perhaps this needs to be considered not
only in North America, but in other countries, like Japan,
which have inherited the "sanctuary church" pattern from
overseas. It would mean radical change for the church in
many ways, and the cost must be counted. But we must also
count the cost of what it might mean in the long run if we
are unwilling to make any radical changes necessary.

There are many other churchmen whose thinking is similar
to Miller's. One of these is Charles M. Olsen in his
stimulating book, *The Base Church*. Olsen believes that for

the renewal of the institutional church to take place, there
is a need for new forms and models, and that many such
options exist. In his own words, some of the things he
states are:

> The Reformation model of congregation, with its
> authority/dependency style of functioning and family-
> oriented approach to enrollment, imposes formidable
> limits. The *base* of the congregation is simply a
> collection of individuals or families.

> I advocate a church "base" which consists of dy-
> namic, cellular groups of people who gather out of
> their common experience of Christ to learn and live
> out his love together. I advocate a church "base"
> which is a connectional organism of living cells of
> Christians. I choose to call these small groups
> "base" groups. Base groups provide the foundation
> for any church superstructure (1973:6).

> Base groups are not a means to another end -- they
> themselves are life! They can incorporate into them-
> selves the full marks of the church, which include
> mission, worship, nurture, and fellowship (13).

> Although small groups have been *utilized* as a
> church renewal scheme, they have rarely been *legiti-
> mized* as a full expression of the church. ... We have
> been so oriented toward the *gathered* congregation
> that the small group is relegated to serving as a
> means to a larger end -- that is, to stimulate active
> participation in the corporate congregation. In this
> role, the house church cannot become anything but a
> half-way house. ...

> *Let's legitimate the base group!* Let's bring it
> into the center of the congregation's life. Let's
> get our pastors and laymen retrained for new styles
> of leadership (16).

> I insist that base communities must be connectional.
> They must be attached to other clusters or to a
> larger expression of the church. Spontaneous groups
> tend to avoid the issue of authority, becoming
> instead a sectarian law unto themselves. In some way,
> "subjection to the brothers" must be expressed. The
> unity of the church must be expressed in the midst of
> diversity (19).

Without equivocation, I want to affirm a connectional position. Base-church groups must function in relationship with the established church structures. Our task is to find ways in which the connection can be maintained (72).

I have suggested that an impersonal, success-oriented, edifice-centered, and clergy-dominated congregational model of Christian community constricts the creative possibilities in the church. I have suggested that building church structures upon a network of inter-dependent, small, base groups is vital to the renewal of the church, and that the new forms may be constructed within, alongside, or outside the parish congregation. I envision the church in the "promised land" functioning with diverse cells, all bearing the full marks of the church. This church operates within every conceivable stream of society, and it eagerly faces the future (139).

I do not want to start a new denomination or an anti-institutional underground church. I do propose a transition within existing church structures to expand the options for Christian community (141).

What Olsen and Miller both propose may sound somewhat idealistic, but it is not just an empty dream. It is, in fact, already beginning to happen in certain places. An article in a September 1975 issue of *The Mennonite*, in speaking of models of the church to take us to the year 2000, gives some concrete examples. It relates, for instance, that

The Prairie St. Mennonite Church in Elkhart, Indiana, has encouraged existing Sunday school classes to become primary fellowship groups, for personal sharing and decision making. These have been given the status of congregations within the "great congregation" with the powers to "bind and loose" and share the Lord's Supper. Representatives from these congregations meet to bring concerns and suggest directions to those who plan the Sunday morning worship hour of the gathered assembly. This is a good example of what can be done within existing structures to increase accountability and provide a place for caring and discipline.

Perhaps the fastest growing new model in the Mennonite church is the intentional community. Persons coming into this association do so after covenanting to make the church their central, total relationship governing all of their life decisions. This provides a different starting point from that of the established congregation where membership requirements are more loosely defined.

Seventeen years ago Reba Place Fellowship in Evanston, Illinois, pioneered this model of church among Mennonites. Today it continues to grow and has been joined by more than twenty other communities based on variations of a similar model of total accountability. ...

A new middle model of church structure between the established congregation and the communal fellowship is emerging in Goshen, Indiana. Called simply the Assembly, each covenanted member of this congregation is expected to be an active participant in a house fellowship group as well as in the congregation. In this model the house fellowship, meeting at least once a week, becomes the primary group. It is here that personal concerns are discussed, decisions made, the Word studied and acted on, and where members are accountable to each other. But the house fellowships do not stand alone. Weekly they meet together in an assembly for praise, prayer, biblical study, and fellowship.

The agenda for the assembly of house fellowships Sunday morning grows out of the questions being discussed in the individual house fellowships. In order to avoid cliquishness and encourage evangelism, house fellowships welcome newcomers and divide when they become too large (over fourteen). The Assembly also divides into smaller congregations when that group becomes too large for easy communication without a public address system (70-100). The Assembly is now composed of three congregations which meet weekly. The entire Assembly meets every seventh Sunday (a sabbatical) for celebration, keeping in touch, and discussion of new directions (Gingrich 1975:491-492).

While there is no one model which we can say would be best for each and every place, what is happening in these various places may also be relevant to our situation in Japan. That is, most churches in Japan are small. And yet, in spite of their smallness, they tend to follow the

sanctuary pattern rather than the house church pattern.
Small groups within a church are generally not thought of as
being a church. The church is thought of as the larger
gathered congregation. It is true, of course, that the
larger congregation is also a church. But might it not be
fitting in some cases to reorganize and recognize the
smaller groups as the basic units of the larger congregations. In other words, to legitimatize them as a church.

Jesus Himself said that "where two or three are gathered
in my name, there am I in the midst of them" (Matt. 18:20),
which connotes that even groups of two or three are legitimate churches. Individual believers are not churches. But
two or three believers together may constitute a church.
In light of this, perhaps the JMCCC Constitution definition
of a "church" as being "groups with 15 or more resident
active members" (Appendix B:3) ought to be reconsidered.
Should not a church be defined by the relationship of its
members to Christ and one another, rather than according to
how large or how small it is?

The smallness of churches, groups of 25 or 30 on the
average, is often lamented in Japan. But could it not be
just the opposite, that the churches are not too small, but
too large? Could it be that people long for a still smaller,
more intimate fellowship, and that even the present churches
should be broken up into smaller units? Could it be that,
as Olsen affirms, we should be "claiming their smallness as
power, rather than feeling guilty and inadequate because
they do not grow" (1973:146)? In any case, perhaps it would
be well to consider restructuring the larger congregations
into clusters of smaller churches. Also, to begin recognizing small groups which do not yet meet the official
Conference requirement as legitimate churches. Perhaps
12-15 should be seen as a maximum rather than a minimum size.

Most of the models of the church cited in this chapter
have come from outside of Japan. But it is interesting to
note in an article in the July 1975 issue of *Shinto no Tomo*
[The Believer's Friend] that there are different models of
the church in Japan also (Seki 1975). The church referred
to in particular in the writeup is the Shunan Church
(*Kyōdan*, UCCJ) located in Akita Prefecture, on the northern
part of Honshu. The church, or actually churches (as the
church consists of nine separate congregations), is situated
in a rural area with a population of approximately 55,000.
The parent church is in Yokote City, and the other eight
congregations are scattered throughout the area, but all are

served by just one pastor. The pastor, 72-year-old Shigeji
Seya, has been pastoring these various churches for 47 years
since he graduated from seminary in 1928.

The work there was originally begun by an independent
missionary named M. M. Smizer. Smizer did evangelism in the
area from 1914 until his death in 1955 (at 81 years of age).
He itinerated from village to village, but said his objective was not to plant churches. He felt his calling was
rather to just do evangelism and leave the formation of the
churches to someone else. When Pastor Seya came, he began
working at that, and has been doing so ever since. As a
matter of fact, Seya, himself a native of Yokote, was the
initial fruit of Smizer's work, and served as the first
teacher in a Sunday school he opened there. Now, as pastor,
he itinerates, walking to the various groups, having a
meeting somewhere different almost every day.

Seven of the churches all have regular meetings. (Yokote
is the only one, however, having regular Sunday worship.
The other groups usually meet on weekdays, often in the
evening.) Two of the churches hold meetings on an irregular
basis, when people are free. The average attendance for
worship at the various centers is 90, 35, 13, 10, 8, 8, 8,
7 and 15 (1975:13). From this it can be seen that the
majority of the groups are quite small. Most of them meet
in believers' homes rather than a church building. They are
"house churches," yet they are all considered churches.
Each of the branch churches serves as a kind of "base camp"
of the larger Shunan Church.

There is a kind of parent-child relationship between the
smaller churches and the largest church, the Yokote Church.
It serves as the central meeting place for the eight branch
churches. All together there are about 200 members in the
churches, and occasionally they may meet for a laymen's
rally or other activity. Together the churches refer to
themselves literally as the "All-Shunan Church." Yet, like
the Yokote Church, they each have their own name and their
own identity. The groups are all independent. Even though
they share a pastor, they each have their own meetings,
including an annual meeting, their own meeting place, they
take care of their own finances and so on, and have their
own evangelistic program.

It is realized that the pastor cannot do all the work by
himself, and an attempt is made to put responsible laymen in
strategic places to carry on the work in each area. It is

said that the head of the household in each "house church"
is especially important, as people tend to gather according
to the position of the head of the household in the village.
As laymen work and serve in their local setting, evangelism
is said to be always a pioneering effort. Whether such a
pattern might or might not be suitable for our own situation
ought to be discussed. But in any case, here is at least
one quite different pattern found within Japan itself, and
no doubt there are others which could be discovered as well.

The question we are wrestling with here is not whether
Jesus intended to found a visible church or not. I think
we would have to agree with R. Newton Flew's argument in his
book, *Jesus and His Church* (1943:35ff.), that it was His
intention to start such a community. The real question for
us is, what shape should that community take? Must it
adhere strictly to the patterns found in the New Testament?
Do we have liberty to adapt those patterns to the needs of
our own day? If so, what are the options?

We have tried to spell out some of the options in this
section. As the JMCCC begins a new work in Fukuoka and
elsewhere, we need to rethink what a church is and what kind
of church we want to have. Do we plan to start single,
double, or multiple congregations like we have now? Are we
thinking of loosely organized groups, highly organized
groups, or something in between? Have we given any thought
to the possibility of intentional communities? Are we thinking of "house churches" or "sanctuary churches"? Have we
considered the possibility of "base churches" and "cluster
congregations"? What kind of church will enable us to move
away from the "one-church-one-pastor" system toward our goal
of the "priesthood of all believers"? What kind of a church
do we want to start anyway? This will take a lot of hard
thinking, and in the end I believe the question will have to
be decided by our Japanese brethren themselves. But it is a
question that must be faced squarely before we can begin to
think about what kind of leaders such a church would require.

WHAT KIND OF LEADERS DO WE NEED
FOR THAT KIND OF CHURCH?

This whole matter of leadership, as we have suggested, is
intimately related to one's concept of the church. But in
our case, since it has not yet been decided exactly what
kind of church we want to have, we are in somewhat of a
dilemma when it comes to suggesting what kind of leaders
such a church might need. This means that we will be under

certain limitations in discussing this question. But perhaps we can at least begin by taking a look at the kind of leaders we find in the Bible, and then try to compare that with the leaders in our churches today.

When we look at what the New Testament has to say about leaders, the first thing that strikes us is that it says very little. That is to say, the word *leader* almost never appears. There are some exceptions, of course (e.g., Heb. 13:7,17), but as a whole, the New Testament does not have much to say about being leaders. It has a lot to say, however, about being servants. Instead of speaking about leaders and leadership, we might say that the New Testament talks about servants and servanthood. As Jesus told His disciples,

> You know that those who are supposed to rule over the Gentiles lord it over them, and their great men exercise authority over them. But it shall not be so among you; but whoever would be great among you must be your servant, and whoever would be first among you must be slave of all. For the Son of man also came not to be served but to serve, and to give his life as a ransom for many (Mark 10:42-45).

Jesus taught His disciples that true greatness lay in serving. He talked more about serving than about being served. He talked more about following than about leading. He talked more about discipleship than about leadership. And He not only talked about it. He Himself set the example. As the apostle Paul sums it up so beautifully,

> Have this mind among yourselves, which you have in Christ Jesus, who, though he was in the form of God, did not count equality with God a thing to be grasped, but emptied himself, taking the form of a servant, being born in the likeness of men. And being found in human form he humbled himself and became obedient unto death, even death on a cross (Phil. 2:5-8).

If Jesus, the Son of God, gave Himself so completely for us, how much more ought we, His disciples, to give ourselves for Him. As He once said, "A disciple is not above his teacher, nor a servant above his master; it is enough for the disciple to be like his teacher, and the servant like his master" (Matt. 10:24-25a).

We know that Jesus chose twelve disciples "to be with him, and to be sent out to preach and have authority to cast

out demons" (Mark 3:14ff.). We also know that three of
those disciples -- Peter, James, and John -- formed an inner
circle within the Twelve (Mark 9:2). Later on He also
appointed seventy and sent them out "two by two" (Luke 10:1).
In these appointments, we can perhaps see the beginnings of
the Christian ministry. But Jesus Himself did not institute
the ministry as such. That was a later development, following Pentecost, and the birth of the Christian Church. But
even so, the fact is that the words *minister* and *ministry*
are never used in the New Testament in the way in which we
generally think of them. That is, the word *minister* is used,
but it is never used as a title for someone. Paul does
speak of himself as "a minister of Christ Jesus" and of
being "in the priestly service of the gospel of God" (Rom.
15:16), but these were not yet titles. There are no Rever-
ends in the New Testament!

The word *ministry* is not used either with reference to
the leaders of the church, as a particular group within the
church. Ministry refers rather to something the whole
church did. As Paul wrote to the church in Corinth, God
"through Christ reconciled us to himself and gave us the
ministry of reconciliation" (II Cor. 5:18). In this sense,
everyone had a ministry, and everyone was a minister. To be
a minister was to serve; to have a ministry was to serve;
to be a Christian was to be a servant of Christ and in the
service of "the gospel of God." Paul often referred to himself as "a servant of Jesus Christ" (Rom. 1:1). He exhorted
other believers also to be "servants of Christ" (Eph. 6:6).

To be a disciple then was to be a servant. To be a servant was to serve, to minister. And yet, even though all
believers had a share in the ministry of the church, we read
of those who were appointed to special ministries. In
Acts 6, for instance, when the church faced a problem of a
practical nature, the twelve apostles gathered all the disciples together and declared:

> It is not right that we should give up preaching the
> word of God to serve tables. Therefore, brethren,
> pick out from among you seven men of good repute, full
> of the Spirit and of wisdom, whom we may appoint to
> this duty. But we will devote ourselves to prayer and
> to the ministry of the word (6:2-4).

As a result, seven men were chosen to meet that need. They
are often referred to as the first "deacons," although the
word itself is not used here. Interestingly though, the

words used in Greek for "serving" tables and "ministering" the Word both come from the same root *diakonos*, which means basically to serve or to minister (Robertson 1930:73). While the nature of the various ministries differed, the essence was the same -- to serve. They were all service ministries. Besides the deacons, there were also deaconesses in the church (Rom. 16:1).

In addition to the deacons and deaconesses, there were also elders in the churches. We read of how Paul and Barnabas appointed elders in every church, and then committed the whole group to the Lord (Acts 14:23). The elders were the spiritual leaders of the church. Later on Paul also speaks of "bishops" or "overseers" in the church (Phil. 1:1), but the way he uses the term suggests that at least in some cases it may be interchangeable with the word for elders (Titus 1:5,7). Whether there were "elder-bishops" or whether bishop was a separate office, perhaps the governing elder in a congregation, is disputed. In any case, the elders seemed to be representatives of the church, the leading members of the congregation, and together with the church in each place made the necessary decisions (Acts 15: 4,6,22). The elders (or bishops) were not necessarily elderly, but would at least be mature in the faith, and able to manage their own households well (I Tim. 3:4-6). They were evidently appointed by the laying on of hands (5:22). And in contrast to the deacons, the elders and bishops seem to have all been men.

Some of these offices, such as that of deacon, appear to have originated with the development of the Christian Church. Others, such as the office of elder, apparently were inherited. G.S.M. Walker in *The New Bible Dictionary* observes, for example, that

> In the Old Testament the elders of Israel, of the people, or of the congregation are frequently mentioned; Jewish synagogues were normally governed by a council of elders, under the chairmanship of a 'ruler of the synagogue,' whose office was perhaps held in rotation; and the entire Jewish people was subject in religious matters to the Sanhedrin of seventy-one members, in which the high priest, during the New Testament period, was chairman *ex officio*. A similar organization was naturally followed in the Christian Church, and the *zāquēn* (elder) of the Old Testament became the *presbyteros* (Vulg. *senior*) of the New (1962:1027).

Jesus' choosing of the Twelve and the sending of the
Seventy have obvious parallels in the twelve tribes (Gen.
49:28) and the seventy elders (Ex. 24:1) of the Old Testament. As we have just seen, the office of elder has
precedents there too. There were also differences, however.
The elder in the New Testament was not only an overseer. He
was to tend the flock that was in his charge (I Pet. 5:2),
but to also preach and teach (I Tim. 5:17), to do pastoral
visitation (Jas. 5:14) and so on. But while there are these
similarities and differences with regard to the office of
elder, the offices of deacon (and bishop?) seem to be unique
to anything in Judaism.

These are only a few of the offices mentioned in the New
Testament. Actually, there are many others. There is the
list in Ephesians 4, for instance:

> And his gifts were that some should be apostles, some
> prophets, some evangelists, some pastors and teachers,
> for the equipment of the saints, for the work of the
> ministry, for building up the body of Christ (11-12).

This list is of special interest to us as it names what we
might call the leadership ministries of the church. It is
of interest for another reason too, and that is that it
expresses what the leaders are given for. The RSV translation here is unfortunate though, because it implies that the
job of these leaders is twofold: first, to equip the saints;
second, to do the work of the ministry. But the fact is
that there really should be no comma after "saints." This
has sometimes been called the "fatal comma," because of the
impression it gives that the leaders of the church are to do
the work of the ministry, whereas the passage actually says
that the leaders of the church are to equip the saints (all
the believers) for the work of the ministry.

There are other lists in Romans 12:6-8, and I Corinthians
12:4-11, 27-31, in which some of the leadership ministries
are also included. But for the most part these latter lists
consist of gifts such as serving and giving and helping and
the like, as well as the spiritual gifts. The implication
would seem to be that every Christian has a gift, a ministry,
a way in which he or she can serve. As Mennonite theologian
John H. Yoder has put it, in the broad sense of the word,
"no one is not a minister" (1969:85). Some of these ministries are within the church, some outside in the world, but
wherever they take place those with leadership gifts are
responsible to prepare the whole church for its overall work
of ministry.

Exactly how the offices of deacon, elder, and bishop fit together with the other offices or ministries is not clearly spelled out in the New Testament. We are not told, for example, whether an elder sometimes also served as pastor/ teacher or not. Nor is it made clear just how these people were chosen or appointed to their various positions. It is indicated, however, that God does give leadership gifts to the Church. As the Church is the body of Christ, it would seem that it is up to the local church to discern such gifts within its midst. To be sure, it is more than a human endeavor. In the case of Paul and Barnabas, for instance, the Holy Spirit told the church to set them apart for the work to which He had called them (Acts 13:2). In the case of Timothy it is implied that God gave him his gift through the laying on of Paul's hands (II Tim. 1:6). The Holy Spirit certainly had a definite part in the process, as in the case where a matter was decided in a certain way because it seemed good to the Holy Spirit and the church (Acts 15:28). But whether the call to an office came to the individual and then was confirmed by the church, or whether it came to the individual through the church is difficult to say.

In any event, the important thing is that God gives such gifts to the Church. People are called to serve in various capacities. When they are called, they are also equipped with the necessary gift to fulfill that particular ministry. And while there is not a list of qualifications for each of the ministries, we do find lists for bishops (elders?) and deacons in I Timothy 3, and another for elders/bishops in Titus 1. The qualifications vary from spiritual to moral to practical, and the candidates (at least the deacons) are to be tested and proved before they serve (I Tim. 3:10). Perhaps these qualifications would apply to some of the other offices as well. Some of the leaders, such as the elders who labored at preaching and teaching, were partially, if not wholly, supported by the church (I Tim. 5:17-18). At the same time, Paul cautioned that there should be no haste in the laying on of hands (5:22). The gifts God had given would become evident in due time.

In summary, there are many ministries enumerated in the New Testament. A few of them may have had their origin in Judaism, but most were original to the Christian Church. But while all Christians had a part in the ministry of the church, and all were in that sense "ministers," not all were ministers as we define the term today. And even though not much is said in the New Testament concerning leaders, it is

important to note that there is no opposition to leaders and
leadership as such. In fact, there were those who were set
apart for special ministries on behalf of the entire church.
Their job was to enable the others to fulfill their own
particular ministry. None of the ministries, whether
general or special, changed a person's status. They were
for service, not status. But while all had the same status,
not all had the same function, which is why there were some
specialized ministries. Perhaps this is what a scholar like
T. W. Manson means when he concludes that in the church,
"while all believers are priests, all believers are not
ministers" (1958:69).

Another important point to remember is that the various
ministries all have their origin in Christ. Indeed, we can
say it is Christ who is ministering through the Christian.
It is interesting, too, to note how all these ministries
have not only originated with Christ, but have their proto-
type in Him. He is *the* Apostle (Heb. 3:1). He is *the*
Prophet (Matt. 21:11). He is *the* Evangelist (Luke 4:18).
He is *the* Pastor (I Pet. 2:25). He is *the* Teacher (John
13:13). He is Lord and Savior and also our Leader (Acts
5:31). But above all, He is the humble Servant (Rom. 15:8).
And as He spoke to His first disciples, so He speaks to us:
"I have given you an example, that you also should do as I
have done to you. Truly, truly, I say to you, a servant is
not greater than his master" (John 13:15,16a).

In the New Testament, then, there does not seem to be any
one pattern of church organization which we can label as *the*
New Testament pattern. The pattern seems to have been
flexible rather than fixed. Under the leading of the Holy
Spirit, the early Christians seem to have simply structured
themselves in a way that would meet needs as they arose.
There were leaders, but in exactly what relationship they
stood to one another is not precisely laid out. They
evidently saw themselves as servants more than as leaders.
That may account in part as to why the organizational
pattern of the church does not seem to have been highly
structured.

Today, however, as we look at churches we see that there
are basically three types of church government which have
evolved. They are the congregational, the presbyterial, and
the episcopal patterns. And yet, varied as they are, no
doubt each of them feels that their own particular pattern
gets its authority from the New Testament. What M. H.
Shepherd, Jr. asserts in *The Interpreter's Dictionary of the
Bible* may well be true, that

Few subjects in the history of the church have received such disputed interpretations as the origin and development of the ministry. The differences of interpreters stem in part from the meager, and apparently contradictory, notices on the subject in the NT and early patristic sources. To a greater degree, however, they are the result of conflicting theological views respecting the nature of the church, and the necessity or expediency of certain forms of ministry for the essential constitution of the church, both in its inner organic unity and in its outer historic structure (1962:386).

If his analysis is correct, it would appear that our concept of the church determines our concept of the ministry, and also that we tend to read our concept of the ministry back into the New Testament. Which means that if we are not careful, our concept of the church and its ministry may soon become grounded in tradition rather than in the Bible itself. To be sure, our concept of the ministry should be determined by our concept of the church, but our concept of the church should be rooted in the Bible rather than in any given tradition.

In the case of the Mennonite Church, as pointed out in the first chapter, it traces its origin back to the Reformation of the sixteenth century and the Anabaptist movement. The Anabaptists had their origin in a restudy of the New Testament, especially the concepts of discipleship and the church. For the Anabaptists as well as for the other reformers, one of the cardinal principles of the whole reformation movement was "the priesthood of all believers." Luther, for example, in reaction to the hierarchical concept of the church, wanted to do away completely with the distinction between clergy and laity. The only distinctions he felt were valid were those which had to do with office. He was not against ministers per se as long as they were "ministers of the Word" and not "priests," standing between God and man. He affirmed the universal priesthood of believers.

Yet, even with this new concept of the church as a priesthood of all believers, and the reaffirmation of the laity, as Hendrik Kraemer remarks in his book *A Theology of the Laity*, "To the present day it rather fulfils the role of a flag than of an energizing vital principle" (1958:63). He goes on to ask why with this new definition of the church and the ministry it remained largely a concept rather than

becoming a fact, and why the ministers became dominant
instead of the whole congregation. He suggests that some
of the reasons for this may have been that much of the pro-
test was polemical and that it was not felt that the biblical pattern of the church had to necessarily be imitated;
that the laity who had been kept immature for so long could
not suddenly function as spiritual adults; that the tremendous stress on the importance of correct preaching required
a specially qualified group of ministers; and that the
actual organizational reforms could not be carried out
without the help of princes and political magistrates who,
along with the ministers, came to occupy an important place
in administering the affairs of the church (1958:64-67).
Perhaps those are some of the main reasons why Luther in the
end had to lament the fact that he could never find enough
converted people to form what he considered to be a true
Christian congregation.

There was at least one group of Christians, though, which
sought to make the concept of the priesthood of believers a
reality. They were the Anabaptists. It was the Anabaptists,
above all, who made a serious attempt to implement the principle of the "priesthood of all believers." For them this
involved the whole concept of the church, which they saw as
the crucial issue. That is, prior to the Reformation, the
church taught and the people believed that God was mediated
to them (the laity) through a priest (the clergy), as
indicated in the diagram (Figure 5.3).

The reformers, on the other hand, taught that God was not
mediated to the people through the priests, but that each
and every Christian had direct access to God through Christ.
Not only that, but that in Christ, Christians were also
"priests" to one another. Yet while this was their belief,
most of the reformers had difficulty putting it into practice. The Anabaptists attempted to put into practice what
until then had largely only been preached, by placing a
great deal of emphasis on brotherhood.

But in thinking of how they ministered to one another as
priests, it is well to remember that this ministry, like the
others we referred to before, was also first fulfilled by
Christ. He is the great High Priest (Heb. 3:1). There were
of course no priests as such in the Early Church. As New
Testament scholar Leon Morris notes, "It is because of
Christ's one priesthood that Christians can speak (paradoxi-
cally) of 'the priesthood of all believers'" (1964:31).
He goes on to say that "His is the one essential ministry.

All human ministry depends on His ministry, and, indeed, is nothing more than a continuation of it" (1964:32). He also speaks of some churches which suggest that the church cannot exist apart from its human ministry, but concludes by stating that "It is the presence of Christ, not that of the ministry, that constitutes the Church" (1964:34). It is important to keep that in mind as we reflect on this subject.

Figure 5.3

PRE/POST-REFORMATION PATTERNS

Pre-Reformation (Catholic)

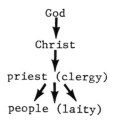

Post-Reformation (Protestant)

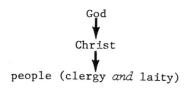

Even though the Anabaptists believed that Christ was in their midst, and sought to embody the priesthood of believers principle, they were not opposed to church leaders as such. For example, Menno Simons, a former Catholic priest, was asked to be one of their leaders after his conversion. In a study paper by George E. Janzen on "The Anabaptist View of the Ministry," he summarizes what they believed about leadership in the following way:

1. The Anabaptists prized church leadership because they believed that it was ordained by Christ himself, and that no church could long exist without leadership.

2. God and the local congregation cooperated in the selection of church leadership.

3. Leaders were responsible to God for the welfare of the Lord's flock. In view of such holy responsibility, the Anabaptists demanded unfeigned holiness of life and purity of doctrine of their leadership.

4. A call by the congregation constituted a call of God, for the congregation made the call only after extended self-examination and prayer. They had complete confidence that God would not permit them to make a wrong choice after such a period of self-preparation and searching for the Lord's will. A member is not in a position to decline the call of the congregation, for then he would be declining the call of God.

5. Leadership came almost always from within the ranks of the local congregation itself.

6. Leadership did not necessarily require extensive theological and other educational preparation. Some of the first leaders were highly educated men, coming mostly from the ranks of the generally well-trained Roman Catholic clergy. Later, however, the emphasis was on holy living, obedience to the Scriptures and faithfulness to Jesus Christ.

7. Leadership was almost totally self-supported. Material stipends were, for the most part, greatly frowned upon. They recognized, on the one hand, the New Testament teaching that ministers of the Gospel have a right to live of the Gospel, but this, on the other hand, was always coupled by a reluctance to use this privilege lest it prove a stumbling block to the acceptance of the Gospel (1965:13).

The Anabaptists were basically congregational in structure. Historically, Mennonite churches stand in the Anabaptist tradition and are also congregational in terms of church polity. But there seem to be many points at which they have departed from the practices of their Anabaptist forefathers, and the concept of the priesthood of all believers. The Anabaptists called leaders out of the local congregation; Mennonites, by and large, call their leaders from outside the local church. The Anabaptists did not require extensive theological education of their leaders; Mennonites usually do. The Anabaptist leaders were self-supporting for the most part; Mennonites as a rule pay their leaders.

Those are only a few of the differences however, and one
important factor which is not mentioned by Janzen is that
the Anabaptist congregations generally had a plural ministry,
whereas Mennonites today have moved toward a single ministry.
In all fairness it should be added this may not be true of
all Mennonites. It is said, for instance, that many Mennonite congregations in Canada have functioned until recently
with a plural, self-supported ministry, and there may be
some that still do. There may even be some in the States
which do, although most of them seem to have made the transition earlier. And there may be some good reasons behind
the changes made. These remarks are not meant to suggest
that some of these changes from the Anabaptist way of doing
things were not in order. The point is that Mennonite
churches, like other Protestants, have been moving toward a
professional ministry. This change has taken place more or
less unconsciously.

What Mennonite educator J. Lawrence Burkholder has said
somewhat facetiously may be true, that we Mennonites seem to
have assumed that

We can adopt a Protestant *form* of the ministry while
having an Anabaptist-free church in *reality*. We can
have a slightly modified Protestant form of ministry
and an Anabaptist ecclesiology with its emphasis upon
brotherhood, priesthood of all believers, and congregational initiative at the same time (1969:13).

The implication, of course, is that the Anabaptist concept
of a believers' church and the Mennonite/Protestant form of
the ministry are practically incompatible. We do not have
room here to discuss the matter further. But it is important to be aware of some of the shifts that have taken place
in the Mennonite Church away from the Anabaptist pattern,
especially since the Anabaptists sought to find their
pattern in the New Testament.

Earlier in this chapter we saw how the Mennonites had
moved away from the house church pattern of the Anabaptists
to the sanctuary pattern. Here we have seen how the
Mennonites have moved away from the Anabaptist pattern of
ministry, especially in the switch from a multiple to a
single pattern. And when Mennonites began to do mission
work in other countries, as might be expected, they took
their patterns with them. This has had a tremendous impact
on the pattern of ministry adopted by the so-called younger
churches. Even though in most if not all cases the objective

was to plant "indigenous" churches, the transfer took place
almost unconsciously.

Take the matter of being self-supporting for example. It
was assumed that an indigenous church ought to be "self-
supporting," but this simply meant that the church was to
support itself rather than be supported by the mission. The
question was never raised as to whether the pastor or pastors should be supported or not. It was rather assumed that
each church ought to have a pastor, to be supported by his
flock. I believe that this process took place in Japan as
much as in other countries where we have been working, and
that is at least part of the reason why there seems to be
the feeling that unless you have a paid pastor, you do not
have a real church. This observation is not intended as a
criticism. It is simply a fact that this is the way things
are, and as a result many small congregations are struggling
to support a pastor whereas, according to biblical standards,
that may not be necessary at all. In any case, before going
any further, perhaps it would be helpful to get an overview
of our leaders, both pastors and missionaries, and then discuss some of the implications.

Of the six pastors (1974), four of them fall between the
ages of thirty-six and forty-five. One is younger and one
is older. They have been Christians anywhere from eight to
23 years, with an average of 16 or 17 years. In no cases
were other members of their families Christian (although
some of them are now). The greatest influence in their
becoming believers seems to have been exposure to the Bible,
followed by a quest for meaning in life, and the experiences
of the war. They have been pastors anywhere from one to 19
years, with an average of 10 years each. The greatest
influences in their becoming pastors were the Bible itself,
wanting to share the Gospel with others, and opportunities
given to serve in the church. At least five of the six view
their call to the ministry as a lifetime commitment. (Note:
In addition to these six, there were at one time two other
pastors also serving the churches, both of whom have since
dropped out of the ministry.)

By way of comparison, seven of the 13 missionaries fall
between the ages of thirty-six and fifty, four are younger
and two are older. The missionaries have served anywhere
from one to 23 years, with an average of almost 15. The
greatest influence in their becoming missionaries seems to
have been the testimonies of missionaries on furlough,
followed by other people or home influences, short-term

experience abroad, a definite call, and the Great Commission. By way of contrast to the pastors, only four of the missionaries viewed their call to missionary work as a lifetime commitment; two said No; seven said "not necessarily." (See Appendix J for the Missionary Questionnaire.)

In terms of training for the ministry, as we noted earlier most of the pastors have been to Bible college, and a few of them also have some university or seminary training. According to the questionnaire they filled out, almost all of them have also had some secular work experience before becoming pastors. I was not aware of this before, but two of them were public service workers, two were company employees, one a bank employee and so on. They worked at these various occupations anywhere from two to 12 years, with an average of six. One point worthy of attention here, however, is that none of them are working at those occupations now. They all gave up their "secular work" for the ministry.

Again, by way of comparison, most of the missionaries have graduated from a liberal arts college or university. Almost two-thirds of them have spent at least some time at a Bible college or Bible institute. Almost half of them have spent two or more years at seminary. At least two of the missionaries are graduates of college, Bible college, and seminary. All of the missionaries have spent at least some time in one or more of the various Mennonite schools. But one of the striking contrasts to the pastors is that many of them do not seem to have had much secular work experience. Another is that all of the missionary wives except one have had some biblical or theological training, whereas most of the pastors' wives have not, at least not formally. In spite of all this education though, over half of the missionaries said they did not feel it was adequate for their work, which suggests that education is not everything. And even one who did feel it was adequate mentioned that "experience is also a good teacher."

As far as their work is concerned, the pastors are all pastoring churches. Three of them have pastored only one church; one of them has been a pastor of two different churches; two of them have been pastors of three different churches, which means the pastors have pastored an average of about two churches each. Their pastorates have ranged anywhere from one to 16 years, with an average of six. As mentioned before, two of them are serving their home churches.

By comparison, three missionary couples and one single
missionary are pioneering and pastoring churches. Two other
couples are pioneering, and two single workers are assisting
churches with outreach. The missionaries have worked with
anywhere from one to four of the different Mennonite
churches. The average number of churches they have served
is between two and three. The length of time spent with a
given church has varied from one to 13 years, the average
being about five years.

The pastors are all considered full-time pastors by the
churches, but most of them receive part of their support
from elsewhere. Four of the six pastors are working part
time to help support themselves. Some of them do this by
teaching English or some other subject; others by doing
writing or translation work. Anywhere from six to 15 hours
per week is spent in such activity, with an average of nine.
Five of the pastors are married but none of them reported
that their wives are presently working (outside the home).
Only one of the six receives his entire support from the
church. The other five receive from 35 to 80 percent from
the church, with an average of about 60 percent.

The four who are working part time receive from 20 to 65
percent of their income from self-support, with an average
of a little over 40 percent. This means that almost half of
their support comes from part-time work rather than from the
church, yet they are considered full-time pastors of the
churches. One of the pastors (for health reasons) does not
work to support himself, but instead receives 40 percent of
his support from the various other churches through the
Church Conference. The missionaries, by comparison, are
full time and fully supported, receiving their support from
the churches in America. Husbands as well as wives receive
equal support, although usually the husbands spend more
time in direct evangelistic work than the wives do.

When asked what the most difficult problem was they face
as pastors, there were replies such as: "human relationships"; "how to understand and communicate the Gospel in our
day"; "building up a church that is strong enough to reproduce itself" and so on. Their main concerns seem to center
around communicating the Gospel and building up the church.
For the missionaries, on the other hand, their questionnaires
reveal that the most difficult problem they face seems to be
the language, mentioned by over half. Other concerns are
the indifference to the Gospel, Christian dropouts, loneliness, remaining spiritually alive, lack of cultural understanding, children's education and the like.

This is in general a profile of the pastors and missionaries and what they are doing. We have looked a bit at the factors influencing their call, at the training they have had, at how they are supported, and a few of the problems they face. But there is one more dimension that needs to be considered, and that is the situation as it is in comparison with what the pastor and missionary ideals suggest it ought to be. That is, by comparing the ideal and the reality we may be able to view more objectively what kind of leaders our churches really need. It is here perhaps more than anywhere else we can begin to sense areas in which some change may be called for. It is in the replies to a number of such questions asked that one can feel a certain discrepancy between the way things are, and the way they would like them to be. Some of the answers are quite revealing.

One of these areas was that concerning the whole support structure. When the pastors were asked, for example, "Would you like to be self-supporting if possible?", two of them said Yes, four of them No. In other words, over half of them preferred to be supported by the church. Most of them did not give a reason for this although one of them said that the reason he did not want to be self-supporting was that "it is difficult to do both." So the majority wanted to be supported. But in answer to another question as to how large a church ought to be in order to support a full-time pastor, the answers ranged from 40 to 100, with the average about 55. The missionary answers to the same question ranged all the way from 10 to 100, with an average of almost 40. Some added that "it depends on the quality," or that it should be "when the church feels it needs one," or that they are "not sure that it is ever necessary."

The fact is, however, that only one of the ten churches is as large as the pastors feel they ought to be to support a man full time, and even it is not giving its pastor full-time support. Whether that is because it cannot or because the pastor wishes to be at least partially self-supporting, I do not know. I suspect it is the latter, as some of the pastors hesitate to take more than a certain percentage of the offerings. But the fact remains that on the average our churches are less than half the size the pastors feel they ought to be to support a man full time, and yet the pastors are considered to be full-time workers. Is there not some contradiction here? If the majority of pastors feel that full-time support is the ideal, but in reality are only supported partially, and if further they feel that a church ought to have over 50 members in order to have a full-time

pastor and our churches are on the average only about half
that size or less, does this not say something about the
kind of leaders we need? It seems to me there is a definite
discrepancy here which needs to be dealt with.

I am not suggesting that we do not need any full-time,
fully supported pastors. I am not saying that I think all
of our pastors should be part time and self-supporting. I
am not suggesting either that the people in the churches are
not giving as much as they should or could. Compared to the
so called "new religions" of Japan, Christians, including
the Mennonites, are giving quite well. This was brought out
in an article by Robert L. Ramseyer in which he compared the
giving of Christians to adherents of the New Religions. One
of his observations was that

> The most obvious financial difference between the
> New Religions and the Christian churches is the level
> of per member giving. Although the three Christian
> congregations [United Church of Christ, Anglican
> Episcopal, Mennonite] come from radically different
> ecclesiastical traditions, all three show patterns of
> giving which are qualitatively different from the New
> Religions. In this the New Religions closely resemble
> the traditional religious bodies in Japanese society.
> In this area of Japan [Miyazaki Prefecture] the annual
> per household dues for temple or shrine vary between
> 120 and 240 yen [$.40-$.80] per year, and when the
> higher figure prevails there is much grumbling about
> the high cost of religion. All other income for these
> religious bodies comes from fees for specific services
> rendered or from property held. Comparing this with
> giving of 12,000 yen to 32,000 yen [$40-$110] per mem-
> ber (not household!) just for the support of one's
> religious group without expectation of specific bene-
> fits for fees paid, the contrast between Christian
> and non-Christian patterns is obvious (1972:89).

In other words, the people are giving and giving liberally.
But though they are giving, due to the small size of the
churches, it still may not be enough to support a pastor and
his family adequately. If it is, the chances are there
would not be much left over for outreach and other expenses.
Concentration on supporting a pastor may at times even
divert a church from getting on with the primary task of
doing evangelism. Be that as it may, all I am suggesting
here is that in light of the apparent contradiction between
the pastors' ideals and the reality, this whole matter of
the paid ministry needs to be looked at again.

With regard to this question, we really do not have space to deal with it here, but it perhaps should at least be pointed out that the New Testament itself presents something of a paradoxical picture. That is, on the one hand, it says that "the Lord commanded that those who proclaim the gospel should get their living by the gospel" (I Cor. 9:14), but in the very next verses, Paul declares that he for one is not going to make use of that right so that he can present the Gospel free of charge (I Cor. 9:15ff.).

Moving on into later church history, in an article on "The Support of the Clergy in the First Five Centuries" (1956), W.E.B. Ream tells us that while the deacons, bishops, and widows were largely supported by the church, the elders were expected to be mostly self-supporting, and even bishops sometimes supported themselves. Following that period, the clergy came to be increasingly supported, in many cases by the state as well as the church. But at the time of the Reformation, as we have already seen, the Anabaptists and perhaps some other groups, while recognizing the validity of a supported ministry as taught in the New Testament, sought to go back to a self-supporting ministry. Menno Simons, for one, exhorts the person who is called by the church to preach or teach, saying,

> If this takes place, brethren, then pastor diligently, preach and teach valiantly, cast from you all filthy lucre and booty; rent a farm, milk cows, learn a trade if possible, do manual labor as did Paul, and all that which you then fall short of will doubtlessly be given and provided you by pious brethren, by the grace of God, not in superfluity, but as necessity requires (Wenger 1956:451).

The Anabaptists favored a self-supported ministry, but the Mennonite churches today have moved by and large toward a supported ministry, and taken these patterns with them in doing their mission work. I cannot speak for the other countries where the General Conference has worked, but the ideal, at least in Japan, seems to have been a supported ministry from the beginning.

Back in 1958, for instance, at their Spring Conference, the missionaries passed the following resolution with regard to pastoral support:

> Resolved that we enter into the following three-year contract with the churches in order to encourage

churches to secure their own pastors and become self-
supporting:

	mission	church
first year	50%	50%
second year	35%	65%
third year	20%	80%
fourth year	0%	100%

(GCMM, Resolution 11, 1958:2)

That plan may have looked good on paper, and no doubt it was
felt necessary at the time, but several years later, at
another Spring Conference, it was reported that

> ... beginning in April aid to the Nango Church for
> pastor's support is to drop, according to mission
> policy, from 35% to 20%. Because the Nango Church
> is unable to make up the balance at this time Voran
> requests that we continue the present 35% aid to the
> church for another year (GCMM, March 1964:6).

The request was granted (Resolution 17). But even so,
after three or four more years, the church being assisted
was not able to sustain itself any longer and decided it
would be best to merge with another nearby congregation
which it then did. But may not part of our problem today
still be that in cases like this, even when we saw that it
would be extremely difficult for churches to support a full-
time pastor, we kept right on trying to do it, rather than
changing our ideal to correspond with the reality.

Both Mission and Church minutes reveal that there has
been considerable discussion of this matter of support over
the years (as recorded, for example, in the detailed
minutes of the JMCCC Annual Conference, 1969:11-13), including proposals for a minimum standard of living and partial
support from the Conference treasury where necessary, but
no basic changes in the overall support structure have come
out of it. It would seem that this whole issue should at
least be reexamined once more in the light of the ideals and
realities current today.

There are a few like missiologist Roland Allen who have
held strong convictions about this matter. Allen contends
that

> The stipendiary system grew up in settled churches
> and is only suitable for some settled churches at

some periods: for expansion, for the establishment
of new churches, it is the greatest possible hindrance.
It binds the church in chains and has compelled us to
adopt practices which contradict the very idea of the
Church (1960:137).

As related earlier, however, the majority of our pastors
seem to feel that the paid pastor system is best for them
and the church. Whether their ideal comes from the New
Testament, or has grown out of their own experience, or both,
I do not know. But if they feel freer doing the Lord's work
by being fully supported, perhaps they should be. There are
in fact some denominations in Japan, such as the Immanuel
Church, where pastors are not allowed to do any secular work
to earn their livelihood, and this may be one of the factors
contributing to their outstanding record of growth (from 8
members in 1945 to over 7,000 in 1967) (Johnson 1967:9).

On the other hand, some of the Mennonite pastors do not
feel that system is ideal. They would rather be self-
supporting. And if they really feel that way, perhaps they
should be encouraged to do so. In any case, this is one of
the big questions that needs to be considered as we think
about the kind of leaders our churches need. Will they be
full time or part time? Will they be fully paid, partially
paid, or not paid at all? Will they be supported or self-
supporting or both? This needs to be discussed openly and
frankly.

Another question asked the pastors was, "Do you think it
is possible for a pastor to serve two or three small churches
at one time?" Five of the pastors said Yes. The sixth one
said No, but in his case it may have been for health reasons. Anyway, almost all of them said that they felt that
it would be possible to serve several small churches at the
same time. When the missionaries were asked, "Do you think
it would be possible for a missionary to serve two or three
churches at one time?", about two-thirds of them also said
Yes. A few of them felt it would be "easier than for a
pastor" or could be done "if there was lay leadership too."
Others felt it would be "spreading oneself too thin" or that
it "depends on the situation." But where churches are
geographically close, most of them seemed to feel it would
be possible.

The discrepancy here is that practically none of the
pastors or missionaries are serving more than one church,
depending on how you define "church." Most of them are

working with one church in particular. As noted before,
seven of the ten churches are pastored by the six pastors;
three of them by missionaries (1975). This suggests that
perhaps we need to also rethink the whole use of our workers.
Are we going to have one pastor or missionary per church?
Are we going to have two or three churches per pastor? Or
are we going to have two or three pastors per church? And
where will the missionary fit in? Will he pastor or pioneer
or what will he do? Will he work with one church or
several? These are some of the questions that need to be
answered as specifically as possible.

One of the most important aspects of this problem may be
whether or not a multi-pastoral system is desirable in Japan
or not. There are a number of Mennonite churches in the
U.S. and Canada, and perhaps other places too, where a few
churches have begun to move away from a single toward a
multiple pastor system. As an illustration of this,

   The Prince of Peace Church, a forty-five member
   congregation in Richmond, British Columbia, a suburb
   of Vancouver, decided last January to move to a shared
   ministry pattern when Waldy Klassen resigned as pastor.

   Mr. Klassen is still serving in the congregation,
   but as part of a six-member unsalaried team. Each team
   member is leader of one of the general "ministries" of
   the church: administration and communication, congregational life, education, outreach and service, personal
   growth and counseling, and worship.

   All members of the congregation are encouraged to
   commit themselves to be a specific resource to at
   least one of the six areas of ministry. Mr. Klassen,
   director of worship ministries, leads the service at
   least once a month, but other members of the congregation also preach (Barrett 1975:638).

In the same article, there are examples of other larger congregations also moving toward a multiple leadership pattern.
This pattern can include both salaried and unsalaried
leaders, but it is said to release much more of the churches
financial resources for various projects, and allows many
more people to be involved in ministry.

With regard to the question of whether or not a congregation ought to have both lay *and* professional pastors,
professor Elton Trueblood states his conviction that *"There*

can be no vital Church without a multipastoral system"
(1967:54)! He naturally is speaking out of an American context, but it is enlightening to note that Tetsunao Yamamori,
in the conclusion to his study on church growth in Japan,
says something very similar. He declares that one of the
clues to rapid church growth is when the church "develops a
multiple leadership structure which mobilizes its entire lay
membership" (1974:138-139).

Assuming this is true, it raises another question, and
that is, what kind of leaders and how many leaders do we
really need? Educational consultant Lois McKinney, in her
study of church leadership needs, suggests that a realistic
ratio of leaders within congregations might be "one leader
for every five members of the church. In other words, a
congregation with 50 members would probably need at least
10 leaders" (1975:186). This would include Sunday school
teachers, church treasurers, evangelists and so on as well
as those who exercise preaching, administrative or other
functions within the local congregation. Lest that seem
like a high ideal, it is interesting to hear that one of the
fastest growing churches in America (from zero in 1955 to
approximately 7,000 in 1974), the Garden Grove Community
Church, Garden Grove, California, is working at this
already. Their church has a "seminary for the laity,"
called the Center for Advanced Lay Leadership, and their
goal is to eventually have 1,000 trained lay persons,
graduates of the school, to shepherd that great congregation
(Schuller 1974:67). They are planning to have one lay
pastor for each of many small groups of people.

While churches in Japan are, to be sure, on a much
smaller scale, that does not necessarily mean they do not
need a multiple leadership system. It is a matter of
structure, not size. As Japan missionary K. Lavern Snider
points out in his study book entitled, *Whose Ministry?*, the
really important thing is that each and every believer discover and develop his or her gift, and use it to minister to
others. As he puts it, "The magnitude of the task alone is
sufficient reason for the engagement of a maximum number of
persons in ministry" (1975:12).

One of the ironic things today is that as a number of
Mennonite churches in North America are beginning to move
away from a single to a multi-pastoral pattern, and are
experimenting with new forms of the church, in Japan most
churches still tend to cling to the old patterns brought by
North American missionaries without seemingly questioning

whether it is really best or not. But is it not possible
for churches here to create original patterns of their own,
patterns that actually fit Japan? The whole matter of the
possibilities of a multiple leadership system, thinking not
only of pastors but of teachers, evangelists, counselors,
Bible study leaders, church planters and other leadership
gifts, deserves a great deal more attention than it has
received up till now.

This is not to imply that nothing has been done in the
area under consideration. In fact, one of the Mennonite
pastors, Takashi Yamada, seems to have given considerable
thought to this, and after reflecting on the matters of the
kind of church we ought to establish and how we ought to
carry on our work, concludes that

> ... we need at least three kinds of gifts of the
> Spirit for the expansion of God's work and the growth
> of the Church; *some strategicians* who can look at and
> think through the whole situation from the overall
> point of view, and *some practicians* who are creative
> and flexible enough to cope with the changing situa-
> tions and develop some practical methods and means to
> carry out the strategy set up by the strategicians.
> These are some extra blessings of God for the Church.
> And then, we need *many local leaders* who can faith-
> fully make use of those methods and means and bring
> actual results working together with church members
> closely, giving them inspiration and encouragement all
> the time through their sacrificial services (1972:6).

There are some stimulating proposals here, and one would
hope that they can actually be followed up on. To my knowledge, there has not been much if any effort put into producing especially the first two types of leaders suggested,
but it would surely seem worthwhile to make an attempt to
do so. Perhaps this should be high on our agenda of things
to think about, and not only to think about, but to
actually do if at all feasible.

A third question asked on the questionnaires was, "How
long do you think a pastor should stay in one church?" The
pastors' answers ranged from five to 10 years, with an
average of about seven and a half years. On this same
question, the missionaries felt a pastor should stay in a
church anywhere from two to 15 years, or even as long as a
lifetime, but the average was about eight and a half years.
Some felt it should be "as the Lord directs" or "as long as
the church and the pastor both feel it is God's will."

The discrepancy here is that two-thirds of the pastors have already been in their churches longer than they feel they should be. One over twice that long! Does this mean that some of the pastors feel a need for a change? If so, why have they not changed? Again, I personally do not know. But in answer to another question as to whether they would be interested in moving to a new area to do evangelism, at least four of them said Yes. One of them said No, but as with some of his other answers, perhaps it was because of his health. But indications seem to be that there is a desire on the part of some for a change. And we need to ask, what is preventing it?

Is the support system holding some of them back? One of them, for instance, when asked what one change he would like to make most in his ministry if he could, said that "when doing evangelism in new areas of Japan, it is important to have a special skill so one can be economically self-supporting." Could that be what is holding him back? If he wanted to change, could he? Is there a mechanism for change? Another said he would like "to make himself a freer servant from and to the church." How can he be freed? Do others feel the same way? The pastors are the only ones who can answer that question. But it is no doubt easier for missionaries to move if they want to, than for the pastors.

As far as the missionaries being willing to move into new situations to do pioneer work, some of them felt they were doing it already and others said they were not ready to move yet, but almost all of them indicated a willingness to do so in the future "as the Lord leads." Concerning the question of what one change the missionaries would most like to make in their work if they could, it is interesting that about one-third of them wrote "do less English teaching" or "cut out English teaching," which is precisely what many of the pastors have to do to support themselves. The missionary, of course, has more of a choice about this as he is fully supported, whereas most of the pastors are not. But if the pastors have to at least be partially self-supporting, perhaps the missionaries should be also. In any case, one of the missionaries suggested she would like to "start over!" Another said that he would like to have "a church without problems." I do not know if you can get much more idealistic than that! But is it not great that we can still love the church, in spite of all its imperfections.

In looking at the work of the pastors and missionaries, we have tried to point out some of the inconsistencies that

are apparent between the ideal as they see it and the way
things really are. But that only serves to point up some of
the problems. What we want are not only problems, but also
potential solutions. What we perhaps need more than anything else is to see some alternative models that have been
effective elsewhere. But before looking anywhere else, we
need to realize that there have actually been a number of
experiments with new forms of leadership in our own
churches. Some of these have been by choice. Others by
necessity.

As a case in point, several years ago, the Aburatsu
Church found itself not having either a pastor or a missionary. As a result, the laymen had to continue the work of
the church alone. Once a month or so, a pastor or missionary from one of the other churches came to help out, but
most of the work was done by themselves. One or two of the
laymen did much of the additional work as lay leaders, and
it was not always easy. But in taking greater responsibility, they said they discovered much about what it meant
to be the church. They became very interested in the
pattern of the churches in the book of Acts, where the
churches were led by laymen. They discovered that they
could be "a church without a pastor," and operated this way
for two or three years. In the end, though, they felt it
was too difficult for them to handle everything effectively,
and so called and received a full-time pastor again
(Isobe 1973:E-6). Some of the other churches have also
made considerable use of lay leaders while their pastor was
studying abroad for a year, or when the missionary went on
furlough. But these decisions to experiment have been more
of necessity than by choice.

There is at least one group, however, the Kirishima
Christian Brotherhood (Kobayashi Church), which has done a
considerable amount of experimenting with new methods of
evangelism voluntarily. The Kirishima Brotherhood is made
up of a number of smaller groups, some of them meeting in
homes and led by laymen, with the pastor visiting occasionally. These groups meet in a few of the towns surrounding
Kobayashi, which serves as the central meeting place. One
example of what they have done began in 1967 when a young
layman and his wife volunteered to move from the city of
Kobayashi to the much larger city of Kagoshima, in connection with his work. So the church decided to invite a
young couple from the States to live and work there also.
These two couples, with the assistance of the pastor, would
try to start a new church there. They began working as a
team in 1970.

The result of their efforts was the emergence of what has been called an "amoeba church" (Liechty 1973:E-7). That is, the form of the church consists of cells of believers who gather at different times and places during the week for worship, study, and fellowship. There are various groups such as English teachers, doctors, women and so on which meet separately on weekdays. There is also a group which meets in the more traditional way on Sunday with different members of the group leading. But an attempt has been made from the outset to operate in a very decentralized way.

This type of approach has much to commend for it in trying to take the church to where the people are. It is very flexible. It also has its drawbacks, as when the lay couple soon moved away and the group was left without Japanese leadership, except for the pastor who went down once a month or so. Distance has also been a problem in this respect, the new group being over two hours away from the mother church. But one of the biggest problems has been finding suitable leaders for the "amoeba churches." It was hoped that these small groups would be self-perpetuating, not having to rely so much on a pastor or missionary, but it appears that they will need more leadership than anticipated. In any case, it will be interesting to see what direction these groups take in the future. (Note: As of 1976, the work in Kagoshima was terminated, at least on a formal basis.)

A slightly different pattern from those used in Kyushu which is being followed by the Mennonite churches of Hokkaido is that of the "tentmaking ministry." In the last chapter, we referred to Marvin Miller's paper on the subject, and would like to quote him once more. In his case study he says,

> We have had tentmaking leaders in the churches for fifteen years and tentmaking expatriates for the last ten years. No Japanese leader receives support from abroad or has for more than ten years. At present all are tentmakers, none of them fully supported by their congregations.
>
> The pattern wherever possible is a shared plural ministry as the ideal, developed as Spirit-given gifts are recognized. In the fifteen churches there are thirty men who preach, of whom eight do nothing but preach. The remainder baptize, give communion, teach and administer programs (1974b:15).

The conviction with which these men continue their tentmaking varies. Some are convinced and hope to continue indefinitely. Others are restless for full support, more distance between themselves and the laity -- neither concepts that we have taught, although perhaps as missionaries have inadvertantly demonstrated. Others are somewhere on the continuum between (16).

Many of us in the Japan Mennonite Church commend the tentmaking pattern for both church and mission for reasons primarily theological, but also for reasons eminently practical. It fits the New Testament concept of the church-as-intended and it works, even in Japan. We are hopeful that as more plural ministries develop in the churches it will be possible as other priorities permit to have overseer-type ministers either fully supported or tentmakers whether as members of teams or as ministers to a number of tentmakers or teams (19).

The Mennonite churches in Kyushu also have a number of men besides the pastors who do preaching and perform other pastoral duties. But one difference between the churches in Kyushu and those in Hokkaido would seem to be that in the latter "tentmaking" (self-support) is seen as the ideal, whereas in the former it is not, at least not for the majority of the pastors. In Kyushu, most of the pastors are doing part-time work, but not because they want to. Their answers seemed to indicate rather that they do it because they have to. In other words, "tentmaking" in Hokkaido is done deliberately, whereas in Kyushu it is done reluctantly. The churches in Hokkaido have demonstrated, however, that "tentmaking" is a workable option. It seems to them to be closer to the New Testament ideal, and to fit their situation. Yet they are also open to supported ministers if the need arises. What works in Hokkaido may not necessarily work in Kyushu, but what others are doing should certainly give us food for thought.

It would seem then that as we rethink this matter of leaders for our churches, some of the questions that will need to be wrestled with are: whether the leaders will be full time or part time; whether they will be self-supporting or supported (partially or fully); whether they will participate in a single or a plural ministry; whether they will come from inside or outside the congregation; whether they will be ordained or unordained (this topic will be dealt with to some extent in Appendix K).

As we consider such questions, we need to also try to think in terms of the social structure within which we find ourselves. Chie Nakane, in her book *Japanese Society*, maintains that

> ... Japanese group affiliations and human relations are exclusively one-to-one: a single loyalty stands uppermost and firm. ... Thus, an individual or a group has always one single distinctive relation to the other. ...

> ... in Japanese society not only is the individual's group affiliation one-to-one but, in addition, the ties binding individuals together are also one-to-one. This characteristic single bond in social relationships is basic to the ideals of the various groups within the whole society (1972:21-22).

If what she says is true, that in Japan "an individual or a group has always one single distinctive relation to the other," that Japanese society is basically a vertical organization (see Figure 5.4) and follows what she calls the "vertical principle," what does this mean for us in terms of leaders and church structure? Are our churches structured along these lines? Ought they to be? Some of the new

Figure 5.4

VERTICAL STRUCTURE OF JAPANESE SOCIETY

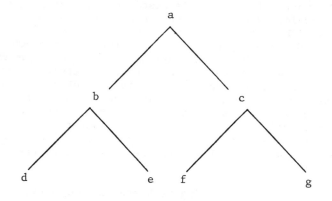

(Nakane 1972:42)

religions such as Sōka Gakkai, which have shown such
fantastic growth in the postwar years, seem to have taken
much greater advantage of the social structure than have
the Christian churches. Nakane goes on to remark,

It is not without significance that Sōka-gakkai is
organized along vertical lines, to which the movement
itself has given the name *tate-sen* (literally, vertical
lines). The *tate-sen* are the result of the extension
of direct lines built between two individuals. The
individual's place along the *tate-sen* is determined at
the time of his conversion to Sōka-gakkai, and this
tate-sen eventually reaches up to the president at the
apex, ... The astonishing success of these new
religious groups, which have grown so large and so
rapidly, seems to be attributable mainly to their
system of vertical organization (1972:61).

In speaking of this same movement, sociologist Tetsunao
Yamamori observes that

The Sōka Gakkai is a lay movement ... It has no
priest. Only the president and some two hundred
people working in the publications department are on
the payroll.

The organizational structure is cellular in nature.
The social relations of the laity are promoted through
the vertical, horizontal, and diagonal groupings of
the members.

The vertical grouping is based on conversion ties.
The grouping extends from the individual, to the *kumi*
(squad with 10 to 15 members), to the *han* (company with
30 to 100 members), to the *chiku* (district with 500 to
1000 members), the *shibu* (region), the *soshibu* (general
region), the *chiho hombu* (local headquarters), and the
hombu (central headquarters, located in Tokyo). This
can be compared with the kinship ties which are so
important in Japanese culture. Member A, converted by
Member B, belongs to the *kumi* of the latter person
even after the former gets his own *kumi*. A *han*, therefore, is made up of those who are converted by the same
group of people.

The horizontal grouping is based on geography.
Japan's mobility rate is growing larger and larger.
The geographically-based structure called the "block

system" has been devised in order to combat the membership loss by mobility. The members in the same geographical unit keep close contact with each other,
which is in itself an attack on the *anomie* created in
today's rapidly changing society.

The final grouping (diagonal) is based on age, sex,
and/or interest. There are various groups and activities in this category: one group each for young men,
young women, college students, and housewives, athletic
groups; a culture organization called *Min'on* for music,
drama, dance, and cultural activities; and a political
party called the Kōmeito (1972:164).

... The Sōka Gakkai claims the equality of all
members at the time of their entry. Neither one's
age, nor his sex, nor his social position matters.
The male and the female, the young and the old, the
rich and the poor are all put on equal footing. On
the basis of his individual effort and capability, the
convert advances toward a higher rank, from an ordinary
member to the rank of "Professor" through variously
graded titles. According to his rank, he is put in
charge of responsibilities of various degrees of importance. The function of this ranking system is quite
contrary to the reality of Japanese society where
differences in sex, age, and social position greatly
influence his road to success. In the Sōka Gakkai,
the function of ranks is thought of as being socio-
psychological in that the system gives status to
those whom the world has overlooked. It means that
the system is value-creating for the individual
member (163-164).

After describing the organizational aspects of the Sōka
Gakkai, Yamamori goes on to suggest that at least two of the
implications of this for church growth are:

... Protestantism in Japan must mobilize the laity
for evangelism. The key to the Sōka Gakkai's success
is due largely to its ability to mobilize the entire
membership for the propagation of its faith. The
doctrine of the "priesthood of all believers" must be
taken more seriously and put into practice. Every
Christian is under God's mandate to *minister* to
others -- Christian *as well as* non-Christians -- for
their spiritual well-being.

... the church must devise a multiple leadership
structure. The Sōka Gakkai created the variously
graded positions of leadership for the more able members. These leaders are unpaid and therefore the
structure is readily reproducible. Since they come
from the group, they know their people and others like
them intimately and are more capable of communicating
to them. In the Japanese church, the topic of lay
leadership has often been discussed but largely
remained an item of theological interest. Consequently,
the monolithic structure with the pastor as the sole
leader has prevailed and is the most common pattern
today. Is it not conceivable to develop, for example,
an army of unpaid part-time lay evangelists -- with
proper status given them -- whose task is to evangelize the unevangelized? These men and women may be
assigned to full-time pastors of various churches.
Not all the pastors and evangelists need to be full
time and B.D. or M.Div. graduates. ... The various
segments of society demand different types of ministers with varying degrees of experience and education.
The church must consider seriously the establishment
of levels of ministry -- paid and unpaid, full and
part-time -- with due status given to all (167-168).

What does all this mean for our churches? In light of
the structure of Japanese society, what kind of church organization should we have? Would it be the same or different
from what we have now? What kind of leaders would be
needed to fit into such a structure? Have the discussions
up till now been just talk, or are we really serious about
actually trying to change the structure of our churches?
If so, in what way and how can it be done?

Most of us perhaps have not given enough attention to
this matter, but there have been a few, like Neil Braun in
his book *Laity Mobilized*, who have proposed variations to
the pattern most churches are currently following. With
reference to his own denomination (Japan Advent Christian
Church), Braun advocates continuing to have "fully ordained
ministers" (*seikyōshi*) and "preparatory ministers" (*hokyōshi*,
under preparation for ordination as full ministers) as they
do now. But he also suggests creating a new role of
"pastor-teacher" (*bokkai-kyōshi*) between those two. The
"pastor-teacher" would be "recognized as qualified to do
pastoral work," and "ordained and authorized to perform the
sacraments" within their district only (1971:124-125).
Usually two or more such persons would serve as the unpaid,

part-time pastors of a church. Candidates for this office
would have to complete a prescribed course of training,
including some classes taught by the fully ordained ministers, and after a number of years of faithful service and
perhaps some further theological training, they could eventually become fully ordained ministers themselves if they
so desired.

In addition to these offices, elders would also be chosen
from each congregation and ordained, and be "qualified to
conduct the sacraments within their own church." The elders
too would be unpaid and might serve on a rotating basis.
Besides these, men and women would also be appointed to be
deacons, lay preachers, exhorters and so on. They would
ordinarily be both unpaid and unordained. Braun feels that
his proposal would likely have to be adjusted to fit various
situations, but that if followed, it would both "guard the
educational standards of the clergy," and "permit the
recruiting of a varied leadership" to provide the necessary
pastoral care for rapidly growing churches. He does not
infer anywhere that this particular pattern is the only one
that would be acceptable. But he does state his conviction
that

> The issue church leaders must wrestle with is: How
> do *you* propose to free the Church to provide pastoral
> care and the sacraments for people, in whatever num-
> bers, whenever and wherever they can be persuaded to
> acknowledge Jesus Christ as Saviour and Lord (1971:126)?

In conclusion, one of the most important insights, for me
anyway, that has come out of this brief study on leadership
is that we cannot just think in terms of training leaders
for the ministry. Leaders *are* needed, but regardless of the
kind of leaders we may feel are necessary, we must not forget, as Mark Gibbs and T. Ralph Morten assert in their book
God's Frozen People, that there is no essential distinction
between clergy and laity. As they point out, "It is literally correct, therefore, to say that all *clergy* -- of any
type -- are part of the 'laity,' the *Laos*, the People of
God" (1964:15). This does not mean that leaders are
unnecessary. It does mean that we must always keep in mind
what we are training them for.

What is the ministry for which leaders are trained?
This is the most fundamental question, for the style
of training must be determined by the nature of the
ministry. Ministry is the purpose and training is a
means (Chao 1977:L).

We need to constantly remember that what is needed is not
just to train a ministry, but to train a ministry which in
turn can train the rest of the church for its ministry.

Some people may feel threatened by this kind of talk. In
many ways it goes against what both the clergy and the laity
have for too long considered their roles to be. Often the
clergy have been only too willing to dominate the church,
and the laity content to remain passive. But we can no
longer afford to ignore what the Bible teaches with regard
to this matter. As churchman Hans-Ruedi Weber contends,
"We need to get back to a fresh vision of (1) the true
ministry of *the whole people of God*, and (2) the true ministry of *those set apart* for a special function (the clergy)"
(1963:17). And there is no need for either the clergy or
the laity to feel threatened by any change in roles, for as
Weber goes on to declare, "A high doctrine of the laity
does not exclude, but rather demands, a new high doctrine
of the clergy" (1963:17).

As we have suggested then, what we need to do first of
all is to take a good hard look at what the church is.
After we have done that, we can begin thinking about the
kind of ministry it needs. As we have tried to bring out
here, the Bible seems to indicate that not only the clergy
but the whole church has a ministry, and that the task of
the leaders is to train the laymen for their ministry in
the world.

WHAT KIND OF TRAINING DO WE NEED
TO PRODUCE THAT KIND OF LEADERS?

In the last section we dealt briefly with the kind of
leaders we might need for the kind of church we may want to
have. Having considered the prior questions of the church
and its ministry, we now wish to talk about what kind of a
training program might be suitable to produce such leaders.
As with the previous two sections, we are somewhat handi-
capped in not knowing exactly what kind of church and what
kind of leaders we do need. But if as we have said the
Church is the people of God who exist for the world, and if
each Christian has a ministry and it is the leader's job to
train the believers for their ministry in the world, then on
the basis of that we want to try to suggest the broad outlines such a training program might take.

Once again, we will take the New Testament as our starting point. In looking at the New Testament, we see first of

all that along with preaching and healing, teaching or
training was an extremely important aspect of Jesus' ministry (Matt. 4:23). It occupied a great deal of His time, and
He was thought of as a great teacher. He was, in fact,
often addressed as Rabbi or Teacher (John 1:38). And yet,
as Ralph Covell notes in his chapter on "Jesus, the Model
Teacher,"

> The New Testament presents Jesus as a teacher who
> is both different from and similar to other teachers
> of that period. In common with other teachers or
> rabbis, he had disciples. ...
>
> Jesus was different from other rabbis in the first
> century in that he did not establish a formal school
> for the teaching of his disciples. In common with
> other rabbis, he had a definite content to impart,
> but he claimed that his teaching was directly from
> God. He did not depend on the authority of a particu-
> lar school nor upon the ordination of an important
> rabbi for its validity. He taught his disciples
> important truths, but the crux of all his doctrine
> was that his disciples should be committed to him as
> a person (Covell and Wagner 1971:34).

Jesus had disciples; He taught them; but as Covell brings
out, His teaching centered primarily on Himself. His "I am"
sayings are a good illustration of this. He naturally made
use of the Scriptures (the Old Testament), but here again
He said that they pointed to Him, and that people must come
to Him in order to have life (John 5:39-40). He claimed
that His teaching fulfilled the law and the prophets (Matt.
5:17). People wondered where He got all of His learning
when He had never been to school, and He said that His
teaching was not His own but came from God, His Father
(John 7:15-17). In fact, He went so far as to say that He
and the Father are one (John 10:30). While to some of the
religious leaders this was nothing short of blasphemy, the
Bible says that the common people heard Him gladly because
He taught as one who had authority and not like their
scribes (Matt. 7:28-29).

The Scribes and the Pharisees had their own schools, but
Jesus had not attended them. And even though He was a
popular teacher, He did not start a school of His own.
Rather, He taught people at various times and places, wher-
ever they happened to be. He taught early in the morning
(Luke 21:38); He taught at night (John 3:1ff.). He taught

daily in the Temple (Luke 19:47); He taught on the Sabbath
in the synagogue (Luke 4:31). He taught sitting in the
mountains (Matt. 5:1ff.); He taught from a boat on the sea
(Mark 4:1); He taught while journeying from place to place
(Luke 13:22). He taught crowds publicly (Mark 10:1); He
taught in homes privately (Luke 10:38-39). He especially
spent a great deal of time teaching the Twelve (Matt. 11:1).
He sometimes gave specific instructions, as when He sent
out the Twelve or the Seventy (Luke 9:1ff.; 10:1ff.). He
taught not only by word, but also by example, resulting in
further requests to be taught (Luke 11:1).

One of His favorite teaching methods was the parable, and
we are even told that He did not teach without using para-
bles (Matt. 13:34). The disciples did not always understand
what He said (Luke 18:34), but one of the main reasons He
chose the Twelve was simply to be with Him (Mark 3:14), to
learn from Him. And when He was no longer going to be with
them in the flesh, He gave them instructions to teach
others all the things which He had commanded them (Matt.
28:20). He never wrote a book Himself. But His disciples
were good learners and wrote down what He said and did,
which we have in the New Testament today (e.g., Luke 1:1-4).
And even though His teaching spanned only three short years,
more books have been written about Him and His teaching than
any other person who ever lived. As John puts it in his
Gospel, if we were to write everything that could be written
about Jesus, not even the whole world itself could contain
the books that would be written (John 21:25). Truly He was
an incomparable teacher.

In the Early Church there was also a great emphasis on
teaching. From the very beginning it is said that the
Christians "devoted themselves to the apostles' teaching"
(Acts 2:42), and that "every day in the temple and at home
they did not cease teaching and preaching Jesus as the
Christ" (5:42). Few of the believers were highly educated,
and yet as Jesus had promised, the Holy Spirit brought to
remembrance the things He had said to them (John 14:26), and
enabled them to speak boldly (Acts 4:13).

There soon came to be some, however, like the apostle
Paul, who had been educated at the best Jewish schools of
the day (Acts 22:3). Paul had been trained as a Pharisee
before his conversion, and was an expert on the law (Phil.
3:5-6). But he claimed that he had not been taught his
knowledge of the Gospel, that it was a direct revelation of
Jesus Christ (Gal. 1:11-12). He became an apostle, preacher,

and teacher of the Gospel (II Tim. 1:11). He presented the
Gospel as the word of God (I Thes. 2:13). His teaching,
like that of his Lord, was Christ-centered (I Cor. 2:2). He
especially stressed the death, burial, and resurrection of
Christ as of primary importance (I Cor. 15:3-4). And yet,
while he was such an influential teacher in the Early Church,
he did not attempt to start a school, but simply taught whoever and wherever and whenever he could. Paul (Saul) and
Barnabas were two of the first teachers at Antioch, where
they met with the church for a whole year, and where the
disciples were for the first time called Christians (Acts
11:25-26).

Like Jesus, the apostles sometimes taught in the Temple
as early as daybreak (Acts 5:21). We are told that Paul
occasionally taught from morning to evening at his lodging,
supporting himself and welcoming all who came to him (28:23,
30-31). There were even times when his speeches went as
late as midnight, or even all night long (20:7,11). He
taught publicly and from house to house (20:20); he taught
in synagogues and in halls (19:8-9), or even in the market
place (17:17). He also itinerated, staying in one locality
only a few weeks, or as long as a year and a half (18:11)
or two years (19:10). The object of his teaching was to
develop men and women "mature in Christ" (Col. 1:28), and
to build up the church (Eph. 4:12ff.). He taught not only
by word but by deed (Phil. 3:17), exhorting others to
imitate him as he did Christ (I Cor. 11:1). Another
objective was to persuade unbelievers, and he often argued
from the Scriptures to prove that Jesus was the Christ
(Acts 17:1-3ff.). Some were persuaded and some were not
(cf. 28:24). But passing on the traditions was extremely
important to Paul, and he taught both by word of mouth and
by letter (II Thes. 2:15). His letters themselves in time
became a part of that tradition (II Pet. 3:15-16).

Paul also instructed others such as Timothy to teach what
he had learned, and even though he was young, to set the
believers an example (I Tim. 4:11-13). He also exhorted
Titus to "teach what befits sound doctrine" (Titus 2:1).
In both cases he also gives specifics as to what he means.
He did not permit women to teach men, although they may
have taught other women (I Tim. 2:12). In a general sense
he implies that all are teachers (Col. 3:16). Yet he also
sees teaching as a gift, listing it in three different
places: Romans 12:7, I Corinthians 12:28, and Ephesians
4:11. Above all, these teachers were to pass on what they
had heard to other faithful men who could in turn teach

others also (II Tim. 2:2). That is, the whole aim of their
teaching was not just to impart knowledge, but to teach
those who could train others. To that end, the Scriptures
were profitable (3:16), and the teacher was to be a workman
who "rightly handled the word of truth" (2:15). It was a
great privilege and at the same time a grave responsibility,
and that is perhaps why James discourages people from becoming teachers unless they really feel called (Jas. 3:1).

In brief then, while there were no Bible schools or
seminaries in New Testament times, there was a lot of teaching going on. The training took place somewhat informally
by our standards, but there were leaders who needed to be
trained, and they were trained to meet the needs of the
churches. Christ seems to have set the pattern that was
followed. It goes without saying that He is the greatest
teacher of all time, and yet He did not establish a school.
He rather taught people when and where they were free, concentrating especially on small groups such as the Twelve.

Paul and the other teachers in the young churches
followed a similar pattern. Their teaching was Christ-
centered and Word-centered, but they were very flexible as
to the time and place of their teaching. In fact, their
whole approach seems to have been characterized by great
flexibility. Their overriding concern was to enable people
to grow in the faith. And as for teachers, the main objective seems to have been to teach those who would in turn be
able to train the rest of the church for its ministry.
Teaching was one of the gifts given to build up the members
of the body of Christ for their work in the world, and was
sought to be used as such.

When it comes to the later development of theological
schools, Origen founded an advanced theological school in
Alexandria (Egypt) in about the year A.D. 230 (Niebuhr and
Williams 1956:45). In the centuries which followed, theological education took various forms. Some pupils were
trained in monasteries, others in episcopal schools where a
group of students were tutored by a bishop, and later on
there was the emergence of the universities in Europe where
theology was also taught. As noted earlier, the Anabaptists
did not especially stress education for their leaders,
although some of their first leaders were also highly educated men. They had been trained as priests, university
professors, or for some other occupation. But gradually, as
persecution continued and many of them were put to death, it
was impossible to have schools of any kind and so Anabaptist
leaders came to be less educated than in the beginning.

As the years went by, however, and persecution lessened, there was the desire on the part of some for a more highly trained leadership. This resulted in the formation of schools such as the Mennonite Theological Seminary of Amsterdam, which was founded over 200 years ago (Smith 1957: 220). As Mennonites migrated to America they also came to feel a need for trained leaders, and as was related before, one of the main reasons for the organization of the General Conference Mennonite Church was for the purpose of education. It was to that end that The Christian Educational Institution of the Mennonite Denomination was founded at Wadsworth, Ohio, over 100 years ago (1957:681).

The Wadsworth school opened its doors in January, 1868, with two teachers and 24 students. Later the same year a professor from Germany was called to teach theology. The aim of the institution was primarily "to train young men for Christian work," but secular subjects were also part of the curriculum. It was a three-year course of study. Students were given an entrance exam, and the only other qualifications were that they had to have a good character and be between the ages of 18 and 30. The instruction was principally in German, which was the language most of the churches used for worship. The school was at first only for men, although some wanted to make it coeducational, and later on women were also reluctantly admitted.

An attempt was made to combine the practical with the intellectual, and students were expected to spend three hours a day in some kind of manual labor for their physical and mental well-being, as well as to benefit the institution. Assignments included such things as doing stable work, peeling potatoes, running errands, carpentering, shoe-making, cutting wood and so on. Costs were not high -- tuition, board, room and washing came to only a hundred dollars a year. But even though expenses were low, the school was never able to attract many more students each year than the first year of its operation. And because of factors such as poor financing, personal differences among the faculty, and disagreement among some of the churches as to proper management, the school closed in 1878, just 10 years after it began, with a heavy debt. This experiment was not a total failure though, as this was where the first missionaries and many of the later Conference leaders received their initial training (Smith 1957:680-682).

The next experiment took place in 1914, when Bluffton College in Bluffton, Ohio, which had been founded by the

General Conference in 1900, was enlarged to include a
seminary known as Mennonite Seminary. This involved the
cooperation of several different groups of Mennonites. In
1921, the seminary separated from the college, and went
under the name of Witmarsium Theological Seminary (named
after the town where Menno Simons was born). But like its
predecessor, the Witmarsium school lasted only 10 years,
closing in 1931, not having enough interest or support to
keep it alive.

The Conference, however, kept working on this matter, and
in 1945 once more opened a Mennonite Biblical Seminary and
Mennonite Bible School affiliated with the Bethany Biblical
Seminary (Church of the Brethren) in Chicago (Smith 1957:
761-762). After 13 years, in 1958, the Mennonite Biblical
Seminary moved to its own campus in Elkhart, Indiana. There
it began cooperating with the nearby Goshen Biblical Seminary (of the Mennonite Church), with which it finally merged
in 1969 to form the Associated Mennonite Biblical Seminaries
(AMBS). The association continues today with a student body
of approximately 200 -- about 40 percent General Conference
Mennonite, and 60 percent Mennonite Church (AMBS 1976:2).
This includes a considerable number of women, part-time, and
non-Mennonite students. There are approximately 15 full-
time members on the faculty.

Actually, the development of seminaries and the professional ministry are both quite recent phenomena in American
church history. Many of the early ministers acquired their
training informally, under the supervision of an older
clergyman, or attended one of the established colleges such
as Harvard or Yale where they also received some theological
training. Other forms of training, such as William Tennent's
famous "log college," combined features of both the established schools and more personal instruction. But it was
not until the early 1800s that seminaries as separate institutions began to be founded on a large scale (Niebuhr and
Williams 1956:242-243). Thus the seminary itself is a
rather late development in America for the training of a
professional ministry.

As far as Mennonite churches go, for many years they
relied more or less on an untrained ministry, simply calling
people from within the congregation to serve as ministers
were needed. But as indicated elsewhere, in recent years
Mennonite churches have been moving rapidly toward a trained,
professional ministry. When they have gone to other countries to do mission work, they have naturally taken with

them the patterns used at home. In Japan, for example, even though the typical church is small, the ideal seems to be having a full-time pastor, trained at a Bible school or seminary, and to that end we have sent young people off to school for such training without giving too much further thought as to whether this is really the best way to provide leaders for the churches.

Some of these patterns, of course, were here before the Mennonites ever came. The first Protestant church in Japan was established in Yokohama in 1872 (Iglehart 1959:43). The training of the ministry began in the same city already in 1875 (1959:49), although the first independent Protestant theological seminary, the Tokyo Shingakusha, was not founded until 1904 (1959:124). In an article on "Protestant Theological Education in Japan," Hidenobu Kuwada points out that at present theological training institutions can be classified basically under five types:

1. Those which have been accredited by the Japanese Government's Bureau of Education as universities; 2. those seminaries which, while not thus accredited, do nevertheless rank high in quality; 3. those called Bible seminaries; 4. those officially ranking as junior colleges; 5. those called Bible schools (1957: 374).

At the time he wrote, there were five seminaries which were qualified by the government to confer the Bachelor of Divinity degree, and three of them were also permitted to grant the Doctor of Theology degree (1957:373). There may be more such schools by now, although Tokyo Union Theological Seminary is said to be the only church seminary (non-university-related program) which offers a post-B.D. (Th.M. and Th.D.) training (TEF 1973:176).

The majority of teachers in these various types of institutions are Japanese, and a considerable number of them have done graduate study overseas, which no doubt has added to the western influence on these schools. Kuwada also notes that "In proportion to the total number of believers, which is rather small, the number of seminaries and Bible training schools is large" (1957:374). Some of these schools naturally are very small, having only a handful of students, but others are said to have a sizeable enrollment, up to 200 or so. Part of the reason for the large number of schools is that many denominations try to maintain their own individual training program.

Up till now, most of the Mennonite pastors have gone to a Christian college or Bible school somewhere. More recently, though, some of them have gone to a college or university first, then on to seminary. The trend seems to be toward getting more education if possible. This tendency perhaps is the result of the fact that most of the present pastors feel that their education has been inadequate for their work. In addition to their answers on the questionnaires, the fact that this is so comes out clearly in some of the minutes.

Back in 1970, for instance, at the Church's Annual Conference there was discussion concerning the establishment of a fund for the training of full-time Christian workers. It was suggested that this fund not only be made available for those contemplating full-time Christian service, and for university students who may want to go on to seminary and become leaders in the churches, but also for the "retraining of present workers." There seemed to be a definite feeling that training programs in the past had been insufficient, and that it was time to restudy the whole matter of theological education. The minutes contain expressions such as the following:

- As for the training of church workers who will be leaders of the entire Church Conference, they should choose to follow a high school - university - seminary course of study.

- The word "seminary" [in Japanese] is vague, for in Europe and America, Bible schools and Christian colleges are schools for laymen. Since the pastors of our churches are mostly graduates of T.C.C., they should have an opportunity for further training (JMCCC 1970:7J).

From this I think it is quite clear that many of the pastors are not entirely satisfied with their training. They feel a need for more, especially when compared to the level of training pastors in other countries receive. If they feel inadequately prepared, surely something should be done about it. But our concern here is not only with the training of pastors. It is also with that of laymen, especially lay leaders. As was observed before, there are several people in each of the churches who are considered "potential lay leaders." These are mature men and women, of various occupations, age levels, and abilities. But one of the pastors mentioned to me later he did not include among

them those who were already serving in his church, which
means that there may be a total of considerably more than
the 40 or so we referred to earlier. Whatever the number,
many laymen are even now deeply involved in the work of the
church.

That this is so came out in the responses to a questionnaire distributed to the churches. In each of the ten
churches, for example, laymen are sometimes, if not always,
chairman of the worship service. This also includes women,
who in half of the churches sometimes chair the service. In
addition, laymen also sometimes preach in each of the
churches. Again, this includes women. Four of the ten
churches reported they occasionally have women preachers.
It would appear from this that laymen may be involved more
in leading worship services in Japan than they are in many
churches in the States, which is something we might not
expect from churches so small in size and with a trained
ministry.

The fact that the lay people are doing a lot is also
brought out in a questionnaire that was given to the church
members. Out of 115 responses, 33 have taught Sunday school;
45 have led morning worship; 14 have preached; 30 have led
a Bible study; 16 have led a women's meeting; others have
served in various capacities such as visitation evangelism,
organist, youth work, treasurer, junior church and so on.
But when asked whether they had had any training for their
various responsibilities, only about 10, or less than 10
percent, said they had, and some of them indicated this was
lay training at the church. One other person said he had
received some training through "self study." But, in general, it looks like the laymen are doing many things but
have not been specially trained for their respective duties.

Some of the members live as close as 50 meters to the
church (or even in the church building in the case of some
pastors and their families); others, as far as 40 kilometers (25 mi.) away. About one-third of the members live
within one kilometer of the church; two-thirds within five
kilometers (3 mi.). It takes them anywhere from a couple
of minutes to an hour to get to the church. They come by
car, bus, train, bike, on foot, or a combination of these.
Almost 70, or well over half, attend church at least once a
week; 30, or about one-fourth, attend twice a week; several
attend three or more times weekly. But overall, approximately 90 percent of those who responded attend at least
once a week. At any rate, distance did not seem to make too

much difference in attendance in some cases, as take the
case where one person who lived 45 minutes away said he
attended church three times a week, just as did one who
lived only three minutes away. That may be an exception,
however, and as a rule one would imagine that those who
lived closer to the church would be able to attend more
often.

About 10 percent of the families had children in Sunday
school. A few of the others said No, or that their children
had already "graduated." When asked whether they sometimes
read the Bible and prayed together as families, all of the
families replied in the positive. In fact, over 100 persons,
or about seven-eighths of those who responded, indicated they
did so. One of the surprising things was that many, even
from non-Christian homes, and the only Christian in their
family, said they sometimes read the Bible and prayed
together, but this was perhaps a reference to the fact that
they have personal devotions (as a few noted) and not to
family devotions as such. One said that he did "every morning and every night." The question itself may not have
been as clear as it should have been.

In answer to whether they had ever had a Christian meeting in their home, 39, or over one-third, indicated they had.
Fifty-nine, or about one half, said they had not, but of
those 59, at least 36 said they would be willing to. About
10 said No, they would not be willing to have a meeting in
their home, although one indicated this was because he was
"boarding with someone else and can't." In some cases it
was not clear if they would be willing or not. But generally speaking, laymen appear to be quite active in their
churches and interested in doing evangelism. A few of them
are also active at the conference level, serving as the
representative of their church, as Conference secretary or
treasurer, or on camp, bookstore, kindergarten and other
committees.

When asked how long they had been Christians, 37, or
about one-third, said it was five years or less. Several
indicated they had been Christians for only a month or so.
Another 38, or approximately one-third, replied they had
been Christians from six to 10 years. Thus almost two-
thirds of the church members have been believers for only
10 years or less. Seventeen said they had been Christians
from 11 to 15 years. Another 17 indicated it had been anywhere from 16 to 25 years. Only four had been Christians
for more than 25 years. One of them said he had been a

believer for over 40 years. But for the most part the churches seem to be made up of relatively new Christians, which is what one might expect as the churches themselves are still quite young.

As to whether they were from Christian homes or not, 75, or about two-thirds, replied No. Twenty-nine, or slightly over one-fourth, replied Yes. But as with a few other questions, there seems to have been some confusion as to whether the question referred to the past or present, the family they grew up in or their family now. If people were not thinking of the religion of the family they grew up in, the chances would probably be that even a greater percentage would be from non-Christian families. Whatever the case, as would be expected in Japan, a good many did indicate that their family religion had been Shintoism or Buddhism. One said it had been Buddhism and Christianity (a case no doubt where only one of the parents was Christian). Another stated frankly, "my parents don't believe anything."

When asked what the greatest influence was in their becoming Christians, by far the greatest number replied that it was the influence of other people. Almost 20 percent of those who answered the question recalled that this was the major factor for them. Some of their answers were as follows: "led by my brother"; "influence of my elder sister who is a Christian"; "persuaded by my father"; through my mother's faith"; "I believed in Christ because my husband was a Christian"; "leading of my wife"; "because my daughter was going to church"; "led by my child who attended Sunday school"; "introduction of a church school teacher"; "testimony of an intimate friend"; "the guidance of a missionary"; "the wonderfulness of Christian fellowship." One could add more, but here already we have a dozen different relationships through which people became Christians. Simply by reading these replies I think one can sense the importance of such connections.

Next in order of frequency, with regard to the greatest influence in their becoming Christians, were personal or family problems. Over 12 percent listed this. Their replies included such things as "anxiety because of illness"; "troubles of life"; "death of a child"; "human relationships"; "because I was a heavy drinker"; "when I was faced with bankruptcy," and so on.

Tied for third and fourth place were a desire to know the truth and a consciousness of sin. Each of these was

mentioned by slightly over 10 percent of the respondents.
The former included answers like, "was seeking for the
truth"; "seeking for salvation"; "I was convinced that
Christianity was indeed the true salvation." The latter
included replies such as "I found that I had no real love to
friends"; "because I came to know my own helplessness";
"because I was convicted of my own deep sinfulness."

Tied for fifth and sixth were the emptiness of life and a
desire to improve oneself. A little under 10 percent of the
answers fell into each of these categories. Regarding the
former, there were expressions such as "loneliness"; "life
was empty"; "despairing of life"; "I wanted to know the real
meaning of life"; "I wanted to believe something." With
regard to the latter, there were replies like, "disappointed
in myself"; "I hated my own character"; "wanted to change my
personality"; "to improve myself spiritually"; "wanted to
live an upright human life"; "because I wanted to be gentle
like Jesus."

In seventh place, with almost 8 percent, was a longing
for peace of heart. Expressions here ranged from "wanting
peace" to "forgiveness of sin and peace of heart" to "seeking my own true happiness." Coming in eighth with about 7
percent were evangelistic meetings: "tent meetings," "young
people's meetings," and so on were mentioned. And tied for
ninth and tenth with about 5 percent each were the love of
God and the words of the Bible. As to the former, people
expressed themselves in ways such as "I experienced God's
love"; "God's love and a consciousness of sin"; "I came to
know both the depth of sin and God's love." Regarding the
latter, there were statements like, "I was attracted by the
words of the Bible"; "as I began reading the Bible";
"through a verse from the Bible written on a poster adver-
tising Christian evangelistic meetings."

In addition to the replies which fell into one of the 10
categories listed above, there were also some which did not
seem to fit into any particular category -- responses such
as "eternal life," "just inevitably," and "I don't remember."
But most of the replies fell into one or another of the
categories. As pointed out, the most outstanding influence
in these various individuals becoming Christian appears to
have been the influence of other people, especially their
own circle of family and friends. It would certainly seem
that in light of this that family or household evangelism
should be encouraged even more. The significance of this
factor for the growth of the church ought not to go unno-
ticed.

In answer to the question, "What is the biggest problem you face as a Christian?", there were various replies. But by far the largest number indicated that their greatest problem was the evangelization or salvation of their family and friends. Over 30, or more than 25 percent of the replies, were in this category. Some of the responses were: "spouse is not a Christian"; "salvation of family"; "I'd like to help my friends believe in Jesus"; "the difficulty of personal evangelism"; "how to witness to non-Christians," and so on. Another area in which there seemed to be a need for help was with their daily walk as Christians. Over 10 percent mentioned this. Their answers included such things as "putting faith into practice"; "living consistently"; "how to live in this world as a Christian"; "living dynamically as a Christian in one's home life," and the like. Still a third category in which there were several replies had to do with lack of faith or commitment. About 5 percent stated this. The answers here involved matters such as "faith is weak"; "more committed Christian"; "perseverance in the faith."

In addition to these three main categories, there were others who indicated that their major problem was "time (including Sunday employment)," "lack of understanding by the family," "conflict of Japanese customs and Christian ways," "inadequate Bible knowledge," or just a "longing to see revival break out." Answers were many and varied. In a few cases it was not clear from their reply exactly what their problem was, or they did not list any. There were a few who said they had "none." But most of the believers were confronted with problems, the nature of which can be seen in their replies.

One would hope that on the basis of the problems which the believers seem to face, any training program that is inaugurated would first of all seek to meet the felt needs of the people. Ironically, while the greatest felt need seems to be getting help with evangelism, few of the churches have chosen to cooperate with the "Total Mobilization Evangelism" program (*Sōdōin Dendō*, Japan's equivalent of Evangelism-in-Depth) being carried on throughout Kyushu from 1974 on. When asked whether they were cooperating with this program, seven of the ten churches said No. Of the other three, one said Yes; one said they were "cooperating, but not cooperating formally"; the third gave no reply. Just what the reasons are why the majority of the churches are not cooperating is not known to the author. Perhaps some of them have their own programs instead, or are cooperating

partially. But if this is one of the needs felt by many of
the people, certainly something should be done about it.

Perhaps we should also ask, however, why the evangelization of one's family and friends is listed as the greatest
problem of many when at the same time a high percentage also
stated that the greatest influence in their becoming Christian was another person, often a member of their own family.
Have they in fact really reflected deeply on how they became
Christians themselves? Are they possibly trying too hard to
win members of their own family? In any event, if personal
evangelism seems to be so difficult in Japanese society,
perhaps we should be concentrating more on things that can
be done together -- home or hospital visitation, literature
evangelism, film evangelism and the like. Or if, as indicated, a large percentage of the people do not now have home
meetings but would be willing to do so, perhaps training in
leading home Bible studies or group counseling would also be
useful. And if as we saw earlier a large number of people
are already teaching Sunday school, chairing worship, preaching, leading Bible studies or women's meetings, but have not
been trained for these things, then surely some training
would be in order there too.

Many people are no doubt doing a good job already, but
with some training they could undoubtedly do even better.
Whatever kind of training is offered, we must think not only
in terms of training evangelists and preachers and teachers.
We must also think in terms of the real needs people feel
now, and help them with those. This could perhaps also
include guidance in such things as how to study the Bible,
pray, lead family devotions, visit the sick, present simply
the plan of salvation, give one's own testimony, and make a
simple presentation of the history of one's church. Above
all, any training program should be as practical as possible.

The fact that people desire practical training was also
brought out in the replies to a question as to which of the
following courses they would choose if they were offered as
part of a training program. The twelve courses are listed
in the order they were given on the questionnaire, with the
number who chose each one. People were to check the three
courses they would like to take most. About 20 people did
not answer the question, or their answer was incomplete.
This list includes only those who checked the three courses
which most interested them.

Church History	25	Other Religions	9
Bible Study Methods	65	Mennonite History	32
Christian Ethics	26	Old Testament Intro.	15
Personal Evangelism	33	Teachers' Training	10
Jehovah's Witnesses	6	Prophecy	10
Prayer	36	Christian Doctrine	24

Simply by looking at the list of courses above, and those which people checked most often, you can see the tremendous interest in practical courses. Out of 97 responses, over two-thirds checked Bible study methods. Prayer and personal evangelism each claimed over one-third of the votes. The only other course which also received almost a third, but is not necessarily practical, is Mennonite history, although here again it may meet a practical need in terms of identity, in knowing where their church has come from. Thus, three of the four courses which received the greatest number of checks were all of a practical nature. Following these in order of ranking were Christian ethics (also practical), church history, Christian doctrine, Old Testament introduction, prophecy, teachers' training, other religions, and lastly, Jehovah's Witnesses. The only course of a really practical nature which did not rank very high was teachers' training. But overall those who responded seem to lean toward more practical courses.

If the courses are to be of a practical nature, it means that people ought to be involved in the work of the church as they study. It probably means that most students would not go off to Bible school or seminary somewhere. Instead, they would likely remain at home with their families and continue to work at their regular jobs. As they learned, they would have opportunity to put their learning into practice, to see if it works. There may be some experiments going on in Japan along these lines, but other than what is being presented in this study, I am not familiar with them. If there are, information on them should be published. But whether there are or not, there have been experiments in other parts of the world from which I believe we can also profit.

One of these is a Bible Institute which has been operating in Buenos Aires, Argentina, for about the past 20 years. I would like to try to summarize what Edward C. Pentecost, who spent a summer ministering in the area, has to say about the school (1972:34-37). The school, he says, "came into being for the purpose of preparing professional people for the ministry of the gospel." It was started by an

independent group of evangelical Christian churches. Before
opening their school, they studied Bible institutes and
seminaries in other countries, but felt the patterns were
not suitable for them. So they started their own school
after their own pattern, which is based largely on the seminar approach, and geared to meet the needs of the individual
student.

There is a definite program of study, but it is not fixed
for any given year. It rather seeks to fit into the students work and family structure. The student studies at
home during the week, and on weekends meets with his professor. Most of the sessions are held on Saturdays when
people are relatively free, anywhere from 8 a.m. to 10 p.m.
There are no textbooks, the material being prepared in
separate lesson form. Each lesson must be completed satisfactorily before going on. The student progresses at his
own speed, taking as many or as few courses as he feels he
can carry, but it takes at least four years to complete the
program. Some take as long as 10 years. But whenever they
finish, they are given a diploma in recognition of the work
they have done. Some of the classes have several students
in them, which gives opportunity for small group interaction.

As said, this program is geared largely for professional
people who also have a desire to minister. Among the students are doctors, dentists, businessmen, and accountants.
This plan allows them a twofold ministry: daily witnessing
at work; serving as respected pastors and ministers. They
support themselves, and since the churches do not have to
support their pastors, they send out their own missionaries,
both men and women, to towns in the area which have no
evangelical church. These missionaries are naturally graduates of the school. In this way, over a dozen new churches
have been planted. All the graduates are pastors of congregations. The institute began in 1953 with 14 students. It
now has some 40 students, taught by five full-time Argentine
teachers. It is supported entirely by student fees and
freewill offerings from the churches that have been blessed
with pastors trained at the school.

Another program which is somewhat similar, this one in
the U.S., is a weekend seminary run by the Episcopalians
(Schonberger 1967). It is called the Bloy House Theological
School, and is located in Pasadena, California, but serves
the greater Los Angeles area. Bloy House has been operating
since 1958. It is a program for ministerial candidates who
are not sure whether or not they really want to give up

their professions and enter the ministry full time. The
students remain at their places of employment, and have
intensive study on weekends at the school. Instruction is
on weekends only. It is a four-year course, and after the
four years, the student can decide if he wants to enter the
ministry full time or not. If he does, he goes on to a
regular seminary for a year of further training. If not, he
remains at his business or profession and perhaps serves as
a part-time priest. It is reported that about half of the
candidates take that path after two years or so of training.

The student body is small -- only about 20 at the time of
writing -- and they want to keep it that way to preserve the
concept. Those enrolled include bankers, actors, physicists,
company presidents, attorneys, electricians and so on. It
is hoped that through getting men with experience like this,
they will be more "down to earth" than the ordinary clergyman, and able to minister in more practical ways. This program is unique not only in reaching more of the real
leaders of the church, but also in giving them the option of
entering or staying out of the ministry. It permits them to
remain laymen if they so choose. It is, in short, an
effective way of testing a person's call to the ministry.

A third program, this one functioning in Chile, may also
have something to commend itself to us. It is operated by
the Pentecostalists and is more specifically for those who
desire to eventually become pastors. According to sociologist, Christian Lalive d'Epinay, who has written up the
report, the Pentecostalists have a saying that "Protestant
pastors are 'trained by the seminary'; Pentecostalist
pastors are *'trained by the street'*" (1967:188). That is,
while the Protestants stress education, the Pentecostalists
stress evangelization in the training of their pastors.
Anyone in their churches who wishes can theoretically become
a pastor, but to do so, he must pass through an apprenticeship system. It may take a long time, and there are many
rungs on the ladder, but the system is effective in separating those who are truly called from those who are not.

Some of the steps in the process are as follows (1967:188-
189): Soon after a person's conversion, he starts proving
his convictions by preaching in the street. Then he is
given responsibility for a Sunday school class (for adults,
as well as children). After this he accedes to the status
of preacher, and has the right to lead worship. If he per-
forms satisfactorily, he may be given the opportunity to
open a new preaching place in his neighborhood. If he is

able to gather a small group, this is regarded as proof of
his charisma or calling. At this stage, which may be years
after he began his climb, he can tell his pastor that he
feels called to the ministry, and at the Annual Conference
of Pentecostalist pastors, his name is proposed as a "worker
for the Lord." If accepted, he will be sent to build up a
congregation in an unevangelized area. Again, he has to
prove that God is working through him, and he will not be
appointed as a "pastor-deacon" unless he can gather a flock.
"If he fails, he returns to the ranks." But if he can
gather a congregation large enough to support himself so
that he can give up his secular occupation, he has passed
the final test, and can become a full-time pastor. The
selection process is then complete.

As elaborated above, it usually takes many years for a
candidate to climb the seven rungs on the ladder -- from
street preacher to Sunday school teacher to preacher to new-
preaching-point preacher to "worker for the Lord" to pastor-
deacon to pastor. But the result is thought to be supernatural, a work of the Holy Spirit. And not only is the
pastor tested, but the church is too. It is not permitted
to have a pastor unless it can support him full time, which
gives them both a sense of mutual responsibility. This
practical system of pastoral training, open to any member of
the church (even those of advanced age) is thought to contribute much to the success of Pentecostalism. And while
they are growing rapidly, they do not seem to be faced with
a chronic shortage of pastors as many Protestant denominations are.

As for the bearing of this latter example on our churches,
there are two or three things that might be noted. One is
that we are short of leaders. That is, in 1974, when this
research was done, only six of the ten churches had Japanese
pastors. Another is that according to the questionnaire
filled out by the churches, eight of the congregations have
had pastors at one time or another -- some just one, some
two, or some as many as three different pastors -- but two
of the newest churches have never had a pastor at all,
although they may be as large or larger than some of the
older churches. (Note: As of 1977, the two churches
referred to here now have their own pastors, but due to
some shifts in personnel, there are still three churches
without a Japanese pastor.) The churches which have had
pastors have averaged about two pastors each.

Still another thing worth noticing is that of the six
pastors, three of them have come out of the same church; two

out of another; one out of a third. In other words, the
pastors have all come out of only three of the ten churches!
Surely there must be those in some of the other churches who
also have the gift to pastor, but perhaps they have never
had a chance to prove themselves. Or even if they have, perhaps there has been no mechanism whereby they can go on to
become recognized as pastors even if they would like to be.
Maybe this is where we can learn from the Chile system and
try to set up a practical way in which gifts can become evident, and by which they can be recognized. If this would be
done, perhaps not only would all the congregations have
pastors, but we would also see God raising up pastors out of
all ten churches rather than just a few.

Regardless of the kind of training program that might be
felt suitable for Japan, one of the big needs will be for
teachers. In addition to instructors who may come from
recognized schools, it would perhaps also be logical to make
use, if possible, of the pastors and missionaries who are
currently serving the churches. Not all of them may have a
gift for teaching, of course, but those who do should certainly be given an opportunity to exercise it. In this way
it would soon become clear who has the gift and who does not.
This would no doubt involve teaching not only in one's own
church, but in other churches as well. There is, in fact,
some sharing of leaders already. For example, when the
pastors were asked if they ever preached in other churches,
four of them said Yes, two of them said No. Those who did
said they did so "once a month," "every other month," or
only "occasionally." In response to the same question, five
of the missionaries indicated they also preach in other
churches occasionally, their answers ranging from "once a
month" to "once every three months" to "once in a long while."

When asked whether they have ever taught a course in
another church, three of the pastors replied Yes; three, No.
Those who had said they taught about the church, evangelism,
and other subjects, in various times and places -- Mennonite
as well as non-Mennonite. When asked if they would be
willing to teach a subject in other churches, two said Yes,
three, No, and one, "if invited, I would accept." The subjects they would be most interested in teaching included
such things as Christian ethics and church music. When
missionaries were asked if they ever taught in other
churches, almost all of them replied No, except through
preaching and a little teaching in English. With regard to
whether they would be willing to teach a course in another
church, seven said Yes, two, "yes, if it was in English,"

one, No, and three did not reply. Some of the subjects they
would be interested in teaching were Bible courses, the
Christian home, Christian education, cults, current issues,
music and the like. Thus, depending on the subject, pastors
and missionaries could be a potential source of teaching
personnel.

Students naturally want a teacher to be someone who knows
more about the subject than they do. But if extension
methods were followed, the teacher would not necessarily
have to be an expert on the subject, but could serve more as
an enabler or a resource person. As someone has said, however, anyone interested in teaching in this sort of training
program should have at least three essential attributes:
"commitment to Christ and the church; the ability to listen;
and the ability to communicate effectively" (*Ministry*, 1965:
27). In short, he or she should be able to demonstrate that
they indeed have been given the gift of teaching. It goes
without saying that those who do not have the gift ought not
to teach.

As we have seen then, some of the pastors and missionaries are willing to teach in such a program. Not only that,
but some of them are interested in teaching in the very same
areas in which the church members indicated an interest in
learning. Along with regular professors, several of the
pastors or missionaries could perhaps also serve as
teachers. But while that may be a partial solution to that
problem, another problem we soon run into is, who will be
the teacher's teacher? That is, as we pointed out earlier,
it is not only the laymen who are interested in study. Most
of the pastors would like to further their training as well.
From their own experience, they report that the courses
they have found most helpful in their ministry are systematic theology, listed by half, as well as Bible exegesis and
church history. When asked in what area they would like to
continue their studies, three of the six mentioned the
biblical languages (Hebrew or Greek), three of them said
Bible or theology, and there were other replies such as
evangelism, Christian ethics, church history, and church
music.

By comparison, the missionaries, in their experience,
have found biblical studies to be the most helpful. Eleven
of the 13, or over three-fourths, listed it. Other subjects
mentioned were missions, Mennonite history, psychology,
religions of the world, and music. But as noted previously
in our study, while most of the missionaries felt their

studies were basically adequate, others felt they had "weak
areas" and "needed more," or "needed a refresher." When
asked if they would be interested in continuing their study,
five said Yes, one, No, others said "possibly," "not
formally," or that they had "no plans." Those who wished
to continue their studies mentioned areas such as the Bible,
Bible study or Bible teaching, history, missions, cultural
areas such as art and music, Asian studies (especially
Japanese history), and counseling. There may be some areas
in which pastors and missionaries could study together, and
be enrolled in the same class. It could be an exciting
learning experience for both. But qualified teachers will
need to be found before it can happen.

Another subject in which one would expect the pastors
might have some interest is that of English. Six of the
churches report that they use English as a means of evangelism. Three do not. One says they did when a missionary
was there. As to its effectiveness, some of the churches
say they have gained no members in this way; others report
they have received as many as 10, with an average of three
or four. The missionaries, as might be expected, all use
some English in their work, teaching anywhere from one to 15
hours a week, with an average of about eight. This includes
direct evangelism through English Bible classes and more
indirect evangelism through straight English classes, some
of them at junior colleges or universities. Ten of the
missionaries felt the use of English was of "considerable"
importance for evangelism; two, "small"; one, "great."
There were also comments such as that it is important for
us but, "as we learn more Japanese, the importance of
English should decrease"; that it is "good, especially when
we teach English Bible"; and that it "can be important to
meet and learn to know people."

The pastors do not use English as much in their work. In
fact, only one of the pastors said he did; two said No; in
three cases it was not clear whether they did or not. Three
of them did say though that they are studying it. Yet, when
the pastors were asked whether they were interested in continuing their study of English, there was no response,
perhaps because those who might be interested may be the
same as those already studying. In any case, when asked
further how important they felt English was for evangelism,
three said "considerable"; two, "small"; one said, "it
depends on how it is used." A few of the pastors themselves have become Christians through English classes, but
by and large the pastors do not seem to be using English

much for evangelistic purposes. Some of them no doubt are
using their ability in English though as a means of support.

But while on the surface their interest in the study of
English does not seem to be too great, in response to a
question as to whether they are interested in participating
in the General Conference "Overseas Church Leaders Study-
Service Program" (a year of study abroad), five of them said
Yes (three of them have already done so as of 1978). The
sixth said he was not interested, but that is possibly
because he has already spent some time overseas. So there
may be some interest here, especially on the part of those
who will be going abroad in the future, to "brush up their
English." This may be an area in which the missionaries can
be of some help. In any case, whatever the pastors are
going to be doing, whether it is pastoring or teaching or
doing something else to earn a living, insofar as possible,
an attempt should be made to find a way to make it possible
for them "to be accredited in both civil and ecclesiastical
worlds" (Winter 1967b:12). And if they are going to study
abroad, any credit they may receive for work done there
should also be made applicable toward that end.

Exactly what all this data means in terms of the kind of
training program we need for lay leaders and pastors is hard
to say. It is difficult because we ought to be interested
in having a program which is based on our concept of the
ministry, which in turn is based on our concept of the
church, but as we have said over and over again, neither of
these have ever been clearly spelled out. It is not probable either that many institutions have given serious thought
to these concepts before setting up their current programs.
They have more than likely simply copied models from elsewhere, which of course is the easiest thing to do. But
we are trying to think in new directions here, not necessarily opposed to what is already being done, but hoping
to find a better way to train leaders for our churches.
Unfortunately, as we have said, there are few models in
Japan to guide us.

In addition to the morning and evening core classes
offered at the Covenant Seminary in Tokyo, and the decentralized program of the Eastern Hokkaido Bible School, the
only other really creative experiment I have run across is
what one pastor is doing locally to make theological education more relevant to the needs of his people. Richard P.
Poethig reports on that program as follows:

In Chiba Prefecture outside Tokyo, Pastor Minoru
Ishimaru has brought theological education out of the
seminary classroom into the activities of his people
in the rapidly growing Keiyo industrial complex which
houses 750 companies. Pastor Ishimaru began teaching
his people by using seminary notes and curriculum outlines. He soon found that his people's own experiences
raised more pertinent theological questions and provided more profound encounters with modern society than
the classroom material he had collected. His people
have grown through the theological dialogues and in
turn have become teachers. They have organized themselves to confront the issues raised in the Keiyo
industrial complex (1972:65).

Poethig also mentions in passing the existence of centers
like the Kansai Seminar House on the edge of Kyoto, which
"bring laity together around occupational concerns or to
discuss particular issues" (1972:64). There may be some
other experiments like this which are being conducted in
Japan, knowledge of which could benefit the rest of us.
But they would appear to be few and far between, and mostly
local in nature.

There is one church, however, with which I am slightly
acquainted, which incorporates a number of features that we
have been talking about in this chapter. It is not a perfect example by any means, but as with the other examples
cited in these pages, there are things we can learn from it.
For that reason, I would like to share something about its
program here. The church being referred to is the Nukui
Minami Cho Christian Church, located in western Tokyo. It
was started 10 years ago by missionary John W. Graybill,
who is working with the Brethren in Christ Church. The
information which follows is taken from an interview with
Graybill on May 8, 1974, and a letter of May 24, 1975.

To begin with, a religious survey was taken in the
community and about a dozen Christians were found. Starting
with those 12, the first home meeting was held in April 1964
(Graybill 1966:31), and since then the group has grown to
have 100 members. Of these 100 members, 58 are official
members (baptized locally), 18 are associate members
(baptized in another fellowship, but are now attending this
fellowship, serving the group, and giving offerings), and
24 are seekers (people who attend at least once a month, are
not baptized, but are listed as "members" for prayer purposes).

Out of the 58 "official" members, 14 are transfers from
other churches. One is from a Brethren in Christ church,
one from a Mennonite church, and the others from various
other denominations. Thus only about 25 percent of the full
members are from other churches. It was mentioned that
Japanese do not transfer memberships easily, and yet since
the church has its own new building, a good number have done
this without much suggestion from anyone. As pointed out,
there are also quite a few "associates" who have membership
in another church as well. And there is a good group of
"seekers," potential members for the future. This potential
is very important too, as 17 people are said to have moved
away from the church during the past year. It is sometimes
thought that rural people feed the city churches, that
people in the cities do not move as much, but this is not
necessarily true. Mobility is also a problem for the urban
church.

In April 1974, just 10 years after it began, the average
attendance at Sunday worship was 53. Forty-two are tithers,
and about 12-15 attend the midweek prayer meeting. Home
meetings are also held. At one time there were 13 of them.
Some met weekly, others biweekly, monthly or whenever it was
convenient to get together. About half of them were in
Christian homes, the other half in non-Christian homes. In
the case of Christians, the meeting was usually held for non-
Christian members of the family. In the case of non-
Christians, it was mostly for family and church people in
the area. In the fall of 1973, it was decided to move the
home meetings to the church building until spring, and then
start again in homes, but most of them have not started up
again. There are only four or five home meetings now. Most
of them are led by laymen, but it depends on the home. If
the person is not spiritually mature, it is led by someone
from the church. The Graybill's also have a group that
meets in their home Sunday evenings, called the Kodaira
Fukuin (Gospel) Center, which was organized into the Yayoi-
dai Christian Church in May 1975.

The congregation has leaders, but it does not use the
word "pastor" for them. Instead, it has four "teachers,"
one woman and three men. The main teacher, Hirotoshi
Hashimoto, has been trained at Japan Christian Seminary and
graduated in June 1974. He has been commissioned as an
evangelist. He can marry, preach, and do the work of an
evangelist, but he cannot baptize or serve communion. He is
commissioned, but not yet ordained (there is no set rule,
but it is said this usually takes three to five years). For

support he teaches music two days a week. Half of his
support comes from that, the other half from the church.
The church also pays his room and transportation. The other
three teachers are supported by personal employment, one
being an English teacher, another the owner of a small
apartment, and the third is self-employed. The woman
teacher does a lot of the visiting, counseling, and teaches
at the ladies meeting.

As far as leadership training goes, there is no definite
program. But on Sunday afternoons, a seminary professor
holds leadership training classes at the church. These are
held from 12:30-2:00, and include theological training,
Bible surveys and so on. Also, before baptism, candidates
are taken through four or five of the Navigator Bible Study
books, and after baptism they try to take them through books
six to ten, with emphasis on leading others to Christ, leading Bible studies and the like. This preparation takes a
lot of time, it is usually done on a one-to-one basis, but
it is reported to have largely eliminated the "backdoor"
problem that many churches have. They also have a marriage
course they have worked out, with 12 hours (six sessions)
before, and several sessions after, marriage. These cover
very practical subjects such as how to budget one's money,
family devotions, and sexuality. In addition, the church
has a literature evangelism program going too.

The church also sponsors an English school in two different centers. They have a total of about 150 students.
Sixty-five students are enrolled at Koganei, 70 at Kodaira,
and 15 at an extension point in a Veterinary Institute. The
school year is divided into three quarters, classes meeting
once a week at different levels. At present they have 55
minutes of English conversation, and 10 minutes of Christian instruction using the Akira Hatori *"Yo no Hikari"*
[Light of the World] radio tapes. They say they are attempting to just "make friends," but already 14 of their members
have been a result of English classes.

The church's goals for 1975 are:

1. The beginning of an early morning or daytime
   prayer meeting
2. Two "personal witnessing" seminars (summer and
   winter)
3. S.S. Bible class for adults before worship time
4. Beginning of Men's Fellowship in church

5. Launching of new morning worship service in
    Kodaira (begun May)
6. Two new children's Bible classes in believers'
    homes
7. Two new adult preaching points in believers' homes
8. 10 baptisms
9. 10% increase in worship attendance
10. Pay back 1,500,000 yen [$5,000] on the church debt
11. Week of evangelism efforts in fall, when celebrat-
    ing 10 years (1975:1).

Compared to other churches that I am familiar with, this
one has had an excellent record of growth, mainly conversion
growth. Some of the factors that might help to account for
this would be the nucleus of Christians that was found in
the beginning, the "cell" approach, the use of homes, the
involvement of laymen, the careful baptismal and marriage
preparation, leadership training classes, multiple leadership, the supporting ministry of their English centers,
suitable facilities and so on, all used in some way or
other by the Holy Spirit. One wonders, though, now that
they have a "head teacher" and their own building and have
moved somewhat from a "cell-centered" program to a more
"church-centered" program, if the group will continue to
grow as rapidly as it has up till now. It is, of course,
hoped so. But future developments should be followed with
interest.

As said before, we are not suggesting here that this
particular congregation ought to be construed as a perfect
example for others to imitate. But it does seem to be
following a definite concept of the church, one which
involves both large and small groups. It also seems to
have a definite concept of the ministry, having several
leaders rather than just one. And while they do not have
an extensive leadership training program, they do see its
importance and are working at it. The church also has
clear goals for the future, and is involved in starting
another group in a nearby area. Being located in a large
city, their program and their problems would certainly be
somewhat different from those encountered by more rural
churches. Yet their example is commendable, and other congregations, rural or urban, can surely profit from studying
growing churches wherever they are.

Having looked at the different facets of church, ministry,
and training, we are now ready to consider what sort of
training program might be suitable for the Japan Mennonite
Christian Church Conference.

THE MAIN ELEMENTS OF SUCH A PROGRAM

On the basis of our study thus far, we may well ask at the outset, is there any one model which might help us to formulate a program to meet our own specific needs? As has been intimated throughout this study, the author believes there is, and that it is found in the recent efforts made in the area of Theological Education by Extension, better known as TEE.

We are at somewhat of a loss, however, to propose a specific program for the churches of the JMCCC. One reason is that I am of the conviction that before we can even begin thinking about such a program, we need to consider two prior questions: What kind of church do *we* want to have? What kind of leaders do *we* need for that kind of church? Only after we have wrestled with those two questions are we going to be in a position to talk about what kind of a training program *we* need to produce that kind of leaders. I also feel quite strongly that any decisions regarding a program will need to finally be made by those who will be responsible for carrying them out, and not by one person alone.

It is, in fact, rather presumptuous to even try to propose a program at all without first consulting our national brethren and having an answer to the two questions noted above. But going on the assumption that a decision made by the Church Conference back in 1969 is still valid -- that is, that we ought to move away from the "one-church-one-pastor" system toward a true "priesthood of believers," and that in order to do that some kind of training program is necessary -- I would like to at least try to suggest what some of the major elements of such a program might be.

First, it would seem that a small-scale extension program on the Bible college or Bible school level would be in order. This would be primarily for the training of lay leaders or lay pastors. Whether it would be for the whole church or not would have to be decided, but it should at least be made available to those laymen serving the churches now, and any additional potential lay leaders within the congregations. A congregation might well designate those it felt could benefit most from the training. Those trained might in turn be able to teach the rest. In any case, to conduct this kind of program the churches would need to tie up with a recognized school. The students would study by extension. They would continue to work as they studied. As they studied they would be able to put their learning to

work. They would receive credit from the school for work
completed, which could eventually lead to a degree. Provision might also be made for brief periods of study in
residence. But a program of this type would avoid many of
the problems we have had before such as an uncertain call,
financial support, undesirable influences, non-return, and
readjustment upon return.

Second, it would seem that a small-scale extension program on the seminary level would also be in place. This
would be primarily for those who are already pastors (or
missionaries). The training most of them have had at Bible
college has been helpful, but the majority have expressed a
desire to continue their education. Until now it has been
very difficult to do so. But in Japan, where education is
so important, it would seem that we should by all means try
to provide these pastors with the training they desire. As
in the case of the lay leaders, the pastors would also
receive credit for their work, which could eventually lead
to a degree on a higher level. They might also be able to
teach the courses they take back in their own churches. In
any event, this program too would have to be tied up with a
recognized seminary. It would be basically a continuing
education program, but might also incorporate short periods
of residence study. Those who complete the first program
over a period of years could naturally move on into the
second if they so desired.

Both of these programs would be vitally important. If
the first was offered without the second, it could be very
threatening to the pastors. If the second was offered without the first, it would only serve to widen the gap between
clergy and laity and make things worse. Ideally, we would
start both at the same time. And in addition to these two
programs, there would no doubt be a few who would occasionally go on to study at a residence school in order to become
Bible teachers, Christian education workers, or to specialize
in some other field. No distinction would be made between
those who studied in residence or by extension. But normally,
most education would take place locally. The churches would
recognize the students for study completed by gradually giving them greater responsibilities.

Even if these programs were on a small scale to begin
with, however, there are several matters that would need to
be worked out with regard to them. I can only mention them
briefly. As indicated earlier, the details of any program
will ultimately have to be worked out by those who would be
participating in it.

The first thing, of course, that would need to be done is to find schools which are willing to sponsor an extension program. There is no TEE in Japan at present. This means that we would need to find schools who are willing to launch out in a new venture. It may take some time to find the right school or schools. But education is extremely valued in Japan, and without being tied to a recognized institution, any program would lack for credibility.

A second thing that would have to be worked out is teachers. Since we are so far from the larger schools, it would likely not be possible for the professor to come every week. Perhaps the regular instructor would come only once a month or so, or at the beginning and end of a term, or some other arrangement would have to be made. Pastors or missionaries may be able to help out with the teaching too. In some cases, special seminars or concentrated courses might be offered. Or, as has already been suggested, it perhaps should be made possible for both laymen and pastors to spend some time in residence as well as in extension study. Again, there undoubtedly could be many options if schools are willing to cooperate.

A third thing that would have to be dealt with is the problem of materials. This was something we ran into in trying to start our own schools before. For extension it may be even more critical. There is a lot of good literature available in Japanese, so programmed texts may not be necessary. It may be possible to produce workbooks to go with regular textbooks and thus have semiprogrammed texts. Cassette tapes and video tapes or other modern means of communication might be useful too. But a way would need to be found to provide students with materials for home study.

A fourth thing that would need to be decided is the distribution of extension centers. Ideally, each of the ten churches would be an extension center in itself. But depending on teachers available and so on, it might be desirable to double up in two or three cases where churches are close to each other. It would also have to be decided whether there would be a regional center or not. And as we are quite a distance from the schools we would likely tie up with, it is hard to say exactly where the headquarters might be. But the program could look something like the accompanying diagram (Figure 5.5) with anywhere from four to 10 centers.

Figure 5.5

PROPOSAL FOR EXTENSION CENTERS
FOR THE JMCCC

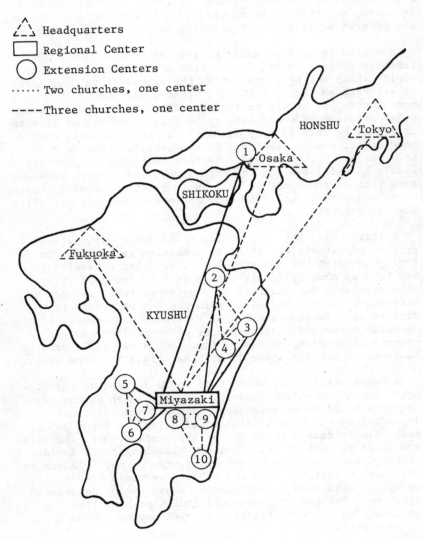

(Note: Honshu and Shikoku are not drawn to scale. Symbols
borrowed from Winter 1969:435.)

That is, if each of the churches served as an extension center, there would be 10. If in some cases (such as 3 and 4, 6 and 7, 8 and 9) where churches are geographically close to one another, they combined to have one center, there would be seven. Or if three churches in an area (such as 2-3-4, 5-6-7, 8-9-10) combined even further, there would be only four. As most of the churches are concentrated in the Miyazaki area, it is assumed that if a regional center was deemed necessary, perhaps Miyazaki City could serve as the place. The headquarters would probably be in one of the larger cities such as Fukuoka, Osaka, or Tokyo. There could no doubt be many other variations to this pattern, and it is proposed here merely as one possibility.

A fifth thing that would have to be considered is whether we worked by ourselves or cooperated with others. There may be other groups on Kyushu as well as elsewhere in Japan who are also interested in extension studies. Especially with regard to materials, it would seem only reasonable to try to cooperate wherever feasible. This is something that would have to be worked out together with other groups who wished to participate.

In any case, all we have been able to do here is sketch the broad outlines an extension program might take. The details would have to be spelled out on the basis of our concept of the church and its ministry, and by those who would be involved in this or any such training program. But in so far as possible, as we have tried to stress all along, the whole program should be of, by, and for the Japanese themselves.

6

A Realistic Vision

The primary interest of our study thus far has been in TEE,
and the possibilities it may have for Japan. More specifically, we have been interested in the feasibility of such a
program for the Japan Mennonite Christian Church Conference.
To determine whether it might be feasible or not we have
looked at the major problems which the Conference has faced
with regard to leadership training, and attempts that have
been made to resolve them. We have considered TEE as an
alternative, and tried to show how it might help solve some
of the problems that still remain. We have also reflected
on the concepts of the church and its ministry, on which
any training program should be based, and attempted to propose the basic outline of a program which could meet our
needs. Now we must try to pull all of these things together
and see how realistic this vision actually is when compared
with the reality of the Japanese situation.

VISION AND REALITY

When we came to Japan for the first time, in 1964, we
lived in Miyakonojo City, located in Miyazaki Prefecture in
southern Japan. It was a city of over 100,000 population.
As we were both from small towns in Ohio, towns of about a
thousand people or less, it seemed to us like quite a large
place. It was hard for us to understand why the Japanese
kept referring to it as the country, as if it were a small,
rural town. To us it was a big city. But the second time
we went to Japan, we began to see their point. We were
invited back to work in the same city, but before that, we
spent a year and a half living in Tokyo while we went to

language school. After that experience, when we went back
to Miyakonojo, our first thought was, "Boy, this really is
the country, isn't it!" Our perspective had changed, and we
began to see things more the way they really were. It made
me realize that things are not always what they seem. A
whole lot depends on our perspective, which may often be
more visionary than realistic.

As another illustration of this, after our language study
we were involved in a church planting ministry. We were
working with a young Japanese church and its pastor, and
together with them were trying to start a new group in an
unchurched area of the city. Before beginning our work, I
wrote down my vision for the kind of church that I felt was
needed there. It included several things such as a church
made up of small, radical fellowships (that is, "radical" in
the sense of being radically different from the ordinary
church structure); that we should think in terms of dozens
or even hundreds of such fellowships; that one pastor could
serve many groups; that the missionary should act primarily
as a catalyst; that we should operate on a team approach;
that lay training is essential; and that churches should
multiply by dividing (when they got too large to meet in a
house).

That was my original vision. But as the work developed,
and I compared my vision with the reality, it became clear
to me that in some respects I had been much too visionary,
especially in terms of the number of groups that could be
started. In the end I came to the conclusion that if we
could get two or three, or even just one such group started,
we would be doing well. I had a new appreciation for the
realities of the situation. I had a new appreciation of all
that had already been accomplished by those who had labored
before us. I also had a new appreciation of the words of
our Lord, "apart from me you can do nothing" (John 15:5).

I sometimes think, though, that God gives us visions,
even if they are not very realistic, just to get us moving.
In the case of our work, for instance, if God had not given
us a vision of what we felt a church ought to be like, we
probably would have never even given it a try. And when we
first began working, I remember not only asking the Lord to
help us begin that kind of church, but to help us do it in
three years (since that was all the time we had before we
were due for furlough). We wanted to be optimistic. The
pastor we were working with, on the other hand, suggested
that if we could have even one or two solid Christians by

the time we left we would be doing well. At the time I
thought he was being rather pessimistic, but later I saw
that he was in fact simply being realistic. He knew the
situation much better than we did. The Lord began to say
to me, "It usually takes longer than three years to plant a
church in Japan. Just hang in there and be faithful!" The
vision may be one thing. The reality may be quite another.

Now while vision and reality may not always be one and
the same, I do not want to give the impression that vision
is unimportant. In fact, just the opposite is true. It is
extremely important, for as the Bible says, "Where there is
no vision, the people perish" (Proverbs 29:18a, KJV). While
we need realism, we also need vision. God gives different
visions to different people in different places. In Korea,
for example, the Southern Presbyterians have had a vision of
planting a Christian church within walking distance (4 km.)
of every group of 100 houses. After a seven-year program of
systematic church planting, that goal has almost been
reached in one area, and they are beginning to move into
other areas to extend the pattern (Rader 1973:311). In
Taiwan, the Presbyterian Church had a vision for a 10-year
"Double the Church Movement." As the result of careful
planning and hard work, the number of churches increased
from 400 in 1954 to 800 in 1964 (Covell and Wagner 1971:21).
In the Philippines, God gave a vision of starting 10,000
home Bible studies as part of the "Christ the Only Way"
movement. These were so successful from the start that the
goal was soon doubled to 20,000 home Bible studies (Wagner
1972:3)! God gives people visions. He helps them to carry
them out. We need visions, while at the same time we must
take into consideration the realities of the situation.

Japan, of course, is not Korea or Taiwan or the
Philippines. Japan is Japan. Its problems are unique. But
so are its possibilities. This is especially true of TEE.
The Japanese are a highly educated people. There are many
fine theological schools in Japan with capable faculties.
There is said to be a higher percentage of trained pastors
per members here than in any other country in the world
(Drummond 1961:456). But there is much more potential in
the churches which needs to be released in a new way. More
than anything else, I am confident that TEE could help bring
it about.

I believe then that if we have a vision for it, the
possibility of TEE being successful in Japan is realistic.
Without a vision, however, if we only look at the realities,

it could appear to be rather difficult. But churches here as elsewhere need to have both a visionary and a realistic perspective. What is being suggested is that in thinking about a training program for the JMCCC or other churches, we should try to keep vision and reality together. We must think big in terms of what we feel ought to be done. We must think small in terms of how we might begin doing it. Perhaps even before that, the first thing we need to do is ask ourselves once again, should something like the program outlined in Chapter 5 really be done? Is it needed?

SHOULD IT BE DONE?

In deciding whether it should be done or not, we need to think in terms of what is best for both churches and schools. As for the churches, when Dr. Donald McGavran visited Japan in 1968, he shared his conviction that "The laymen is [*sic*] the untapped wealth of the Churches of Japan" (1968:20). Our study would confirm that, for as we have seen, there are many potential lay leaders within our own churches in addition to those already serving, but they have not been trained. The odds are that they will not be trained in the future either without something like TEE. It is perhaps the only way that the leadership potential within the churches is going to be released. As Donald Hoke has stated, he believes that TEE is "the key to unlocking the power of the laymen here" (Hoke 1975b:3). Indeed, it may be just that.

But, as we have also shown, it can be every bit as useful in providing those who are already pastors with the advanced training they desire. In addition, thinking in terms of outreach, without more leaders expansion will be difficult if not impossible. So in terms of providing adequate leadership for small churches, in terms of continuing education, and also in terms of reaching out, it is a method that has great potential. It has potential not only in increasing the quantity and quality of leaders in rural churches, but in urban ones as well.

As far as schools go, this is an area with which I personally am not very well acquainted. All I can do is go by what others have said or written. And if what a person like Akira Demura says about the crisis in theological education in Japan is true, then many schools are in big trouble. He notes that "theological education in this country ... is facing an acute crisis," and goes on to explain that

> One tangible sign of this crisis is the marked
> decline in enrollment in almost all of the theological

schools, whether formally accredited by the Ministry of
Education or not. Kwansei Gakuin School of Theology,
for example, which is one of the three accredited
Kyodan-related seminaries with graduate programs, last
spring [1972] could admit only two students to its freshman class although, of course, there were more applicants. And Seinan Gakuin, affiliated with the Southern
Baptist Church and with a system that is somewhat different from other schools, reportedly does not have any
students in its first-year class. Even Tokyo Union
Theological Seminary admitted only seven freshmen whereas
up until some ten years ago its freshman class used to
have nearly thirty students (1973:117).

In addition, he maintains that Christian educators are also
concerned about the quality and qualifications of theological students. A clear-cut objective, too, seems to have dis-
appeared from theological education, and because of the
diversification of patterns and types of Christian ministry,
it is hard to define precisely the role of a minister. Much
of the theological curriculum is also said to be rather
"medieval" in its nature and objective, and that unfortunately it is hard for theological educators to easily change
their frame of thought.

As a result, there are some schools such as the Doshisha
School of Theology, which have "liberated" admission requirements and no longer require students to submit proof of
membership in a church, a baptismal certificate, or a
recommendation from a pastor. Thus almost anyone who passes
the stiff entrance examinations can enter, although it is
said applicants are carefully screened in an interview with
some of the faculty. The Department of Christian Studies at
Rikkyo University is even more "progressive," and is said to
differ little from departments of religious studies in the
secular universities. Partly as a result of this, Rikkyo has
many times more applicants than other institutions. Not
only lack of students, but finances are also a serious problem for many schools. Because of this, the Kanto Gakuin,
one of the more famous schools in Japan, decided in 1973 to
discontinue its theological school, the Kanto Gakuin School
of Theology. A short time later, another famous school,
Aoyama Gakuin University, made a decision to suspend admis-
sions to its Department of Theology on both the graduate and
undergraduate levels (Demura 1973:117-118).

In a follow-up article on the closing of seminaries, however, Takaaki Aikawa points out that most of the teachers

and students in those schools were not Christians anyway,
and that perhaps we should not lament their passing in that
there are still far too many schools for the number of
Japanese Protestants. He says, too, that to reopen seminaries in those two universities would be next to impossible,
and that to make Tokyo Union Theological Seminary a real
"union" seminary is also almost too much to expect (because
of differences between denominations). In wondering what to
do about it, he concludes that the current seminary situation is best described by the Japanese expression *anchū
mosaku*, "groping about in the dark" (1974:110).

The fact that theological schools face some very serious
problems is also reinforced by the summary statement on
theological education in Japan made for the International
Congress on World Evangelization held in Lausanne, Switzerland, in 1974. In the profile of Christianity in Japan,
prepared for the Congress, it is reported that

> There are more than 40 Bible schools and seminaries
> in Japan. Recent enrollment is down by 40% in many,
> reflecting a drop from the 1,400 previously recorded.
> Five of the schools have closed because of lack of
> students (ICWE 1974a:4).

This perhaps is not as shocking to those of us who have been
working in Japan as to those who have not. Many of us are
undoubtedly familiar with schools which have almost as many
faculty as students, or a very high faculty-student ratio.
There are many small Bible schools in Japan which are having
a hard time of it. But the striking thing here is that now
it is not only the small schools which are in trouble. So
are the big ones.

The situation makes one wonder if some kind of an extension program might not bring new life not only to the
churches, but to the schools as well. It has happened in
other countries, and it would not be surprising if schools
in Japan could also easily double or triple their enrollments with a program such as this, with little additional
expense. It may be just what they need. Rather than be a
threat to them, it could be one of the greatest things that
has happened in a long time. Theological education taking
place right in the churches could be exciting! The problem
is not so much that people are not interested in theological
education, but that in many cases they cannot go to the
schools even if they want to. As a result, the schools
suffer and the churches suffer. And after all, is not the

purpose of theological education to serve the church? When
it begins to do that, rather than just maintain itself, a
lot of good things could happen.

Actually, when one stops to think about it, we are dealing
with a very complicated problem here, and I do not feel the
blame can be placed entirely on either the churches or the
schools. It must be shared by both. That is, as pointed
out in the last chapter, many of the structures of both
church and school have been imported. They were brought
from other places and were adapted to Japan. But while they
may have been useful when they were first brought here, they
probably have undergone little change. Many of them are now
outdated, and need to be reworked. The fact that this is so
is sometimes hard to see when you are immersed in a situation,
but when Dutch churchman Hendrik Kraemer came to Japan in
1960, he suggested that Japanese church structures were 80
years behind!

> ... Dr. Kraemer emphasized his conviction that the
> Japanese Church, while it constituted one of the most
> creative factors in the life of the nation sixty to
> eighty years ago, and was then a culturally explosive
> element which gave moral seriousness and new vision
> in human relations, had now become tightly bound to
> the pattern of structure, conceptions and forms which
> were developed at that time. The Japanese Church,
> while priding itself on its modernity over against the
> remnants of feudal thought and practice still widely
> existant in the nation, was in fact modern only with
> the modernity of eighty years ago (Drummond 1961:452).

Whether churches (and schools) in Japan are actually
that far behind is not for me to say. There are many things
in the churches and theological schools of the West that
also need to be reexamined. Western schools and churches
need updating in many ways too. And we must not forget that
many of the structures being followed in Japan today originally came from the West, and that is part of the problem.
But the point to be made here is that it is not just the
schools which are to blame for the situation. How can they
change unless churches change? On the other hand, how can
churches change unless seminaries change? It would seem
that schools are simply trying to provide the kind of
leaders they feel the average church wants. So the problem
is mutual. But as we have suggested, our training program
ought to be based not on tradition, but on our concept of
the ministry, which in turn should be based on our concept
of the church.

Someone has said, "if the ministry of the Church requires to be reshaped, the only way this can effectively be done is by the refashioning of theological education" (W.C.C. 1965: 70). But how can theological education be reshaped without the consent of the churches? Do not the churches also have a responsibility here? If the churches feel they need a different sort of ministry, should they not say to the schools, "This is the kind of leaders we need. Can you help us produce this kind of leader?" If the churches would do that, it would be easier for the Bible schools and seminaries to change. Or, on the other hand, schools should also be asking the churches, "What kind of leaders do you need? What kind of leaders do you want us to try to produce? How can we do a better job?" There needs to be constant dialogue on this matter if any change is going to come about.

At a deeper level, of course, are the problems associated with a professional ministry. Extension expert Ross Kinsler reminds us of this, saying, "the ministry is not fundamentally a profession; it is a function of the body of believers" (1978:14). But he goes on to assert that too often the seminaries "have created a profession of the ministry. So the church has remained as a sleeping giant" (1978:24). He challenges churches as well as seminaries to do some serious reflecting on the situation, and rightly so. For without a willingness to change on the part of the churches, the schools hands are tied. Without a willingness to change on the part of the schools, the churches cannot do much either. A much greater degree of consultation and cooperation is called for.

As we consider this matter of whether TEE should be initiated in Japan or not, there is one other important factor which ought to be kept in mind and that is the future. Granted that at present only about 1 percent of the population is Christian, but what would happen if revival were to break out. If revival came to those who already profess to be Christians, and awakening to many of those who are not, would the churches be able to handle all the newcomers? Would the schools be able to train sufficient leaders quickly to care for them? Or might they be lost to the Church because churches and schools were not ready.

This may sound like a very hypothetical situation to some, but revival has come to Japan in the past. Charles W. Iglehart, in his book *A Century of Protestant Christianity in Japan*, notes that in the period of rapid growth from 1882-1889, church membership increased rapidly. "In seven

years," he reports, "the adult membership rose from a little
over four thousand to thirty thousand" (1959:76). The number of churches, ministers, and evangelists also increased,
but not in as great a proportion as the membership. Another
writer, Tetsunao Yamamori, in his book *Church Growth in
Japan*, states that in one denomination, the Japan Holiness
Church, communicant membership climbed rapidly from about
3,000 in 1925 to almost 20,000 by 1932 (1974:118). That is
well over 500 percent in seven short years!

To be sure, this was not a nationwide phenomenon. But as
Eric Gosden points out in an article on "Revival," "While
there has been no nation-wide movement of the Spirit of God,
there have been local movements." He goes on to declare
that "We still await the day when the Holy Spirit so works
throughout the nation, that it is manifestly demonstrated
that God is One and the Living God," and asks, "Are conditions ripe for this?" (1974:43). His answer, on the basis
of a detailed study, is that

> ... we may hold a strong conviction that God will
> work in Japan. Add to the number of existing Chris-
> tians the tens of thousands who have attended mission
> schools, been to church, attended Bible classes, and
> there is a tremendous potential upon which the Holy
> Spirit can work. Once revived, Christians will move
> out in witnessing and evangelism and all Japan can be
> moved (1974:48).

If such events have happened before, what makes us think
they might not happen again? Would it not be wise to at
least try to anticipate what might take place in the event
of revival, to pray for it, and seek to prepare for it?
Even as recently as the period from after World War II until
about 1960, many churches in Japan experienced quite rapid
growth compared to now. (For more details, see for example
"Brief Survey of Mission History," Ariga, 1973.)

The Mennonite churches in Japan, like many other churches,
are still small. And yet, even the Mennonites have enjoyed
fantastic growth in some other parts of the world in the
last decade or two. Take Indonesia, for instance. During
the first 100 years of their existence, the Mennonite
churches in the Muria area experienced considerable persecution, and as of 1950 the total baptized membership was still
only about 2,000. But by 1969, only 19 years later, it had
reached approximately 20,000, or 10 times as many (Shenk
1973:28)! Much of this growth is reported to have taken
place in the 1960s.

An interesting sidelight here is a comment made 20 years ago by a Mennonite missionary in Columbia to one in Japan. In his letter he says, "It seems as if you are going the pace of a rabbit and we the pace of a turtle" (Stucky 1958:1). At the time that was no doubt true. Things were going much better in Japan than in Columbia. Today the situation is somewhat reversed, and things seem to be moving much faster in Columbia than in Japan. But what if Japan would open again?

What would happen if the Mennonite churches in Japan suddenly showed a tenfold increase, as in Indonesia? Suppose the Japan Mennonite Church Conference grew from 600 to 6,000 in the next 10 years or so. Would churches be able to handle all the people? What part would schools play in training the new converts? How could it best be done? Surely the present leaders could not begin to do it all. But if by TEE the potential leaders who are already within the churches were trained, if revival should come, as we hope and pray it will, not only would there be many more leaders available to help conserve the increase, but it would make it possible to train many more new ones besides. If there were always an adequate number of trained leaders, it would make even further unlimited expansion possible. "Hindsight is always better than foresight," we say, but surely the time to get ready is now.

I cannot speak for other churches or denominations, but reflecting on our own situation, it does not seem to me there is any question as to whether something like TEE is needed or not. As we have shown, we are already short of trained leaders. Some of our present leaders feel inadequately prepared. Our expansion is severely limited because of a lack of leaders. Even apart from the possibility of revival coming to Japan, in so many ways something new is called for in terms of tapping the potential already available within the churches. With enrollments dropping and schools closing, is it not time that we look at some of the basic questions again? Church, ministry, and training are three of them. And if we are really honest with ourselves, I believe it will become obvious, if it is not already, that some drastic measures are called for if the churches are to be the Church, and the schools to serve the church. As has been well put, "Change may be difficult; the status quo is impossible."

But assuming then that some changes are in order, and that TEE may be able to make a contribution, can it be done? That is, even if we feel it should, could it? Or are there some unsurmountable obstacles in the way?

COULD IT BE DONE?

Whether TEE could be done or not may depend to a large
degree on what we would try to do with it. If perchance we
could start over from scratch, we would likely want to try
to do many things differently. As James F. Hopewell,
Director of the Theological Education Fund, contends,

> If we faced a *tabula rasa* situation in which noth-
> ing was known about the form and function of seminaries
> as they now exist, we probably would not create in
> that void a training structure that would resemble
> the present theological school (1967:158).

But that is a big "if." If we could start completely over,
that would be one thing. But the fact is, with a multitude
of schools already in existence, that would be next to
impossible to do. In planting new churches, we might to
some extent be able to alter the structure to conform more
with our ideals. But with schools which have existed for a
long time already, it would no doubt be much more difficult
to change completely. And it might not even be desirable,
as surely there are many good things we can learn from the
schools that already exist.

Our concern here really is not with how to dismantle the
schools there are, but with how to make them more effective.
As we have said before, TEE is not out to destroy. It is
not an attempt to supplant, but rather to supplement what is
being done already. Indeed, as noted elsewhere, it would be
impossible for TEE as we have defined it to function without
residential schools. TEE is but a geographical extension of
the program of a recognized theological school. It may, of
course, be necessary in some cases to modify the program or
course content in some ways to meet the needs of the
churches. But basically it is a way of starting where we
are, with what we have, in an attempt to make it more as we
would like it to be.

Theological schools in Japan have for the most part
traditionally been residential. But as has been pointed out
in this study, there are now schools in many parts of the
world which operate both residential and extension programs.
While there would not need to be any attempt to duplicate
exactly what is being done in other countries, surely there
is much we could gain from them. In a sense, it would be
another imported pattern, just like the present one is.
Yet even in the United States, while it did not begin there,
many schools have been using extension programs effectively.

Fuller Theological Seminary in Pasadena, California, for example, since 1973 has had Extension Centers in the San Francisco area, Seattle, and other cities along the West Coast, as well as in the Los Angeles area where the school is located. It is a full-fledged theological program, and students, mostly laymen, can take up to the equivalent of a full year in residence (12 courses) by extension. In addition to the theological instruction, the program also includes supervised on-the-job training in ministry, and opportunities to experience and create "koinonia" or real Christian fellowship. Those who finish the program can either go on to complete their seminary study in residence, or receive a "Certificate of Graduate Studies in Ministry" (Goddard n.d.:1). It normally would take at least two years' time to complete the program, but it is felt to be an effective way of clarifying a person's call as well as preparing people for a greater ministry. As of 1977, an M.A. in theology can also be earned at two of the extension locations by completing the 24 courses necessary for that degree.

But while many schools like Fuller are now offering extension studies, one thing that most people perhaps are not aware of is that Fuller's first "extension program" was actually in Japan! It began, in fact, way back in 1962, one year before TEE even got started in Guatemala. To be sure, it was only a summer program and on a much smaller scale. Nevertheless, in an article entitled "Fuller Summer Seminary," we can read the details concerning the third summer session (1964) of the Japan branch of Fuller Theological Seminary (Hoke 1963c:25). According to the article, the summer school was to be held for about two weeks from the middle of July on the campus of the Karuizawa Bible Institute at Karuizawa, Nagano Prefecture. It goes on to say that

> Two divisions are held simultaneously: a college-level division, and a seminary-level division. Qualified applicants in the seminary-level division are granted full transfer credits to the Fuller Theological Seminary in the United States, upon successful completion of the courses here (1963c:25).

The curriculum for the summer was to include courses on "The Doctrine of God," "The History of the Doctrine of the Person of Christ," "Philosophy of Education," "New Testament Introduction," and "Lectures in Practical Theology" in the seminary division. The Bible school division was to have courses in "Barthianism," "The Life and Ministry of Paul," "Miracles," "Matthew," and "The Prison Epistles of Paul."

There were a couple of foreign lecturers scheduled for the
sessions, such as Dr. R. Kenneth Kantzer and Dr. George
Peters, although the program was directed in Japan by Dr.
Hideo Aoki. Several of the courses were also to be taught
by Japanese or foreign instructors from a Japanese Bible
school or seminary. The courses were open to ministers of
any denomination. There were a number of scholarships
available, and it was anticipated that there would be a
capacity enrollment of 80 students.

The above program, as indicated, grew out of Fuller
Seminary's Summer School Program. But Fuller Seminary's
summer program in turn had grown out of the Winona Lake
School of Theology (WLST), Winona Lake, Indiana. That is,
back in the early 1960s, Fuller did not have a summer program of its own, so the two merged and the Winona Lake
School's summer session (continuing education) program
became Fuller's official summer program. WLST had already
operated for a few years previous to this. After the merger,
Fuller Seminary then launched a summer program in Japan,
providing a building, lecturers and so on. But according to
Dr. John Huffman Sr., who was president of the Winona Lake
School at the time of the merger and who became the director
of the Fuller Summer School Program, while there was at
least one American scholar in Japan for the sessions each
year, an attempt was made to also keep the program as
indigenous as possible. One problem, he said however, was
that there were few good books available. Another was that
there was not much of an evangelical program in Japan at
the time. But in spite of such problems, courses were
offered in various ways -- in English, for those who could
handle it, and in Japanese, or translated into Japanese,
for those who could not (Huffman 1975).

One of the values of the program he felt is that it gave
the students a taste of real seminary study. It only
functioned for several years, but it was a full-fledged
seminary program for which students who completed the work
could receive full credit. Dr. Huffman asserted that "as
an experiment it was reasonably successful." Why then did
it stop? Why did it not continue? The main reason, he
recalled, is because "Fuller's Summer School Program
reverted back to the Winona Lake School of Theology." There
may also be the fact that there came to be more and better
evangelical schools in Japan. But at any rate, we can
rightfully say that extension has been done in Japan
already, and done successfully. In that sense, it is
nothing new. If it can be done from overseas, surely there

is every good reason to believe it could be done at home as
well.

In our look at schools in Japan, we observed that there
are none which have genuine TEE programs according to our
definition of it as *the geographical extension of the program of a recognized theological training institution.* But
while that may be true, we did see that the Covenant Seminary
in Tokyo, for instance, has been experimenting with something
similar to it in the form of morning and evening classes for
laymen. It differs from TEE though in that it is not a geographical extension of the school.

We also saw that one school in particular, the Eastern
Hokkaido Bible School, has many of the characteristics of a
TEE program. The teacher goes to his students in several
different centers. Classes are offered on various levels.
The student gets credit for work completed. One big
difference, however, from TEE, is that the program is not
connected with a recognized institution (that is, an institution which is recognized at least in theological circles,
even if not fully recognized by the government). But if
there would be some recognized schools which would be willing to recognize such a program or the programs of many
other small Bible schools scattered throughout the country,
one would think that transition to an authentic TEE program
could be made fairly easily. In areas where there are no
such schools, it might take more time to get started. But
hopefully, in either case, whether starting from scratch or
with programs which already exist, there would be recognized
schools willing to experiment with it for their own sake as
well as for the benefit of the churches.

My own interest in something like TEE began back in 1966,
when I first sensed a need for some sort of Bible training
program for the Mennonite churches in Kyushu. At the time
it seemed to me that if we were to ever start a training
program, there were several characteristics which it ought
to have. Looking back at what I wrote down then it should
be Biblical, academic, evangelical, interdenominational, and
headed by a Japanese. That was how I felt at the time, and
personally, I was interested in the possibility of teaching
in such a program. But when I shared this vision with the
pastors and churches, they said they did not feel the need
for a Bible school yet. It was not until about three years
later that they decided to start a school of their own, but
as we have seen, that never got off the ground.

In any event, a year or two after being given a vision
for this I had the privilege of studying at Fuller Seminary's
School of World Mission, and taking a course entitled
"Training the Ministry" from Dr. Ralph Winter. That was my
first exposure to TEE and, needless to say, I was excited
about it. Here, I was convinced, was the kind of program
that could help meet the needs of churches in Japan, and
provide all of the qualities a training program ought to
have. There are undoubtedly other characteristics one could
mention, but as I reflect on those that occurred to me, I
still feel they are valid, although of the five perhaps the
hardest one to make a reality would be the "interdenominational" part.

If the program was tied up with an interdenominational
Bible school or seminary, it would naturally in a certain
sense be interdenominational already. But in terms of something which would actually be interdenominational on a local
level, which would bring Christians together for serious
study, this might take some doing. Whether it could be done
or not is premature to say. Yet I do believe it would
definitely be worth working toward as an ideal. The answers
to some of the questions on the church, pastor, and missionary questionnaires may give us a better idea of how
realistic such a proposal might be.

As far as the churches go, when asked if they ever got
together with other Mennonite churches for fellowship, five
said Yes, four No, and one did not reply. As to how often
they have done so, in most cases it was only "once" or
"twice," although in one case it was "five or six times."
The responses may reflect to some extent the geographical
distance between congregations, but from the questionnaires
alone that is hard to know. Be that as it may, there does
seem to be at least a little inter-Mennonite church fellowship.

When it comes to fellowshipping with non-Mennonite
churches, two of them said Yes, seven said No, and one did
not answer. One of them who has said they have done it
only once. Another said they have done so about six times.
So there also appears to be a little interchange with non-
Mennonite congregations as well, although it is very limited
and presumably only for fellowship. In response to whether
they have had a city Christmas program with other churches,
only two of them said Yes. Eight said No. Some have done
so before, but for various reasons have discontinued doing
so. With regard to the World Day of Prayer, the response

was a little more positive. Five of the churches said they
do get together with other churches for that occasion. Four
said No. One did not answer. But if it is difficult to get
cooperation among churches for something like a "city
Christmas," one wonders if it would be possible in something
like TEE. Of course, it would be only for those who were
interested, and as it would involve a third party (the sponsoring institution) so to speak, perhaps it could work. But
this is something that would have to be worked out in relationship with the school and other local churches.

In reply to a question regarding whether they participated in a city pastors' meeting or not, five of the
Mennonite pastors said Yes. One of them said No. Those who
meet say they do so "once a month" or "every other month."
In reply to the same question, four of the missionaries said
Yes; nine, No. They also seem to meet for the most part
"every other month," or in one case, only two or three times
a year. One of the missionary wives also mentioned that she
meets with the other pastors' wives who get together once a
year. In other words, there does seem to be at least some
sharing among the leaders of the churches at this kind of
more informal gathering.

As to whether TEE could be done, if desirable, as we have
tried to indicate, the answer would seem to be in the affirmative. As recounted, it has in fact already been done in
the past from overseas in a small way. It is also being
done to some degree today in a limited way, even though
according to our definition it ought not to be classified as
a genuine TEE program. But suggesting that it could be done
does not mean that there would not be any problems along the
way. As noted before, there would be such matters as sponsoring schools, extension centers, teachers, materials,
cooperation with other churches and so on which would all
have to be worked out. Yet the Japanese are a creative
people, and surely under the guidance of the Holy Spirit
they could find ways to solve these various problems.
Indeed, perhaps they should be seen as challenges rather
than problems. As George Bernard Shaw once put it,

Some men see things as they are and say, "why?"
I dream of things that never were and say, "why not?"

If then TEE is something that ought to be done, and
seemingly could be done, the next question to consider is
how can it be done? What would it take to make something
like this not just a vision but a reality?

HOW IT COULD BE DONE

In order for a program like TEE to work, the first thing
that is needed is to believe that it can be done. If we
lack confidence that it can be done, the chances of its
being successful are small. Confidence leads to success,
and we need to be convinced that there is a way to do it.
This does not mean that we should naively assume there will
be no problems involved in doing it. We have run into problems before in trying to establish our own schools, and
there is certainly no guarantee that there would not be
problems in starting a program like TEE. In fact, as we
have brought out repeatedly, there are certain matters that
would have to be resolved if the program is to be successful.
But while there may be problems, we should not be so pessimistic as to believe that they cannot be solved. Anything
worthwhile doing usually involves some hurdles. But what is
called for first of all is an optimistic spirit, taking into
consideration the realities of the situation, and a conviction that it can be done. As we have tried to indicate,
there is every reason to believe that it can be done if
given a fair trial.

Second, if TEE is going to work in Japan, we need to be
agreed that it ought to be done. This is basically a
matter of consensus. If we really believe that it can be
done and must be done, then it could be done if we are
totally committed to it. But we will have to be willing to
follow through on our conviction. Back in 1963, for example,
when the school that was proposed did not have the full
support of the pastors and churches, it was simply dropped
rather than trying to work through the problems. Or again,
in 1970, when the committee that was responsible to make
preparations for the opening of a Bible school ran into
problems such as materials and the like, it was again simply
dropped rather than trying to work it through. And also,
especially in this latter case, part of the failure no
doubt lay in the fact that hardly any money had been
budgeted for the school, with the result that no one could
be released to devote most of their time to it, and that
certainly did not help matters any. If TEE is going to be
done, and be successful, we will not only have to agree on
the fact that it must be done, we will also have to "put our
money where our mouth is." We will have to give it priority.
We will have to give it the support it deserves both in
terms of finances and personnel.

Related to all of this is an interesting article in the
Harvard Business Review on "What We Can Learn From Japanese

Management." In that article, Peter F. Drucker notes that one of the most important concerns of top management is making effective decisions, but goes on to make the observation that

> ... the Westerner and the Japanese mean something different when they talk of "making a decision." With us in the West, all the emphasis is on the *answer* to the question. ... To the Japanese, however, the important element in decision making is *defining the question*. The important and crucial steps are to decide whether there is a need for a decision and what the decision is about. And it is in this step that the Japanese aim at attaining "consensus." Indeed, it is this step that, to the Japanese, is the essence of the decision. The answer to the question (what the West considers *the* decision) follows its definition.

> ... Thus the whole process is focused on finding out what the decision is really about, not what the decision should be. Its result is a meeting of the minds that there is (or is not) a need for a change in behavior (1971:111).

Now if what Drucker says is true, that a decision in Japan may often be only the definition of the question, and not actually a decision to do something about it, might this not in some measure be helpful in explaining what happened to the proposed Bible school in 1970? According to the record, a "decision" had been made in 1969 to start such a school. But might it not be possible that that decision was more a definition of the problem or of the need for a school rather than a decision to actually go ahead with one. If so, that may explain partially at least why the whole thing was dropped so suddenly when there were some problems. Perhaps it was not felt that the decision was binding enough to have to be followed up on.

But there is another factor at work too, which Drucker touches on when he points out that "Only when all of the people who will have to carry out the agreement have come together on the need to make a decision will the decision be made to go ahead" (1971:112). In the case we are dealing with here, the decision to start a school had been made by the Conference. There was a consensus of opinion. A committee was appointed to begin making preparations to carry out the decision. But, as we saw before, there were some differences of opinion within the committee, and as a

result they could not make the extra decisions necessary to
actually carry out the earlier decision made by the Conference. In other words, even though a so-called "decision"
was made at the conference level, a number of additional
decisions were called for in order to carry out the original
decision, and when they were not made the whole thing
naturally fell through. And as there was no accountability
built into the system, or what little accountability there
should have been (to at least the Conference Executive
Committee) was not followed through on either, it is not
surprising that the project ended the way it did.

Whether this is in fact more or less what happened in
that case may be questioned by some, but could it not be
that one of the greatest weaknesses in the decision of 1969
is that it may not have been so much a decision to really do
something as it was a definition of the problem. As a
result there was not much follow through which may also
indicate some serious weaknesses in the structure of the
conference setup itself, namely, a lack of power to actually
carry out what it decides. In any event, whether some of
the previous Conference decisions have been merely a definition of the problem rather than an actual decision to do
something may be debatable. But if it is decided to go
ahead with some kind of a TEE program, we are going to have
to do more than just define the problem. We are going to
have to work out an actual plan whereby our decision can be
carried out. Accountability will also have to somehow be
built into the system. In short, we will need to know not
only what we want to do and how we are going to do it, but
also how we are getting along so we can modify our program
if necessary and not end up as before. As educator Kenneth
B. Mulholland has brought out, even with TEE, it may be
necessary to make some "in-flight corrections" (1976:112).

In addition then to believing it can be done, and must be
done, thirdly, we need to begin making plans to do it. This
involves a need for establishing goals. Many of the local
churches are doing this already. For example, in response
to a question as to what their goal was as a church for the
year 1974, there were various replies. Some of them were
very specific, such as "three or more baptisms"; "each one
win one to Christ"; "attendance of 35-40 at worship, 15 at
prayer meeting, 50 at Sunday school, and 15 baptisms";
"pray for five baptisms this year, attend prayer meeting and
offer earnest prayer, holding a special evangelistic meeting
in fall and for that purpose do preparation evangelism each
month, have interest in and pray for the bookstore work."

Other replies were less specific, like "become a praying church, become counselors to each other, become trained, Spirit-filled witnesses, each one win one to Christ"; "'Bear one another's burdens, and so fulfill the law of Christ' (Gal. 6:2), deepen our fellowship through four or five spiritual retreats during the year, produce as many baptisms as possible." Still others were quite general, such as "start some home meetings"; "everyone join their hearts together in witnessing for Christ"; "obedience to the Holy Spirit's promptings." One of the churches had not set any goal, saying that "nothing in particular was decided on."

When it comes to goals, it seems to be somewhat easier to establish them on a local level than as a Conference, although as we have seen even at the local level they are not always so clearly defined. Whether these various goals were reached or not is hard to say. But perhaps even more important than that is whether one can tell *if* a goal has been reached. In other words, when one has a general goal, how do you know whether you have reached it or not? The more specific the goal, the easier it is to measure whether it is being realized or not. That is, goals should be both realistic and realizable. They should also be measurable.

In 1967, for instance, when the churches set a goal of 60 baptisms for 1968, it proved to be both realistic and realizable. To have set a figure of 6 or 600 would not have been realistic. The figure was modest as it was based on past experience, but as it was specific, it was also measurable. It was a good goal. Whether the goals listed above were realistic or not is for each church to judge. But few of them would appear to be measurable, which makes evaluation difficult, if not impossible. It is naturally safer to set a vague goal, because there is no danger of losing face if you do not happen to reach it. It is risky to set specific goals because we are not always sure if we can reach them or not, but at least then you know if you are getting anywhere, and if not, there is a greater possibility of remedying what is wrong.

On the Church Conference level, as suggested, it appears to be even much more difficult to establish really concrete goals. This is revealed vividly in an article entitled "Goals Set in Taiwan and Japan," which was published in *The Mennonite*, the General Conference paper. In 1972, the General Conference Mennonite Church had a Goals, Priorities, and Strategy (GPS) Conference in Chicago, and this article dealt with follow-up conferences in Taiwan and Japan which

were attended by pastors, laymen, and missionaries. As the
result of the "mini-GPS" conference in Taiwan in November
that year, it was reported that the following ten-year goals
were established:

1. Increase membership to 1,500. Present membership
    is 600.
2. Establish five new churches.
3. Have every member tithe.
4. Have all churches financially independent of North
    America. Six now are.
5. Hold a Sunday school teachers' training workshop
    every year.
6. Have 300 totally Christian households, compared to
    120 now.
7. Purchase a building for the Mana Bookstore in
    Hwalien.
8. Find lost members and bring them back into the
    fellowship of the church.
9. Emphasize lay leadership training.
10. Send at least one new ministerial student to
    seminary each year (GCMC 1973:54).

From this, one can see that the Taiwanese churches spelled
out their goals quite specifically. But what about Japan?
What goals were set there? Well, perhaps the title of the
article is somewhat misleading, because it does not report
on any goals being set in Japan. It does, however, refer
to a two-day seminar that was held, at which the author was
also present. Yet, while there was a lot of vigorous discussion at the meetings, nothing concrete ever came out of
it, which is why there were no goals to report. No goals
were set, even though that apparently was one of the main
reasons for getting together.

The article goes on to report that the secretary of
General Conference Mennonite mission work in Asia, who also
attended the seminar, said that

> The most important thing we did in Japan was to
> establish good relationships with the pastors and
> church leaders. We found that we had given the impres-
> sion that Newton [Kansas] was the headquarters of the
> Kyushu [now Japan] Church Conference. But we told
> them that this was not so and that we want to respect
> their autonomy and maintain a brotherhood relation-
> ship (1973:54).

So rather than establishing goals, the emphasis seems to have shifted to establishing good relationships, which, of course, is important also. And the fact that no goals were set may reflect the fact that there were still a number of unresolved tensions which hindered the decision-making process. It may also reflect on a difference between Japanese and Taiwanese attitudes toward setting goals. But if we are going to move forward with TEE or church planting or whatever it is, we are going to have to dare to set some goals. Specific goals. Goals that are realistic, realizable, and measurable.

It is interesting to note now, several years after the above goals were set in Taiwan, how they are doing in at least one area. One of their goals, as you remember, was to establish five new churches by 1982. As of September, 1976, another article in *The Mennonite* reported that this goal had already been met, and the group (FOMCIT) had decided to add two more churches to their original goal (GCMC 1976:643)! Would these new churches have been started without that goal in mind? Probably not. To be sure, responsiveness in Japan does not seem to be nearly as great as in Taiwan. But does that mean we do not need goals? Surely not. Perhaps that is all the more reason we do need them.

In 1968 for example, when we were working toward a specific goal, as indicated earlier we had our best growth ever. There may have been other factors involved, but it is naive to assume that we are going to get anywhere without setting some definite goals and working toward them. The decision to open new work in Fukuoka, Hiroshima, and elsewhere is a step in that direction, but even there it does not seem to be very clear just what we want to do and how we plan to do it. But can we really do what we want without planning for it? As someone has put it, "Failing to plan is planning to fail." Or, to state it more positively, as in *The Living Bible*, "We should make plans -- counting on God to direct us" (Prov. 16:9). Indeed we should. And part of making plans is setting goals, and how we intend to reach them.

Providing then that we believe TEE can be done, that it ought to be done, and begin making plans to do it, the final thing we need to do is to start putting our plan to work. This is easier said than done, but we must begin somewhere, even if it is just on a small scale. Whether we actually go ahead and do it is perhaps fundamentally a matter of the will. As to whether we really have the will to do it, it seems to me we are at least moving in that direction.

Back in 1967, when I personally first became interested
in returning to Japan, possibly to do Bible teaching, and
asked the Conference Executive Committee how they felt about
the possibilities of such a ministry, there did not seem to
be much enthusiasm. As the minutes sum up the feelings of
the group, "Right now there are no definite plans for a
central Bible school. This would only come when the need is
felt and not because a teacher was available" (JMCCC,
March 12, 1967:1). It was felt rather that it would be
better if I came back willing to do whatever needed to be
done, rather than limiting myself to a teaching ministry.
It was on that basis I returned. But several years later,
in 1973, when I shared with the Executive Committee my
interest in doing further study at the School of World
Mission at Fuller Seminary in the area of Theological Education by Extension, especially with reference to the needs of
the JMCCC, there seemed to be a much greater openness to
something like this. As is recorded in the minutes, "The
Church Conference welcomes this, and hopes he [Sprunger]
will be able to make practical implementation of these
studies after furlough" (JMCCC, November 11, 1973:1).

If this is truly indicative of a change in attitude
toward the need for some kind of training program, one
would hope that we would indeed have the will to do it. It
should not be presumed though that TEE is something that can
be done by one person or even a small group of persons. If
it is to be done at all, it must have the backing of not
only pastors and missionaries, but also of the laymen in the
churches. Without firm support, it is not likely that such
a program could succeed. But if everyone involved really
has the will to do it, then perhaps we are already halfway
there. "Where there is a will, there is a way," the saying
goes. The will must precede the way if TEE is to be a
success.

Before we get started on any program, however, as we
have oftentimes hinted, the matters of church, ministry, and
training all need to be worked through in order to develop a
training program to meet our own specific needs. In 1965,
there was a pastors' seminar on the theme of "The Pastor."
Various other seminars have been held since then. Perhaps
another one is called for at which we seriously consider once
again some of the basic questions, and not only consider them,
but seek to put down as specifically as possible how we would
answer them, and what this means in terms of future strategy,
including the possibilities of TEE. If we were to do something like this, it would hopefully not only help to clarify
our goals, but give us something more concrete to work toward.

As we make our plans, we should not feel bound to set up exactly the same kind of program undertaken in other countries. Any program which might be initiated should be kept flexible. As was affirmed in "The Lausanne Covenant," leadership training is needed and there is a great need to improve the theological education of church leaders. But there is no need for such programs to be patterned after any one system. As the Covenant states,

> In every nation and culture there should be an effective training program for pastors and laymen in doctrine, discipleship, evangelism, nurture and service. Such training programs should not rely on any stereotyped methodology but should be developed by creative local initiatives according to biblical standards (ICWE 1974b: 10).

Training programs ought to be biblical, but they need not be stereotyped. We need to be reminded of this time and again lest we fall into another rigid pattern.

Yet there have been many experiments in theological education over the past decade or so, and no doubt there is much to be learned from their successes and failures. (See, for example, *Learning in Context*, TEF, 1973). Even among the Mennonites there has been some experimenting. As an illustration, several years ago the AMBS began a "Seminary Without Walls" program, in which some of the professors go to off-campus study centers in Mennonite communities during the inter-term month of January. During the same period, there are also inter-term courses on campus for three weeks or so in which pastors and others are urged to enroll (AMBS 1973:6).

There are also a number of Mennonite groups around the world participating in or beginning their own TEE programs. Perhaps the most recent of these is what is being done in Zaire where an extension education program is being launched by the Mennonite Bible Institute at Tshikapa. According to an article on this program, it is planned to set up regional centers in the various language areas and the number of extension centers will depend on how many students there are in a particular locality. One of the reasons given for starting the program was a lack of sufficient leaders in the Mennonite churches, and also that many of the pastors have not had enough theological training to deal adequately with the problems they face in their congregations. The TEE program will be the same as that offered

at the residential institute, to which it is attached, and
it is said that

> The program will be available to all pastors and
> deacons who want to improve on their previous knowledge.
> It will also give basic training to those who have had
> no biblical training without requiring them to leave
> their present occupations (GCMC 1975a:674).

This program was scheduled to begin in March 1976. There
has also been a move in this direction in Latin America
following the closing of the Evangelical Mennonite Biblical
Seminary (inter-Mennonite) in Montevideo, Uruguay, at the
end of the '74 school year (GCMC 1975b:B-59-64). At this
writing, the details of that program have not yet been made
clear.

Any program which is launched in Japan must definitely be
tailored to fit the Japanese situation. It would need to be
"contextualized." Exactly what that means would have to be
spelled out by the cooperating schools and churches. But if
such programs can be done successfully in other parts of the
world, there is no reason why it could not be done successfully here also. In fact, a somewhat similar program in
secular education is already being planned in Japan for 1979.
It is called a "University on the Air," and will be offering
courses through radio and TV programs.

According to the article on it, this university will be
an authorized school with a Liberal Arts Department. In
addition to lectures being given via broadcasts, periodicals
will also be mailed to the students. It is also said that
some experiments and other lessons will be given regularly
at study centers about once a month. The program will
follow a four-month semester, and credit will be given to
students who successfully pass the examinations at the end
of each term. This proposed "University on the Air" is
being sponsored by the Education Ministry, and broadcasting
is scheduled to begin in several areas of the country in
1979 or 1980. About 450,000 people are expected to enroll
in this new university (*Asahi Evening News*, January 10,
1976:3). In many ways this program resembles TEE. If such
an undertaking can be done in secular education, why not in
theological education as well, although, of course, it
would have to be on a much smaller scale.

Whether any subsidy for personnel and so on might be
needed to help get such a program underway is naturally

premature to say. But at the GPS Conference referred to
earlier, the number two priority (next to "Evangelism and
Church Planting") agreed on for the next decade was "Leadership Training." As the statement itself explains it, this
means that where requested the General Conference Mennonite
Church would be ready to "Assist the Mennonite churches
related to COM to extend and improve national leadership
training, giving particular attention to lay leaders"
(GCMC 1972:1). In light of this, one would trust that, if
needed, such assistance would be available. There are also
organizations such as the Asia Theological Association (ATA),
which has as one of its main aims "to assist folk engaged in
TEE as requested" (Harrison 1975:1). Although ATA has no
TEE program itself, it is willing to help develop such, and
no doubt in the future there will be many other resources
provided.

To begin with, however, what is most needed is, as we
have tried to say, to believe TEE can be done, ought to be
done, to make plans to do it, and to begin working our plan.
If we can only get started, there is every good reason to
believe TEE will succeed in Japan.

A REALISTIC VISION

Some people are visionaries, some are realists. We need
both realists and visionaries, but perhaps what is needed
most is a happy combination of the two. As for TEE in
Japan, there are no doubt some skeptics who are not sure it
can or ought to be done. There are undoubtedly many others
who think it has great potential and that it could be done
easily without any problems. Yet we need not go to either
one extreme or the other. We need the best of both.

Let us be honest with ourselves though, and admit first
of all that at times our goals are rather unrealistic.
There are perhaps those today who would like to go back to
the "good old days" in the 1950s, when people came to tent
meetings literally by the hundreds and there were many
decisions for Christ. As an example of this, it is reported
that in 1955 there was an average attendance of about 120
adults and over 200 children at tent campaigns held in five
different places (GCMM, Evangelism Committee Report, Annual
Conference, 1955:2). It might be nice to go back if we
could, but times have changed, and to think that apart from
a special moving of the Spirit we can return to those days
is simply not being realistic. It is to deceive ourselves.

We cannot live in the past. But neither should we live
too far in the future. A well-known Japanese evangelist,
for instance, has said that "If every Christian would become
an active Christian and be able to capture one soul a year
and make that new soul productive, Japan would probably be
evangelized in seven years" (Hatori 1968:6). I am glad he
qualified that statement with the words "if" and "probably."
I imagine he is too, because here it is well over seven
years later and in spite of great efforts the percent of
Christians in Japan is just about the same as before. As
pointed out earlier, the percentage of the Japanese population which is Christian today is in fact less than it was
over 350 years ago! That is a reality we need to take into
consideration.

Or, as in our own experience, having had a vision of
starting a church in three years, we soon discovered that in
reality it may take considerably longer. To be sure, there
are exceptions, as in the case of Martha and Ann Classen,
who were able to turn over their work in a *danchi* (a vast
new housing area) to a pastor after only a year and a half.
They have a real vision for "*danchi* evangelism," and yet at
the same time are realistic in adding that their next
experience seems to be taking much longer (Classen 1974:27).
So each situation is different, and while we need to have
dreams and visions, we must be careful or we may often be
dreaming dreams that are much bigger than reality permits.
Dreams and visions are important, but we must also take into
consideration the realities of the situation. In this respect, TEE is no exception. We must start where we are, with
what we have, rather than where we wish we were. In short,
what is called for is a realistic vision.

In the case of the JMCCC, we are just one little denomination in Japan. We have our struggles as well as our
successes. But as indicated at the beginning of our study,
three of the biggest problems that are faced today by the
Conference are lack of growth, lack of leaders, and lack of
goals. We have also been so forward as to suggest further
that a solution to the second problem, that is, the lack of
trained leaders, could well be the key to solving the other
two as well. In other words, as was summarized in Chapter 1,
the heart of the problem is that

When churches do not grow, there is no need for more
    leaders;
When there is no need for more leaders, few new leaders
    are produced;

When few new leaders are produced, few new groups can
    be started;
When few new groups are started, churches do not grow.
When churches do not grow ...

What is being advocated here is that in order to solve this
problem, the process must somehow be reversed. That is, if
we start with leaders,

When many new leaders are produced, many new groups
    can be started;
When many new groups are started, churches will grow;
When churches grow, there will be a need for more
    leaders;
When there is a need for more leaders, many new leaders
    will be produced.
When many new leaders are produced ...

One of the keys to making such a reverse possible, to
getting us out of the vicious circle we are in, may be TEE.
Through a TEE program, we would be able to discover and
develop many of the lay leaders already within the churches.
By giving them a kind of in-service training, where they
would also be expected to use what they learn as they go
along, it should also make it possible to start many new
groups. As such groups were started and began to grow, it
would create a need for even more leaders to repeat the process. With a felt need for a greater number of leaders, it
would strengthen a program like TEE even more, and make it
possible to produce the leaders needed for growing churches.

Churches in Japan, as a general rule, seem to remain
quite small, especially rural churches, and this is often
lamented. But if that is the way things are, would it not
seem reasonable to try to start many small churches, instead
of attempting to establish such large ones? There is, of
course, nothing wrong with large ones, but size alone does
not make a church a church, and if churches are going to
plateau at 10, 20, or 30 members, then why not follow rather
than fight the pattern, and seek to establish many more
small churches.

Yet if this is to be done, it will also mean some changes
in the whole leadership structure of the church. It will
mean perhaps a redefinition of what a pastor is and what he
does. It may involve the creation of new roles. It may
require moving toward a multiple leadership structure and
so on. Both laity and leaders alike need to give serious

thought to what constitutes a church, and to what sort of
church and ministry and training program is most needed in
our own particular situation. This will not be easy. But
as missiologist Donald A. McGavran states with regard to
leadership,

> We are not called on to create a static ministry
> for static Churches content to remain at their present
> size in the midst of millions of the winnable. We are
> called to create a ministry which will keep growing
> Churches growing and start non-growing Churches on the
> road of great growth (1966:142).

We might add to that, we are called to create a ministry
which can make the planting of new churches possible.
McGavran goes on to ask, "What happens when the existing
church has come to a standstill?" and replies, in his own
words,

> In part, the answer lies in the creation and support
> of leaders who fit *new* congregations. Such leaders
> should be turned out as fast as new congregations can
> be gathered, at the point where they are being won,
> from among the men and women who compose them (1966:
> 143).

Exactly! Many more new congregations are needed, and many
more leaders to shepherd them. By beginning to produce more
leaders than we need at present, it would make it possible
to start many new congregations, out of which other new
leaders would emerge and need to be trained. That is where
TEE comes in, to train the leaders who are already there, to
begin reversing the cycle, and to keep on doing so.

If TEE can help us solve our leadership problem, as we
are suggesting it can, that could also go a long way toward
helping solve our non-growth problem as well. By having
more leaders (including many church planters), it would be
possible to start many more groups which in turn could add
considerably to the overall growth of the church. It is
often said that it is easier to start new groups than to
enlarge the old ones, and assuming that is true, it would be
all the more reason to try to work that way. This is said
to be one of the secrets of how TEAM was able to plant 16
churches in 19 years in a difficult rural area of Shikoku
(Cox 1974:26).

A solid training program could perhaps enable each
church to start at least two or three new groups, and those

in turn to reproduce. But if we do move in that direction, it will mean that people will need to be trained to lead such groups. To train them will require some sort of training program. In this connection, Ralph Winter raises the question of whether the extension system can really promote church growth. He answers in the affirmative saying that by hunting down the leaders who are most significant for the growth of the church, by fitting its program to train effective church planters, by building church growth theory into the curriculum, and by having professors who are church planters themselves, he believes that an extension seminary can indeed make a real contribution to the growth of the church (1969b:48-51).

While we might agree such a program could contribute greatly to church growth, it would be folly to assume that if we simply adopt a TEE program, our churches will automatically begin to grow. Yet it is also being naive to assume that our churches will grow without something like this. Training *is* important. An article confirming this appeared in the weekly paper, *Kurisuchan Shimbun* (The Christian, January 18, 1976:2). It reported that in 1975 the Takadanobaba Church in Tokyo had 53 baptisms, an amazing number in one year for any one church in Japan. Two years before that it also had the same number. The subtitle of the article is, "The Key to Church Growth is Lay Training!" A lot of lay training is apparently done in that church. If training is really one of the keys to such phenomenal growth, as the article implies, then it is high time we get going on a systematic, coordinated training program. Producing more leaders may not lead to growth in all cases. But one thing is sure. Without more leaders, it is going to be almost impossible for our work to expand. If it does grow, it will not be because of, but in spite of, the present setup.

Besides helping us solve the leadership and growth problems we have, something like TEE may also be a partial solution to our lack of goals problem. It could give us a focus to rally around as churches and as a Conference. By having a unified program in which we could all cooperate, it would give us a common goal, something to work toward, to draw us closer together. There could be many benefits in such a program, not only for the Mennonite churches, but for any and all who might want to join in. At the same time, we must not be so unrealistic as to think that this alone can unify the churches. But one would hope it could at least contribute toward that end.

As pointed out in the last section, local churches often set goals. On the conference level, however, it seems to be much more difficult. Yet the Conference is made up of local churches and their members. In reply to a question as to how important they feel the Church Conference is, of the 99 who answered the question, 50, or over half of the members, said "great." Forty-six said "considerable," and only three replied "small." In other words, at present, the Conference seems to have a great deal of support at the local grass-roots level. It would seem that as much as possible, this should be used to good advantage. With that kind of support, one would assume that if we could all rally together around a program like TEE, it could possibly even increase support for the overall work of the Conference.

But, if TEE is undertaken, it will need to have the whole-hearted backing of the Conference. It will need to be thought of not as a second-rate program, or as only suitable for laymen, but as a full-fledged theological training program. As Wayne Weld asserts, if it is to succeed, "Extension must become at least one of the official pastoral and lay training programs of the denomination" (1973:64). If it did, not only could it help us begin solving some of our problems, but it could also help us to become more purpose-oriented rather than problem-oriented. It could give us a concrete goal toward which we could all pull together. Needless to say, it would likely not be a panacea for all our ills, but more than anything else might it not be the very sort of thing we need.

As we make plans for the future, we need vision. We need to see new possibilities. At the same time our visions must be balanced with reality. We have had visions before, not only for Bible schools, but for several kindergartens, Christian centers and so on. Yet for various reasons, none of them ever became a reality. Perhaps part of the reason is that some of them were not realistic enough. But whatever the reasons, we, too, need to beware lest we also get carried away with what may be unrealistic visions.

When it comes more specifically to the planning of the JMCCC, an article in *The Mennonite* notes that the overall goal of the Conference is "outreach evangelism." It goes on to explain that there are two aspects to this. The first involves "outreach by existing churches into surrounding areas and nearby cities"; the second involves "outreach into more distant areas." In relation to the latter, it is stated that "We want to start work in major cities all over

Japan." Truly, in light of our growth thus far, that is indeed an ambitious goal. Yet it is somewhat balanced with realism when it is added that, "To be sure, it is a long-range goal" (Isobe 1975:E-5).

One of the main reasons for considering expansion into the larger urban areas seems to be that many of the people, especially young people from the churches in Kyushu, tend to gravitate toward the big cities. But it is also worth noting that while the Conference eventually hopes to begin work in numerous large cities, it is planning to start in only one, Fukuoka, the largest city in Kyushu. As observed earlier, the work there is in fact underway. If more personnel were available, perhaps it would be possible to begin working simultaneously in several other places as well. But vision must take into consideration such realities, and perhaps the important thing is getting started, even if only in one place for now. How long it will be until we can get going in other cities, only time will tell. (As of late 1979, I am happy to report that work has also been begun in the city of Beppu, near Oita, in Hiroshima, and in the smaller town of Sadowara, Miyazaki Prefecture.)

While there are plans to reach out in these various ways, the writer, then chairman of the Conference, also mentions that "we are looking forward to establishing a Mennonite Christian Center in Tokyo, Japan's largest city." He goes on to say that this center could "serve as a fellowship center for all Asian Mennonites as well as a center contributing to evangelism and church expansion throughout Asia." He concludes, "To strengthen the Christian fellowship between Christians of all Asian lands, we urgently feel the need for such a center" (1975:E-5). While that certainly is a worthy goal, one immediately wonders if such a center might not also be a good meeting place for the several Mennonite groups working in Japan, and undoubtedly that is part of the thinking behind it.

But, in addition, perhaps it could become not only a kind of fellowship center for the Mennonites in Japan, but also a study center, a research center, and even in some way fit into a TEE program. That is, while it would not necessarily have to be an extension center as such, might it not be possible for those who are already pastors and others interested to go to such a center in Tokyo for brief or longer periods of residential study. As TEE can include both residence and extension work, it would seem that here too there might be some possibilities which ought to be explored in working out a comprehensive vision. (Note: Since this was originally drafted the Japan Anabaptist Center, or *Nihon Menonaito Kyōdai Sentā* in Japanese, was launched in Tokyo in spring, 1977. It provides a meeting place, special lectures, library, lodging and so on primarily for members of the Mennonite and Brethren in Christ churches, but also available to others.)

It is not yet clear what directions this Anabaptist Center will take in the future, but perhaps it too could have a bearing on the kind of training program we feel would be appropriate. Informal seminars have in fact been held occasionally by interested groups, and at one time in the past there was even talk of possibly opening a joint school together. But might it not be feasible for the Center to serve as a short-term residential study center for both laymen and pastors? Or as a sponsoring agency or clearing house for courses offered in Mennonite churches throughout Japan, with an exchange of teaching personnel by local churches or groups as desired? Or what about it perhaps serving as a missionary training or orientation center to prepare Japanese for service abroad, or to train missionaries from other countries for service in Japan? Such a program might even have the possibility of eventually being much broader than just Japan, even international in scope. Much will depend on our vision and what we do to make it happen.

What the Mennonites will do with the proposals contained in this study is an open question. But personally, I believe we stand at a crossroads in Japan. We can continue to drift along as we are, uncertain of our direction, and seeing little growth. Or we can begin to make bold plans to reach out, and not only talk about them, but actually begin to put them into operation. There is a Japanese proverb which goes, *"Chiri mo tsumoreba, yama to naru"* (literally, "Dust collected becomes a mountain"), with the meaning that our efforts add up. The important thing is to get started. What the first step will be is hard to say, but if we are to get anywhere it will have to be taken. We can choose to be followers or leaders. We can experiment or maintain the status quo. We can be pioneers or traditionalists. But choose we must. To decide not to do anything would be a decision. But to not decide at all would be "a decision to do nothing." What is called for is some decisiveness and action.

We have seen how in many instances the Anabaptist vision and the Mennonite reality are quite different things. Still,

it does not seem realistic to think we can go back to the
Anabaptist vision. We must go forward with one of our own.
As Pastor Takashi Yamada has expressed it, "we need to
create our own unique visions in the particular cultural
backgrounds of our own lands and nations, strikingly
inspired by the original experiences of the early Anabaptists" (1976:7). To do that, perhaps we will have to begin
as they did with another look at what the Bible says the
church is, what the ministry is, and how it can best be
trained. Whether the Mennonites will be among the first to
launch out with TEE in Japan remains to be seen. But
whether they are or not, the point is that we must try to
hammer out a vision that is both realistic and realizable.
A vision that combines vision with reality.

While we have been talking primarily about the Mennonites
throughout this book, what has been said with reference
to them is surely applicable to many other churches or
denominations as well. The problems that we have encountered in our work could no doubt be verified many times over
in the minutes, letters, and records of numerous other
missions and churches working here also. The problems that
have been spelled out here are not unique to us. In fact,
I imagine one could almost say they are universal to the
churches of Japan.

Yet, in TEE, may it not be that we have one of the
secrets for releasing the potential that is locked up within
so many churches? Might this not be just what churches
need? As Masao Takenaka says with regard to reforming the
structure of churches in Japan, "We must find the way to
make the Christian Church not a static, building-centered
religion but a people's movement, a company of new humanity
making a joyful pilgrimage on earth" (Bates and Pauck 1964:
209). Might not TEE be one of the things that makes this
possible? Or at least a little more probable? The answer
will depend on what we do with it.

What is being suggested here then is that we must be
realistic about the problems that may be encountered in TEE.
At the same time we need to be optimistic about its possibilities. We need to think in terms of what it can do for
both churches and schools. Hopefully it could bring new
life to both, through helping us solve some of our basic
problems. But even though the possibilities are great, we
must not underestimate the cost of undertaking it. It
would no doubt mean some basic structural changes in our
churches. It would likely involve some role changes on the

part of both laity and leaders. It would mean that both
churches and schools would have to take a good hard look at
what they are doing and why and how. There would be many
areas in which change would undoubtedly be called for. As
Jesus taught about building a tower, we must first sit down
and count the cost and see whether we will be able to finish
it, lest people laugh at us if we are not able (Luke
14: 28ff). So to be sure, we must count the cost of going
ahead. At the same time, we must also try to count the cost
of what it might mean if we do not. What will it mean in
the future for churches and for schools if they are left
just as they are? How can we help them become more what God
wants them to be? Might not TEE be a vital part of the
answer?

TEE for Japan. Visionary? Realistic? Or both? As I
am sure you, the reader, have gathered by now, I for one
definitely believe it is both, and that if we work at it,
if we really wrestle once more with the basic questions of
church, ministry, and training, it is possible to come up
with a vision that will be both visionary and realistic --
in short, a "realistic vision." Just what the details will
be has yet to be seen. Any such program will have to be
put together in Japan, primarily by the Japanese. It
should look "made in Japan." When it does, and when we
begin to see it happen, that will indeed be something for
which to give praise. May our prayer be:

"Oh God, give us a realistic vision, and help us to
make it a reality!"

Appendices

Appendix A

Personnel who have Served in Japan with the General Conference Mennonite Mission

Name	Home Community	Service
Leonore G. Friesen	North Newton, KS	1951-1968
William C. Voth (d) Matilda Voth	Newton, KS Whitewater, KS	1951-1955
Verney Unruh Belva Unruh	Bloomfield, MT Freeman, SD	1951-1966
Esther Patkau	Hanley, Sask.	1951-1974
Peter Voran Lois Voran	Pretty Prairie, KS Pandora, OH	1951-1971; 1978-
Paul W. Boschman LaVerne Boschman (d)	Petaigan, Sask. Aberdeen, ID	1951-1971
Bernard Thiessen Ruby Thiessen	Whitewater, KS Whitewater, KS	1952-
Ferdinand Ediger Viola Ediger	Drake, Sask. Inman, KS	1953-
Anna Dyck	Drake, Sask.	1953-
Martha Giesbrecht Janzen George E. Janzen	Waldheim, Sask. Mission City, B.C.	1953-1980 1959-1980
Robert L. Ramseyer Alice Ruth Ramseyer	Bluffton, OH Bluffton, OH	1954-1972; 1978-
Peter Derksen Mary Derksen	Abbotsford, B.C. Virgil, Ont.	1954-

Name	Home Community	Service
Raymond Reimer (d) Phyllis Reimer	Steinbach, Man. Freeman, SD	1957–1969
Dennis Epp	Rosthern, Sask.	1958–1961
Virginia Claassen	Whitewater, KS	1959–1964; 1967–
Franzie Loepp Dorothy Loepp	Turpin, OK Whitewater, KS	1961–1964
Ivan Regier Anne Regier	Madrid, NB Freeman, SD	1962–1964
Carl Liechty Sandra Liechty	Berne, IN Peninsula, OH	1963–1966; 1969–1974; 1978–
Agnes Dueck	Clearbrook, B.C.	1964–1967
W. Frederic Sprunger Ellen Sprunger	Kidron, OH Smithville, OH	1964–1967; 1970–
Arlin Jansen Ruth Jansen	Redlands, CA Redlands, CA	1966–1968
Doyle Preheim LaDona Preheim	Freeman, SD Marion, SD	1966–1969
Ray Kliewer Loralee Kliewer	Pismo Beach, CA Pismo Beach, CA	1967–1970
Terry Lehman Louise Lehman	Berne, IN Souderton, PA	1968–1971
*Frank Becker *Rachel (Becker) VanWingen	Wayne, NJ Buhler, KS	1968–1971
*Allan Teichroew *Kathryn (Teichroew) Gaeddert	Mountain Lake, MN Geneva, NB	1969–1971
*Robert Loewen *Anne Loewen	Grande Prairie, Alb. Manitou, Man.	1969–1972
*Marvin Linscheid *Elma Linscheid	Aberdeen, ID Aberdeen, ID	1969–1972
Ethel Kambs Umble	Elkhart, IN	1970–1971
John Sommer Sharon Sommer	Garden Grove, CA Orosi, CA	1970–1973
Delvyn Epp Lucille Epp	Henderson, NB Winkler, Man.	1973–1976

Name	Home Community	Service
Henry Kliewer	Winnipeg, Man.	1976-1980
Nellie Kliewer	Winnipeg, Man.	
*Ronald Rich	Washington, IL	1977-1979
*Elaine Rich	Kokomo, IN	
Stanley Butler	Spokane, WA	1977-1980

*
Served only in Tokyo, outside the sphere of the JMCCC.

(Sources: Pannabecker 1961a:60; Ediger 1975:1)

Appendix B

Constitution of the Japan Mennonite Christian Church Conference

The proclamation of the Gospel is the most important and foremost calling of the Church, the body of Jesus Christ. Called by Jesus Christ, we, the churches of the Japan Mennonite Christian Church Conference, by the divine assistance and guidance of God, here formulate the following Church Constitution, not to hinder the free operation of the Holy Spirit, but to further the growth and advance of the Church Conference, believing that "all things should be done decently and in order." (I Cor. 14:40)

ORGANIZATION: GENERAL RULES

Article I.   Name: This organization shall be called the Japan Mennonite Christian Church Conference (referred to as the "Church Conference" below).

Article II.   Purpose: The purpose of this organization shall be to unite all of the Mennonite churches in Kyushu, to encourage fellowship with the worldwide body of Mennonite believers, and to assist the churches in their programs of work.

Article III. Confession of Faith: Accepting the Holy Bible as the authoritative rule of faith and life, and confessing the Apostles' Creed, we believe:

1. In one God, eternal, omnipotent, omniscient, omnipresent.

2. In God the Father, Creator of heaven and earth.

3. In Jesus Christ, the only begotten Son of God, appointed as the Savior and Lord of the world, His atoning death on the cross, His resurrection from the dead, and His triumphant return.

4. In the Holy Spirit, graciously sent by the Father to lead men to the truth in Christ, to comfort and strengthen the believer, and to equip the believer with power to live the Christian life and to proclaim the Gospel.

5. In man, created in the image of God, who through the sin of pride and rebellion has fallen out of fellowship with his Maker, and stands in need of redemption and reconciliation.

6. In salvation through the grace of God who mercifully forgives the repentant sinner through faith in Jesus Christ, and through conversion to a life of humble obedience to Christ and the Scriptures.

7. In the Holy Bible as the only authoritative revelation of God, given by the inspiration of the Holy Spirit, a completely trustworthy guide of faith and life.

8. In the Church as the body of Christ, the fellowship of those who have repented of their sins and have covenanted themselves to a life of obedience to Christ and the Scriptures, who seek diligently to strengthen and comfort one another, and to proclaim the salvation in Christ to the unbelieving world.

9. In the Christian life as expressing itself in sincere love to God and man, a life dedicated to obedience and holiness, propagating itself through diligent prayer and the searching of the Holy Scriptures, through the fellowship of believers and aggressive evangelism.

Article IV. Membership: 1. The Church Conference accepts the above Confession of Faith and this Constitution, and welcomes into the participation of its fellowship churches cooperating in the total program of the Conference.

2. The Church Conference will not interfere in the government of the local participating churches. However, participating churches will regard the decisions of the Church Conference morally binding and will seek to conscientiously execute these decisions.

3. New churches desiring membership in the Church Conference shall make formal application stating their desire. Application shall be made in writing at least three months prior to the annual conference of the Church Conference, and presented to the Chairman of the Church Conference who will in turn present the matter to the Executive Committee. Following investigation by the Executive Committee, formal recommendations shall be made to the Church Conference.

4. Self-propagation, self-government and self-support are considered necessary qualifications of member churches, and groups with 15 or more resident active members are to be considered member churches, while those with less than 15 are termed evangelistic centers.

Article V.   Officers: Officers shall consist of Chairman (1), Secretary (1), and Treasurer (1). The Chairman shall be elected by the recommendation or election of the Church Conference at the annual meeting, and the Secretary and Treasurer shall be appointed within the Executive Committee.

Article VI.   Executive Committee: To carry out the decisions of the Church Conference, the Church Conference shall appoint an Executive Committee. The Executive Committee shall be made up of one member from each of the participating churches, and upon the approval of the Church Conference at the annual meeting, shall assume responsibility of this position.

Article VII. Auxiliary Committees: The Church Conference is authorized to call into existence various auxiliary committees, as the need arises. These may be chosen by the Annual Conference, by the Chairman, or by the Executive Committee, or they may consist of volunteers.

<u>Article VIII</u>. <u>Amendments</u>: Any amendment of the above constitution must be done by the consent of at least two-thirds of the representatives present at the annual conference.

<u>Article IX</u>. <u>Supplementary Rule</u>: This Constitution shall be in effect from the day of its adoption.

<u>BY-LAWS</u>

1. <u>Annual Conference</u>: The highest authority in the Church Conference shall be the Annual Conference. The annual meeting shall be held at least once a year.

   a) <u>Delegates</u>: Churches participating as members of the Church Conference shall send laymen, missionaries and pastors as delegates to the annual meeting. Member churches may send 3 delegates for the first 25 resident active members, and one additional delegate for every additional 25 resident active members in the congregation. The member churches shall register the names of their appointed delegates with the Executive Committee prior to the annual conference.

   b) <u>Observers</u>: Active church members, missionaries and pastors who are not chosen as official representatives to the annual meeting may attend as observers.

   c) <u>Voting Privileges</u>: Every official delegate to the annual meeting shall have one vote. Substitutes and votes by proxy shall not be recognized. Observers also shall not be granted voting privileges.

   d) <u>Decisions</u>: In order for decisions to be made at the annual meeting, an attendance of at least two-thirds of the possible vote-holding delegates shall be required. Decisions shall be made on the basis of a two-thirds majority vote of those present.

2. <u>Executive Committee</u>: The Executive Committee shall, as a general rule, meet once every two months, and is authorized to hold special meetings whenever deemed necessary. The Executive meeting shall be called by the Chairman of the Church Conference, and may meet for the official transaction of business when more than half of the membership is present. Auxiliary committees or the participating member churches may also call for special

meetings of the Executive Committee through the Chairman
or through the members of the Executive Committee.

a) Observers: Observers to the Executive Committee
   shall follow same rules as apply to observers at the
   annual meeting.
b) Voting Privileges: follow same rules as apply at
   annual meeting.
c) Term of Office: The term of office for members of
   the Executive Committee shall be one year. However,
   the term of office for the Secretary and Treasurer,
   chosen from within the Executive Committee, shall be
   two years. Members of the Executive Committee are
   eligible for re-election.
d) Decisions: same rules shall be followed as at
   annual meeting.

3. Auxiliary Committees: a) Committee Members: in accor-
                             dance with general rule #7.
                          b) Term of Office: undetermined.

4. Duties of Personnel: (Officers)

   a) Chairman: The Chairman calls the Annual Conference
      and Executive Committee meetings, as well as chairs
      the meetings. He serves to guard the interests of
      the Church Conference, encourages its unity, visits
      the member churches in the interest of their spiri-
      tual welfare and growth, and may seek to give help-
      ful counsel wherever and whenever a situation calls
      for it. In cases where no special representative is
      chosen, the Chairman shall always represent the
      Church Conference. The member churches and the
      Executive Committee shall respect the counsel and
      direction of the Chairman, in accordance with the
      decisions of the Annual Conference.

   b) Secretary: The Secretary shall act as assistant to
      the Chairman, shall record all the minutes of the
      Annual Conference and the Executive Committee, pre-
      serve them in a file, and duplicate and distribute
      all minutes and announcements.

   c) Treasurer: The Treasurer shall have charge of the
      treasury of the Church Conference, and shall perform
      all duties relating to financial bookkeeping. The
      Treasurer, in accordance with Annual Conference
      decision, shall pay out all sums requested by the

various committees and the member churches. The
Treasurer is authorized to collect all annual dues
from the member churches, in accordance with Annual
Conference decision. The Treasurer shall be responsible to prepare financial reports, have his books
audited once a year, and present his report to the
Annual Conference.

d) <u>Executive Committee</u>:

- (i) Shall act to execute the decisions of the
  Annual Conference, and all necessary business
  transactions that shall arise between annual
  conferences.
- (ii) Shall prepare recommendations and a proposed
  budget for presentation to the Annual Conference.
- (iii) In the event that its officers (or the members
  of any of the other committees) cannot continue in their position for some reason, or
  business arises which they cannot handle, the
  Executive Committee shall appoint substitute
  personnel.
- (iv) Shall appoint qualified personnel to audit the
  treasurer's books.
- (v) In the event that problems arise within the
  member churches shall actively assist in finding solutions, in accordance with the need.
- (vi) Shall give counsel to church leaders (missionaries and pastors) concerning placement and
  type of service.

5. <u>Annual Dues</u>: All member churches shall be responsible
to contribute annual dues to the Church Conference. The
annual dues shall be calculated on the basis of one-
tenth of the local churches total annual income. Without the express decision of the Annual Conference, the
Church Conference may not lay any additional financial
burden on the member churches.

6. <u>Amendment of the By-Laws</u>: Same rules shall apply as are
binding in connection with the General Rules.

(This constitution was approved at the annual session of the
JMCCC, October 1968. Since then a few minor revisions have
been made, and the name changed from "Kyushu" to "Japan" at
a session held March 19-21, 1976.)

Appendix C

"Statement of Understanding Between the Japan Mennonite Christian Church Conference and the General Conference Mennonite Mission in Japan"

The basic purpose of the General Conference Mennonite Mission in Japan is to work with the Japan Mennonite Church Conference and other Mennonite congregations in Japan in making Christ known and in building His Church. However, to meet the peculiar needs of missionaries, periodic meetings to consider problems such as the following will be necessary:

1. Children's education
2. Missionary housing
3. Transportation
4. Fellowship
5. Language study
6. Activity outside of the sphere of the Japan Mennonite Church Conference.

In order to implement this, we agree to have an Executive Committee consisting of Chairman, Secretary, Treasurer, and Alternate, who are elected annually. It shall be the duty of this committee to call a meeting of all missionaries at least once a year for fellowship and necessary business, and to transact any business that comes up in the interim between business meetings. The specific duties of the members shall be:

Chairman:
1. To chair business meetings.
2. To carry on correspondence between field and COM.
3. To inform all missionaries of all correspondence between field and COM.

Secretary: 1. Keep minutes of all official business
              meetings.
           2. Circulate minutes among all missionaries.

Treasurer: 1. Keep financial records.
           2. Provide quarterly and annual reports.
           3. Have records audited at least once a year
              by two responsible persons appointed by
              the Executive Committee.

Alternate: 1. Attend all Executive Committee meetings.
           2. Be prepared to assume the duties of any
              of the other three Executive Committee
              members as the need arises.

(This statement was approved by the GCMM at its December
1972 annual session, and by the JMCCC at its February 1973
annual session.)

Appendix D

Churches and Pastors Affiliated with the Japan Mennonite Christian Church Conference (1978)

Name*	Address	Pastor
Aburatsu Christian Church	170-8 Sonoda Cho Nichinan Shi Miyazaki Ken 887	Naoki Hidaka
Atago Christian Church	2-3-2 Atago Cho Nobeoka Shi Miyazaki Ken 882	Takeomi Takarabe
Baba Cho Christian Church	5-2 Baba Cho Kobe Shi Hyogo Ken 652	
Hyuga Christian Church	2-11-19 Tsuru Machi Hyuga Shi Miyazaki Ken 883	
Kirishima Christian Church@	+2-20 Kirishima Miyazaki Shi Miyazaki Ken 880	Hiroshi Yanada
Kirishima Christian Brotherhood	3 Shimonishi Cho Kobayashi Shi Miyazaki Ken 886	Takashi Yamada
Namiki Christian Church	1-20-7 Kamikawahigashi Miyakonojo Shi Miyazaki Ken 885	Hiroshi Isobe

Name	Address	Pastor
Oita Mennonite Christian Church	2-7-1 Nakatsuru Oita Shi Oita Ken 870	Shozo Sato[x]
Oyodo Christian Church	2-7-4 Yodogawa Miyazaki Shi Miyazaki Ken 880	Hiroshi Yanada
Takajo Christian Church	328 Homanbo Takajo Cho Miyazaki Ken 885-12	Tsugio Matoba

[*] Note: In addition to the churches listed here, there are also "evangelistic centers" in Miyakonojo and Miyazaki, and "churches" in Fukuoka (1976, Takeji Nomura pastor) and Beppu (1978), although not yet officially recognized by the Church Conference as churches. Work was also initiated in Hiroshima[z] in 1979, as well as the town of Sadowara, Miyazaki Ken.

[@] This church has been without a regular pastor since the beginning of 1979, but will be served on a part-time basis by Pastor Mitsuo Shimada from April 1980.

[x] Will terminate as pastor of the church in March 1981 and begin serving in the Minami Miyazaki area. Junji Sasaki will assume pastoral duties from April.

[z] Tadayuki Ishiya will begin working with this group as of April 1981.

[+] official Conference address

Appendix E

A Sample of Programmed Material on "The Mennonites in Japan"

The following material was prepared as part of the assignment for a class in Programmed Instruction, taken at Fuller Seminary in the fall of 1974. It is by no means to be construed as a perfect example of what programming is or how it ought to be done, but is simply presented here as one way of doing it. For the reader who would like to get a better feel for this educational technique or this type of material, I would suggest that you simply sit down and work through it yourself. Starting with the pre-test, continuing with the course itself, and following it up with the post-test should take no more than half an hour or so at the most.

According to my instructor, Fred Holland, if a course is well written, "the student should score low on the pre-test, and 100 percent on the post-test." That is the ideal. But in this case it should perhaps be mentioned that this little course was written primarily with non-Mennonites or new Mennonites in mind. Therefore anyone with Mennonite background should do a lot better on the pre-test than someone who is from a different tradition. Be that as it may, it is probably better not to worry too much about how you score on the test, about whether you pass or not. If you just take a little time, I think you will have fun working through it. And you are the only one who will know how you have done.

PRE-TEST

1. Who are the Mennonites named after? _____

2. The founder of the Mennonite Church was from _____.

3. What does the word "Anabaptist" literally mean? _____

4. The main reason Mennonites migrated to America was because of _____.

5. One reason for several Mennonite groups is _____ difference.

6. When did the Mennonites go to Japan? _____

7. The _____ coming of Christianity to Japan was after the war.

8. Put the initials of the various Mennonite groups in the circle on the island where they are working.

   GC - General Conference
   MB - Mennonite Brethren
   MC - Mennonite Church

   Hokkaido

   N

   Honshu

   Kyushu

9. One type of work all three Mennonite groups are doing is _____.

10. There are about _____ Mennonite Christians in Japan.

THE MENNONITES IN JAPAN

So you've never heard of the Mennonites. Don't feel bad. Neither have a lot of other good people. But I think it would be a shame if you didn't learn a little about who the Mennonites are, now that you have a chance. I guess I feel that way partly because I am one of them, and I'd like you to know something about myself as well as my people.

I trust that this little course will not only help you to discover something about who the Mennonites are, but also to find out a few things they've been doing in Japan. As you might guess, we've been Mennonite missionaries to that country for several years. To us it's our second home. Japan is a fascinating country. The Mennonites, an interesting people. I hope you will enjoy learning a little more about both in this mini-course on "The Mennonites in Japan."

Perhaps I should also say a little about how to use this course before you begin. It's actually an experiment with a new way of learning. The method of learning is called "programmed instruction," but it is really not as complicated as it might sound. In contrast to the more traditional lecture-quiz method of study, in programmed instruction the content and the questions regarding the content are integrated as you go along. The answers to the questions are also in the text. I am sure you will enjoy this new method of study.

All you have to do is start reading and follow instructions as you proceed. For example, when a question is followed by a blank, simply write in the answer. If any questions are not clear, reread the preceding paragraph, and try again. If you still cannot answer, something is likely wrong with the material, so just leave it blank and go on.

At the end there will be a brief test consisting of 10 questions to see how both student and teacher have done. If you work through all the material first, the test should be no problem. Nine out of 10 correct answers will be considered a job well done. The entire course ought to be completed within 30 minutes. Good luck!

1. Christians belong to many different denominations. It might be Baptist, Lutheran, Mennonite, Methodist, Presbyterian or something else. And in many cases, denominations are named after persons. For example, the Lutherans are named after Martin Luther. The Mennonites

are named after Menno Simons. Not all denominations are named after a person, but many of them are.

Who do the Mennonites get their name from? . . . .

2. That's right. The Mennonites get their name from Menno Simons. Menno Simons was born in 1496. He died in 1561. Menno Simons is not as well known as the other leaders of the Protestant Reformation. But like Calvin, Luther, and Zwingli, he was one of the reformers.

Menno Simons was one of the leaders of the . . . .

3. The Mennonites are named after . . . .

4. As you just answered, assuming that I taught you correctly, Menno Simons was one of the leaders of the Protestant Reformation, and the Mennonites are named after him. Actually, it was not Menno's intention to start a Mennonite Church any more than it was Luther's to start a Lutheran Church. But just as Luther's followers were called "Lutherans," so Menno's followers came to be called "Mennonites."

The . . . . Church gets its name from Menno Simons.

5. Yes, even though it was not Menno Simons' intention to found a church, looking back historically, that is the way things developed, and so we have the Mennonite Church today. As we said, Menno was one of the reformers. The Reformation, as you know, began in Germany, but Menno Simons was not from Germany. Menno was from Holland. He was one of the leaders of the Reformation there.

Menno was from what country? . . . .

6. Circle the correct answer:

The founder of the Mennonite Church was from
France   Holland   Germany .

7. Right again. Menno Simons was from Holland. But the Mennonite Church really had its beginning earlier in the Anabaptist movement in Switzerland, which began in 1525. The Anabaptist movement spread from Switzerland to Germany, Holland, and other countries. It was in Holland that Menno Simons was asked to be a leader of

one of the Anabaptist groups. The Mennonite Church gets
its name from Menno Simons, but actually had its origin
in the Anabaptist movement. This means that the Mennonites are one of the oldest Protestant denominations.

What church has its origin in the Anabaptist movement?
....

8. Correct! While different churches have different begin-
    nings, the Anabaptist movement was the origin of the
    Mennonite Church. The word "Anabaptist" literally means
    to "re-baptize." Anabaptists were Christians who were
    rebaptized Christians. They had been baptized as infants
    in the Catholic Church, but they did not believe that
    baptism was valid. As a result, they rebaptized one
    another on personal confession of their faith in Christ.

    Those who "rebaptized" one another were called ....

9. Check the right answer:

    The word Anabaptist means ( ) rebaptizer.
                               ( ) reconfirm.
                               ( ) an analytical Baptist.

10. As we have just seen, those Christians who rebaptized
    one another at the time of the Reformation were called
    "Anabaptists," which means "rebaptizers." The Anabap-
    tists simply tried to practice what they believed the
    Bible taught. But they were persecuted for their faith,
    both by the other churches of their day, and by the
    state. As a result, the Anabaptists were forced to
    leave Switzerland, and moved to other countries in
    Europe.

    In a word, why were the Anabaptists forced to flee to
    other countries? ....

11. That's right. They were forced to move because of per-
    secution. That is how they got to Holland, where Menno
    Simons became one of their leaders. The Mennonite
    Church, which grew out of the Anabaptist movement was
    also severely persecuted. The result was that the
    Mennonites fled to places such as Russia, where they
    were promised religious freedom. But when freedom there
    came to an end, they began migrating to the United
    States and Canada, where many of them live today.

Who were persecuted and migrated first to Russia, later to America? ....

12. True or false:

..... The main reason the Mennonites went to America was because of persecution.

13. If you answered "true," you were a hundred percent correct. It was because of persecution or loss of religious freedom that the Mennonites came to America. And as they came, they brought their faith. As Tertullian observed, "The blood of the martyrs is the seed of the Church." They also brought their different cultures. Culture is one of the main reasons there are so many different Mennonite groups today.

What is one of the main reasons for so many Mennonite groups? ....

14. That's right. One of the main reasons for the existence of different Mennonite groups is different cultures. We have already learned how the Mennonites originated in the Anabaptist (rebaptizers) movement which began in Switzerland, how they spread to other countries such as Holland where Menno Simons became one of the Anabaptist leaders, how the Mennonite Church came to be named after him, and how because of persecution many of them came to America. And when they came, they brought their various cultures with them. The Mennonites from Switzerland brought their Swiss culture. The Mennonites from Holland brought their Dutch culture. The Mennonites from Russia brought their Russian culture and so on. Their cultures were of course different, which led to differences.

The various Mennonite groups all brought their different .... with them.

15. Select the best answer:

One of the reasons for different Mennonite groups is
..... cultural difference.
..... racial difference.
..... doctrinal difference.

16. Correct again. There were cultural differences, and that is one of the reasons for so many different

Mennonite groups today. But the Mennonites also work
together in various ways, especially in the areas of
relief and service and peace. They are also very interested in missions. Many of them have their own mission
programs, such as the three Mennonite groups working in
Japan. They all went to Japan after World War II.

After World War II, how many Mennonite groups went to
Japan to do mission work? ....

17. That's right. Three Mennonite groups went to Japan
     after World War II. At that time Japan was very re-
     sponsive to Christianity. Before the war, Shintoism had
     been the state religion, and the emperor was thought to
     be divine. After the war, however, when Emperor
     Hirohito declared that he was not a "god," it left a
     religious vacuum. Mennonites, as well as many other
     Christian groups, sought to meet that need.

     Did the Mennonites go to Japan before or after World
     War II? ....

18. The three Mennonite groups working in Japan went after
     ....

19. Right on! There were three Mennonite groups who went
     to Japan. They all went after World War II. The pe-
     riod immediately after the war was actually the third
     coming of Christianity to Japan. The first two comings
     had been the Catholic and the Protestant, in that order.

     The post-World War II period was the .... coming
     of Christianity to Japan.

20. Right again. That was the third coming. The first was
     by the Catholics back in 1549. The second was by the
     Protestants in 1859. The third was after World War II.
     These are the three eras of Christianity in Japan.

     The third era of Christianity in Japan was after ......

21. Given the following three dates, put the proper date in
     front of each of the three main comings of Christianity
     to Japan.

     1549   ..... Protestant
     1859   ..... post-World War II
     1945   ..... Catholic

22. The correct order was Catholic, Protestant, post-World
War II, chronologically. If you happened to get the
Protestant and Catholic comings reversed, don't worry.
It won't be on the final test. But
you may want to go back and read
No. 19 and No. 20, where we talked
about that. Anyway, as noted, there
were three Mennonite groups that
went to Japan after World War II.
Below is a map of Japan. Three of
the main islands are Kyushu (pronounced "cue-shoe"), Honshu, and
Hokkaido.

Hokkaido

MC

N

Honshu

MB

Kyushu

GC

Write the names of three of the main   . . . .
Japanese islands (you may look back   . . . .
if you need to):   . . . .

23. The three Mennonite groups working in Japan are the
General Conference Mennonites (GC's), the Mennonite
Brethren (MB's), and the Mennonite Church (MC's). They
work on three different islands. From south to north,
Kyushu, Honshu, and Hokkaido, respectively.

Write the full names of the three   . . . .
Mennonite groups working in Japan, ...
from south to north (again you may   . . . .
look if you need to):

24. As we said, the three Mennonite groups work on different islands. The GC's work on Kyushu. The MB's on
Honshu, and MC's on Hokkaido. By putting their initials
in alphabetical order (GC, MB, MC), you can remember on
which island they work, if you remember the order is
from south to north. If you reversed the order, you
would still get one right.

Put the initials of the proper
Mennonite group in the circle on
the map in the area where they
are working (don't look back
unless you have to):

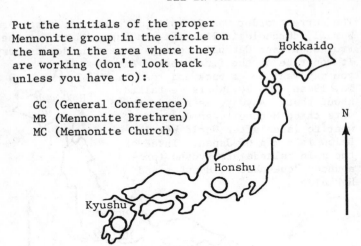

GC (General Conference)
MB (Mennonite Brethren)
MC (Mennonite Church)

25. These three Mennonite groups, while working in differ-
    ent areas, are doing many of the same things. One
    thing they are all doing is church planting. That is,
    they are all trying to start new churches in areas
    where there are no churches or not enough churches.

    What is one thing all three groups are doing? ....

26. That's right. The Mennonite groups are all doing
    church planting. But there are other things only one
    or two of them are doing, such as bookstore work, Bible
    schools, and radio evangelism. Since Japan is an
    advanced country, there is no need for churches to
    operate schools or hospitals as in some other lands.
    Therefore they are not doing medical or educational
    work. But they are all doing church planting.

    What are two kinds of work the Mennonites are not doing
    in Japan? ....

27. Circle the one type of work all the Mennonite groups
    are doing: Bible school
                bookstore
                church planting
                radio evangelism

28. If you circled the words "church planting" you chose
    the right answer. Some of the Mennonite groups have
    Bible schools, bookstores or radio work, but not all.

And none of them are into medical or educational work.
But they all are engaged in church planting. The
Mennonites would like to do more things together, but
it is quite far from southern Kyushu to northern
Hokkaido. In fact, about 2,400 kilometers (1,500 mi.).

About how far is it from Kyushu to Hokkaido? ....

29. Japan is sometimes thought to be just a small country,
but it is actually very long and narrow. It's not easy
for the Mennonites to get together. They went to their
various areas because they were some of the neediest
areas, the most unchurched areas. They have been working there for over 20 years now. All together there
are probably about 2,000 Mennonite Christians in Japan.

About how many Mennonites are there in Japan? ....

30. Underline the correct answer:

There are approximately   1,000   2,000   3,000
Mennonites in Japan.

Two thousand did you say? Right again. And that brings
us to the end of this little course. We have seen how the
Mennonites are a group of Christians. They got their name
from Menno Simons, one of the reformers. Menno Simons was a
leader of the Anabaptist movement in Holland. The Anabaptists, who originated in Switzerland at the time of the
Reformation, were persecuted because they "rebaptized" one
another. The Mennonites were also persecuted, and as a
result migrated first to Russia, later to the United States
and Canada.

We have seen how they brought their various cultures as
well as their faith with them. Cultural differences led to
the formation of different Mennonite groups. Three of these
groups went to Japan after World War II. That was the third
coming of Christianity to Japan. We have also seen how the
three groups are working on three different islands. From
south to north, the General Conference Mennonites on Kyushu,
the Mennonite Brethren on Honshu, and the Mennonite Church
on Hokkaido. They are all involved in church planting.
There are about 2,000 Mennonite Christians in Japan today.
These are just a few of the things we have learned.

Now it is time for the test. As mentioned before, it
is not only to see how well you have done but how well *we*
have done. Good luck with the test, and God bless you!

P.S.   The Brethren in Christ (BIC) are another Mennonite-
          related group working in Japan, but due to the
          limitations of this brief course were not included.
          No discrimination is intended. After all, we are
          all "brethren" in Christ.

P.P.S.   If you would like to read more about the Mennonites,
          a good book to start with would be *An Introduction
          to Mennonite History*, Cornelius J. Dyck, ed.

POST-TEST

1. Who are the Mennonites named after? _____

2. The founder of the Mennonite Church was from _____.

3. What does the word "Anabaptist" literally mean? _____

4. The main reason Mennonites migrated to America was because of _____.

5. One reason for several Mennonite groups is _____ difference.

6. When did the Mennonites go to Japan? _____

7. The _____ coming of Christianity to Japan was after the war.

8. Put the initials of the various Mennonite groups in the circle on the island where they are working.

    GC – General Conference
    MB – Mennonite Brethren
    MC – Mennonite Church

9. One type of work all three Mennonite groups are doing is _____.

10. There are about _____ Mennonite Christians in Japan.

Appendix F

Eastern Hokkaido Bible School Student Questionnaire

1. Name of your church? .... (198)[@]

2. Age: 15–25 .... 26–35 .... 36–45 .... 46–55 ....
56–65 .... 66+ .... (198)

3. Sex: male / female Single? ... Married? .. (198)

4. Occupation? .... (198)

5. How long have you been a Christian? .... (198)

6. Do you ever teach Sunday school?   ....
                 lead Sunday worship?   ....
                 preach?   ....
                 lead Bible study?   ....
                 lead women's meetings? ....
                 other?   ....

    If so, have you had any training for this particular
service? .... (199)

7. Have you received any Bible school or seminary training?
.... If so, when? .... where? .... (199)

8. Are you planning to be a pastor? .... (199)

9. How long have you been a student in this school? ....
Studying presently? ....
If married, is your partner also studying? ...... (199)

10. How far do you live from the school? .... (199)

11. What courses have you taken? Course   Length   Place
                                  ....
                                  ....
                   (199-200) ....

12. About how much time did you spend per week in preparation for these courses? .... (200)

13. What course has been most helpful to you? ....
    Why? .... (200)

14. What is one course you would like to take if offered?
    .... (200)

15. Next to the Bible, what Christian book or periodical do you find most helpful? .... (413-414)

16. Did you study with Dr. Charles when he taught in Japan?
    .... (200)

17. What concrete suggestions do you have to make the Eastern Hokkaido Bible School even better? ....
    (200)

@ Indicates page on which information is used.

Appendix G

Church Questionnaire *

1. Name of church? .... (96)@ Reporter .... (367)

2. Year church began? .... (96)

3. Present active membership? .... (96)

4. City in which located? .... (96)
   Population........ Growing? .... (220)

5. Weekly meetings: Meeting   Place   Leader
   .... (200-
   .... 221)

6. Monthly meetings: ....
   .... (221)

7. Is the chairman of Sunday worship a layman? ....
   Sometimes a woman? .... (277)

8. Do laymen ever preach? ...... Sometimes a woman? ......
   (277)

9. About how many potential lay leaders are there in the
   church? .... (96)

10. Has the church had a lay training program in the past?
    ....

If so, what courses were taught? By whom? For how
long? How many students?

....
....
....
Did you feel it was worthwhile? .... Any special
problems? .... (96-97)

11. Does the church have a lay training program now? ......
     If so, please describe as above. (If you need more
     space, please use the back.) (97)

12. Does the church have church officers? .... If so,
     what positions are there? ....
                          .... (378)

13. Does the church have elders? .... If so, how many? ....
                          deacons? ....   "   ....
            (378) deaconesses? ....   "   ....

14. What form of baptism does the church practice?
     Sprinkling? .... Immersion? ....
     Do you give candidates a choice of form? ....
     Do you have a pre-baptismal course?........ If so,
        what content? .... How long? ....
     Do you have a post-baptismal course? .... If so,
        what content? .... How long? .... (392)

15. What are the requirements for church membership? (If
     you have a statement, please attach it to this sheet.)
     .... (393)

16. Have you had any problems with transfers to other
     churches? ...... If so, of what nature? ...... (393)

17. How often do you have communion? ...... Regular or
         special service? ....
     Are unbaptized believers also allowed to participate?
     ....
     Have you ever had a love feast? .... (397-398)

18. How many unmarried girls are there? ...... Unmarried
        men? ....
     Does the church marry Christian and non-Christian? ....
     Does the church marry non-Christian and non-Christian?
     ....
     If so, have any of them become Christian? ...... (400)

19. How many Christian families are there in the church?
...... (400)

20. Have there been any cases of discipline in the church?
..... If so, what for and by whom? .... (400)

21. Have any "gifts of the Spirit" (I Cor. 12) been manifested in the church? ....
If so, which ones? .... (410)

22. Have any members been lost to the Jehovah's Witnesses?
.... If so, how many? ....
Mormons? .... If so, how many? ....
Tōitsu Kyōkai [Unification Church]? .... If so,
how many? .... (416)

23. Do you ever get together with other Mennonite churches
for fellowship? ..... If so, how often? ..... (314)

24. Do you ever get together with non-Mennonite churches
for fellowship? ..... If so, how often? .....
Does your city have a "city Christmas?" .....
World Day of Prayer? ..... (314-315)

25. Does the church use English for evangelism? .....
If so, about how many members have come through this
means? ...... (289)

26. Does the church have any special booklet they give
first-time visitors? ..... If so, what? ..... (416)

27. Does the church have a simple pamphlet explaining its
history, beliefs, practices? ..... (416-417)

28. How many pastors has the church had?   Name   Term
....
(286)   ....

29. How many pastors have come out of the church? ....
Name   Present position
....
....
If they are still pastors, but serving in another
denomination, what do you feel is the main reason?
.... (118)

30. Is anyone from the church in training now to be a pastor? ....
           Name   School   Expected graduation
          ....
          ....
    If so, what do they plan to do after graduation?..(119)

31. Is the church participating in the Kyushu "Total Mobilization Evangelism" (*Sodōin Dendō*) program? .... (281)

32. What are the church's goals for this year (1974)? .... (318-319)

*Answered by the following for each of the churches:

Aburatsu	:	Munetoshi Hirakawa
Atago	:	Takeomi Takarabe
Baba Cho	:	Takeji Nomura
Hyuga	:	Tsugio Aratake
Kirishima	:	Ichiro Kawakami
Kirishima Brotherhood	:	Takashi Yamada
Namiki	:	Hiroshi Isobe
Oita	:	Peter Derksen, Katsuhiko Kurimoto
Oyodo	:	Hiroshi Yanada
Takajo	:	Anna Dyck

@Indicates page on which information is used.

Appendix H

Church Member Questionnaire *

1. Name of church? .... (348-349)[@]

2. Age: 15-25 ....   26-35 ....   36-45 ....   46-55 ....
           56-65 ....   66+   .... (122)

3. Sex: male / female   Single? ....   Married? ....
   If married, is your partner also Christian? ...... (122)

4. What is your occupation? .... (122)

5. How long have you been a Christian? .... (278-279)

6. Was your family religion Christianity? .... (279)

7. What was the greatest influence in your becoming a
   Christian? .... (279-280)

8. Were you baptized in this church? .... (393-394)
   If not, what church did you transfer from? ....

9. How far do you live from the church? .... (277)

10. On the average, how many meetings do you attend a
    week? ....
    If you have children, do they attend Sunday school? ....
    Does your family sometimes read the Bible and pray
    together? .... (277-278)

11. Do you ever teach Sunday school? .....
                 lead Sunday worship? .....
                 preach?   .....
                 lead Bible study?   .....
                 lead women's meeting? .....
                 other?   ....
    If you have filled any of the positions listed above,
    have you received any special training for them?
    .... (277)

12. Have you ever participated in any kind of lay training
    program? ..... If so, what? ..... when? .....
    where? ..... (121)

13. If the following courses were offered, which ones would
    be of most interest to you? (Please check three.)

    ... Church History   ... Other Religions
    ... Bible Study Methods   ... Mennonite History
    ... Christian Ethics   ... Old Testament Intro.
    ... Personal Evangelism   ... Teachers' Training
    ... Jehovah's Witnesses   ... Prophecy
    ... Prayer   ... Christian Doctrine (282-283)

14. Have you ever had a Christian meeting in your home?
    ..... If not, would you be willing to? ..... (278)

15. What is the biggest problem you face as a Christian?
    .... (281)

16. Next to the Bible, what Christian book or periodical
    do you find most helpful? .... (413)

17. What do you think of the "*Tomo yo Utaō!*" [Let's Sing,
    Friend!] songs? .... (411-412)

18. Did you go to see "*Shio Kari Tōge* [Pass]"? .....
    Would you recommend it to others? .... (412)

19. How important do you feel the work of the Church
    Conference is?
             small ...   considerable ...   great ... (330)

___

*
Answered by members of each of the ten churches listed in
Appendix D.

@
Indicates page on which information is used.

Appendix I

Pastor Questionnaire *

1. Name .... (372)[@]

2. Age: 25-35 ... 36-45 ... 46-55 ... 55+ ... (248)

3. How long have you been a Christian? .... (248)

4. Was your family religion Christianity? .... (248)

5. What was the greatest influence in your becoming a Christian? .... (248)

6. What is your home church? .... (286-287)

7. How long have you been a pastor? .... (248)

8. What was the greatest influence in your becoming a pastor? .... (248)

9. Do you view the pastorate as God's call for a lifetime? .... (248)

10. Did you do any other work before becoming a pastor? .... If so, what kind? .... How long? .... (249)

	School	Dates	Degree
11. Have you attended university?	......	....	......
Bible school?	......	....	......
(120) seminary?	......	....	......

12. What was the biggest problem you faced as a student?
.... (117–118)

13. Do you feel your training was adequate for your work?
.... (120)

14. What courses have you found most helpful? .... (288)

15. Would you like to continue your education? ...... (120)
If so, in what area? .... (288)

16. Have you been ordained? ...... If so, when? ......
where? ...... By whom? ......
If not, do you pronounce the benediction? ....
                   baptize? ....
                   serve communion? ....
                   conduct weddings? ....
       (380) conduct funerals? ....

17. What does ordination mean to you? (If you need more
space, please use the back.) .... (381–382)

18. What churches have you served as pastor?
    Church   Period
    ....
    .... (249)

19. Do you also do part-time work? ....
If so, what? .... Hours per week? .... (250)

20. If married, does your wife work? ......
If so, what? ..... Hours per week? ..... (250)

21. What percent of your support comes from the church?....
                                    self-employment?....
                    (250) the Church Conference?....

22. If possible, would you prefer to be totally self-
supporting? ...... (251)

23. Do you feel it is feasible for one pastor to serve two
or three small churches? ...... (255)

24. How large do you feel a church should be to support a
full-time pastor? ...... (251)

25. Do you ever preach in other churches? ......
If so, how often? ...... (287)

26. Have you done any teaching in other churches? ....
    If so, what? ..... when? ..... where? ..... (287)

27. Would you be willing to teach a short course in other
    churches? .....
    If so, what is an area of special interest to you?
    .... (287)

28. Do you participate in a city pastors' meeting? ....
    If so, how often? .... (315)

29. How long do you think a pastor should stay in one
    church? .... (258)

30. Do you have any interest in moving to a new area to do
    pioneer evangelism? .... (259)

31. What is the most difficult problem you face as a
    pastor? .... (250)

32. Do you use English in your work? ......
    Are you studying English now? ......
    If not, are you interested in continuing your study of
       English? ...... (289)

33. How would you rate the importance of English as a
    method of evangelism?
       small .... considerable .... great .... (289)

34. Are you planning to participate in the "Overseas Church
    Leaders Study-Service Program"? ...... (290)

35. If you could make one change in your ministry, what
    would it be? .... (259)

36. What do you feel is the greatest need of our Church
    Conference? .... (31-32)

* Answered by the following pastors: Tsugio Aratake
                                       Hiroshi Isobe
                                       Takeji Nomura
                                       Takeomi Takarabe
                                       Takashi Yamada
                                       Hiroshi Yanada

@ Indicates page on which information is used.

Appendix J

Missionary Questionnaire *

1. Name .... (376)[@]

2. Age: 20-35 ... 36-50 ... 51-65 ... (248)

3. How long have you been a missionary? .... (248)

4. What was the greatest influence in your becoming a missionary? .... (248-249)

5. Do you plan to "bury your bones" in Japan? (That is, do you view your calling to be a missionary in Japan as a lifetime commitment?) ...... (249)

	School	Dates	Degree
6. Have you attended college or	......	......	......
university?	......	......	......
Bible school?	......	......	......
seminary?	......	......	......

If married, has your partner had any formal Bible school or seminary training? ...... (249)

7. Do you feel your training was adequate for your work? ...... (249)

8. What courses have you found most helpful? ...... (288)

9. Would you like to continue your education? ......
If so, in what area? .... (289)

373

10. Have you been ordained? ......
     If so, when? ...... where? ...... By whom? ......

     If not, do you pronounce the benediction? .....
                         baptize?   .....
                         serve communion?   .....
                         conduct weddings?   .....
          (382-383) conduct funerals?   .....

11. What does ordination mean to you? (If space is inade-
     quate, please write on the back.)............ (383-384)

12. Are you a member of a Japanese church, American church,
     or both? ...... (395)

13. How large is your home church? ...... (409)

14. Is the chairman of Sunday worship in your home church
     a layman? ...... Ever a woman? ......
     Do laymen ever preach? ..... Sometimes a woman? .....
     (408-409)

15. Does your church have a lay training program (besides
     S.S.)? ......
     If so, please describe. .... (428)

16. Does your church have church officers? .....
     If so, what positions are there? ....
                                       ....
     Does your church have elders?   .....
                         deacons?   .....
                         deaconesses?   ..... (379-380)

17. What form of baptism does your church practice?
                    Sprinkling or pouring?   .....
                    Immersion?   .....
                    Both?   .....
     If both, are candidates given a choice of form? ....
     Is there any problem with transfers to or from other
     churches? ....
     How old were you when you were baptized? ....
     Did you have a pre-baptismal course?   ....
                    post-baptismal course?   .... (394-395)

18. How often does your church have communion? ....
     Regular or special service? ....
     Are unbaptized believers also allowed to participate?..
     Has your church ever had a love feast? ...... (398-399)

19. Does your church marry Christian and non-Christian?....
    two non-Christians? ..... (401)

20. Have there been any cases of discipline in your
    church? ....
    If so, what for and by whom? .... (400-401)

21. Have any "gifts of the Spirit" been manifested in your
    church? ....
    If so, which ones? .... (410-411)

22. Have any members of your church been lost to the
    Mormons? ...... Jehovah's Witnesses? ......
    Other? .... (416)

23. What different churches have you worked with in Japan?
    Church   Period
    ....
    .... (250)

24. Do you ever preach in other churches? ......
    If so, how often? ...... (287)

25. Have you done any teaching in other churches? ....
    If so, what? ...... when? .... where? ...... (287)

26. Would you be willing to teach a short course in other
    churches? ..... If so, what is an area of special
    interest to you? .... (287-288)

27. Do you feel it is feasible for a missionary to work
    with two or three churches at one time? .... (255)

28. How large do you feel a church should be to support a
    full-time pastor? ...... (251)

29. How long do you think a pastor should stay in one
    church? ...... (258)

30. Do you participate in a city pastors' meeting? ....
    If so, how often? ...... (315)

31. Do you have any interest in moving to a new area to do
    pioneer evangelism? ...... (259)

32. What is the most difficult problem you face as a
    missionary? .... (250)

33. Do you use English in your work? ......
     Approximate hours per week? ...... (289)

34. How would you rate the importance of English as a
     method of evangelism?
         small .... considerable .... great .... (289)

35. If you could make one change in your ministry, what
     would it be? .... (259)

36. What do you feel is the greatest need of our Church
     Conference? .... (32)

* Answered by the following missionaries:
       Virginia Claassen   Martha Janzen
       Mary Derksen   Esther Patkau
       Peter Derksen   Ellen Sprunger
       Anna Dyck   Fritz Sprunger
       Del Epp   Bernard Thiessen
       Lucy Epp   Ruby Thiessen
       George Janzen

@ Indicates page on which information is used.

Appendix K

Implications of a Theological Education by Extension Program for Other Urgent Matters

In this study, reference has often been made to the Anabaptists, the spiritual ancestors of the Mennonites. As has been pointed out by church historians, one of the most recent images of the Anabaptists is that they were the "Bible Christians of the Reformation" (Dyck 1967:314). That is, more than any other group they took the Bible seriously as their rule of faith and practice. As descendants of the Anabaptist movement, Mennonites today tend to pride themselves on the fact that this is part of their heritage, and perhaps rightly so. Yet, it is not enough to just pride ourselves on our background. From time to time we need to reflect on how close our life really is to the Scriptures. To what degree do Mennonites, in fact, reflect Anabaptist ideals? To what degree do they actually reflect the New Testament itself? These questions need to be raised not only by the older churches, but by the so-called younger churches as well.

In relation to this, some of the data gathered in preparation for this paper reveals to some extent, I believe, a few of the current practices in the member churches of the JMCCC, as well as some of their North American counterparts from which the missionaries have come. While this matter cannot by any means be dealt with adequately here, especially with regard to a comparison of New Testament materials, I would like to present the information supplied me in hopes of at least raising a few of the issues involved, and hopefully to stimulate further thinking on them. There

are half a dozen or so areas into which the data falls, and
we will try to consider them as briefly as possible one at
a time.

STRUCTURE

By structure is meant the leadership structure of the
churches. When asked whether they have church officers or
not, six of the ten churches replied they did, three said
they did not, and one did not answer the question. As to
the way they are set up, one said their church simply has a
chairman, a secretary, and a treasurer. Another was a
little more complex, saying their officers consisted of
church representatives, secretary, treasurer, evangelism
committee members, and education committee members. A third
reported they had two treasurers (sharing the responsibility?), youth group officers, a person in charge of their
Total Mobilization Evangelism (*Sōdōin Dendō*) program, and a
person in charge of the library. One said they have deacons,
church officers, women's and young people's groups. Still
another mentioned that "as far as office work goes, there is
only a treasurer. The chief work of the church officers is
spiritual leadership. There are three members."

In reply to whether they have elders or not, of the nine
churches who answered, one said Yes, eight, No. Two of
them have deacons; seven do not. One of them said they have
a deaconess, eight of them not. The churches who said they
have deacons each reported that they have two, but one
commented that "we don't use the title deacons. They are
called church officers." The same would be true of the
deaconess who is also a member of that particular church.

Thus there appears to be considerable variety in the
structural setup of the churches. There is a total of about
10 different positions, including that of pastor. There are
few elders, deacons, or deaconesses in the churches,
although in some cases it looks as if there are persons
serving the same function even though the identical terms
may not be used. Some of the congregations would seem to be
structured more or less functionally, with committees to
meet the needs of various groups such as young people and
ladies. Most of the church structure is seemingly to take
care of internal affairs. Included here would be such functions as an educational committee. Also, there seem to be
only two churches with any kind of outreach committee. But
as churches are still rather small in size, perhaps outreach as well as internal matters can be handled fairly well

with just a few church officers. In any event, this is more or less how the churches are structured. In cases where there were reported to be no church officers, presumably most of the necessary business is carried out by the pastor himself, or in consultation with some or all of the members of the congregation. Yet even in cases where there are officers, it is not clear to what degree they actually lead the church, and the great variety in patterns and situations makes this even more difficult to assess.

By way of comparison, when asked whether their home churches in North America have church officers or not, 12 of the 13 missionaries replied theirs did. In one case it was not clear whether it did or not. As to the makeup of this group, four of them said that their church had a chairman, secretary, and treasurer (plus a few other positions such as vice-chairman in some cases). One said that the leading committee in her church consisted of a chairman, secretary-treasurer, trustees, chairmen of the faith and life, missions, and education committees, and also included the pastor. Another said his had a ministerial council made up of deacons and trustees and pastors, with an executive committee elected from that body. One other mentioned that his church simply had a spiritual council. In some cases, the respondents noted that they had been away from home so long they did not know or were not sure how their church was structured any more.

As to whether their churches have elders or not, seven said Yes, five, No, and again one was not clear. Eleven of the churches have deacons; two do not. Two have deaconesses, nine do not, and in two cases it was not apparent whether they do or not. Thus over half of the churches have elders, over three-fourths have deacons, but only a couple have deaconesses. Of these three categories, one church has only elders. Four have only deacons. Five have both deacons and elders. One has elders, deacons, and deaconesses. Another has only deacons and deaconesses. In one case, there are no elders, deacons, or deaconesses.

It may be that in some cases elders and deacons are almost interchangeable terms, used for the same office. In other cases they may be quite clearly distinguished, as where one person stated that in his church "elders look after the spiritual welfare of the church; deacons look after the physical welfare of the church." Also, it is hard to say whether the offices of elder and deacon are restricted to men, or in certain cases may include women.

One person observed that in the case of her church, "The
members of the executive committee do the 'desk' work but
decisions are made by the congregation as a whole. Business
sessions are open to both men and women, although women are
usually silent." So it is not exactly clear what the role
of women is in this area.

At any rate, there seems to be considerable variety in
the structure of local congregations, some more simple and
some more complex. This may depend somewhat on the size of
the church, but there is a total of close to 10 positions,
including the pastor, found in the various churches. Almost
all have deacons or elders, some have both, although just
what the duties of these offices entail is not spelled out.
In many ways the churches appear to be structured functionally, yet almost all the structure would seem to be for the
purpose of carrying on internal affairs, and only one
indicated they had a mission committee for outreach. The
others may too, although it may not be called exactly that,
and it's hard to really know the structure of a congregation
on the basis of such meager data. While all of the churches
have some kind of leadership structure, it is not evident
how much leading these leaders actually do and how much is
left to the pastor.

On the basis of this data alone, it is also difficult to
say how much influence the structure of North American
churches has had on church structure here in Japan. In
light of the great variety in structure, the nature of the
various positions listed, the inward looking nature of the
structure and so on, it would appear at first glance that
the influence may be considerable. But before elaborating
any more on that, perhaps at least one more area ought to be
explored and that is how leadership is designated in the
church. In other words, what place does ordination have?
To that we turn next.

ORDINATION

In answer to whether they had been ordained or not, only
one of the six pastors gave a positive reply. He was the
first pastor called, and was ordained in 1959 (at the
Aburatsu Church, Nichinan) by the missionary elders. The
other five pastors replied they have not been ordained. Yet
in response to a related question as to whether they pronounce the benediction, baptize, serve communion, conduct
weddings or funerals, they all answered Yes. Which says
that even though most of them have not been ordained, they

still carry out all the functions we usually expect of ordained leaders. This situation, of course, raises many questions. Why was the first pastor ordained and the others not? Have any of the others desired ordination? If so, why have they not been ordained? If not, why not? In short, what does ordination mean to them?

When asked, "What does ordination mean to you?", the pastors (1974) gave various replies as follows:

"I have not studied much about the significance of ordination. But as long as it is mentioned in the Bible, it must have some significance. As for me, I don't have any idea yet."

"I don't have any special problems with it."

"I can recognize the significance of ordination as a service of appointment to the ministry, but I cannot see it as a service appointing a person to the status of pastor. This understanding of ordination, as marking the appointment of a person to the status of pastor (as someone specially set apart with some authority above others), is found today in post-reformation Protestant groups as well as in Anabaptist-Mennonite circles. It is also existent in practice in the latter, and what is worse, it is tied up with authority within the church. For that reason, I cannot accept it."

"It does not have much meaning. Rather, it has many negative aspects. One of these is that it gives a consciousness of special privilege toward the pastor's position. There are many big questions about being able to perform the ordinances of the church just because one has received ordination. Rather than such formalism, we ought to give greater weight to the more real issues (such as a pastor's call, experience, and service to the congregation)."

"I do not feel there is any special meaning in ordination which is practiced by many religious organizations today. If the meaning of ordination were made clear on the basis of the Bible, and if it were performed with a proper purpose, standard and method, it might be different but ..."

"I do not feel it has any special meaning. (This is also true from the fact that in the case of our

organization non-ordained pastors are also able to
perform the ordinances.)"

On the basis of the above statements, it is clear that
ordination does not seem to have much meaning among the
pastors. Even the pastor who was ordained said he felt it
did not have any particular meaning. One did suggest, however, he felt it may have some significance, although he had
not had a chance to really study it yet. Others mentioned
it may have significance if the meaning is made clear from
the Bible. But it is quite evident that there is a general
consensus that ordination should not be tied up with the
status or authority of a pastor. This being so, there may
be other things which are felt to be more worthy of consideration at this time. And with the pastors all performing
the functions of ordained men already, perhaps it makes the
situation more understandable. But the question still
remains, why are things the way they are? Is not something
like ordination necessary for order in the churches? Why
does ordination seem to have meaning in some denominations,
and not in others? Why does ordination seem to have so
little meaning among the JMCCC churches? Does this stem
from a study of Scripture, or perhaps from some other
source?

By way of comparison, when it comes to the missionaries,
only five of the 13 (1974) replied that they had been
ordained. One noted that while he was not ordained, he had
been "licensed"; another, that while she had not been
ordained, she had been "commissioned" as a missionary. Perhaps most of the others also were at least commissioned.
But of the five who had been ordained, three of them were
men, two were (single) women. It is perhaps noteworthy
that none of the missionary wives have been ordained. This
may suggest a slightly different role for them than for the
single workers.

In any event, all of those who reported they had been
ordained received their ordination in the 1950s -- four of
them in Canada, one in the U.S. Two of them were ordained
more than once. In fact, one of the two reported that he
had been ordained three times! Once as a minister, then as
a missionary, and finally as an elder. The first two ordinations took place in Canada, the third in Japan. The other
missionary who was ordained more than once also received his
second ordination in Japan. The ordinations in Canada were
performed by elders. It may have some significance that
each of the Canadian missionaries was ordained at one time

or another by the same elder (J. J. Thiessen). The ordinations in Japan were performed by already ordained fellow
missionaries.

It should perhaps also be pointed out that in addition to
the earlier missionary wives, none of the later missionaries,
men or women, married or single, have been ordained. Whether
this is just a temporary phenomenon or indicates a trend may
be of value to pursue. At any rate, when those who have not
been ordained were asked if they pronounced the benediction,
baptized, served communion, conducted weddings and funerals,
in most cases the answer was No. There were two who said Yes,
they did pronounce the benediction. One said he also performed the other functions. But except for the benediction,
seven of the eight said No, they did not perform these functions. One of them did indicate though that she would feel
free to do so if the situation required it.

What then does ordination signify to the missionaries?
Why is it that all of the older missionaries (men and single
women) are ordained, but none of the younger ones are? Is
it because the earlier missionaries or the pastors (most of
them also unordained, however) are carrying the responsibilities of the usual ordained leader? Has ordination lost
its meaning? Or is it simply being neglected? How do the
missionaries feel about ordination anyway? What does it
mean to them? When asked this question, they replied as
follows:

"Ordination indicates the acceptance of certain responsibilities."

"A setting apart for a given task -- by the Lord more
than by man, although man is used as the instrument."

"Confirmation, by the church, of God's call to service."

"A recognition by me and the church as having the gift
of teaching, preaching, and witnessing and being set
aside by God and the church for that purpose."

"Primarily it means to me that the church has accepted
me to minister to its needs in the capacity of leadership."

"A way of designating (setting apart) a leader of a
congregation. I don't feel it should be permanent but
rather be an active office while the person is actively
engaged in pastoral work. This calling (setting apart)

of a leader should take place within the context of a
congregation in consultation with the wider fellowship
(conference). It would and should often follow certain
training (but need not necessarily be so)."

"Designates leader of a group. Don't think it should
involve special powers to baptize etc., but rather from
an organizational point of view."

"Given the blessing of fellow believers to lead in
certain functions of the organized church. To me it
means not an investment of power or authority but the
responsibility to give guidance and leadership when
asked to do so and when necessary, so that the group
of believers can function orderly and be about its
business of worshipping and witnessing."

"A lifetime promise to serve the Lord faithfully in
the tasks and areas He assigns. Though the person has
the right to baptize, etc., it is not necessarily a
must that he should exercise these rights; on the other
hand, I believe those not ordained should question themselves why they exercise the right without ordination."

"I'm not sure. That's the reason I'm not ordained.
The other is that the pastor I work with has not been
ordained either. If I was and he wasn't, I would probably be expected to perform the ordinances he does
now. But why should I get ordained if it doesn't seem
to have any meaning in the Japanese context?"

Three of the missionaries did not reply to the question
of what ordination meant to them, but from the replies given
one can get a general idea of how the missionaries feel.
Compared to the pastors it seems to have greater meaning for
the missionaries, even for some of those not yet ordained.
For the most part they seem to see ordination as a functional thing, designating or setting apart the leader or
leaders of a congregation. It is a confirmation by the
church of gifts given. Also of God's call. Some feel it is
a temporary thing; others suggest it is permanent. But in
any case, it seems to me what is significant is that while
this setting apart is felt to be necessary or good for the
organization of the church, the status of the one set apart
is not changed. It is not felt ordination gives a person
greater power or status. Rather, it is seen as the setting
apart of a person for service. In a very real sense perhaps
we could say it is the setting apart or designating of the
church's servants, rather than of its leaders.

What does all this imply? It is difficult to say on the basis of a limited study like this. But when most of the older missionaries are ordained and the younger are not, when some have been ordained as often as three times and others not at all, and most of the pastors have not been ordained either and yet are performing the same functions as ordained persons, it makes one wonder if it is maybe not time to restudy the whole matter in greater depth. Why were the first missionaries ordained but the later ones not (just as in the case of the pastors)? To what extent have the churches patterned themselves after the missionary pattern (or lack of it)? Or to what extent have the churches themselves influenced the pattern? Why is it that ordination seems to have so little meaning in our circles? What does the New Testament actually have to say about the topic? If we could again take a good hard look at it, perhaps it would not only be helpful with regard to the work of the churches in Japan, but in America as well. And especially to some like myself, for whom the meaning of ordination is not all that clear.

Note: After having compiled the above material on ordination, I subsequently discovered that this subject has, in fact, had considerable attention before. In a folder on "Ordination" found in the Mission file, there is a report, for example, on a "Conference on Ordination" held at the Mennonite Biblical Seminary in Chicago in July 1957. This was sponsored by the Committee on the Ministry of the General Conference Mennonite Church. One of the papers presented in connection with that conference was a good study on "Ordination in Biblical and Historical Perspectives," by Erland Waltner. In a report by the Findings Committee of the conference, there is also a brief statement on some of the implications of the historical developments for the ordination of ministers in the General Conference.

There is also a copy of a paper from a few years later, 1962 to be exact, entitled "Some Theses Concerning Ordination," by Cornelius Dyck. This was a rather detailed presentation made to introduce the topic for joint faculty discussion at the Associated Mennonite Biblical Seminaries (Elkhart, Indiana). It was a study made in relation to the larger question of the Christian ministry. There are other papers in the file and much correspondence also with regard to the whole matter of ordination.

One of the most comprehensive reports was a "Statement on Ordination, Commissioning, and Licensing," along with

"Procedures for Ordination and Certification of Ministers,"
both of them by the Committee on the Ministry (GCMC 1964).
These statements were apparently drawn up for presentation
to the triennial session of the General Conference in 1965.
But it was actually not until nine years later, at the
session in 1974, after such statements had been worked and
reworked many times, that the Conference finally passed a
Resolution on Ordination. In a condensation of it from *The
Mennonite*, it

> Affirms both the priesthood of all believers and
> the designation of leadership roles. Ordination implies
> function, not status, and is available to persons,
> regardless of race, class, or sex. No sinful act
> should permanently disqualify a forgiven person from
> serving a congregation (GCMC 1974:488).

From this brief review of developments, you can see it
has taken quite a long time to arrive at any sort of consensus on the subject in the North American General Conference
churches. But the above resolution was finally adopted, and
no doubt will be an important guideline for the future.

In Japan the subject of ordination has also received
much interest over the years. As a matter of fact, way
back in 1956, at the annual missionary meeting, a resolution
was passed with regard to the qualifications of a minister.
For a person with training, it read as follows:

1. The man must be called by the church.
2. He should complete 3-4 years of Bible school or
    seminary.
3. He should work as assistant pastor or under the
    supervision of a missionary or experienced pastor
    for a minimum of 2 years after graduation.
4. Upon the recommendation of the supervising pastor
    or missionary and upon completion of the minister's
    entrance examination he is eligible for full ordina-
    tion.
5. He must be a Christian for 7 years before he is
    ordained (GCMM, Resolution 4, Annual Conference,
    1956:4).

For a person without training, the qualifications were the
same except that if he was a young man he was strongly
urged to get some Bible school or seminary training, and
would need to have at least three years of supervised
experience.

A questionnaire for examining ministerial candidates was also drawn up. It had to do with one's personal Christian experience, God's call to the ministry, previous work experience, educational training, doctrinal beliefs, familiarity with Mennonite history and so on. Thus there appears to have been from the beginning a good deal of attention given to the whole question of ordination.

As mentioned previously, the first ordination of a pastor took place in 1959. In 1964 there were requests from two churches for their pastors to also be ordained. So the Elders Committee took up this matter. But instead of approving the ordination of these two leaders right away, they began to rethink what ordination was all about. This resulted in an historical decision, which is included in a report from the Elders Committee to the 1965 annual meeting of the Kyushu (Japan) Mennonite Church Conference, as follows:

CONCERNING OFFICIATING
AT THE OBSERVANCE OF THE SACRAMENTS

In June, 1965, the Elders Committee of the Kyushu Mennonite Church (in our group the elders committee is composed of the missionaries and pastors who have been ordained) met to discuss the applications for ordination for two pastors. At the time, the committee considered anew the meaning and condition of ordination, the relation of ordination and the administration of the sacraments and other related matters. The result of that discussion is the following decision:

"We believe that each congregation is responsible to the Lord Himself and therefore each congregation, under the leadership of the Holy Spirit, has the authority to administer Baptism and the Lord's Supper."

Now a word concerning the need for such a decision. Up until now, whenever the sacraments were observed, an ordained missionary or pastor has always officiated. For this reason a church, served by a pastor who is not ordained, and which has no ordained missionary working with it, could not have baptism or communion unless it invited an ordained man from another place to come and officiate. From various angles this has been troublesome and inconvenient and has denied churches the spiritual blessings connected with the

observance of the sacraments. When the elders committee discussed the matter in this light the question of
who may officiate was raised and the above decision
was reached.

The purpose behind this decision is that, even in
cases where churches do not have an ordained pastor or
missionary, the congregation, under the guidance of
the Holy Spirit, may choose a suitable leader to
officiate at the sacraments. Concretely this decision
means:

1) That an unordained pastor or missionary also,
may, following the leading of the Holy Spirit and
the decision of the congregation, officiate at the
sacraments.
2) A church, if it is so led, may choose a suitable
person from among the laymen, to officiate at the
sacraments.
3) The church may, if the need is felt, call a
person from another place, to officiate at the
sacraments.

However, any congregation which wishes to exercise
its authority, based on the above decision, and choose
a leader to officiate at the sacraments, must carefully
and fully consider the following:

1) It is understood that the church will do this
only after it is assured of the leading of the Holy
Spirit through heart-searching prayer and faith.
2) There must be a thorough effort to teach the
meaning and observance of the sacraments so the
entire church fully understands what it is doing.
3) While each congregation may choose the leader it
is important that, if necessary, it have the counsel
and advice of the wider fellowship of our Mennonite
churches in order that they will not make a wrong
decision in this matter.
4) The elders committee stands ready to counsel and
advise each congregation, when so requested (JMCCC,
Elders Committee Report, Annual Conference, October
1965:1-2).

The above statement, or rather, the decision of the
Elders Committee was approved by the larger Conference. As
intended, in some cases it undoubtedly made it easier for
the local churches to conduct baptism and observe communion.

At the same time, it raised anew the question, what then
does ordination mean? This question had in fact been asked
earlier, in a letter to his fellow elders that was written
shortly after the original proposal had been made:

> The decision to cease making ordination a requirement
> for the administration of the Lord's supper and baptism
> received my approval. However, I think we made the
> decision rather hastily without having time to think
> through just what this might mean. If ordination
> before, among other responsibilities, also brought with
> it the "authority" to give communion and baptize, what
> really does it mean now? If it still means primarily
> a symbolical confirmation of the call of God to the
> ministry then we should ordain as pastor or "dendoshi"
> [evangelist] soon after being called by a church. If
> this would be done then we would simply be saying that
> baptism and the Lord's supper can be administered with-
> out eldership ordination. In our decision the other
> day have we not gone to the other extreme now for in
> practice we are saying a man can serve a congregation
> indefinitely now without ordination of any kind. I am
> afraid there will be a tendency to postpone ordination
> as elder now because there is no practical need for it
> in the church. We already have one man that is serving
> the third church without any ordination. Will the
> church see the need for ordination and will the pastor
> himself see the need? Who will now encourage ordina-
> tion, the church or the board of elders (Boschman,
> June 1965:1)?

In response to this, one of the other members of the
committee prepared a rather detailed study on the "Biblical
Qualifications for Ordination" (Unruh, July 1965), for consideration by the elders. There may have been other input
also. At any rate, there seem to have been diverse points
of view expressed within the committee of elders itself, but
in spite of this they went on to make their recommendation
to the Conference, which was then passed unanimously. The
concerns expressed above appear to have been valid however,
as the two men for whom ordination had been requested were
not ordained. And although the number of pastors has
increased (to eight in 1978), there have been no further
ordinations since the first one.

There have been requests though from the churches for the
matter of ordination of pastors and elders to be taken up
again by the ordained brethren at the Church Conference

level. There was such a request in 1968 (JMCCC, Annual
Conference, 1968:12). In 1969, there were two more requests
for local pastors to be ordained. Correspondence indicates
that the Elders Committee began working on this, and seemed
favorable to the request, but it never led to the ordination
of these men either. One of them had even submitted an
84-page handwritten answer to the Ordination Examination
questions, yet for some reason or other was never ordained!
Just what happened is unknown to me. The matter seems to
have been dropped rather suddenly. Perhaps some of those
who were involved could shed more light on why things turned
out the way they did. But one wonders if the decision of
1965 might not have had something to do with the outcome.
Its intention was to provide local churches with the ordinances, and perhaps was seen as a temporary measure. Yet in
light of the fact that there have been no ordinations since
that time, it looks as if it may have become permanent.

There are, of course, many Christian denominations in
Japan which practice ordination. They no doubt feel they
have a good basis for it. As we have seen, however, the
JMCCC does not seem to attach much importance to it. The
same thing could be said of the Japan Mennonite Church (JMC)
congregations in Hokkaido. Even though they have studied
the subject to some degree and apparently reached a consensus that ordained leadership is needed in their congregations (as affirmed in their statement on "Study of Ministry
and Ordination," 1964), still only two or three of their
church leaders are reported to be ordained. The meaning of
ordination is said to be the big problem -- the meaning to
the leader and the meaning to the congregation.

Nevertheless, there are exceptions to this pattern.
In 1973, for instance, an inter-Mennonite congregation in
Tokyo requested the ordination of their pastor. Following
a study of the topic with representatives from several
other Mennonite-related groups in the area, the decision was
left up to the local church and the pastor was ordained.
Even in the JMCCC churches, while no pastors have been
ordained in the last 20 years, there is at least one case of
a layman being ordained as elder in one of the churches,
said to be hopefully the first of a board of elders (Thiessen
1969:1). So there are exceptions, to be sure, but for the
most part there does not seem to be much interest in con-
ferring ordination. To the contrary, there seem to be a
lot of questions about what it means.

What does ordination mean anyway? T. W. Manson, in speaking of the ministry of the church, touches on this. He concludes:

> The first and essential factor in ministry is the giving by Christ to the Church of the man whom He has called to the ministry. The second is the acceptance of Christ's gift by the Church and the formal recognition of the man whom the Lord has called. In the Church this recognition may be given by bishops, or a presbytery, or the local congregation. We call it ordination (1948:96).

To Manson the meaning of ordination appears to be clear. It is simply the formal recognition of a person God has given to serve the Church. And perhaps the important thing is not whether it is called "ordination" or not. If we are hung up on the word, perhaps it would be better not to use it at all. It is not a biblical term anyway.

But there are others who see ordination as implicit in baptism. That is, by virtue of their baptism, that all Christians have already been ordained to serve. Be that viewpoint as it may, it seems to the author that perhaps there ought to be a way, a place, and a time for the recognition or confirming of gifts too. Also, that such confirmation ought not to be limited to pastors or missionaries or other leaders already recognized within the church. What about Sunday school teachers? Lay evangelists and preachers? Bible study leaders? The church treasurer? The secretary? The Conference chairman? Church representatives? The bookstore workers? The kindergarten principal, its Christian teachers and so on? Is there not a place for a recognition of God's call to them also? And not only a confirmation of their call, but a promise to pray for them and give them our support? It goes without saying that this suggestion would include women as well as men.

I certainly cannot spell out all the implications of the above data with regard to ordination, especially here in Japan. But it does seem that we should at least know where we stand. If we are going to practice ordination or something like it, we should know why. If not, we should know why not. We need to have a basis for our practice as well as our faith. Whether the current practices were borrowed from America, whether they originated in Japan, or whether they may be a combination of the two may be debatable. But in light of this additional information we have just considered, it would tend to confirm the conclusion we arrived at earlier, that it may be time to once again take a look at the subject and try to reach some consensus on it.

BAPTISM

Turning now from ordination to some other church practices, the churches reported as follows with regard to baptism. As to form, all ten of the churches say they practice pouring rather than immersion. When asked whether they give candidates a choice of form, five of them said Yes, although one of them indicated that in their case anyhow up till now no one has requested immersion. Three said No, they do not give a choice. Two did not say.

As to whether they have a pre-baptismal course, all of the churches replied in the affirmative. With regard to content and length, there seems to be quite a variety. Two of them said their candidates study doctrine for three months; another, basic doctrines from three months to a year, depending on the person. Two groups use a Mennonite catechism book, one of them for only one or two sessions to six months, the other from three to six months, again both depending on the circumstances and the person. One of the churches does a study of the Apostles' Creed anywhere from two to six months, differing according to the needs of the candidate. One stated that the Bible is the center of their course, which lasts about a month. Another has two to four sessions with their candidates on faith and church life. Still another says they have a three-session course (using a simple booklet *"Senrei e no Michi Shirube"* [Preparing for the Road to Baptism], worked out by their former pastor) to acquaint people with the church's doctrines and beliefs. One church simply replied that the content and length of their course varies according to the person, as was mentioned in many of the above cases also. So while all the churches have something, the content seems to vary from basic doctrine to the Bible to the Apostles' Creed to a catechism or the use of some other brief course. The average length is about three months.

When asked whether they had a post-baptismal course, only one replied in the positive. The content is said to be a continued study of basic Christian doctrine, but there are no special limits as to length. Seven other churches said they did not have such a course. Two did not reply to the question, but presumably they do not either.

In response to what their requirements are for church membership, the eight churches who answered replied as follows:

"Faith."

"Believing in and following Christ."

"Repentance of sin and belief in Christ as one's Savior."

"A person who believes in Christ as God's Son with all his heart."

"'If you confess with your mouth the Lord Jesus Christ and believe in your heart that God raised him from the dead' -- faith in Christ as Savior and Lord."

"A sincere acceptance of the Apostles' Creed, and especially a personal experience of Jesus Christ's atonement for one's sin."

"Confession of faith based on the Bible; faithful attendance at the various meetings of the church."

"Believing in salvation through the Lord Jesus Christ; fulfilling one's duties as a church member, following the rules of the church, honoring the Lord's supper."

Belief in Christ and following Christ appear to be central to the requirements. Promising to be a good church member also comes through quite strongly. Related to the matter of membership, two churches did not respond to the question, but none of the churches appear to have a specific statement of faith of their own. They may rely on the Conference statement, or a confession like the Apostles' Creed instead.

As to whether they have problems with transfers to other churches, eight of the churches said No; two, Yes. One indicated it was a "problem of baptism." Another said that in their case, "it appeared to be form of baptism problem at first -- but basically it turned out to be spiritual state of the church. The problem is resolved." Otherwise, no major problems were listed.

In connection with this are the replies of the church members as to whether they were baptized in the church to which they belong at present. Seventy-six, or about

two-thirds, replied Yes; 33, or less than one-third, said
No. There were several who did not reply, or from their
answer "not yet" revealed that they apparently were unbaptized believers. Of those not baptized in their present
church, seven were transfers from other Mennonite churches.
Twenty-four were transfers from non-Mennonite churches, and
in a couple of cases it was not clear which it was from.
At least a few of these transfers from non-Mennonite
churches were from other local churches. Several were from
other prefectures, and there were also a small number from
Osaka or Tokyo. About 10 of the transfers came from various
denominations such as Alliance, Baptist, Church of Christ
(Christian Church), Free Methodist, Immanuel, United Church
of Christ (*Kyōdan*) and so on. In over half of the cases,
what denomination they transferred from was not identified.
There do not seem to have been any special problems, though,
transferring into the Mennonite churches. Any problems the
churches mentioned were connected rather with transferring
out (and perhaps related mostly to the matter of form of
baptism as noted in one case above).

By way of comparison, when the missionaries were asked
what form of baptism was practiced in their home churches,
eight of them said sprinkling or pouring; one, immersion;
four, both. One commented that his church practiced both
"although sprinkling or pouring are more common." Another
said that immersion was "upon request by the candidate,"
and still another that they occasionally immersed but that
it was "done in a neighboring church." Those who practice
both were also asked if they give the candidates a choice of
form. All of them said Yes. Another one remarked that
while his church did not practice both forms, candidates
"would be immersed if it was requested."

With regard to how old they were at the time of their
baptism, all the missionaries were between the ages of 12
and 18. The average age of baptism was fifteen, but the
most common ages were thirteen (2), fourteen (2), sixteen
(3), seventeen (3), and eighteen (2). As to whether they
had a pre-baptismal course, 11 of them said Yes; two, No.
But the replies as to whether they had a post-baptismal
course were almost the opposite. Ten said No; one, Yes,
"in Sunday school"; two "did not remember" or did not reply.

When asked whether there were any problems in their home
churches regarding transfers to or from other churches,
eight said No or "I don't think so," "not sure, not that I
know of." Three answered Yes; two did not say. Of those
who had problems, one reported that it was just "sometimes,"

another that it "depends on the receiving church," and a
third that they did "sometimes to [certain] churches." One
added a note of explanation on her baptism, saying,

> I was baptized in an evangelical Mennonite Church. We
> were given a choice of baptism form. In this group all
> chose to be immersed. Basically, my reason for being
> immersed was that transfer of church membership may be
> simpler.
>
> Another thing that I appreciated and continue to wish
> it were being done so in other churches is that baptism
> did not automatically make one a church member. In
> this church baptism was one step -- then if one chose
> at that time or later to become a member of the church
> it was another service, ritual or whatever it might be
> called.

As far as church membership goes, two of the missionaries
are formally members of a Japanese church only, four of
American churches, and seven of both.

From this comparison of practices in Japanese churches
and the churches from which the missionaries have come,
there are both similarities and differences. With regard to
baptism, most of the churches practice pouring, although
some say they give a choice when requested. Almost all have
pre-baptismal courses. But almost none have post-baptismal
courses. In both cases, there have been a few problems with
transfers to other churches, but this appears to be mainly a
problem of transferring out of rather than into the
Mennonite churches themselves. There would seem to be many
similarities with regard to the practice of baptism.

Traditionally, pouring has been the most common form of
baptism practiced among Mennonites, although as we have
observed there are exceptions, and other forms are recognized as well. As James H. Waltner has well stated in the
book, *This We Believe*, "The symbol is of less importance
than that which it symbolizes" (1968:143). That is, what
matters is not so much that a person has been baptized by
one form or another, but that he has "died with Christ" and
been "raised to a new life." The really important thing is
faith in Christ as Lord and Savior. This is something
Mennonites have stressed through their emphasis on believers'
baptism. That does not necessarily mean adult baptism. As
we have seen, some of the missionaries themselves were
baptized quite young. But it does mean the presence of

faith as a prerequisite to baptism. This is where the Anabaptists too placed the emphasis, on faith rather than form.
Today among their descendants also, with the exception of
one group in particular, outward forms have for the most
part not been stressed. Yet the form is a symbol, it
symbolizes something profound, and one wonders if perhaps
more attention should not be given to this aspect as well.

In the African Independent Churches (AICs), for example,
baptism is said to usually be by immersion in running water,
three times in the name of the Trinity (Brown 1972:169).
And yet, among these same churches, there are some which
have no baptism (cf. *Mukyōkai* in Japan); others practice
"dry baptism," without water; and still another group bap-
tizes using water that has been mixed with the blood of a
dove (1972:177-178)! Water baptism there is often connected
with cleansing, or is closely related to the baptism of the
Spirit. Baptism is almost always a separate service. It is
a solemn occasion, and yet also an occasion of joy for the
observers as well as the one baptized. There is no one form
that is followed. There are many forms, each designed for a
given culture. But to the people of that culture, the
symbol or the form, whatever it may be, is said to be important. It makes the rite even more meaningful.

Here in Japan, with an abundance of water, and with the
rite of cleansing also being an important aspect of the
traditional religions, especially Shintoism, one wonders why
there have not been more such original forms developed in
the Christian churches. Or why is there so much emphasis on
baptism with water, and so little on the baptism of the
Spirit? Cannot these two be combined? As Robert Friedman
asserts in his book on *The Theology of Anabaptism*,

> Baptism then is the external attestation for the
> internally experienced new birth. ... In this sense
> baptism is far more than a mere sign. It has a
> testimonial quality, *the attestation for a previously
> experienced "baptism" with the Holy Spirit*. There
> can be no question that in the early period of Ana-
> baptism adult baptism had this profound spiritual
> connotation (1973:136).

If water baptism really attests to a previous "baptism,"
as Friedman maintains, how can this best be illustrated in
actual practice, in the ceremony itself? Must our forms be
limited to sprinkling, pouring, or immersion? Why not work
at developing some new forms that may be even more meaningful

to the people of this land and culture? The form, to be sure, may be less important than what it symbolizes, yet it too can be full of meaning. Or, if the form is occasionally a problem as we have seen, might it not be well to consider adopting a form that would be acceptable anywhere? Writing out one's own personal confession of faith to be read at the baptism ceremony (as is done in some cases already) can also make the occasion more meaningful than simply giving assent to a fixed creed. And surely there are many other modifications which could be made. Perhaps an open sharing of innovations which have already been made here and there would be a good place to begin.

It may be of interest to add, in closing this section, that the first few baptisms in the first General Conference Mennonite church in Japan were by immersion, using a Baptist church, the thinking being that it might be easier to join other churches in the area later on. The switch to the practice of pouring, however, soon took place, perhaps from reasons of convenience more than anything else. But maybe this should be looked at again, from a biblical and theological as well as a practical point of view.

COMMUNION

When it comes to communion, there is considerable variation with regard to frequency. One of the churches says they have it every month. Another has it eight times a year. A third, approximately once every two months. Other churches report they have it six, four, or three times a year. Some, that they celebrate it two or three times a year, two times a year, or just once or twice a year. One group mentioned that the frequency of communion in their church is not fixed, but the average seems to be about five times a year. Almost all the groups have communion as part of a regular service. There are exceptions to this, though. The group celebrating it eight times a year, for instance, said that two of those are special services (Christmas and Easter?). Another indicated that their church often has communion after a baptismal service.

As to whether unbaptized believers are allowed to participate in communion, four of the churches said Yes; six, No. One of those whose church allows this commented, "they may take part in the communion in cases where it is deemed proper." It may be that this is considered on a case-by-case basis in the other groups also.

In reply to whether they have ever had a "love feast,"
four of the groups said Yes, five No, and one did not respond. Whether it is exactly a love feast or not is hard to
say, but one of the groups who responded in the affirmative
said that they eat lunch together every week after church.
Perhaps some other groups do this too, if not every week,
occasionally, although it was not brought out in their
replies. But still there may be some question as to the
definition of a love feast, as to whether simply eating
together can be considered a love feast or not. Thus the
number who have actually had a love feast may not be as
large as appears at first.

As for the frequency of communion in the missionaries'
home churches, their replies varied from two to six times a
year. The most common pattern seems to be having communion
at least three to four times a year, as mentioned by eight
of the missionaries. Only two reported they have it more
than four times in a year. Three did not answer the question, but on the average of those who did, communion appears
to be held about four times during a year. In reply to
whether this is part of a regular service or is a special
service, one said it was regular, five said "special" or
"usually special." Four said they had both kinds of services; three did not respond.

When asked whether unbaptized believers are also allowed
to participate in communion, one missionary said, "yes, if
they know the Lord personally." Ten said No; two did not
reply or "not know." Of those who said No, one was not sure,
saying, "don't think so." Another that it was "not as a
general principle, but there are exceptions." Still another
pointed out that in the case of his church, "those present
are asked to decide for themselves but usually only includes
church members." Thus as a general rule unbaptized believers would not seem to be allowed or at least not encouraged
to participate in communion, but there also may be exceptions to this.

In reply to whether their church has ever had a "love
feast" or not, there was one Yes, seven No, and five who did
not answer or had a question about it. One of the No
answers, for example, was "not to my knowledge." Others who
were not sure made such comments as "depends what you mean,"
or "I'm not sure what you mean by love feast. The congregation several times a year has meals together at church
(outside of weddings and funerals)." There does not seem to
be a clear consensus as to exactly what a love feast is, and

hence some may have found it difficult to give a direct answer to the question. Yet the one who gave a positive reply as to whether they had love feasts or not in her church simply said, "yes, often, but they are not called love feasts! Love is manifest!" And in the end, perhaps that is the most important thing.

From this comparison of communion practices in the missionaries home churches and the churches in Japan, again we can see similarities and differences. As to frequency, the most common pattern seems to be to have communion several times a year. In the North American churches, this is often a special service. In Japan, it is usually a part of a regular service, although in one case it was mentioned that it was held after a baptismal service. In Japan, unbaptized believers seem to be permitted in many cases to participate in communion (believers' communion versus baptized believers' communion), whereas in the American churches it appears to be rare. To the best of my knowledge, however, children in the Mennonite churches in Japan do not take part in communion even though they may be believers, whereas there are cases in the North American churches where they do, although that would no doubt still be the exception rather than the rule even there.

The question about whether love feasts were held or not may not have been as clear as it should have been, so it is difficult to make a comparison on that. But eating together or at least drinking tea together seems to be a lot more common in Japanese churches than among their counterparts overseas, where people so often rush home after services, and it makes one wonder if it might not be well to take advantage of this practice and try to work communion into it more frequently.

Just to what degree the churches here have followed the practices brought from overseas is hard to determine. There have naturally been some adaptations made. But it seems to me quite significant that none of the churches here have communion every week, or every time they meet, as is done in some other traditions. This may indicate that overseas influence is greater than we might think. But at any rate, perhaps as with baptism, an attempt should be made to find new forms for celebrating communion -- forms which may be more fitting to the Japanese culture. How this could actually be done is not for me to say. But I do believe that if we had the will, there would be a way, and it could be more meaningful for all.

DISCIPLINE

We turn now from the ordinances to the matter of church discipline. Each of the churches was asked whether there had been any cases of discipline in the church. If so, what for, and by whom. In reply to this, two of the churches said Yes; six, No; two did not answer. As to the purpose of the discipline, one church replied it was "for the sake of the person concerned." The other one said it was "to separate the person from false teaching, and to protect the flock." In both of these cases it was carried out by the church officers.

Related to this topic is the question, for instance, of whether a church would marry a Christian and a non-Christian. Six of the churches say they do; four, they do not. One of them said it was done on a case-by-case basis. Another, "We haven't had a case like that so far, but if one should arise, we would talk it over thoroughly with the unbelieving partner, and if that person was a serious seeker, would give consideration to performing the ceremony." As to whether they would marry two non-Christians, four said Yes, six said No. One said they do this also on a case-by-case basis. When asked if any of the non-Christians who had been married in the church later became Christians, two of the churches reported that one or two had done so, one replied No, and still another said they "didn't know."

There are a number of Christian families in the churches already. Some reported having only one, others up to seven. The average number of Christian families per church was between four and five, with a total of 37 (including a few widows in one case) for the eight churches who answered the question. But one of the striking figures was the number of *un*married girls -- 44! Another, the number of *un*married men -- 32! The different churches had anywhere from one to 16 unmarried girls, with an average of almost five. They had from zero to 11 unmarried men, with an average of between three and four. In light of this, one wonders if more attention should not be given to these singles, to the possibility of getting some of them together, and establishing more Christian homes. Perhaps a marriage committee could be set up to act as a "go-between." In any event, there seem to be various attitudes toward the marriage of Christian and non-Christian.

With regard to the same question as to whether there have been any cases of discipline in their home churches, 10

of the missionaries said Yes; two, No; one did not reply.
As to what the discipline was for and who dealt with it,
there were the following: "premarital sex; (dealt with by)
church board"; "adultery; (dealt with by) congregational
action, but initiated by pastor"; "girls pregnant at marriage
who didn't confess were excommunicated; also know of cases
where confession was made, and accepted; don't know how it's
dealt with now"; "those who joined armed forces -- not
allowed roles of leadership in church; those who became
pregnant outside of marriage -- publicly ask for forgiveness"; "in many forms, mostly counseling with unwed pregnant
girls, people who can't get along, etc."; "a group of
brethren have gone to individuals to talk to him as a
brother when there has been a problem"; "discipline in the
form of warnings -- presently often re excesses in the
charismatic movement -- i.e. speaking in tongues"; "if we
don't pay our church dues we are not allowed to vote at the
annual meeting."

   The answers given by the missionaries were more specific
than those from the churches. Several cases of sexual sin,
for example, were mentioned. Also, joining the armed
forces. In some of the cases it was noted that such problems were dealt with by the elders, the church board, or a
small group of brethren, but at other times it was taken up
by the whole congregation. There was one case also which
went so far as to speak of actual excommunication. On the
other hand, confession, forgiveness and acceptance were
also recollected.

   As to the marriage of Christian and non-Christian, four
missionaries said their churches did, two said they did not,
and seven said they "didn't know." When it came to the
marriage of two non-Christians, none said Yes; two said No,
and 11 did not know. This reflects the additional fact, I
believe, that most of these missionaries have been away from
their home churches for many years, and so do not know the
real situation anymore with regard to certain practices.
That this is so comes out in their vague replies to a number
of other questions too. However, one also brought out that
as to whether these things are done or not, it "depends more
on the pastor's viewpoint." Thus the pastor would seem to
play a key role here.

   When it comes to discipline in the New Testament, the
classic passage often referred to is Matthew 18:15-17. In
it Jesus speaks of going to a brother who has sinned, or
taking one or two others along, or even taking the matter

to the whole church when all else fails. The word *disci-*
pline does not occur in these verses, it is in fact not even
a New Testament word. But the concept is there. There are
passages about not being conformed to the world but being
transformed (Rom. 12:2), about being holy as God is holy
(I Pet. 1:15-16), or stressing the purity of the church,
"without spot or wrinkle" (Eph. 5:27). The practice is also
there. The apostle Paul, for instance, went to the extreme
of saying there were times when a person should even be
"delivered to Satan" (returned back to the world?) as a
disciplinary measure (I Cor. 5:4-5). Such a move would
hopefully cause the person in question to eventually repent
and be saved. Much emphasis is given to restoring an erring
person back to his or her rightful place in the church (e.g.,
Gal. 6:1). So while the word itself may not be used, the
idea and the practice of discipline are there in the life of
the Early Church.

As time went on, though, there came to be a double
standard practiced in many churches -- a higher one for the
clergy, another lower one for the laity. There was nothing
biblical about this, of course, and so at the time of the
religious reformation there were some groups like the Anabaptists who sought to go back to the practice of the Bible
itself. Discipline was, in fact, a very integral part of
Anabaptist belief and practice. The second article of their
"Schleitheim Confession" exemplifies this. It reads as
follows with regard to the ban (excommunication):

> We are agreed as follows on the ban: The ban shall
> be employed with all those who have given themselves
> to the Lord, to walk in His commandments, and with all
> those who are baptized into the one body of Christ and
> who are called brethren or sisters, and yet who slip
> sometimes and fall into error and sin, being inadver-
> tently overtaken. The same shall be admonished twice
> in secret and the third time openly disciplined or
> banned according to the command of Christ. Matt. 18.
> But this shall be done according to the regulation of
> the Spirit (Matt. 5) before the breaking of bread, so
> that we may break and eat one bread, with one mind and
> in one love, and may drink of one cup (Lieth 1963:
> 284-285).

From this it can be seen that discipline was closely
related to participation in communion or the breaking of
bread. The rest of the Confession too has primarily to do
with practice rather than belief -- with separation from

the world, non-use of the sword, the oath and so on (1963:
282-292). These practices were tied in with their concept
of the church as a carefully disciplined group of believers
and followers of Christ. Submission to the group was a part
of their commitment to the brotherhood.

As for today, a survey of "practices and trends" in
General Conference congregations was taken in 1955. This
was for a study conference on "The Believers' Church."
Maynard Shelly, who summarized the data, reports the following with regard to discipline in churches in both the United
States and Canada. Seventy-four percent have a provision in
their constitutions for church discipline. The remainder do
not, or do not have a written constitution, yet many of this
latter group are said to still practice some type of discipline. While the churches generally have a high ideal of
discipline, not all of them by any means appear to adhere to
it very closely. Some apparently always do, 40 percent say
they usually do, but 10 percent admit they never do.
Matthew 18 is the most frequent scriptural basis given for
discipline. In some cases there is partial exclusion of
offenders first, with total exclusion only as a last resort.
Restoration is made through public confession or confession
to at least the church council. While the pastor is closely
involved, the church council is said to be the key group in
administering most discipline.

The acts most commonly subject to discipline are said to
be the following: "immorality, criminal offense, remarriage
after divorce, divorce, membership in secret societies,
departure from true Christian belief, unethical business
dealings, and entrance into military service," in that
order. Immorality seems to be the chief cause for disciplinary action. Divorce, and remarriage after divorce are
also high on the list. Some churches also discipline for
marrying a non-Christian, and various other reasons such as
non-support or non-attendance at church, violence, drunken-
ness, irreconcilableness, and resorting to court trials.
Within a five-year period, 376 people were disciplined in
the General Conference for various causes. Forty-five
percent of those were disciplined for immorality. Thirty-
nine percent for "doctrinal error or departure from true
Christian belief." The number of individuals disciplined
varied from district to district, but it is reported that
over half of the congregations had subjected at least one
or more members to discipline in the last 10 years. Larger
churches (over 300 members) are said to discipline more
frequently than smaller ones. As a result of disciplinary

action, about half of the people are said to have been
successfully restored to the church. A fourth or so were
"lost to other congregations," and about the same number
"lost to all religious activity" (GCMC 1955:35-39).

While at first glance there may seem to have been numerous cases of discipline, considering the number of churches
(229 congregations which responded), and the secular society
we live in, one might expect even more. As we also noted,
however, there are congregations which do not practice much
if any discipline. This phenomenon is naturally a cause of
concern, and should make us reflect on what it really means
to be the Church. What meaning does church membership
actually have when there is no discipline, when there are no
doubt unbelievers as well as believers on the roll, when it
is not clear who is and who is not in the church? To be
sure we cannot be the ultimate judge of that, yet it would
seem the local church has a responsibility to do what it can
to ensure that it is a believers' church. It might also be
commented that in cases such as those enumerated above,
discipline is largely left up to the individual churches,
with the Conference serving only in an advisory capacity as
requested.

As we have seen, there also appears to be little discipline in the Japanese Mennonite (JMCCC) churches, although a
couple of instances were mentioned such as departure from
the teachings of the Bible. There is also in the Mission
file a letter reporting on a Christian kindergarten teacher
who was dismissed for talking against a *Seichō no Ie* (one of
the New Religions) kindergarten, while helping its principal
find teachers for the school. She even recommended one of
the young Christians recently baptized in the church to be
one of the teachers (Voran 1956:1). This seems to be an
exception though, and as a rule discipline would appear to
be rather lax.

That there is a lack of discipline is apparent in some
churches in relation to inactive members. Also, when it
comes to such things as a Christian marrying a non-Christian.
This may have something to do with the number of partners
available within the churches. It may also have something
to do with Japanese society. But nonetheless, we should
perhaps be reminded that this is a far cry from the belief
and practice of the early Anabaptists. As Anabaptist
scholar William Keeney points out,

> Dirk [Philips] especially would argue that there
> are only two valid marriages, between two nonbelievers

or between two believers. The possibility of marriage
between a believer and a nonbeliever was impossible.
... One is a Christian marriage; the other is not and
most Anabaptists felt that there was no middle ground
(Bethel College 1962:20).

What the Anabaptists believed and practiced sounds more like
what Paul taught on the subject (I Cor. 7) than what is
being practiced in many circles today. The Japanese situation is admittedly quite different from that in Europe or
North America, yet if marriages between Christian and non-
Christian are permitted, even on a case-by-case basis,
should not the basis for that practice at least be made
clear so everyone knows where we stand and why.

There are other areas such as not smoking, not drinking,
tithing, keeping the Lord's day and the like which are
strictly enforced among certain churches in Japan. While
these practices are perhaps implicitly rather than explic-
itly taught among the Mennonites as well, ought not some
reasons also be given for our stand with regard to such
things. Not that all the Christians or all the churches
need to conform to a prescribed standard, but that we at
least consider why we do what we do.

The word *discipline* no doubt has different connotations
to different people -- some of them positive and others
negative. As observed earlier, the word itself is not used
in the New Testament, but the concept and the practice are
both there. The need for discipline continues today as
well. One reason for this is simply to obey Christ's
command with regard to it. Another is for the sake of the
church, to maintain its purity. Still a third, and perhaps
the most important of all, is for the sake of the person
himself, to seek to restore him (or her) to his place among
God's people. Other reasons could be given, but perhaps
these are some of the main ones to reflect on. Discipline
in a negative sense is of course also a reminder to the
other brethren of the seriousness of discipleship, and one's
commitment to the brotherhood. It is not something to be
taken lightly.

Along with this, mention must be made of Marlin Jeschke's
book entitled *Discipling the Brother*. The book is about
discipline, but the title itself is positive, not "disciplin-
ing," but "discipling" the brother. And is that not what
discipline is all about? It is meant to be a part of the
discipling process. As Jeschke states,

> Church discipline is part of the gospel. ... Church
> discipline is the act of attempting to disciple a
> brother who is in danger of abandoning the faith
> through any particular act or attitude. Such an act
> of discipling is the corollary of evangelism, which is
> the initial act of discipling (1972:38-39).

In other words, he feels discipling is but the continuation
of evangelism.

To some, discipline is no doubt a disgraceful act, but
Jeschke shares his belief that "Congregational discipline
will not be considered a disgrace if it is carried out
redemptively instead of punitively" (1972:186). As he says
elsewhere, "In the final analysis the church is interested
in the recovery of the discipled life" (1972:90). Thus he
sees discipline in a very positive light. Yet, if all
efforts at reconciliation fail, he realizes that excommunication may be necessary, as painful as it may be. As he
puts it, "excommunication is really the reverse of baptism"
(1972:104). Just as we practice one, we may need at times
to practice the other.

The Anabaptists believed much the same thing. As William
Keeney asserts, to them church discipline

> ... is but the negative side of the positive doc-
> trine of the church. If a gathering of believers out
> of the world into a fellowship is the true church and
> body of Christ, then a separation back to the world is
> required whenever someone no longer is a believer
> (Bethel College 1962:22).

Much more could be said with regard to this or concerning
other beliefs and practices today. But for those interested
in reading further on this subject about the vision and the
practice in our own day, *Studies in Church Discipline* (GCMC
1958) is recommended as a good place to start.

As far as practices in Japan are concerned, I do not feel
it is in place for me to suggest what ought to be done.
With regard to marriage, however, as hinted earlier, it
might be well to try to establish some way whereby eligible
unmarrieds within the church can get together and make it
possible to establish more Christian homes. This could add
greatly to the stability of the churches.

There are also cases where half or more of the members
have dropped out, moved away, become inactive, or are active

elsewhere, and yet remain on the rolls of Mennonite churches. While church discipline can be carried to extremes, and we must be careful to avoid that pitfall, is there not also a place for prayerfully and carefully purging the rolls as best we can to make membership in a local church more meaningful?

Then too, one wonders if it might not also be in place to have some kind of an annual "recommitment service" in each of the local churches. This would be a time when those who are active would reaffirm their baptismal vows, their commitment to God and to each other. Those who were not an active part of the fellowship any longer could be invited to renew their commitment also. If they should fail to do so, they would be so to speak, "returned to the world." Such a process would make it possible to know more who was in the church and who was not. To refuse to include oneself would be to exclude oneself. At least one of the churches does have something similar to this in their local constitution, where after five years of being inactive and there has been no response to initiatives on the part of the congregation to bring them back, such people are automatically dropped from the membership list. If something like this was decided everywhere, and actually followed through on, it would no doubt give church membership new meaning. It would hopefully restore to fellowship many who had fallen away. It might also help to improve the image of the church in the eyes of the world.

Exactly what the nature of this annual commitment would be would have to be worked out. There are some groups in other parts of the world where people commit themselves to pray, give, worship, serve, witness, study and the like. The details of the commitment would need to be hammered out, but I for one am persuaded something like it is necessary. What journalist Richard Halloran contends may generally be true, that

No decision or agreement is ever an absolute commitment to the Japanese. They believe that an agreement is valid only so long as the conditions under which it was made continue to obtain (1969:93).

Yet people need to be made to realize that commitment to Christ is not just a temporary thing, but ought to be permanent -- the commitment of a lifetime. Also one's commitment to God's people.

There are some churches in the States which separate
church membership from baptism, especially in the case of
children. Such a setup may make membership more significant
for them. In Japan, where most baptisms are adults anyway,
that might not be a very helpful solution. But to make
membership more meaningful surely something is needed. Some
kind of discipline. We need to openly talk, pray and decide
how, when, and where to begin.

WORSHIP

From the matter of discipline we next move to the area of
worship. This has already been touched on very briefly in
relation to our discussion on baptism and communion practices. Even much earlier in our study, we dealt with the
degree of involvement of laymen in the worship service. We
noted that most worship services are usually if not always
chaired by laymen, often by women as well as men. Laymen
also sometimes preach, including women in some cases. All
in all, the impression we got was that laymen are quite
active in leading worship and serving in other ways in the
churches affiliated with the JMCCC.

By way of comparison, when the missionaries were asked
whether the chairman of Sunday worship in their home congregations was a layman or not, seven replied Yes, four said
No. Of those who answered in the affirmative, two said it
was only "sometimes," another that it was "quite often." Of
those who replied in the negative, one observed that only
occasionally did a layman do so. One of the missionaries
said she did not know, another that "there is no special
worship chairman."

As to whether the chairman was ever a woman, one said
Yes; nine, No. Of those who responded negatively, one did
say they occasionally do have a woman chairman, another
indicated that it was "not unless ordained," and a third
commented, "not yet." As in the case of laymen in general,
one reported they did not have a special "worship chairman,"
another "didn't know," a third person gave no reply.

As for whether laymen ever preach, 12 said Yes, and one,
No. Two of the 12 said it was only "occasionally." As to
whether women sometimes preach, six said Yes; five, No. Of
the other two, one said she did not know, and one did not
answer. Of those who replied in the affirmative, two said
"occasionally" or "very occasionally," one said, "if
ordained, yes!", and another added that "I suppose if a

woman wants to it is possible." Of those who answered in
the negative, one remarked, "no, at least not for many
years"; another, "only women missionaries."

From this brief survey it would appear that American laymen (including women occasionally) are also quite active in
leading worship services, although not perhaps as much as
their Japanese counterparts. This is evident in particular
with regard to the worship chairperson who in Japan is almost
always a layman, whereas in the United States and Canada,
this would seem to be true only about half the time, if
even that, depending to a large degree on the church of
course. One notices also that women there only rarely seem
to lead in worship, although recent trends indicate that
pattern may slowly be changing.

It is noteworthy too that in North America in cases of
women chairmen as well as preachers, whether they are asked
to serve or not seems to be contingent (in at least certain
cases) on whether they have been ordained or not. The same
was not stated of men, however. In the case of Japan, as
we have seen, ordination does not seem to have much meaning
in Mennonite circles so this is not especially a problem.
At any rate, it is obvious that laymen on both sides of the
ocean often lead worship or preach, apart from whether they
are ordained or not, and this is perhaps one indication of
lay activity with regard to worship.

As to how much these practices are dependent on the size
of a congregation it is hard to say. The American congregations are generally much larger in size than those in Japan.
The missionaries reported home congregations consisting of
anywhere from 150 to 1,200 members. Some of the figures
given were qualified as being "approximate," but even so,
the average size of their home churches would appear to be
well over 350. Size is not everything though, and we might
well ask, are laymen really more active in larger congregations, and less active in smaller ones?

From our limited study the impression would be that this
is not necessarily true. Actually, it may be just the
reverse, that the smaller congregations such as here in
Japan are where the laymen are most active. In fact, it may
be that percentagewise for their size the Japanese churches
are considerably ahead of their American counterparts when
it comes to the amount of lay involvement in certain areas
of church life. In any case, this might be a subject worthy
of study in a term paper somewhere.

When it comes to the content of worship, there were no
direct questions asked, but related to this there was a
question as to whether any "gifts of the Spirit" (I Cor. 12)
had been manifest in the churches or not. And, if so, which
ones? In reply to this, five of the churches said Yes; one,
No; four made no answer. Those who responded affirmatively
noted that the gifts of faith (2), healing (2), and tongues
had been manifest (one church did not give any concrete
examples). Another mentioned "serving the church," which,
while it may not be a "spiritual" gift, is certainly one of
the "service" gifts mentioned in the chapter. The question
was not as clear as it should have been, and there was no
doubt some confusion at this point between these different
kinds of gifts. In any event, it can readily be seen that
in some, although apparently not in all the churches, some,
if not all of the gifts of the Spirit, have come to
expression.

When it comes to the missionary replies to the same
question regarding manifestation of "gifts of the Spirit" in
their home churches, there were eight Yes; one, No. Those
who gave a positive reply listed the following gifts:
"prophecy, tongues, healing, etc."; "teaching, preaching,
tongues -- but not in church"; "gifts of leadership";
"forgiveness and restoration; gifts of music, teaching";
"glossalalia [tongues] most common, but also some 'prophecy,'
some instances of healing"; "prophets, teachers, helpers,
administrators, wisdom, knowledge, evangelists, pastors";
"speaking in tongues, healing, prophecy, teaching, preaching!
love!!"; "gifts of teaching, serving, etc., but as far as
gifts of tongues or healing I am not aware that these have
been manifested."

Here again in these various replies we see a confusion
between service and spiritual gifts, undoubtedly due in
part to the ambiguity of the question. While these are of
course all given by the one and same Spirit, one wonders if
it might not be more helpful to distinguish between the two
kinds of gifts. Or does this mixing them all together perhaps reflect something about the situation in the churches
from which these missionaries have come?

There were a few other comments also. The one who
replied negatively commented that, "if you are referring to
the charismatic movement -- not that I know of." Two
others did not give a direct Yes or No but made the following remarks: "probably -- really have lost touch with
what's happening"; "a recent openness towards charismatic

movement by some members, but not the pastor (present)." Of the two remaining, one did not reply, the other said, "I don't know."

From this you can see that as in the Japanese churches, in the American churches, too, a number of spiritual gifts have been manifest. Among the most common are tongues (4), prophecy (4), healing (3), wisdom, and knowledge. Some other gifts were not referred to at all. It raises the question, why are some gifts more common than others? Also, why have some churches experienced these and others seemingly not at all? How would so-called "charismatic churches" compare to this? Would they experience more the whole range of gifts, or would certain ones appear to be more prominent?

There do not seem to be any striking differences though between the gifts as experienced by Japanese and American Christians. Tongues and healing were mentioned most frequently. The gift of faith was listed in Japan, and prophecy in America, but not vice versa. The data is insufficient, however, to draw any specific conclusions from that. Also, to what extent these various expressions take place in smaller or larger groups was not revealed in the questionnaire. Be that as it may, there does not seem to be an overemphasis in the Mennonite churches on gifts of the Spirit, and it makes one ponder what influence the more openly "charismatic" churches may have in the long run on those who do not emphasize this dimension of the Christian faith as much.

As far as music in the churches is concerned, it is assumed that all the churches use the *Sambika* (Japanese hymnal) or *Seika* (revival songbook), or a combination of the two. Besides this, there is more contemporary music also, such as the *"Tomo yo Utaō!"* songs [Let's Sing, Friend!], Christian folk-type songs written mostly by Japanese young people. When church members were asked what they think of these, 24 replied they felt they were good songs, 11 others said they felt they were good, especially for young people, and 22 said they felt they were "really great." Only a couple said, "I don't like them very much." In other words, there seems to be a very positive feeling toward them. Just how much they are used in worship is difficult to say, but one person suggested that the songs would be "suitable for people who come to church for the first time."

Some others made comments such as "wonderful," "really fresh," "they are songs that touch my heart." As for

singability, a few said "there are many melodies and they
are easy to sing"; another, that they are "very enjoyable,
easy to become familiar with, and give a good feeling." A
couple mentioned that they would be "especially good for
times when we have open-air meetings," or "very good and we
must use them for evangelism." One stated they would be
"good for informal young people's meetings," and still
another said, "because there are many good songs, they
should be not only for young people, but it would be good if
they spread to the older people and were sung by them as
well."

In short, while there were a couple of members who did
not care for the songs much, and 15 or so others who did not
know of them, were not well acquainted with them, or were
not sure about them yet, generally speaking there is the
impression of overwhelming support for them. Perhaps this
is mainly because they are new and fresh and different and
singable, but whatever the reason, one would hope that the
churches would seek to make the best use of them in worship
as well as other ways. By doing so, music can also become
an effective means of evangelism.

Another question, which is not directly related to worship but has an indirect bearing, is whether the church
members had gone to see the film *"Shio Kari Tōge* [Pass],"
and whether they would recommend it to others. In reply to
this 47 or nearly half said they had seen it, 31 said they
had not. As for whether they would recommend it, 52 said
Yes. The reason this figure is higher than the number who
actually saw it is that there were a few who did not see it,
but indicated they had "read the novel," and their recommendation was based on that instead. There were several
others who said that they had not seen it but would recommend it, perhaps on the same basis. There were also a few
who had seen it but did not say whether they recommended it
or not. Yet, on the whole, the movie was given a very high
rating.

I do not know whether this film has been shown in many of
the churches or not. Some have done so, I know. At least
one person said they would "like to see it." But if it is
such a good movie, and with more and more excellent films
becoming available having been made in Japan and about
Japanese Christians, one would think it would be worthwhile
promoting the showing of these, if not as part of worship,
perhaps as a special service. The positive response might
also hint at the use of more audio-visuals (slides, film

strips, short films, banners, paintings or sculpture and so on) in the worship service itself.

Another question asked which also does not have a direct relationship to worship but is nonetheless connected is, "Next to the Bible, what Christian book or periodical do you find most helpful?" The responses to this fell into five basic categories. (Note: One person listed two different items, one of which fell into the first category, another into the third, so one is listed in each; another person named two items in the second category, but this is counted only once in the total there.)

In first place were personal testimonies (15). The replies here included comments such as "testimonies"; "books written about the Christian life"; "testimonies of Christian believers"; "unexaggerated personal experience." Second were newspapers or magazines (14): *Ketsudan no Toki* [Decision] (1), *Kurisuchan Shimbun* [The Christian] (3), *Shinto no Tomo* [The Believer's Friend] (2), and *Hyakumannin no Fukuin* [Gospel for the Millions] (6) were ones mentioned.

Third were commentaries, expository or Bible study books (11). Remarks were made like "commentaries" or "Bible commentaries"; "expository books on the Bible"; "Bible expository books written from a layman's point of view"; "books useful for Bible study"; "*Kyōshi no Tomo* [The Teacher's Friend]." In fourth place were devotional or spiritual books (8). Here comments were found as "pietistic books, spiritual books"; "Upper Room"; "books like *Streams in the Desert*"; "an anthology of good books on faith."

Fifth were doctrinal or theological books (4). There were such remarks as "doctrine" or "Christian doctrine"; "theological books"; books "about the Holy Spirit." Besides these five categories, a number of general comments were given like "something that's easy for beginners to understand"; "standards for the Christian and books on revival"; "books which are a sincere criticism of Christianity and Christians." There were also a couple who replied "I don't know," or "I can't think of any at the moment."

The same question as to what book or periodical was most helpful (next to the Bible) was also asked of some of the students of the Eastern Hokkaido Bible School. While there were only six (out of 12) who answered this question, the following comments were made: "*Shinto no Tomo*, '*Mikotoba no Hikari*' [Light from the Word]"; "'*Mikotoba no Hikari*' (as my

'daily bread')"; "I have learned a lot from *Mure* [Flock] and
Kurisuchan Shimbun"; "something to strengthen me spiritually"; "Professor Gan Sakakibara's 'Anabaptist Series'."
One of the replies was not clear. It may have been a misunderstanding of the question. Whatever, we see these books
fall into the same kind of categories as above -- magazines
and newspapers or devotional books are mentioned, including
some of the same titles; spiritual books, too; also more
theologically-oriented books. At least some of the same
things are being read in Hokkaido and Kyushu.

Be that as it may, what does all this mean? What can we
learn here? While not all those who filled out the church
member questionnaire responded to the question, over 50 did
so, and from their answers we can see that a lot of reading,
including a lot of serious reading, is being done, and this
by laymen. As we saw earlier, laymen are quite actively
engaged in leading worship. Whether they are doing any
study on the topic of worship is an open question, but might
it not be a good idea to do so and together try to rethink
what worship is or should be all about. Might it not also
be helpful to study various liturgies and try to glean ideas
others have found helpful with regard to worship patterns.
Also practical suggestions for making worship more meaningful such as various ways of involving the congregation in
prayer (sentence, bidding, or unison prayers, for example),
or in giving (not only money, but ideas, service, things,
time), or in the sermon (outlines, note-taking, feedback
afterwards and so on). Or the recent "body life" movement.
How seriously have some of these options been explored?

With the tremendous amount of effort being put into reading, might it not be helpful to encourage study in the whole
area of worship a little more, not just as an academic
exercise, but with the aim of improving our worship, of
making it more meaningful, of getting people involved not
only as spectators but as even more active participants.
The same might well be done in baptism and communion services. Or other special services such as dedications,
weddings, and funerals. Or might there not be the possibility of Christianizing certain Japanese celebrations (like
3-5-7 Day or Adults Day or other such occasions) and making
them a regular part of the church year. Where are the
experimenters who will lead the way in demonstrating how it
can be done?

DENOMINATIONALISM

The last item we want to take up in the appendix is a brief look at denominationalism. That is, throughout this study we have been dealing with the Japan Mennonite Christian Church Conference, and the churches which make up that body. But how "Mennonite" are they, and to what degree is their Mennonite heritage stressed? This is rather hard to put one's finger on, and yet there may be some clues that are found in the church questionnaires.

Actually, the fact is that while the word *Mennonite* is used in the name of the Conference, only one of the ten churches uses it in the name of the local congregation. That in itself may say something. But the original name chosen by the founding mission for its organization was the "*Shinwa Meno Kirisuto Kyōkai*," or "Faith-Peace Mennonite Christian Church" (Voth, February 1952:1). This was later changed to "*Menonaito Senkyōdan*" or "Mennonite Mission," and the Mission itself from almost the beginning seems to have gone by the name of General Conference Mennonite Mission. When the Mission and the churches later on decided to form a conference in 1964, the name Kyushu Mennonite Christian Church Conference (KMCCC) was selected.

Then, a few years ago (1976) when the conference name was changed from the KMCCC to the JMCCC, there was considerable discussion as to whether or not to keep the word *Mennonite*, whether it was biblical to do so or even necessary. And if we did want to continue to stress our denominational distinctives such as an emphasis on peace, whether it might not be better to drop the word *Mennonite* and change that to a more neutral term that would be able to both stress our distinctives and be more Japanesey at the same time. As the reader can see, however, although the word Kyushu was broadened to Japan, it was decided to retain use of the word *Mennonite* in the conference name. One of the main reasons put forth for this was that most other Mennonite groups in the world do so, and for us to do so too would be less confusing than choosing a different word. Also, that historically it could be an important reminder to us (and others) of our Anabaptist-Mennonite background.

While Mennonites have generally sought to maintain their identity or continuity with the Anabaptist movement, they have never been ones to claim that they are the only true church as certain groups do. There are many such groups around -- the Jehovah's Witnesses, Mormons, *Tōitsu Kyōkai*

[Unification Church] to name but a few. One might inquire
what influence these groups have had on the Mennonite
churches. When asked this question, of whether any of their
members had been lost to such sects, two churches said Yes;
five, No; three did not answer. Of those who said Yes, one
said they had lost one member to the Jehovah's Witnesses,
another that their church had lost three members to the same
group. Otherwise no losses were reported, although there
may have possibly been others to these or similar groups.

When it came to the situation in the missionaries' home
churches, in reply to the same question, there was one Yes,
nine No, two who did not answer, and one who did not know.
The Yes answer was qualified with a question mark, but was
to the Jehovah's Witnesses also. Five or six of the No
answers were qualified with statements such as "not that I
know of," "not to my knowledge," or "I'm not sure -- no
steady members as far as I know." This may reflect the fact
that most of the missionaries are probably not really up to
date on what is happening in their home congregations. But
there were also some remarks that while no members have been
lost to any of the cults, some have gone to "other Protestant churches," "some have left due to disagreement in
charismatic expressions," and there are "some no longer
faithful in the church." It is difficult to compare losses
in Japan and North America. Losses to cults seem to be
small in both places. It is intriguing though that all the
losses reported seem to be to one group. Might this possibly reflect some weakness in the theology found in the
churches, or a lack of teaching to acquaint people with the
beliefs of various sects?

In any event, we might well go on to ask how the churches
seek to pass on their faith, especially to newcomers. With
regard to this, when asked whether their church had a booklet of any kind they give to first-time visitors, eight of
the churches replied No, two said Yes. Those who said Yes
indicated it was an "announcement of church activities"
(church bulletin?) or a "locally printed announcement of
meetings." There was no report of any particular literature
being given to new people, although most churches may have
tracts or something people may pick up freely if they are
interested.

Another question that was asked was whether the church
had a simple pamphlet to explain its history, beliefs, and
practices. To this question, eight of the churches answered
No; two, Yes. One of those who answered No added, though,

that they do have "printed copies of our statement of faith."
This is presumably the conference statement, unless they
have worked out their own. Those who replied Yes did not
say what the literature was, but they may have been referring to the booklet on Menno Simons entitled *Mō Hitori no
Kaikakusha* [Another Reformer], published some years ago
(Peachey 1961). At any rate, nothing specific was mentioned.

One wonders, however, if this might not be an area in
which something more is needed. Melvin L. Hodges of the
Assemblies of God reports how in Latin America their
Reglamento Local, or "Standard of Doctrine and Practice,"
has been invaluable to both individual Christians and local
churches. This manual is based on Scripture and teaches new
converts the essentials of the faith. They are taught how
they ought to live, their responsibility to the church and
the world. It is the basis of agreement for the local
church, and a basis of fellowship for the churches in an
area. It deals with basic doctrines, the ordinances, membership, discipline, church organization and the like (for
greater detail of such a standard, see Hodges 1953:140-157).
It is something that laymen can use as well, to pass on
their faith without a long period of training. Next to the
work of the Spirit, Hodges reports that this simple little
handbook has been vitally important in the expansion of
their churches (McGavran 1965:115). Might not something
like this have a place in Japanese churches too? Besides
doctrine and practice, perhaps it could include a brief
history also, and be adapted to the situation of each local
church.

It is interesting to note in passing that while the word
Mennonite is used in many parts of the world today, it is
not used in the country of its origin. As Anabaptist
historian Cornelius Krahn has observed,

> ... in the countries in which Anabaptism originated,
> particularly in the country which gave us Menno, his
> name is at present not attached to the movement, while
> in the rest of the world the descendants of the Ana-
> baptists are known as "Mennonites" (Bethel College
> 1962:60).

Just why this is the case is not spelled out, whether it is
simply the result of historical development, or if there are
theological or other reasons for it. But it may be worth
pursuing by someone.

There are of course those who reject denominational
labels completely on the basis that they are unbiblical.
Watchman Nee, for example, advocates that denominations are
not scriptural, that the basis of the church is local, and
any divisions which take place must be on the basis of geography, not on the basis of sectarian, doctrinal, racial,
national, social or other differences. As he puts it,
"Locality is the divinely-appointed ground for the division
of the Church, because it is the only inevitable division"
(1962:63). This is not the place to debate the issue of
whether denominations are biblical or not. Perhaps a more
helpful question is, what can be done to transcend or even
eliminate these man-made barriers, and are we working at it?

With regard to this, in his study on *The Ecumenical Movement and the Faithful Church*, John Howard Yoder has noted
that the first Anabaptists went to great lengths to establish and maintain "brotherly relationships" with others who
confessed Christ. In fact, he says,

> ... there are good grounds for saying that the Anabap-
> tists were the first ecumenical movement, in the
> positive sense of that word. Alone of all the churches
> of the Reformation, they were truly international (1958:
> 33).

And in speaking of the situation today, he goes on to state
his conviction that

> ... Christian unity is just as clearly a Biblical
> imperative as are evangelization, nonresistance, and
> nonconformity, and that, however delicate the question
> may be, it demands open discussion and action (1958:
> 35).

Back in 1967, one of the Executive Committee (JMCCC)
recommendations was that the matter of whether or not it was
necessary to preserve our Mennonite identity be studied,
also the pros and cons of participating in organizations
like the *Kyōdan* (UCCJ) and the National Council of Churches.
One of the main reasons given for this proposal was to provide an opportunity to discuss the relation of our group to
the rest of the Christian movement in Japan, also the bearing of this on our goal of indigenization, and our future
direction. The result was a resolution that this "problem
be taken up and discussed at the pastor-missionary fellowship meetings" (Decision 6, Annual Conference, 1967:6).
Whether this was actually followed up on or not is not known

to the author. But perhaps it ought to be looked at again.
Why do we feel it so important to preserve our Mennonite
identity anyway? What relation does this have to our
identity in Christ? What might we have to lose or to gain
by seeking to find our identity only in Him and His Church?
These may be a few of the questions that could be asked.
But if, as Yoder affirms, Christian unity is an imperative,
like the Anabaptists, we need to work at it in a positive
way.

While the early Anabaptists may have worked at the matter
of unity, it was not their main objective however. Their
aim was rather to restore as far as possible the New Testament church. Since their time, there have been others,
notably the Campbells, who have also sought to do so.
Richard T. Hughes has written an enlightening article comparing the two named, "A Comparison of the Restitution Motifs
of the Campbells (1809-1830) and the Anabaptists (1524-1560)"
(1971:312-330). He points out that while both movements had
restitution as their central motif, and began with the same
basic presuppositions regarding the Scriptures (that
Scripture was their final authority), the results were
strikingly different.

The Campbell movement seemed to assume that if the
practices of the church as found in the New Testament were
reinstated, the restoration of the church would naturally
follow. The Anabaptists too looked to the New Testament
for their pattern, yet their emphasis was spiritual and more
sectarian, whereas the Restorers emphasis was external and
more tolerant. One of the reasons for this latter fact may
be that restoration for the Campbells was a means toward
Christian unity, whereas the Anabaptists were more interested in a revival of the pure body of Christ. In other
words, the Campbells were concerned with unity, the Anabaptists with purity (creation of a believers' church).

To achieve their end, the Anabaptists concentrated more
on spiritual aspects such as discipleship rather than on the
external aspects of the church. For instance, with regard
to church organization and the ordinances, the Campbells
were explicit, the Anabaptists not. While believers'
baptism was essential to the Anabaptists, they did not also
stress immersion as the Campbells did. References to
these things are found in various Anabaptist writings, but
as Hughes notes, "they sought a restitution of essence
rather than of form" (1971:326). He goes on to say that
while the Anabaptists aim was to restore the church *in toto*,

their failure to do so can be attributed to two reasons:
first, the unregenerate nature of state Christianity (which
made them concentrate on inner reform), and second, the
severe persecution they underwent.

The Campbells concentration on outer reform and lack of
emphasis on the spiritual dimensions of the church was due
primarily to their stress on Christian unity, which they
felt could be achieved by a renewal of external factors.
Also, with their Irish and Protestant background, the need
for a spiritual or moral restitution was not nearly as
pressing as it had been for the Anabaptists. Furthermore,
they did not face persecution to divert them from an outer
to an inner restoration. Thus neither of the groups was
able to actually achieve a total restitution of the New
Testament church as they had hoped to, mainly due to influences of culture. The writer concludes that one thing we
can learn from it is that

> ... this comparison should reveal that restitution --
> or any biblicist motif -- is not immune to cultural
> influences in any generation. To that extent the
> church of Christ will always be the church of the
> world (1971:330).

It goes without saying that there is no "perfect church"
today, never has been, and never will be until Christ comes
again. No matter how faithful they are, churches and the
Church are made up of imperfect people. This does not mean
we should not strive for restoration as the Campbells and
Anabaptists did. It does mean though that as we try to help
make the church more what it ought to be, we need to be
aware of cultural and other influences and realize that we
probably never will achieve perfection, that restoration is
an ongoing activity. In spite of that, we need to continually seek to become more what we believe God wants us to
be. With His help, each and every church can hopefully make
progress toward this goal.

Anyway, one of the signs of imperfection in the church
today is obviously the existence of denominations. Whether
denominations are inevitable or not, and what we ought to
do about them is a moot question. But it may be enough
just to remind ourselves of the fact that literally hundreds
of denominations do exist, including those in Japan. Even
within the Mennonite church alone, there are four different
Mennonite or Mennonite-related groups working here (and a
dozen or so others who are not in Japan). To admit that is
in itself an admission of failure to restore the New

Testament church. In any case, perhaps because of cultural differences as much as anything else, this is the way things are. It is unfortunate to have exported so many or our differences to this country, and yet these various groups have much in common, and at least some of them are trying to do a few things together.

There is, for example, the Japan Mennonite Fellowship (JMF) which seeks to bring these different groups together for fellowship and to cooperate in various projects connected with some of the traditional Mennonite emphases such as discipleship, brotherhood, and peace. It also seeks to promote study of the Anabaptist-Mennonite heritage, and to help the churches relate to the wider Mennonite body in Asia. Several years ago, the Asian Mennonite Conference, made up of churches from Japan, Taiwan, India, Indonesia, and some other Asian countries, formed a mission board called "Asia Mennonite Services." Their first efforts were in Bangladesh. Asian, North American, and European Mennonites also cooperated in the Bangladesh work, although largely due to political problems, that venture has unfortunately been terminated for the time being. Every five years or so there is a Mennonite World Conference too. The last one was in Wichita, Kansas, U.S.A., in July 1978. The Japanese Mennonites from the various bodies were naturally also represented at that. So in different ways, cooperation is going on among many of these groups. Whether it can be broadened or not only time can tell.

Just to insert a personal note here, after our first term of service in Japan, I decided to attend an interdenominational seminary to complete my theological training. As I had already attended our Mennonite seminary for two years previously, there were those who asked why I was not going back there. There were many reasons to be sure, one of the main ones being that I had become interested in doing further study in missions and that our seminary had little to offer in that area. Also, having grown up in a Mennonite community, attended a Mennonite church, a Mennonite college, and a Mennonite seminary, I simply wanted to find out a bit more what it was like outside Mennonite circles. Needless to say, I found many other earnest Christians, and came to realize that the Church was much larger than my own little denomination. That in itself was a valuable lesson.

At the same time, I also came to have a new appreciation of the Mennonite Church, being able to look at it from a distance. And although ideally it would be nice if we could do away with denominations, human nature being what it is,

one wonders if to try to do so might not in the long run
lead to an even greater proliferation than now. Perhaps one
of the most beneficial things we can do is cooperate
together with others of like mind wherever possible, and
show in this way that in spite of some differences we still
do love each other.

As far as the question we began with, How "Mennonite" are
the churches in Japan? this is difficult to say. In North
America and many other places the word *Mennonite* is frequently used in the names of churches -- "First Mennonite"
and so on. Here it is not, as we have seen, perhaps partly
because of the negative connotations the word has when
sounded out in Japanese ("*me-no-nai-hito*," or a "person-
without-eyes"). There is also a possible confusion with
some of the sects such as the Mormons (because of the name
beginning with the same letter). People who have not been
indoctrinated in the faith do not know the difference
between the two, and it can be confusing to them. In fact
the whole raft of denominations, including Catholic and
Protestant divisions, are a source of perplexity too.

Be that as it may, in Japan the name "Mennonite" is used
among our churches on the conference level. It is also used
in at least some cases in the bulletin if not on the sign-
board of the church, as a means of identification of a
particular brand of Christianity. As to whether this is
really necessary perhaps each congregation must decide, but
there does seem to be a considerable degree of Mennonite
identity even though the name may not be used much locally.
This came out in the member questionnaires also with regard
to the subjects people were most interested in studying.
Mennonite history was high on the list. It may be an
indication of seeking for identity in certain cases.

Some churches in Japan such as the *Mukyōkai* play down the
importance of the institutional church. Other churches
claim to be "Christians only, but not the only Christians."
Whether these approaches actually avoid the denominational
pitfall may be debatable. In any event, Mennonites have
traditionally been tolerant of other Christian churches.
Within their own denominations too, there has been the motto,
"Unity in essentials, tolerance in nonessentials, and
charity in all things" (Smith 1957:690).

Such a position no doubt makes for both strengths and
weaknesses in the churches, but that is not the point here.
The point is that it was never Menno Simons intention to

found a denomination in the first place. As he himself
wrote,

> If I should by my teaching gain disciples for myself
> and not for Christ Jesus, seeking my own gain, praise,
> and honor, then indeed woe unto my soul. No, brethren,
> no (Wenger 1956:311).

Nevertheless, although Menno is not revered as a saint, that
the Mennonite denomination was born is an historical fact.
It is hard to turn history back. But perhaps the most important thing is not so much where Mennonites have come from,
but that it be made clear what Mennonites believe and why.
If that could be done, hopefully the emphasis would end up
being where it ought to be, and solidly based on the Bible.
Might that not be the best way to honor Menno, or rather,
as he put it, honor Christ and His Church.

CONCLUSION

This brings us to the end of our comparison of practices
in several areas of Mennonite church life in Japan and
North America. We have noticed many similarities, also
some differences. It is difficult to ascertain in such a
brief survey just how much influence North American churches
have had on Japanese churches. The similarities suggest it
has been considerable. One of the most disturbing aspects
may be that at so many points there seems to be a rather
clear reflection of the American scene. This is apparent
not only with regard to the very structure of the churches
themselves, but even more so when it comes to certain
practices such as ordination.

In that area we noticed a lack of clarity in the American
churches, or one might even say confusion. It is discon-
certing to say the least to see this same confusion
reflected in the Japanese churches as well. Perhaps this
is one of the weaknesses of congregational polity. Yet one
of the most disturbing things is not simply how much
Japanese churches resemble American ones, but at many points
how American Mennonite churches so little reflect Anabaptism
(in areas such as discipline). At any rate, a TEE or similar program could provide a forum for the discussion of some
of the issues raised here, in addition to helping solve a
number of problems in the area of leadership training.

As the church considers these matters (including that of
leadership training), we all need to be reminded again that

the churches are free to work out their own pattern. While "indigenization" is said to have been the goal from the beginning, the fact is that the churches have in many cases seemingly accepted without question the patterns brought by the missionaries. There is of course nothing wrong with adopting patterns from elsewhere, as long as they fit. A good example of this is the Early Church itself which borrowed quite heavily from Jewish structures. But today, as anthropologist A. R. Tippett has asserted,

> The greatest threat to an indigenous Church is the denominational character of Christian missions. We tend to plant denominational structures (1969:134).

In our own case, this would seem to be true not only of local church structure, but with regard to conference structure also. That is, when the churches began to think about working out a constitution for local use, the minutes indicate that the starting point for doing so was apparently a comparison of constitutions of other groups already established in Japan such as the Lutheran, Holiness, and Baptist churches (JMCCC, Church Council, July 9, 1960:2).

As for the development of a conference constitution, when the Conference was first organized (1964), it appears there was heavy dependence on the constitution of the Mennonite churches in Taiwan. Copies of constitutions used by the Mennonites in Columbia, and that of the Japan Mennonite Conference in Hokkaido are also on file, evidently having been obtained for reference. There were all of these influences in addition to that of the General Conference Mennonite Church itself from which the missionaries came. But one of the big questions is, what attempt was made to begin with the Bible, and do the borrowings that were made actually fit the culture? And even though the JMCCC Constitution was rewritten a few years later (1968), was the committee able to start from scratch, or was the pattern already too well entrenched to really break free?

What is true of the structures may also be said of the theology. Much of it has been imported as well -- in its expression if not in its essence. The JMCCC Statement of Faith, for instance, which is part of the Conference Constitution, was drawn up by one of the missionaries. This was done at the request of the Conference. But the original statement was done in English, and while it is a beautiful expression of the essentials of our faith, when translated into Japanese, it loses something, perhaps because it was

not done in Japanese to begin with. The minutes note that
the statement was "designed to be one that will still be
acceptable many years and even centuries from now," and that
"contemporary issues deemed of a temporary nature, as well
as the traditional 'Mennonite distinctives' were deliberately
not included" (JMCCC, Annual Conference, 1968:3). While
that may be well and good, the finished product somehow does
not feel or sound very Japanesey, and is used little in the
churches. This is most unfortunate it seems to me, when we
are trying to communicate faith within the Japanese culture.

Seiichi Yagi from the Kanto Gakuin University in Yokohama
has written an article called, "The Dependence of Japanese
Theology upon the Occident." He says that this dependence
is only natural, with (Protestant) Christianity having been
introduced to Japan from the Occident. At the same time,
while he feels Japan can continue to learn from Occidental
theology, he contends that Japanese need to develop the
courage to think for themselves, to develop a theology which
fits Japan. He goes on to remark that

> Japanese theology, which the Japanese have developed
> by themselves through facing their own problems in
> Japan, may naturally be expected to express its own
> character in a more or less diverse form from that of
> the Occident (1964:261).

Paul T. Lauby of Silliman University in the Philippines
also stresses the need for theological education to be
culturally oriented. He states:

> It is quite obvious there is no such thing, theo-
> logically speaking, as a Filipino gospel or an Indian
> gospel or a Japanese gospel. Nevertheless, it is
> true that theological education must be creatively
> related to the particular culture in which it works.
> There has been a strong temptation to borrow Western
> course content and curriculum structure without much
> thought about whether they are relevant to the Asian
> situation and whether they do an effective job of
> preparing an adequate ministry for the Orient (1962:
> 26).

As Mennonites, we occasionally hear references to Anabaptist theology, even in Japan, as if this were our ultimate point of reference. But may it not be as has been
suggested by others that we need a "by-pass theology," which
is to say, "we may need for the time being to 'by-pass' the

Reformation and its controversies and go back to our common
original source, the Bible itself" (Endo and Kroehler 1966:
174). Is this not exactly what the Mennonite Community in
Zaire is trying to do? A few years ago it accepted the
theme of "Return to the Bible for an Authentic Christianity"
as its watchword for the church as it moves into the future
(Shapasa 1975:7). Might not the same be appropriate here in
Japan or wherever we are?

Franklin H. Littell observes in his book, *The Origins of
Sectarian Protestantism*, that

> In the Anabaptist church view two notes stand out
> from the rest:
> 1. The church must be a voluntary association, taking
>   its spirit and discipline from those who intention-
>   ally belong to its fellowship.
> 2. The church must follow the guidelines of the New
>   Testament as to confession of faith and organiza-
>   tional pattern.
>
> In the history of Christianity there have been some
> who said that the Bible was ambiguous as to doctrine
> and organization. The traditional orthodox view has
> been that it gives clear indications on doctrine but
> is ambiguous as to organizational pattern. The Ana-
> baptists maintained that the New Testament was clear
> both as to the content of the Christian faith and the
> organizational procedures in the true Christian Commu-
> nity (1964:46).

If what he says here is true, that for the Anabaptists the
New Testament was clear on both content and pattern, as
their descendants does it not behoove us to also go back to
the Bible itself.

To do so is difficult. We are all prisoners to a great
degree of our heritage. It is not easy to break free, to
read the New Testament as if for the first time and apply it
to our day. But as we move into the future, it would seem
fitting to give it a try. We need to take to heart what
Latin American missionary Roger S. Greenway has expressed
candidly:

> If patterns of mission work, church organization, or
> anything else Christians seek to do to extend Christ's
> kingdom prove ineffective and actually hinder men from
> becoming members of Christ's church, those patterns

should be abandoned. The norm is the New Testament
with its glorious liberty to adapt to the actualities
of each situation, rather than to the prisonhouse of
foreign tradition (1973:164-165).

Along this line, might it not also be in place for the
American churches to remind the Japanese churches of their
freedom, and to apologize for having unwittingly imposed so
many patterns upon them. Three years ago (1976) was the
25th anniversary of the General Conference work in Japan.
The year before (1975) was the 450th anniversary of the
beginning of the Anabaptist movement. As part of the celebration of that event, it was declared a "Year of Jubilee,"
and in various ways attempts were made to liberate or set
people free from whatever was binding them. Might it not be
fitting to say to the Japanese churches, "While we rejoice
in your birth and growth, in other ways we feel we may have
unintentionally bound you and as a result you are not able
to become all God wants you to be. Please forgive us. As
brothers and sisters in Christ we would simply remind you
that with the Scriptures and the Spirit as your guide, you
are entirely free to develop your own patterns and ways."

How better could we encourage the churches to truly
become indigenous than to remind them they are free, to
liberate them and release them to God. After all, as missiologist Charles H. Kraft has brought out, "indigeneity" is
really a matter of "dynamic (functional) equivalence" rather
than "formal correspondence" (1973:41). If this was our
aim, in the long run might it not help Christianity overcome
some of its foreignness. We may not like to admit it, but
as described by sociologist Robert Lee, in Japan

Christianity is still the Stranger in the land who
has taken up alien residence. ... Like Buddhism,
Christian faith has been imported from the outside,
but unlike Buddhism it has yet to become fully indig-
enized; it is still clothed in Western garb. It has
the taint or the smell of the foreign (*bata-kusai*)
(1967:156).

Who would dare deny the truth of what he says? The
architecture of church buildings, western music, the pattern
of services and the like quickly give that away. Those
within the church are probably even more aware of this than
those outside, or at least were in the beginning. But that
does not mean this handicap cannot be overcome. To be overcome it will need to be worked at -- consciously. But if it

is, we may be confident that the church can become more
indigenous, more Japanesey. It will take time, but it can
be done. Rather than smelling foreign, it can perhaps take
on the aroma of *miso* (bean paste soup).

As the Japanese churches work on this, perhaps the
American churches ought to do so as well. The fact is that
many of their patterns have been imported too, especially
from Europe, and they also need to continually try to find
more effective patterns. As Franklin Littell has commented,
"The restitution is never a finished task, but must be undertaken again and again" (1961:28). And this, not only with
regard to customs, traditions, and practices that have long
been taken for granted, but with respect to the training of
believers as well. That is, most American churches have
Sunday school for adults as well as for children. But is
that indeed adequate? Does it do the job that needs to be
done? Most Japanese churches do not seem to have Sunday
school for adults, although in many cases a midweek meeting
may be something of an equivalent. But do these meetings
really prepare believers sufficiently for their ministry in
the church and in the world?

When asked whether their home churches had any kind of
lay training program besides Sunday school, five missionaries replied No; four Yes. Three others said they did not
know and one gave no answer. Of those who said Yes, one
added that it was simply "instruction for baptism over a
period of several months each year." Another mentioned
their church had "teacher training, Bible training and witnessing courses on Wednesday evening." A third noted they
occasionally had "a series of studies on Christian home, or
book of the Bible in about five sessions or so." One other
stated that they have "no fixed long-term program for all,
but special 'short courses' like Campus Crusade approach,
home visitation involvement (all voluntary participation),
Bible study, etc." Of those who answered No, one remarked,
"not really," another, "not as such," but on Wednesday evening they have general Bible study and prayer meeting, also
several home Bible studies.

So while there are Sunday schools, and some midweek
Bible studies or home meetings, and here and there some
short courses and so on, one wonders if that is really adequate. Many churches evidently have no regular systematic
training program besides Sunday school or a midweek meeting.
In light of this, might not a similar type of program as
that proposed in this study for the churches in Japan also

be applicable to churches in North America -- a supplementary program geared especially to train laymen and lay leaders. As Ralph Winter has summed it up,

The greatest *encouragement* in missions today is that the Christian movement is outrunning traditional methods of ministerial training, but the greatest *tragedy*, both in the U.S. and abroad, is that we are ecclesiastically and institutionally arthritic at the point of *bending* to give appropriate, solid, theological education to the real leaders that emerge in the normal outworking of our internal church life (1967a:13).

May it not be that American churches along with Japanese churches need to rethink their educational as well as evangelistic methodology, and to retool to become more effective, to work at putting their own house in order. To restore a more biblical pattern may mean first of all going back to the Scriptures to see what we can learn there. To do so, to go back to the Bible, to really take it seriously, will no doubt affect some of our practices, perhaps even some of our beliefs. But Menno Simons himself declared that

... the whole Scriptures, both the Old and New Testament, were written for our instruction, admonition, and correction, and that they are the true scepter and rule by which the Lord's kingdom, house, church, and congregation must be ruled and governed. Everything contrary to Scripture, therefore, whether it be in doctrines, beliefs, sacraments, worship, or life, should be measured by this infallible rule and demolished by this just and divine scepter, and destroyed without any respect of persons (Wenger 1956: 159-160).

Again and again Menno sought to bring believers back to the Word of God, to compare its teachings with his own. For example, in another passage from his writings, he pleads,

Therefore I beseech you again by the mercy of God and for the salvation of your souls that you may weigh my doctrine and the doctrine of all men who have written from the times of the apostles, and write now, with the Gospel of Jesus Christ and the doctrine of His holy apostles, lest you be deceived by me or by some other man, ... Is it the Word of God which I teach? Let those who are spiritual judge. In that case they must accept it in the name of the Lord if

they would not be lost. But if it be human doctrine,
then let it be accursed of God. For other foundation
can no man lay than that is laid by the apostles which
is Christ Jesus. I Cor. 3:11 (1956:312).

Menno Simons, a biblicist. The Anabaptists, the "Bible
Christians of the Reformation." And Mennonites today, in
Japan, North America or wherever?? How faithful are they to
the Bible itself? To what extent do they really let it
determine what they believe and what they do -- their faith
and practice? In closing, I feel the words of Mennonite
historian C. J. Dyck would be most apropos:

The calling to be Bible Christians of the twentieth
century in the full sense of the term as the Anabaptists understood it is a major challenge and holds great
promise. Whether the Mennonites can indeed become this
more fully, and witness to its power, remains to be
seen (1967:315).

Glossary

arbeit:	part-time work
ken:	prefecture, geographical unit comparable to a county
*Kyōdan:	United Church of Christ in Japan (UCCJ)
Kyōgiinkai:	Church Council (JMCCC)
Mukyōkai:	"Non-church" movement, founded by Kanzo Uchimura
san:	polite name -- suffix for Mr., Miss, or Mrs.
sensei:	term of respect used instead of *san* for any kind of teacher such as a pastor
shi:	city (pop. over 50,000)
Shūkyō Hōjin:	Religious Juridical Person (legal incorporation of a religious body)

Sōka Gakkai: militant new sect of Buddhism that has
                      grown rapidly in postwar years

yen: basic monetary unit of Japan (in 1979, the
                      average exchange rate was about 220 yen per
                      dollar)

---

*A macron over the ō (or other vowels) indicates a slightly
lengthened vowel sound in Japanese words. For the sake of
simplification, however, it has been omitted in the names
of people or places, and in the case of words such as
Shinto which have become anglicized.

Bibliography

BOOKS
(Sources Cited)

ALLEN, Roland
1960   *The Ministry of the Spirit.* Grand Rapids, Mich.,
        William B. Eerdmans.

BATES, M. Searle, and PAUCK, Wilhelm, eds.
1964   *The Prospects of Christianity Throughout the
        World.* New York, Charles Scribner's Sons.

BETHEL COLLEGE
1962   *No Other Foundation* (Commemorative Essays on Menno
        Simons). North Newton, Kan.

BOSCHMAN, Paul W., ed., BRAUN, Neil, and YAMADA, Takashi
1968   *Experiments in Church Growth: Japan.* Kobayashi
        City, Miyazaki, Japan Church Growth Research
        Association.

BOXER, C. R.
1951   *The Christian Century in Japan, 1549-1650.*
        Berkeley, University of California Press.

BRAGHT, Thieleman J. van
1951   *The Bloody Theater or Martyrs Mirror of the
        Defenseless Christians.* Translated from the
        original Dutch edition of 1660 by Joseph F. Sohm.
        6th ed., Scottdale, Pa., Herald Press.

BRAUN, Neil
   1971   *Laity Mobilized: Reflections on Church Growth in
          Japan and Other Lands.* Grand Rapids, Mich.,
          William B. Eerdmans.

BUREAU OF STATISTICS, OFFICE OF THE PRIME MINISTER
   1974   *Japan Statistical Yearbook: 1973/1974.* 24th ed.,
          Tokyo, Japan Statistical Association.

COVELL, Ralph R., and WAGNER, C. Peter
   1971   *An Extension Seminary Primer.* Pasadena, Calif.,
          William Carey Library.

DRUMMOND, Richard Henry
   1971   *A History of Christianity in Japan.* Grand Rapids,
          Mich., William B. Eerdmans.

DYCK, Cornelius J., ed.
   1967   *An Introduction to Mennonite History.* Scottdale,
          Pa., Herald Press.

FLEW, R. Newton
   1943   *Jesus and His Church.* 2nd ed., London, Epworth
          Press.

FRIEDMAN, Robert
   1973   *The Theology of Anabaptism.* Scottdale, Pa.,
          Herald Press.

GENERAL CONFERENCE MENNONITE CHURCH
   1958   *Studies in Church Discipline.* Newton, Kan.,
          Mennonite Publication Office.

GIBBS, Mark, and MORTON, T. Ralph
   1964   *God's Frozen People.* London, Collins (Fontana
          Books).

GREENWAY, Roger S.
   1973   *An Urban Strategy for Latin America.* Grand
          Rapids, Mich., Baker Book House.

HALLORAN, Richard
   1969   *Japan: Images and Realities.* Tokyo, Charles E.
          Tuttle.

HERR, Willis E., comp.
   1975   *The Sprunger Family: Descendents of Peter
          Sprunger, Born 1757.* Los Angeles, Calif.

HERSHBERGER, Guy F., ed.
1957   *The Recovery of the Anabaptist Vision.*   Scottdale,
       Pa., Herald Press.

HILL, D. Leslie
1974   *Designing a Theological Education by Extension
       Program: A Philippine Case Study.*   Pasadena,
       Calif., William Carey Library.

HODGES, Melvin L.
1953   *The Indigenous Church.*   Springfield, Mo., Gospel
       Publishing House.

IGLEHART, Charles W.
1959   *A Century of Protestant Christianity in Japan.*
       Tokyo, Charles E. Tuttle.

JESCHKE, Marlin
1972   *Discipling the Brother.*   Scottdale, Pa., Herald
       Press.

JUHNKE, James C.
1979   *A People of Mission.*   Newton, Kan., Faith and
       Life Press.

KINSLER, F. ROSS
1978   *The Extension Movement in Theological Education.*
       Pasadena, Calif., William Carey Library.

KIRISUTO SHIMBUNSHA
1979   *Kirisutokyō Nenkan: 1979* [The Japan Christian
       Yearbook].   Tokyo, Kirisuto Shimbunsha.

KLAASSEN, Walter
1973   *Anabaptism: Neither Catholic nor Protestant.*
       Waterloo, Ontario, Conrad Press.

KRAEMER, Hendrik
1958   *A Theology of the Laity.*   Philadelphia, Pa.,
       Westminster Press.

LEE, Robert
1967   *Stranger in the Land: A Study of the Church in
       Japan.*   New York, Friendship Press.

LEHMAN, James O.
1969   *Sonnenberg, A Haven and a Heritage.*   Kidron, Ohio,
       Kidron Community Council.

LEITH, John H., ed.
   1963   *Creeds of the Churches*.   Garden City, N.Y.,
           Doubleday.

LITTELL, Franklin Hamlin
   1964   *The Origins of Sectarian Protestantism: A Study of
           the Anabaptist View of the Church*.   New York,
           Macmillan.

McGAVRAN, Donald Anderson
   1965   *Church Growth and Christian Mission*.   New York,
   (ed.)   Harper and Row.

   1966   *How Churches Grow: The New Frontiers of Mission*.
           New York, Friendship Press.

MANSON, T. W.
   1948   *The Church's Ministry*.   London, Hodder and
           Stroughton.

   1958   *Ministry and Priesthood: Christ's and Ours*.
           London, Epworth Press.

MORRIS, Leon
   1964   *Ministers of God*.   London, Inter-Varsity Fellow-
           ship.

MULHOLLAND, Kenneth B.
   1976   *Adventures in Training the Ministry: A Honduran
           Case Study in Theological Education by Extension*.
           Nutley, N.J., Presbyterian and Reformed Publishing
           Company.

NAKANE, Chie
   1972   *Japanese Society*.   Berkeley, University of
           California Press.

NEE, Watchman
   1962   *The Normal Christian Church Life*.   Washington,
           D.C., International Students Press.

NIEBUHR, H. Richard, and WILLIAMS, Daniel D., eds.
   1956   *The Ministry in Historical Perspectives*.   New
           York, Harper and Row.

OLSEN, Charles M.
   1973   *The Base Church*.   Atlanta, Ga., Forum House.

REISCHAUER, Edwin O.
1964   *Japan: Past and Present.*   3rd ed., New York,
        Alfred A. Knopf.

ROBERTSON, Archibald Thomas
1930   *Word Pictures in the New Testament,* III (Acts).
        Nashville, Tenn., Broadman Press.

SCHULLER, Robert H.
1974   *Your Church Has Real Possibilities!*   Glendale,
        Calif., Regal Books.

SMITH, C. Henry
1957   *The Story of the Mennonites.*   4th ed., Newton,
        Kan., Mennonite Publication Office.

SNIDER, K. Lavern
1975   *Whose Ministry?*   Osaka, Japan Free Methodist
        Mission.

SPAE, Joseph J.
1968   *Christianity Encounters Japan.*   Tokyo, Oriens
        Institute for Religious Research.

THEOLOGICAL EDUCATION FUND
1972   *Ministry in Context: The Third Mandate Programme
        of the Theological Education Fund.*   Bromley, Kent,
        England, TEF.

1973   *Learning in Context: The Search for Innovative
        Patterns in Theological Education.*   Bromley, Kent,
        England, TEF.

THOMSEN, Harry
1963   *The New Religions of Japan.*   Tokyo, Charles E.
        Tuttle.

TIPPETT, A. R.
1969   *Verdict Theology in Missionary Theory.*   Lincoln,
        Ill., Lincoln Christian College Press.

TRUEBLOOD, Elton
1967   *The Incendiary Fellowship.*   New York, Harper and
        Row.

WALTNER, James H.
1968   *This We Believe.*   Newton, Kan., Faith and Life
        Press.

WELD, Wayne C.
  1973   *The World Directory of Theological Education by
         Extension*. Pasadena, Calif., William Carey
         Library.

WENGER, John Christian, ed.
  1956   *The Complete Writings of Menno Simons, c. 1496-
         1561*. Translated from the Dutch by Leonard
         Verduin. Scottdale, Pa., Herald Press.

WINTER, Ralph D., ed.
  1969   *Theological Education by Extension*.
         Pasadena, Calif., William Carey Library.

YAMAMORI, Tetsunao
  1974   *Church Growth in Japan: A Study in the Development
         of Eight Denominations, 1859-1939*. Pasadena,
         Calif., William Carey Library.

BOOKLETS AND PAMPHLETS

BURKHOLDER, J. Lawrence
  1969   "Theological Education for the Believers' Church,"
         Concern No. 17: 10-32. (*Concern* is a Pamphlet
         Series for Questions of Christian Renewal, and may
         be ordered from the Business Manager, 721 Walnut
         Ave., Scottdale, PA, 15683.)

GENERAL CONFERENCE MENNONITE CHURCH
  1977   *Handbook of Information: 1977/1978*. Newton, Kan.,
         Faith and Life Press.

HORSCH, James E., ed.
  1979   *Mennonite Yearbook and Directory* (Vol. 70).
         Scottdale, PA, Mennonite Publishing House.

JACOBSEN, Morris B.
  1977   *Japanese Church Growth Patterns in the 1970's*.
         Tokyo, Japan Evangelical Missionary Association.

KRAHN, Cornelius
  1967   *The Witness of the Martyrs' Mirror for Our Day*.
         Revised reprint of the April 1967 issue of
         Mennonite Life. North Newton, Kan., Bethel
         College (Mennonite Library and Archives).

KRAHN, Cornelius, and GINGERICH, Melvin
1967   *The Mennonites: A Brief Guide to Information.*
        Newton, Kan., Faith and Life Press. (Latest
        edition available from Faith and Life Bookstore,
        Box 347, Newton, KS, 67114.)

LITTELL, Franklin Hamlin
1961   *A Tribute to Menno Simons.*   Scottdale, Pa.,
        Herald Press.

MIYAZAKI PREFECTURAL GOVERNMENT
1966   *Miyazaki, Kyushu, Japan.*   Miyazaki, Japan.

PANNABECKER, S. F., ed.
1961a   *The Christian Mission of the General Conference
        Mennonite Church,* "The Mission Abroad in Japan,"
        55-60. Newton, Kan., Faith and Life Press.

PATTERSON, George
1978   *Obedience-Oriented Education.*   Portland, Ore.,
        Imprenta Misionera.

PEACHEY, Paul
1961   *Mō Hitori no Kaikakusha: Meno Shimonzu* [Another
        Reformer]. Translated into Japanese by Hiroko
        Kanekubo. Tokyo, Inochi no Kotobasha for Nihon
        Menonaito Bunshō Kyōkai [Word of Life Press for
        the Japan Mennonite Literature Association].

WEBER, Hans-Ruedi
1963   *Salty Christians.*   New York, Seabury Press.

WINTER, Ralph D., ed.
1967b   *The Extension Seminary and the Programmed Textbook.*
        Report of a workshop in Armenia, Columbia,
        September 4-9, 1967. ALET: Latin American
        Association of Theological Schools, Northern
        Region. (Copies may be obtained from the editor
        c/o Fuller Theological Seminary, 135 N. Oakland
        Ave., Pasadena, CA, 91101.)

YODER, John Howard
1958   *The Ecumenical Movement and the Faithful Church,*
        Focal Pamphlet Series No. 3. Scottdale, Pa.,
        Herald Press. (Focal Pamphlets may be ordered
        from the Mennonite Publishing House, 616 Walnut
        Ave., Scottdale, PA, 15683.)

YODER, John Howard
    1969   "The Fullness of Christ: Perspectives on Minis-
            tries in Renewal," *Concern No. 17*: 33-93. (For
            information on *Concern*, see under Burkholder,
            J. L.)

ARTICLES

AIKAWA, Takaaki
    1974   "The Current Scene," *Japan Christian Quarterly* 40
            (Spring): 109-111.

ARIGA, Keiichi
    1973   "Brief Survey of Mission History" ("Confrontation
            of Christianity and Nationalism in Japan" -- Part
            Two), *Japan Harvest* 23 (Summer): 22-25.

ASAHI EVENING NEWS (Tokyo)
    1976   "'University on Air' Opening in 1979," January
            10: 3.

ASSOCIATED MENNONITE BIBLICAL SEMINARIES
    1973   "Seminary Without Walls -- 1974," *The Bulletin*,
            October: 6.

    1976   "What Seminary Growth Means," *The Bulletin*,
            October: 2-3.

BARRETT, Lois
    1975   "Congregations Share Ministry Tasks," *The
            Mennonite*, November 11: 638-639.

BRAINERD, Edwin
    1974   "The 'Myth' of Programmed Texts," *Evangelical
            Missions Quarterly* 10 (July): 219-223.

BROWN, Kenneth I.
    1972   "Forms of Baptism in the African Independent
            Churches of Tropical Africa," *Practical Anthro-
            pology* 19 (July-August): 169-182.

CHAO, Jonathan T'ien-en
 1977   "Crucial Issues in Leadership Training: A Chinese
        Perspective," *Mission-Focus*, May: F-0. (*Mission-
        Focus* is published for mission leaders, with
        single copies free upon request from Mennonite
        Board of Missions, Box 370, Elkhart, IN, 46515.)

CLASSEN, Martha
 1974   "Opening the *Danchi*," *Japan Harvest* 24 (Spring):
        24-27.

COX, Ralph
 1974   "Sixteen Churches in Nineteen Years," *Japan
        Harvest* 24 (Summer): 26-27.

DEMURA, Akira
 1973   "The Current Scene," *Japan Christian Quarterly*
        39 (Spring): 117-118.

DRUCKER, Peter F.
 1971   "What We Can Learn From Japanese Management,"
        Harvard Business Review 49 (March-April): 110-122.

DRUMMOND, Richard Henry
 1961   "Hendrik Kraemer in Japan," *International Review
        of Missions* 50 (October): 451-459.

EMERY, James H.
 1969   "The Presbyterian Seminary in Guatemala Three
        Years Later, 1966," in R. D. Winter (ed.): 86-101.

ENDO, Sakae, and KROEHLER, Armin
 1966   "The Urgency of Rural Evangelism in Japan Today,"
        Japan Christian Quarterly 32 (July): 165-174.

GENERAL CONFERENCE MENNONITE CHURCH
 1973   "Goals Set in Taiwan and Japan," *The Mennonite*,
        January 23: 54.

 1974   "Resolutions Passed," *The Mennonite*, August 20:
        488.

 1975a "Extension Education Scheduled in Zaire," *The
        Mennonite*, November 25: 674.

 1976   "Taiwan Churches Set New Goals," *The Mennonite*,
        November 2: 643.

GINGRICH, Ann and Paul
    1975   "Breathing New Life Into the Church," *The
            Mennonite*, September 9: 490-492.

GOSDEN, Eric
    1974   "Revival," *Japan Harvest* 24,25 (Fall-Winter):
            42-48.

GRAYBILL, John W.
    1966   "Are Cell Meetings the Answer?" *Japan Harvest* 16
            (Winter): 31-32.

HARVEY, E. E.
    1970   "New Methods in Theological Teaching," *South East
            Asia Journal of Theology* 12 (Autumn): 74-82.

HATORI, Akira
    1968   "Come Back to Japan" (Part Two), *Decision*,
            October: 6.

HOKE, Donald E.
    1963b   "New Theological School Association Formed,"
            Japan Harvest 13 (Winter): 12-13.

    1963c   "Fuller Summer Seminary," *Japan Harvest* 13
            (Winter): 25.

HOPEWELL, James F.
    1967   "Mission and Seminary Structure," *International
            Review of Missions* 56 (April): 158-163.

HUGHES, Richard T.
    1971   "A Comparison of the Restitution Motifs of the
            Campbells (1809-1830) and the Anabaptists (1524-
            1560)," *Mennonite Quarterly Review* 45 (October):
            312-330.

INTERNATIONAL CONGRESS ON WORLD EVANGELIZATION
    1974b   "The Lausanne Covenant," *Japan Harvest* 24,25
            (Fall-Winter): 9-10.

ISOBE, Hiroshi
    1973   "Church Without a Pastor," *The Mennonite*,
            December 11: E-6.

    1975   "The Church Becomes Urbanized," *The Mennonite*,
            March 11: E-4,5.

JOHNSON, Harold I.
1967   "The Birth of the Immanuel Church and Its Miracu-
        lous Growth," *Japan Harvest* 16 (Spring): 9-10.

KRAFT, Charles H.
1973   "Dynamic Equivalence Churches," *Missiology* 1
        (January): 39-57.

KURISUCHAN SHIMBUN [The Christian]
1976   *"Go Kōmoku ni yoru Dendō Hōsaku"* [Five-Point
        Evangelism Strategy], January 18: 2.

KUWADA, Hidenobu
1957   "Protestant Theological Education in Japan,"
        International Review of Missions 46 (October):
        372-379.

LALIVE d'EPINAY, Christian
1967   "The Training of Pastors and Theological Education:
        The Case of Chile," *International Review of
        Missions* 56 (April): 185-192.

LAUBY, Paul T.
1962   "A Theological Core Curriculum With Reference to
        Asian Needs," *South East Asia Journal of Theology*
        3 (April): 25-36.

LIECHTY, Sandra
1973   "Amoeba Church Evangelism," *The Mennonite*,
        December 11: E-7.

McGAVRAN, Donald Anderson
1968   "Church Growth in Japan," *Japan Harvest* 18
        (Winter): 15-22.

McKINNEY, Lois
1975   "Plan for the Church's Leadership Needs,"
        Evangelical Missions Quarterly 11 (July): 183-187.

THE MENNONITE
1961   "Our Conference," September 5: 574-575.

MINEAR, Paul S.
1962   "Church, Idea of," *The Interpreter's Dictionary of
        the Bible*, I: 607-617. Abingdon Press.

MINISTRY
1965   "Lay Training and Lay Training Centres," 6
        (October): 25-32.

PEACHEY, Paul
    1961   "*Mukyokai-shugi*: A Modern Japanese Attempt to
            Complete the Reformation," *Mennonite Quarterly
            Review* 35 (January): 70-78.

PENTECOST, Edward C.
    1972   "A Bible Training Course for Professional People,"
            Evangelical Missions Quarterly 9 (Fall): 34-37.

PETERSON, Len
    1973   "The New System -- Covenant Seminary," *Japan
            Harvest* 24 (Winter): 11.

POETHIG, Richard P.
    1972   "Theological Education and the Urban Situation in
            Asia," *South East Asia Journal of Theology* 13.2:
            61-67.

RADER, Paul
    1973   "Korea," *Church Growth Bulletin* 9 (March): 311.

RAMSEYER, Robert L.
    1972   "Finances in the New Religions and the Christian
            Church," *Japan Christian Quarterly* 38 (Spring):
            84-89.

REAM, W.G.B.
    1956   "The Support of the Clergy in the First Five
            Centuries A.D.," *International Review of Missions*
            45 (October): 420-428.

ROBINSON, D.W.B.
    1962   "Church," *The New Bible Dictionary*, James D.
            Douglas, ed.: 228-231. William B. Eerdmans.

SCHONBERGER, Ernest
    1967   "The Episcopalians' Weekend Seminary," *Church
            Growth Bulletin* 3 (July): 5. (Condensed from the
            Los Angeles Times, March 11, 1967.)

SCHOWALTER, Paul
    1957   "Martyrs," *The Mennonite Encyclopedia*, III:
            521-525.

SEKI, Shigeru
    1975   "*Mikan no Kaitaku Dendō*" [Unfinished Pioneer
            Evangelism], *Shinto no Tomo* [The Believer's
            Friend], July: 12-15.

SHAPASA, Kabangy
  1975   "Return to the Bible for an Authentic Christi-
          anity," *AIMM Messenger* (Fall): 7.

SHENK, Wilbert H.
  1973   "The Planting and Growth of the Muria Christian
          Churches," *Mennonite Quarterly Review* 47
          (January): 20-30.

SHEPHERD, M. H., Jr.
  1962   "Ministry, Christian," *The Interpreter's Diction-
          ary of the Bible*, III: 386-392. Abingdon Press.

SPRUNGER, Hugh D.
  1974d   "TEE Program Gives Impetus to Theological Training
          of Church Leaders," *The Mennonite*, September 10:
          E-2,3.

STAHL, J. D.
  1973   "Being Church: A Way of Life," *Christian Living*,
          December: 16-21.

WAGNER, C. Peter
  1972   "Christian Missions: Dawn or Dusk?" *Theology,
          News and Notes*, June: 2-3. (Fuller Theological
          Seminary alumni publication.)

WALKER, G.S.M.
  1962   "Presbyter, Presbytery," *The New Bible Dictionary*,
          James D. Douglas, ed.: 1027. William B. Eerdmans.

WARD, Ted, and ROWEN, Samuel F.
  1972   "The Significance of the Extension Seminary,"
          Evangelical Missions Quarterly 9 (Fall): 17-27.

WINTER, Ralph D.
  1966   "This Seminary Goes to the Student," *World Vision
          Magazine*, July-August: 10-12.

  1967a   "New Winds Blowing," *Church Growth Bulletin* 3
          (July): 12-13.

  1969b   "Will the 'Extension Seminary' Promote Church
          Growth?" *Church Growth Bulletin* 5 (January):
          48-51.

W.C.C. Division of Studies
  1965   "What Kind of Ministry? What Kind of Training?"
          South East Asia Journal of Theology 6,7 (April-
          July): 67-72.

YAGI, Seiichi
  1964   "The Dependence of Japanese Theology Upon the
          Occident," *Japan Christian Quarterly* 30 (October):
          258-261.

YAMADA, Takashi
  1976   "The Anabaptist Vision and Our World Mission (II),"
          Mission-Focus, March: 7-14. (For information on
          Mission-Focus, see under Chao, J.T.)

YAMAMORI, Tetsunao
  1972   "The Sōka Gakkai: A Religious Phoenix," *Practical
          Anthropology* 19 (July-August): 158-168.

                        MINUTES AND REPORTS

CHAIRMEN OF MENNONITE MISSIONS (in Japan)
  1958   Minutes, Tokyo, July 2.

CHEN, Stephen
  1974   "Taipei Regional Center Report," May 13. (Mimeo-
          graphed)

GENERAL CONFERENCE MENNONITE CHURCH
  1955   *Proceedings of the Study Conference on the
          Believers' Church* (Held at Mennonite Biblical
          Seminary, Chicago, Ill., August 23-25, 1955).
          Newton, Kan.

  1975b   *1974 Commission on Overseas Mission.* Reports
          presented to the Council of Commission Meetings,
          February 11-13, 1975, Newton, Kan.

GENERAL CONFERENCE MENNONITE MISSION
  1953   Minutes, Annual Conference, September 5-12.
  1954   "   "   "   September 4-9.
  1955   "   "   "   September 12-18.
  1956   "   "   "   October 22-27.
  1957   "   "   "   October 28-November 2.
  1958   "   "   "   October 27-November 1.

GENERAL CONFERENCE MENNONITE MISSION

1959	Minutes, Annual Conference,	October 26-31.
1960	" " "	October 3-8.
1961	" " "	October 2-7.
1961	(Devotional) " "	"
1962	Minutes, " "	October 22-25.
1963	" " "	October 21-24.
1964	" " "	October 19-22.
1965	" " "	October 18-21.

1954	Minutes, Spring Conference,	April 9-14.
1956	" " "	May 2-5.
1958	" " "	April 7-9.
1959	" " "	March 23-25.
1962	" " "	April 16-18.
1964	" " "	March 23-24.

1957	Minutes, Business Session,	January 28.
1957	" " "	April 16.
1960	" " "	June 20.

1954	Minutes, Executive Committee, September 23.

1957	Minutes, Education Committee,	December 2.
1958	" " "	January 4.
1960	" " "	January 23.
1960	" " "	February 11.
1960	" " "	October 1.
1961	" " "	April 18.
1961	" " "	June 12.
1961	" Joint Ed. "	June 27.
1961	" " "	September 23.
1961	" " "	December 12.
1962	" " "	February 23.
1962	" " "	March 12.
1962	" " "	April 21.
1963	" " "	February 19.

1955	Report, Ed. Comm., Annual Conference	(Sept.).
1957	" " " "	(Oct.-Nov.).
1958	" " " "	(Oct.-Nov.).
1959	" " " "	(Oct.).
1960	" " " "	(Oct.).
1961	" " " "	(Oct.).
1962	" " Joint Conference	(Oct.).

1955	Report, Evangelism Annual Conference	(Sept.).
1956	" Committee, " "	(Oct.).

GENERAL CONFERENCE MENNONITE MISSION
```
1957   Radio Report, Annual Conference (Oct.-Nov.).
1958     "      "       "         "    (Oct.-Nov.).
1960     "      "       "         "    (Oct.).
1961     "      "       "         "    (Oct.).
```

1959   Minutes, Missionary-Workers Conference, Sept. 18-19.

1972   "Statement of Understanding Between the Japan
       Mennonite Christian Church Conference and the
       General Conference Mennonite Mission in Japan."
       Approved at the annual session, December 5-7.

JAPAN MENNONITE CHRISTIAN CHURCH CONFERENCE
```
1962   Minutes, Joint Conference, October 15-16.
1963     "       "         "      October 14-15.
1964     "       "         "      October 26-27.
1966     "     Annual Conference, October 21-24.
1967     "       "         "      October 7-10.
1968     "       "         "      October 12-13.
1969     "       "         "      November 15-16.
1970     "       "         "      October 9-11.
1973     "       "         "      February 10-11.
1974     "       "         "      February 10-11.
```

1963   Minutes, Joint Spring Conference, April 17.

```
1958   Minutes, Church Council, October 18.
1959     "     (Kyōgiinkai)    September 19.
1960     "         "           July 9.
```

```
1962   Minutes, Joint Executive Committee, May 14.
1964     "       "         "         "     April 10.
1965     "       "         "         "     October 5.
```

```
1967   Minutes, Executive Committee, March 12.
1968     "         "         "       January 14.
1969     "         "         "       February 2.
1969     "         "         "       September 7.
1973     "         "         "       November 11.
```

1965   Report, Elders Committee, Annual Conf., Oct. 25.

```
1969   Minutes,    Lay Bible School       December 12.
               Administration Committee,
1970     "              "                 March 5.
1970     "              "                 May 30.
```

JAPAN MENNONITE CHRISTIAN CHURCH CONFERENCE
1965-1977, Annual "Church Growth Surveys."

    1968   *Constitution of the Japan Mennonite Christian Church Conference*. Approved at the annual session, October.

    1973   "Statement of Understanding Between the Japan Mennonite Christian Church Conference and the General Conference Mennonite Mission in Japan." Approved at the annual session, February.

SPRUNGER, Hugh D.
    1973   "Report on TEE in Taiwan," May 12. (Mimeographed)

    1974c   "Report on TEE Work in Taiwan," May 20. (Mimeographed)

VOTH, William C., and UNRUH, Verney
    1951   "Kyushu Report." (Typewritten)

LETTERS AND INTERVIEWS

BOSCHMAN, Paul W.
    1965   Letter to Elders Committee, June 12.

EDIGER, Tina Block
    1975   Letter to author, December 30.

GRAYBILL, John W.
    1974   Interview with author, Tokyo, May 8.

    1975   Letter to author, May 24.

HOKE, Donald E.
    1954   Letter to Missions (in Japan), November 8.
    1956   "   " Verney Unruh, January 25.
    1959   "   "   "   "   September 22.
    1961   "   " Missions (in Japan), May 24.
    1963a   "   " Robert L. Ramseyer, October 29.
    1964   "   " General Conference Mennonite Mission, January 23.
    1975a   Letter to author, July 29.
    1975b   "   "   " including "Comments on Theological Education by Extension in Japan," Feb. 13.

HOSTETLER, Elizabeth
    1974   Letter to author, October 27.

HUFFMAN, John Sr.
    1975   Telephone interview with author, Pasadena, Calif.
            to Key Biscayne, Fla., June 7.

JACOBSEN, Morris B.
    1974a   Interview with author, Tokyo, May 7.

    1974b   Letter to author, October 22.

MILLER, Marvin J.
    1974a   Interview with author, Obihiro, Hokkaido, May 1.

OXLEY, H. Dale
    1974a   Interview with author, Hitoyoshi, Kumamoto, May 22.

    1974b   Letter to author, November 4.

PANNABECKER, S. F.
    1961b   Letter to Board of Missions, October 12.

RAMSEYER, Robert L.
    1962   Letter to Verney Unruh, March 13.
    1963a   "   "   Donald E. Hoke, May 17.
    1963b   "   "   "   "   "   October 25.
    1970   "   "   author, February 20.
    1974   "   "   "   November 11.

SPRUNGER, Hugh D.
    1974a   Interview with author, Taichung, Taiwan, June 3,4.

    1974b   Letter to author, November 24.

SPRUNGER, W. Frederic
    1970   Letter to Robert L. Ramseyer, February 24.

STUCKY, Gerald
    1958   Letter to Verney Unruh, March 26.

TANASE, Takio
    1974   Interview with author, Obihiro, Hokkaido, May 1.

    1975   Letter to author, March 30.

THIESSEN, Bernard
    1969   Letter to Elders Committee, (Spring).

UNRUH, Verney
1955   Letter to Donald E. Hoke, April 27.
1956   "   "   John Reid, May 9.
1958   "   "   Donald E. Hoke, March 14.
1959a   "   "   "   "   "   March 9.
1959b   "   "   "   "   "   November 9.
1960a   "   "   "   "   "   February 17.
1960b   "   "   "   "   "   April 2.
1961   "   "   Board of Missions, June 29.
1962   "   "   Education Committee, March 10.

VORAN, Peter
1956   Letter to Education Committee, February 10.

VOTH, William C.
1952   Letter to Board of Missions, February 25.

WILLMS, Peter A.
1958   Letter to Chairmen of Mennonite Missions (in
       Japan), April 5.

YANADA, Hiroshi
1975   Letter to author, January 28.

MISCELLANEOUS/UNPUBLISHED MATERIAL

CHINA EVANGELICAL SEMINARY
1972   "Material for Extension Education Catalog."
       (Mimeographed)

1974   *News Bulletin*, No. 33 (January).

DYCK, Cornelius J.
1962   "Some Theses Concerning Ordination." Presentation
       made at the AMBS for Joint Faculty discussion,
       April 30. (Mimeographed)

EASTERN HOKKAIDO BIBLE SCHOOL
n.d.   Information sheet on new program that began in
       1965. (Xeroxed)

EXTENSION
1977   *The Monthly Air Mail Newsletter*, December.
       (Publication ceased with this issue, but back
       copies to November 1972 may be ordered from
       Wayne C. Weld, c/o North Park Seminary, 5125
       N. Spaulding Ave., Chicago, IL, 60625.)

GENERAL CONFERENCE MENNONITE CHURCH
    1964   "Statement on Ordination, Commissioning, and
            Licensing"; "Procedures for Ordination and Certi-
            fication of Ministers." Committee on the Ministry
            Minutes, September 22-23. (Xeroxed)

    1972   "Commission on Overseas Mission Goals, Priorities,
            Strategy Conference Statement." Chicago, Ill.,
            June 30. (Xeroxed)

GODDARD, Homer L.
    n.d.   "Fuller Theological Seminary Extension Ministries."
            (Mimeographed)

HARRISON, Patricia
    1975   "TEE in Asia and the South Pacific -- Problems and
            Projected Solutions." Report given to TEE Work-
            shop class, Fuller Theological Seminary, SWM,
            January(?). (Dittoed)

INTERNATIONAL CONGRESS ON WORLD EVANGELIZATION
    1974a   *Status of Christianity Country Profile: Japan.*
            Prepared for the ICOWE, Lausanne, Switzerland,
            July.

JANZEN, George E.
    1965   "The Anabaptist View of the Ministry." Study
            paper given at a pastors' seminar, June. (Dittoed)

JAPAN BIBLE PROTESTANT MISSIONS
    1962a   "Hitoyoshi Bible School Notification," January.
            (Mimeographed)

    1962b   "The Hitoyoshi Bible School," May. (Mimeographed)

JAPAN MENNONITE CHURCH
    1964   "Study of Ministry and Ordination." Study report
            prepared by the Education-Literature Committee,
            and submitted to the Annual Church Conference,
            Kushiro, Hokkaido, May 2-3. (Mimeographed)

MILLER, John W.
    1972   "Church Reform and the Missionary Congregation in
            the 1970's." Study document prepared under the
            auspices of the Council on Faith, Life and
            Strategy of the Mennonite Church. (Mimeographed)

MILLER, Marvin J.
    1974b "Pros and Cons of a Tent-Making Ministry." Paper presented at the Hayama Seminar in Japan, January 5-7, 1974, now available in pamphlet form under the title, *The Case for a Tentmaking Ministry.* (Single copies free on request from Mennonite Board of Missions, Box 370, Elkhart, IN, 46515.)

RICHARDS, Joe, and PEACHEY, Paul
    1959 "Seminary and Bible School Study." Report prepared for the Hokkaido Mennonite Fellowship and the supporting mission. (Mimeographed)

SHINAGAWA CHURCH
    1970 "Shinagawa Community Center," March. Address: Shinagawa Church, 7-40 Kita Shinagawa, 4 Chome, Shinagawa Ku, Tokyo 140. (Mimeographed)

SPRUNGER, Hugh D., and LIAO, David
    1971 "Planning for an Extension Seminary Program." Presented by "Consultations on Extension Seminary Programs," November 6, 1970 and January 4, 1971. (Mimeographed)

TOKYO CHRISTIAN COLLEGE
    1955 "Japan Christian College Prospectus."

    1956 "Prospectus: The Japan Christian College."

    n.d. "Tokyo Christian College." (Printed brochure)

UNRUH, Verney
    1965 "Biblical Qualifications for Ordination." Material prepared for Elders Committee meeting, July 20. (Typewritten)

WALTNER, Erland
    1957 "Ordination in Biblical and Historical Perspectives." Paper presented at a "Conference on Ordination" sponsored by the Committee on the Ministry of the GCMC, held at Mennonite Biblical Seminary, Chicago, Ill., July 10-11. (Mimeographed)

YAMADA, Takashi
    1972 "Response 12." Analysis and observations on national church workers' replies to questionnaire from the Commission on Overseas Mission, GCMC. (Mimeographed)

Biblical References

NEW TESTAMENT (CONTINUED)

NEW TESTAMENT (CONTINUED)

Index*

*Numbers in parentheses () indicate a bibliographical reference.

About the Author

W. Frederic Sprunger, better known as "Fritz," was born to
Silas C. and Helen B. (Stockham) Sprunger in Massillon,
Ohio on September 20, 1940. He was raised in Kidron, Ohio
and there became a member of the Salem Mennonite Church.

In 1962, after studying for three years at Bluffton College
(a Mennonite school in Ohio), and for one year at a sister
school, Bethel College in Kansas, Fritz was graduated from
Bluffton College with a Bachelor of Arts degree in sociology.
He continued his education by spending two years at the
Mennonite Biblical Seminary in Elkhart, Indiana. He completed his work for a Bachelor of Divinity degree in 1969
at Fuller Theological Seminary in Pasadena, California,
where he is presently a candidate for a degree in missions
at the School of World Mission. Fritz has contributed
several articles to such publications as *The Mennonite,*
Japan Harvest, and *Japan Christian Quarterly.*

In 1963 Fritz was married to Ellen (Hostetler) Sprunger.
They have been serving with the General Conference Mennonite
Church since 1964 in southern Japan's Miyakonojo City,
Miyazaki Prefecture. They began their service as house-
parents and moved into evangelism and church planting work.
In 1980 they transferred to Fukuoka City to continue working
with the Japan Mennonite Christian Church Conference. They
have two sons, Timothy and Jonathan.

BOOKS BY THE
WILLIAM CAREY LIBRARY

GENERAL

Christ and Caesar in Christian Missions by Wade Coggins and
E.L. Frizen, Jr., 1979, 160 pp.

Church Growth and Christian Mission by Donald A. McGavran,
1965, 256 pp.

Church Growth and Group Conversion by Donald McGavran,
J.W. Pickett, A.L. Warnshuis, & G.H. Singh, 1973, 128 pp.

Committed Communities: Fresh Streams for World Missions by
Charles J. Mellis, 1976, 160 pp.

Crucial Dimensions in World Evangelization by Arthur F.
Glasser, et al., 1976, 512 pp.

Everything You Need to Grow a Messianic Synagogue by Phillip
E. Goble, 1974, 176 pp.

God's Way to Keep a Church Going and Growing by Vergil
Gerber, 1973, 96 pp.

The Indigenous Church and the Missionary by Melvin Hodges,
1978, 108 pp.

STRATEGY OF MISSION

*Education of Missionaries' Children: The Neglected Dimension
of World Mission* by Bruce Lockerbie, 1975, 76 pp.

An Evangelical Agenda: 1984 and Beyond by the Billy Graham
Center, 1979, 234 pp.

Evangelicals Face the Future by Donald E. Hoke, 1978, 184 pp.

Manual for Accepted Missionary Candidates by Marjorie Collins,
1978, 144 pp.

Manual for Missionaries on Furlough by Marjorie Collins, 1972,
160 pp.

Mission-Church Dynamics: An African Experience by Harold
Fuller, 1980, 260 pp.

THEOLOGY OF MISSION

Christopaganism or Indigenous Christianity? by Tetsunao
Yamamori & Charles R. Taber, 1974, 242 pp.

*The Conciliar-Evangelical Debate: The Crucial Documents,
1964-1976* by Donald A. McGavran, 1972, 254 pp.

*The Radical Nature of Christianity: Church Growth Eyes Look
at the Supernatural Mission of the Christian and the Church*
by Waldo J. Werning, 1975, 224 pp.

*Social Action vs. Evangelism: An Essay on the Contemporary
Crisis* by William J. Richardson, 1977, 65 pp.

POPULARIZING MISSION

The Night Cometh: Two Wealthy Evangelicals Face the Nation by Rebecca Winter, 1977, 96 pp.

Once More Around Jericho: The Story of the U.S. Center for World Mission by Roberta Winter, 1978, 272 pp.

Stop the World I Want to Get On by C. Peter Wagner, 1974, 144 pp.

Student Mission Power: Report of the First International Conference of the Student Volunteer Movement for Foreign Missions, 1979, 248 pp.

The Twenty-five Unbelievable Years: 1945-1969 by Ralph D. Winter, 1970, 128 pp.

REFERENCE

An American Directory of Schools and Colleges Offering Missionary Courses by Glen Schwartz, 1973, 266 pp.

Church Growth Bulletin, Second Consolidated Volume (Sept. 1969 - July 1975), by Donald A. McGavran, 1977, 512 pp.

Word Study Concordance and New Testament (2 Vol. Set) by Ralph & Roberta Winter, 1978, 2-Vol Set.

The World Directory of Mission-Related Educational Institutions by Ted Ward & Raymond Buker, Sr., 1972, 906 pp.

HOW TO ORDER

Send orders to William Carey Library, P.O. Box 128-C, Pasadena, California 91104 (USA). Please allow four to six weeks for delivery in the United States.